THE GREAT
RAT RACE
ESCAPE

From Wage Slavery to Wealth:
How to Start a Purpose Driven Business and
Win Financial Freedom for a Lifetime

MJ DEMARCO

Author of the International Best-Seller *The Millionaire Fastlane*

Published by
Viperion Publishing Corporation
PO Box 18151
Fountain Hills AZ 86268

ISBN Paperback: 978-1-7367924-9-0
ISBN eBook: 978-1-7367924-0-7
Printed in the USA

The information presented herein represents the view of the author as of
the date of publication. This book is presented for informational purposes
only. Due to the rate at which conditions change, the author reserves the
right to alter and/or update his opinions based on new conditions. While
every attempt has been made to verify the information in this book, neither
the author nor his affiliates, partners, or associates assume any responsibility for errors, inaccuracies, or omissions.

The fictional story portrayed in this book, including all names, characters, and incidents, are fictitious and any resemblance to any actual per-
sons, living or deceased, is not intended and purely coincidental.

UNSCRIPTED® is a registered trademark with the USPTO
Registration 5,433,559
Unlawful use is prohibited.

ADDITIONAL RESOURCES

THE UNSCRIPTED TEXT NETWORK

Stay motivated, grow your business, mentorship, and more...
Text "Rat Race Escape!" to MJ @ (480) 531-8964
(USA and Canada only, text/data messaging rates may apply)
Outside of North America?
Join MJ on Telegram
t.me/UnscriptedNetwork

CONNECT WITH MJ DEMARCO

https://www.instagram/MJ.DeMarco
https://www.twitter.com/MJDeMarco
https://www.youtube.com/FastlaneMJ
https://www.LinkedIn.com/in/MJDeMarco
https://www.MJDeMarco.com

OTHER BOOKS BY MJ DEMARCO

THE MILLIONAIRE FASTLANE (2011)
Crack the Code to Wealth and Live Rich for a Lifetime
https://www.theMillionaireFastlane.com

UNSCRIPTED® (Book 1 - 2017)
Life, Liberty, and the Pursuit of Entrepreneurship
https://www.getUnscripted.com

WEALTH EXPO$ED (2020)
This Short Argument I Overheard Made Me a Fortune

THE FASTLANE FORUM

Want to Discuss UNSCRIPTED® Entrepreneurship?
https://www.theFastlaneForum.com

CONTENTS

PREFACE

Ugh. I'm an idiot. A masochistic idiot. And I'm proof that anyone can escape the rat race. If this idiot can do it, you can too.

No, seriously. This isn't false humility.

You see, this book, in part, is my first attempt at storytelling. But unlike a normal person, I didn't write a romance. Or a mystery novel. Or something with known archetypes and well-worn story arcs. Nope. You see, this idiot chose to write the hardest story ever. A book that has no genre. A book half fictional story, half nonfiction business book. A book about entrepreneurship, building wealth, and escaping the rat race. A book that has no known example to observe or model.

The first rule of authorship is "show, don't tell." Problem is that business books are mostly "telling"—do this and don't do that. This makes them hard to understand and finish. Hard to demonstrate a "big picture" and change the reader's life. Hard to convince the reader of what is possible. So I challenged myself to deliver a story that not only "tells" but demonstrates the "show."

And a challenge it was. I mean seriously. How exciting could a story about starting a business be?

He had an idea and registered an LLC.

She placed some Facebook ads.

No, this is not my new writing style.

No, I'm not writing like James Altucher because I lost a bet.

Anyhow.

When I began this journey, it was the middle of 2017. I expected this project would take me three months to write. It went nearly four years.

Because I'm an idiot.

This book could have been titled *The Idiot's Guide to Escaping the Rat Race.* But since I don't like lawsuits from the good folks at Penguin Random House, I went with something different: *Unscripted®: The Great Rat Race Escape.*

Inside, you'll witness the rat race poison a marriage and chew up dreams. Inside, you'll find a story about an ordinary couple seeking an extraordinary escape. Inside, you'll get a front row seat to how the 99 percent becomes the 1 percent. Embedded within the story are 120 strategies and principles to show you the way. So you too can have a *Great Rat Race Escape.* And live happily ever after. If this idiot can, you can.

INTRODUCTION

Every day, someone tries to start a business. And every day, someone fails at business. Some people go on to make a decent living with their business, others own a grind that pays the bills for the month, only to repeat until some godforsaken retirement age, or worse, death. But few people start a business as a way to escape the rat race.

Not only will *Unscripted®: The Great Rat Race Escape* show you how, but it will also demonstrate how one married couple (with a baby on the way) makes it happen.

This book is actually two books blended into one. That's right—a "two for one" deal! The first is a fictional narrative, a story of awakening for one family, the Trotmans, who discover that the life they're living isn't the life they've dreamed. As they struggle to navigate the rat race and its pervasive dogma, their journey is chronicled as they leverage Fastlane entrepreneurship for their escape, from idea to launch to execution to scale.

As you can imagine, writing a story with business as the central theme has the potential to be incredibly dull. As such, I've created characters dealing with their own personal demons as they navigate a struggling marriage rife with boredom, bills, and unfulfilling work. Some readers might be uncomfortable with the marital conflicts the husband-and-wife team face, as well as the touchy subjects they address. Caution: Some reader discretion is advised.

As the Trotmans' story unfolds, rat race busting strategies and principles related to their struggles are integrated throughout. Some of these pertain to life itself, not just business because a successful venture alone doesn't automatically translate to happiness. Each concept is prefaced with an icon that represents its informational category.

 STRATEGY: An action or process that can help deliver results, either near-term or long-term to your business or your life.

 PRINCIPLE: A new perspective or belief shift, often questioning or disproving a well-established belief, which itself is often propagandized by the rat race paradigm.

Each strategy and principle is geared toward helping you (and the characters) escape the rat race Unscripted—lasting financial freedom[P11] independent of politics, economics, or stock market returns.

If the tumultuous year of 2020 was good for anything, it's that it exposed the rat race's systemic conspirators, a powerful group of entities from tech tyrants to corporate media professionals to politicians, all deeply invested in grooming an obedient populace subject to submission, suppression, and servitude. In other words, the rat race is the world's economic cult, and every cult thrives as long as enough fools obey its dogmatic preachers.

The good news is you don't have to obey. You don't have to turn on the television and listen to the latest rat race lies, from "save $100 a month for fifty years to retire rich" to "get a college degree and a good job" to "how entrepreneurship is risky," (but outsourcing your paycheck to a non-essential corporation isn't.)

If you're dissatisfied in your life, either with your job or your business, and seek a meaningful new path that rewards your mortal life with deep purpose, soulful happiness, and real financial freedom, read on. If any of the following apply, this book was written for you.

- You hate your job and don't see any path forward.
- You seek to do meaningful, purpose-driven work over meaningless, debt-driven work.
- You would like to control your own destiny with your own business.
- You realize that "saving $100 a week for fifty years" is an untenable idea wrought with peril.
- You don't want to work most of your life only to retire in life's twilight when your energy and health are on the downside.
- You'd love to follow your passions without needing them confirmed by demand, money, or cultural approval.
- You desire a more affluent lifestyle not subject to soul-crushing frugality, disciplined saving, and years of stock market optimism.
- You'd rather invest your time in an effort that could yield financial independence in five or ten years, not 40 or 50.
- You've always been a hustling entrepreneur but never made the leap into six, seven, or eight-figures.
- You're an entrepreneur who has yet to crack the code to a viable idea or a venture worthy of exploding sales.

That said, if you're already an entrepreneur with a growing business and millions in sales, this book, while helpful in some respects, probably isn't going to move your needle. The last thing I want to do is sell someone a Ferrari when they were expecting a Lamborghini. Particularly, *if entrepreneurship has not yet changed your life*, this book is for you. If it already has, then probably not.

Over 25 years ago, entrepreneurship changed my life. And it made me financially independent, to the point where I never need to work ever again. I'm not talking about the latest "early retirement" orthodoxy dependent on lifestyle mediocrity and stock market returns, as most financial bloggers now promote. I'm talking about the kind of "retirement" that is rich in luxury (dream houses and cars are nice!), but also rich in time and resources. For me, going Unscripted meant I could pursue my writing passions free of financial validation and editorial control. Looking back, I wouldn't change a damn thing.

I want to be clear: starting a business is the hardest thing you will ever do. Growing it will be the second. If you're going to challenge yourself with these tasks, you want your reward to be transcendent. Your venture needs to offer a prize that has the power to help you escape the tyranny of the rat race, either through a millionaire-making income or a life-changing liquidation event. This book is the story of how you can do just that, complete with 120 strategies and principles to make it happen.

Don't let the rat race and its demagogues proclaim your life as non-essential. Don't let the rat race entice you to save your life away for the promise of an elderly retirement. Don't let the rat race lull you into a tedious existence medicated by television, video games, and trivial sporting events. Go Unscripted and build a business that not only changes your life, but perhaps also the lives that come after you.

My will shall shape my future. Whether I fail or succeed shall be no man's doing but my own. I am the force; I can clear any obstacle before me, or I can be lost in a maze. My choice, my responsibility, win or lose, only I hold the key to my destiny.

ELAINE MAXWELL

Never forget that life can only be nobly inspired and rightly lived if you take it bravely and gallantly, as a splendid adventure in which you are setting out into an unknown country, to meet many a joy, to find many a comrade, to win and lose many a battle.

ANNIE BESANT

ELEVEN MINUTES
MONDAY, NOVEMBER 10TH, 2008 - 5:34 AM

Jeff Trotman jolted awake, shooting up from bed, panicked. Sweat soaked his nightshirt despite the cold outside. *Did I oversleep?* His old alarm clock on his night stand was retired, replaced with a new iPhone 3G. Was the alarm set correctly? He squinted around the room, but the Monday morning darkness remained. Rain plunked a tormenting chorus against the window, an opera of lost dreams and smothered souls.

He flung his legs to the floor and fumbled for the phone in the dark. Finding the device, he pressed it on. The time cracked the darkness: 5:34 AM, eleven minutes remaining before it was set to scream. He rubbed his face and glanced at the empty sheets. His pregnant wife was not in bed beside him. An ER nurse at Chicago's Northwestern Hospital, she'd left hours earlier for the graveyard shift. While her pregnancy advertised that they were a happy couple who often frolicked in the sheets, they weren't. The last time they made love was the likely conception date of their unborn daughter: a distant six months ago. His marriage, his career, his happiness—nothing was going as he expected.

He lumbered out of bed and toddled to his bedroom window. It was cracked and frosted over, its chaotic fractures stippled like a map of Rome drafted by a drunk cartographer. The shattered glass was a reminder of another thing he had to fix. And pay for.

The acid in his throat intensified. He plunked his forehead onto the glass and gazed vacantly at the empty street, still illuminated by lampposts. The frozen window impaled its chill on his skin. His forehead begged for mercy, but he didn't care. It only exposed what he'd long denied: *he was alive, but he wasn't living.*

A lone van slowly chugged by, newspapers fed to their driveways. The nearby freeway growled with rush-hour traffic. The cold slowly numbed his forehead, robbing him of the only sensation that felt real.

Bella, their black Labrador puppy, snored on her backside near the window, all four of her legs raised skyward. He watched her rhythmic breathing and jealousy singed his brain. *Sleeping without a care in the world.* His wife Samantha, or Sam as everyone called her, had insisted on adopting the dog from a no-kill shelter just weeks ago. If the local law had allowed it, she'd have twenty dogs in their home. There wasn't a living creature that Sam didn't love or try to save, and that included terrifying insects. A melon-sized tarantula could roam the house, and she wouldn't kill it. She'd bottle it up and try to find it a home. Yes, she was that neurotic. She claimed it was compassion.

As for Bella, he suspected his wife wanted the puppy because their three-year-old marriage was lifeless. Their work schedules afforded little time together. They no longer kissed or hugged. Meals were eaten alone. Jeff's jokes, always worth a laugh from his wife, suddenly weren't funny. The passionate banter that had sparked their courtship depreciated into small talk—the weather, household chores, and petty pleasantries. He loved Bella but suspected the dog was an emotional plea, a distracting bribe from his wife to fill the void plaguing their relationship.

The cortisol that abruptly awoke him was now gone, replaced by fatigue and wooziness. Anxiety and regret draped over him like a wet blanket. *He loathed what he'd become*, an obedient bill-paying rat in a meaningless job and a crumbling marriage. Weekend entertainment and mindless shopping could no longer conceal the reality: his life was work, sleep, pay bills, and repeat. His life had been reduced to a commodity, a cog that got its grease each paycheck and every weekend.

He exhaled against the window. His breath condensed on the cracked glass, shape shifting into tombstone. He lifted his head and shook it in disgust. Even the universe taunted at his soul. When Jeff was young, he'd promised himself that he would fight for his dreams. And he had many to choose from. His father taught him woodworking, and by his late teens, Jeff could fashion a Mona Lisa from a tree stump. He saw himself building furniture or carving sculptures for the rich and famous. He also played the saxophone and dreamed of being in a jazz band. If none of that panned out, Jeff saw himself as an author, writing fantasy-fiction novels or realistic science fiction, not the Disney crap that passed for *Star Wars* nowadays. No matter which, he envisioned an exciting future of meaningful work, the kind that could lead to a life of luxury and leisure.

Instead, Jeff abandoned his creative proclivities and earned a college degree in accounting. He was good with numbers but didn't exactly enjoy them. Still, his father would argue, "Accounting is where the money's at!" and Jeff agreed. He loved exotic vacations, fast cars, and designer clothes. Starving artists lived in sheds and drove Priuses.

Right out of college, he snagged a job as a transaction auditor for a large drug company. You know, the one with all the lawsuits. Sorry, I guess that doesn't narrow it down. Unfortunately, his career didn't get him the Ferrari or the Fiji vacation. After four years of number crunching for insurance companies and government bureaucrats combined with pay raises that made inflation giggle, framing houses suddenly appealed more.

The thought of the looming day was suffocating: the stiff suit he had to wear, the frigid drive to the train station, the snow-soaked shoes while waiting on the platform, the hour-long train commute with the other miserables, and the disquieted elevator ride to the 67th floor, where eight grueling hours of trivial number-crunching would unfold.

Jeff and his wife tolerated their jobs, and both were reasonably paid. But both were reasonably unhappy and reasonably broke. Still, they put on quite a show. Between the three-bedroom house in the suburbs and the late model cars, him a BMW 3-Series, his wife a Lincoln Navigator, by all appearances they lived the American Dream. But behind the white picket fence, it was an American Nightmare.

In college, Jeff's wife had wanted to be a veterinarian. But her dream, like Jeff's, would die early. When she couldn't afford medical school, she chose nursing. After graduation, she was hired by a nursing consortium that might as well been a corporate cartel. Nursing proved quickly to be a mistake. Doctors roamed the halls like pharaohs and expected to be fanned with date-palms and robed in gold. Worse, patient care was profit-care—patients were numbers on a clipboard, hurried along as if a gurney was an assembly line.

Jeff lumbered back to the edge of the bed and sat. The sleet continued its heckle through the window. The soft linen sheets joined in the humiliation and tempted him like a cookie would a child: *Why don't you nap for a few moments? You saw your phone, you have eleven more minutes to sleep peacefully, why waste them before going to work? Join me, Jeff, join me, and in that eleven minutes, we can rule the galaxy as father and son!*

He slumped farther to the edge of the bed and rubbed his head, calculating how he would manage the extra eleven minutes. Would he sleep through his alarm? Had he even set it right? If not, could he trust himself to wake up after the eleven minutes? How much time did he really have after all these mental gymnastics? Once he realized he was having a debate with himself, the rain, and Darth Vader masquerading as a bed, he hung his head and damned himself with another question: *is this what my pathetic life has become, a negotiation for eleven minutes?*

"Eleven freaking minutes," he mumbled as he trudged to the bathroom. After brushing his teeth, he confronted his self-hatred in the mirror. Even his reflection radiated hopelessness. Dark circles underlined his brown eyes and gave him the appearance that he'd lost a fight. His posture slumped, his 6'3 stature deflated without confidence. Friends teased him because of his

Jesus-like silky brown hair, but he didn't see a prophet or a savior; he saw a mugshot of Charles Manson, dead stare included. He was only 27 but looked 40. Worse, he felt 70.

He cranked the shower on and sunk to the rim of the bathtub waiting for the hot water, the day's only joy. He glowered at the tub's mildewy drain. It needed to be cleaned, another "to do" on his list. The water swirled into a void, mirroring the first 27 years of his life. He'd followed culture's unwritten rules precisely as designed, only to get sucked into an abyss. He'd gone to college, gotten the good grades, the prestigious degree, the respectable job, the middle-class trinkets, the storybook marriage, and the cute house notwithstanding the 29.4 years of payments remaining. To his peers and his family, he feigned success, but his soul begged his brain for a truthful confession. His life was cursed like a weekly television rerun, broadcasting the same boring episode over and over. It was death by mediocrity.

A quote nagged in his head, something he once heard but didn't under-stand: *Most men die by twenty-five but aren't buried until seventy-five.* The toys meant to bribe his misery or to peacock affluence—a new set of golf clubs, an electronic doodad, a day at Wrigley Field watching millionaires hit a ball—had lost their effect. Like a drug needing bigger doses for the same high, his purchases doped him for days, but their side-effects lasted for years. His only gasp for air was a short vacation subject to his wife's crazy schedule or an occasional staycation, a weekend furlough of freedom which sped time, only to slow Monday morning.

As for retirement, the Trotman's idea of planning were trips to the riverboat casino and Powerball. Retirement was not on their radar; survival was. And how to do it while looking prosperous and well-heeled. But between him and his wife, they had no heel. They were broke, unless you jointly counted the $3,000 in their 401(k)s. With eleven charge cards between them, the credit flowed like the cheap imported goods from China and Mexico. From the Nordic Trac exerciser that sat rusting in the basement to the Louis Vuitton purse he'd bought his wife for Christmas, his spending seemed to spend an eternity with his friends at MasterCard and Visa. They had two car payments, a mortgage, and Mercedes taste on a Mazda budget. Altogether, they had no net worth, no financial plan, and no clue.

With a baby on the way and more responsibility like diapers and doting moms who forget their husbands, Jeff felt the charade he showboated was about to become impossible. He loved the idea of becoming a father, but he hated the game. He hated that the chains that enslaved him to a dying marriage and a suffocating career were about to get tighter. Unless he miraculously won a CEO job with a CEO salary, the hedonistic theatrics and the credit cards that funded the ruse would need to continue.

Ding-Ding Ding... Ding-Ding Ding...

The alarm on Jeff's phone screeched, jarring him from his trance. The eleven minutes were over. And so was his will to live. Like a good little rat, he put on his best suit and drove to the train station. Except he wasn't sure if he would get on the train or step in front of it.

THE CONVENTIONAL WISDOM PRINCIPLE

Conventional Wisdom Rarely Gets You an Unconventional Life

It was 2005. A plumber was at my home to fix a faucet. While he lay on his back and jostled with the pipes, he couldn't stop talking about how much money he was making from real estate. For me, this random moment of insignificance held great significance. I knew in that instant that the great housing boom was at its end. And sure enough, a few months later, the housing market crashed. Trillions of dollars were lost, and millions of bankruptcies followed. Today, a similar scenario unfolds as the stock market exuberantly hits record highs while negative interest rates scour the planet.

In mathematics, "the wisdom of the crowd" has immense value in finding accurate judgments, specifically in mathematically based problems. Unfortunately, while the crowd might accurately guess the number of gumballs in a jar, they won't accurately guess how you can escape the rat race. Conventional wisdom is spewed from the crowd, and the crowd represents the mean, otherwise known as mediocrity. If the crowd knew any better, they wouldn't be two paychecks from broke and wasting half their life in front of a television.

The Conventional Wisdom Principle is about the stone-cold truth: *If you follow conventional wisdom from conventional people living conventional lives, you will get exactly that: a conventional life.* And conventional lives are not underwritten by dreams, but by servitude—*the rat race.* Your penance in this obligatory game is an unfulfilling job. Your cheese? A scant paycheck, a mediocre weekend, and a retirement fantasy that pays forty years later. You know, after the knee replacement, after the receding hairline or the wrinkles, and after most of your life has been wasted in a job you hate.

Look at the people in your life. Family, friends, co-workers, your comrades stuck in traffic. Is anyone living a full life flourishing with meaningful work? Anyone happy on Monday morning? Is anyone walking into the Porsche dealer, pointing to "the red one" and paying cash? Know anyone free of financial stress, someone who doesn't need to finance the furniture for 60 months and the house for 30 years? If you're honest, the answer is likely a resounding NO. And that's because our culture thrives on mediocrity and obedience. It is the world's business model.

Whether you know it or not, your existence has been programmed from diapers to death. Behind this truth a pervasive operating system grinds, a cultural conditioning scheme called the *Script*. And conventional wisdom is its code language. Such "wisdom" like go to college and earn a degree regardless of cost, economics, or employment forecasts. Get a good job with benefits. Work hard Monday through Friday, play harder Saturday and Sunday. Cheer for your favorite football team, watch the hottest Netflix drama and get outraged at the latest news agenda fed to you. Pay your taxes, finance a car, mortgage a house, have a few kids, and eat according to the USDA food pyramid. Drink your milk. Let a billionaire software mogul stick you with a vaccine and stamp you with a digital ID. Wear your mask. Live frugally and invest all your saved pennies at Wall Street firms, preferably in a low-cost indexed fund, where one day, you'll retire rich. Of course, assuming the stock market never crashes, and you survive long enough to enjoy it...

... welcome, my friend, to the operating system of the rat race.

Because this gospel bankrolls the economy, it is deified in every echelon of culture: lower and higher education, news and financial media, entertainment and sports, and government. Worse, you're likely surrounded by Scripted humans, devout believers in the world's economic religion. From famous financial celebrities and educators to family and peers, there is no escape.

But be warned. If you're okay forsaking your youthful dreams for an elderly retirement dependent on thankless jobs, stock market performance, and bankrupted government pension programs, conventional wisdom buys that lottery ticket. Except this lottery ticket is sponsored by the rat race.

The Script is the rat race's puppet master, a cultural existence engineered for herding purposes. And herds—sheep, cattle, pigs, chicken, bees—are organized for economic objectives: slaughter and servitude. Your life is worth more than trinkets, taxes, and television ratings. Don't let the gospel of the rat race, the world's economic religion—the Script—hijack it. If you want to *live* like the 1%, you can't *think* like the 99%.

☑ KEY CONCEPTS

- The "wisdom of the crowd" advocates for the rat race, not for your freedom.
- Question conventional wisdom or have it lead you into a conventional life.
- The Script administers the rat race and is culture's default operating system, bankrolled by powerful institutions and corporations.

THE NEW PEN STRATEGY

Write New Words or Suffer the Same Story

2

In the winter of 1995, I contemplated suicide.

It was nearing midnight, and I was driving a limousine for a small company in Chicago. Only I wasn't driving; I was stuck on the shoulder of the road in a blizzard. Only the rhythmic hum of the windshield wipers played to my disquieting silence. As I waited for the snowplows, I deliberated on my miserable life. I had two business degrees and had graduated near the top of my class. But here I was, stuck working a menial job, a job I could have snagged straight from a high school detention hall. College didn't educate me; it indebted me and gave me the expectation that I deserved more. But the only "more" in my life was more debt, more embarrassment, and more failure. By my mid-twenties, I expected to be moderately successful, in a good relationship, and on my way to financial freedom. But none of that existed. I was broke. Worse, my long-time girlfriend dumped me for a successful radio executive. And yes, she was perfectly justified in doing so as I floundered from one dumb idea to the next. While my college peers were deep into a seemingly successful middle-class life, I was deep into Mom's basement.

If you died today and your life was narrated in a story, how would it read? Would it be a one-star story filled with generically posthumous platitudes like, "Joe was such a nice guy"? Or would it be a compelling tale that someone couldn't put down? Since you're reading this book, I can guess that you aren't happy with how your story is being written.

As I sat on the side of the road, I realized my story was going nowhere.

It was then that I contemplated suicide: how I would do it and the note I'd write explaining it. After a few ominous visions on how I'd murder myself, a .380 to the mouth, or a plastic tube affixed to my car's exhaust, it hit me. *Even suicide and its method of execution was a choice.* I had free will and the power of choice, an endowment that up to that point I had denied. Everything in my life, including how I thought and felt about it, was a choice. If I wanted a different life with a different story, I needed to make different choices. But more importantly, what beliefs were causing me to make those choices? What beliefs were laying the groundwork for the failed choices that were causing my broken life?

Wherever you are: suffering a dead-end job, tolerating a loveless marriage, studying law in college, or living a dream, your existence is moored on one truth. The results you suffer today (or enjoy) unfolded from your beliefs and the choices they conceived. The internal environment—your thoughts—cause the outside environment and acts like a flight plan for your life.

Belief ▸▸ Choice ▸▸ Consequence ▸▸ Your Life

This sequential relationship amounts to hundreds of choices daily. And they all evolve from your beliefs. For instance:

- What food to shove in your mouth…
- What media to feed your eyes…
- Who to be friends with…
- What books to read or not read…
- How to tackle problems…
- How to handle rejection…
- How to feel about money…
- What you do with your free time…

Altogether, your beliefs and the choices they compel write *The Book of You—your story*. In your book, the various pens writing your story are your beliefs. Each word penned to the paper would be a thought, each sentence a choice, each paragraph an action, each chapter a habit. Your life story is the total of your actions (or inactions), which in turn are caused by those pens transcribing your beliefs. If you're armed with a pen that believes drinking three Dr. Peppers every day is okay, what kind of story gets to the paper? A tale of health, or a tale of diabetes?

While each of us is born into varied circumstances, we retain the rights to the pens writing our story. A rich kid might choose to squander his privilege in heroin while the poor kid decides to be the one dealing it. If you don't like your life's station or where it leads, you need to change the pens writing your story. And the only way to change those pens and the choices they write is to change your beliefs. Namely, you need to expose your *poison pens*—Scripted beliefs that are condemning your life to mediocrity, misery or worse, death.

For example, a family friend is battling morbid obesity, high blood pressure, and diabetes. He refuses to change his diet despite a heart attack, multiple stent surgeries, and a dozen prescription medications. His "diet" is a combination of fast food and gas station fare: donuts, fried chicken, and wieners that have been roller grilled for six days. The last time his mouth saw a vegetable was when the Berlin Wall fell. If two heart attacks and multiple hospital visits aren't enough of a crisis to compel a dietary change, what crisis is? Stroke? Death? When asked this question, he revealed his flawed belief. *My poor genetics cause my health problems, not my food choices.* In other words, he believes a Nigerian prince needs his bank account number to help him flee a military coup.

Sadly, this flawed belief will have a big cost, and I'm not talking money. The worst poison pen is the one that will kill you. Fact: *The harsh truth doesn't care about your beliefs.* If you believe you can fly, you'll jump off a cliff and die. Truth is independent of belief.

The same applies to freedom from the rat race. If a broke blogger says "doing what you love" is the secret to success, and you believe him, you might fail twenty businesses. If you believe relying on a faceless corporation isn't risky to your freedom, but relying on your business is, you'll settle for the job. When beliefs misfire action, reality has a way of smacking you in the face. As such, misfired beliefs have fiery consequences and write dire stories. In self-help circles, they call them "limiting beliefs," but clinically speaking, they're delusions.

Give me 30 seconds (or 30 words when it comes to my forum), and I can immediately predict if someone will be a lifetime rat racer. No, I'm not clairvoyant. But after interacting with tens of thousands of people over the last decade, I can spot a headspace that precedes failure. The internal environment—your thought words—cause the outside environment—the story. If you're packing poison pens from the rat race, you won't write the blockbuster.

For example, as a teenager, my poison pen was that only a specific group of people could get rich quickly, and hence, get rich young. People capable of this feat were celebrities, athletes, and musicians. If I didn't aspire to act, dribble, or sing well, I was out of luck. Wall Street's fifty-year plan of saving patience would be my fate. That is, I'd end up a perfect rat.

Luckily for me, I exposed this poison pen in my teens. Everything changed when I encountered a young man who owned a ridiculously expensive sports car—the Lamborghini Countach. Popularized by the classic Burt Reynolds movie *Cannonball Run*, the Countach was my dream car because it was closest to a *Star Wars* land-speeder. After spotting the car at an ice cream parlor, I stalked the owner in the parking lot. When a young man approached the car, I boldly asked him what he did for a living. Expecting to hear something relating to my false belief (actor, athlete, et al.), he revealed he was an inventor. What, an inventor? I was stunned, and the poison pen was exposed. And then replaced. At that moment, I knew I could "get rich young" because "get rich quick" existed outside the box of celebrity. New belief, installed. I had a new pen and as such, new choices with which to write a new story. And it did, at least until I got stuck on the side of the road and contemplated suicide.

Two more poison pens lurked behind my struggles, however, corrupting my story. Yes, I knew entrepreneurship could produce financial freedom fast. Except I wasn't pursuing business ventures with my own grit and creativity. Instead, I skipped from one inferior business scheme to another. Things like network marketing, low-rent franchise opportunities, and real estate investment strategies plucked from late-night infomercials. I falsely believed that there was a turnkey plug-and-play system that could lead to success. Turns out, the only people getting rich from these "systems" were the entrepreneurs peddling them. I had a gun but was loading blanks. Which is why I wasted years failing.

Second, I suffered from seasonal depression. If the sun wasn't shining and I wasn't working, you could bet I was sleeping. Or doing nothing productive. A belief deep inside my head was responsible for my lack of progress: I believed that I couldn't emigrate from Chicago because I was born and raised there. Arguments heckled my brain, things like *You can't leave Chicago, your family is here!* or *You love the Chicago Bulls, how could you abandon them?* As if an NBA franchise cared about my fandom.

After canceling my suicide, I confronted these two poison pen beliefs and killed them. First, I vowed never to rely on a third-party for my business success. No MLM or affiliate bullshit. No franchise opportunities or late-night business schemes. Second, I severed the invisible handcuffs that kept me in Chicago. Within a few months, I moved to Arizona. And because I crushed these two beliefs, my life instantly changed.

If the winds of mediocrity are directing your life, ask the hard questions. What Scripted beliefs are writing your story? And who is reinforcing those beliefs? Your parents who insist you become a doctor because it carries a certain cultural status? Is it an educational system that advocates spending $120,000 for a medieval theology degree? Is it that hypocritical guru who made millions selling motivational seminars and yet, tells you that millions can be made by patient investing?

The point is, are the witches of conventional wisdom[P1],the *Script*, poisoning your story with sub-plots amenable to rat race outcomes?

Building a business is risky!

Saving $100 a month will make you rich!

You can be happy living in a shed down by the river with no plumbing or electricity!

The rat race is filled with liars. Your first step is to stop lying to yourself.

☑ **KEY CONCEPTS**

- The internal environment—your thoughts—cause the outside environment and is like a flight plan for your life.
- The Book of You is your life as it is today, an aggregate of your beliefs and the choices they created.
- Truth doesn't care about your beliefs.
- Every day you make thousands of choices, including what to think and feel. These choices are like the words, paragraphs, and chapters of your unfolding story.
- Poison-pens are Scripted beliefs that are responsible for the poor outcomes in your life.

THE BRIBE

Jeff boarded the train four more times that week. Each day's commute further deadened his soul. He didn't read the newspaper or people watch; he slept. On Friday's commute, he fell asleep and dreamt he was eighteen again after high school graduation. It was the happiest summer of Jeff's life, before college, expectations, and responsibilities. That summer, he played tenor saxophone in a jazz trio at a local wine bar. The invite was for one weekend only, but after playing to sticky crowds with big wine appetites, the bar asked them to play all summer. Still, Jeff's parents were adamant that he attend college for business, or as Jeff's dad would say, "where the money is." Despite having a talent for music and storytelling, Jeff agreed. Seth, Jeff's older brother, passed on college when his drug habit stole the opportunity. Jeff's parents insisted their kids go to college and "do better" than either of them. His father was a framing carpenter nearing retirement, not because it was time to quit, but because his aching back could no longer do the work. His mom worked as a retail manager at Dillard's, code for overworked and underpaid. With an income at the poverty line, Jeff's parents had easy access to federal grants and student loans. This shifted the costly burden of college to Jeff, and then to Kaycee, his younger sister, who would attend two years later. When the passenger next to him nudged him in his ribs, Jeff woke up docked at Union Station. After collecting himself back into reality, it was as if he had blinked, and ten years had disappeared, just like his hopes for a life worth living.

At home on Sunday afternoon, Jeff sat stooled at the kitchen island and stared aimlessly at a television commercial. After watching the Bears get slaughtered 37-3 by the Green Bay Packers, he felt the tension start to grind its way up into his chest. His sporting distraction was over, and only reality remained. He hated Sunday night as he felt like a Scottish Jacobite waiting to be hung by a redcoat. At least those Scotsmen had their agony end. For him, he felt a perpetual noose around his neck: hung every Monday, loosened Friday, retightened Sunday night, rinse, repeat.

He looked around and felt ashamed. *First-world problems*, he thought. By all measures, he and his wife were successful. They had a beautiful home, nice cars, a refrigerator filled with food, and good-paying jobs. He even had Bears tickets for their next home game.

But deep down, he knew the truth. His soul whispered in moments of quiet reflection, during a hot shower or alone in his car. If the last five years foretold the next fifty, he was going to die a bitter, regretful old man. After three different jobs since graduating college, it was clear his career might as well been a job on an assembly line during the industrial revolution. Except he didn't assemble parts or pull levers, he moved numbers and audited inventory manifests. Heck, he didn't even believe in the drugs his company manufactured. He felt like an infantryman who would die on the front line waging a war he didn't believe in. *There has to be more to life than filing reports and waiting for a weekend football game,* he thought. And now he was about to become a parent. He worried for his unborn child who, if things didn't change, would have a walking corpse for a father. With his marriage taking on water, Jeff knew it was time to confront his wife about his feelings.

His wife was heating a plate of beans and rice at the microwave. She was in her "off day" pajamas, a shabby pink flannel ensemble with smiling lambs for polka-dots. Jeff thought his wife's PJs were cute when he first saw them years ago, but now they were as homely and unappealing as an unflushed toilet at O'Hare Airport. While normal wives liked dogs and dolphins, his wife had a thing for lambs. They were like her talisman, and she would adorn her world with them, from necklaces to shirts to hairpins. The hundred or so lambs screen-printed on her tattered PJs were so faded that they now resembled dirty snowballs.

After some idle chat about hospital gossip, Jeff spoke about his morning battle with his alarm. "Eleven damn minutes!" Jeff shouted over the buzz of the microwave as he sat on the kitchen stool. As Sam waited, Jeff continued, "I sincerely would have sold my soul to stay in bed. Not sure how much more I can take doing what I do, or this job." The microwave dinged off. He continued, "And riding that damn train every morning into the city. Did you know that on Friday I fell asleep and the guy next to me had to wake me up?" He didn't let Sam answer and picked up a pile of envelopes stuffed in the kitchen's organizer. He filed through them and sneered, "Mortgage, electric bill, water bill, car insurance, property taxes, it never fucking ends. We're like rats on a treadmill."

Sam chuckled, "You're having a mid-life crisis at 27?"

"I'm serious Sam. We should talk."

She put her plate of beans down and wiped her hands on a dish towel. Her crystal blue eyes narrowed as she leaned her tall and slender frame against the granite counter. "Uh oh," she remarked crossing her arms.

Not a good sign, Jeff thought.

She quipped, "Is this about Carolyn?" Jeff's boss was a dead-fish he likened to Nurse Ratched of accounting.

"It's about everything. My job. My boss. Your job. Our life. Becoming parents." He paused and clenched his jaw. "And our finances are a shitshow. We owe so much money, and it's never going away. We both hate our jobs, and I never see you. And..." His voice trailed off.

Sam sat next to him now, eyes piqued and asked, "And?" she asked, fidgeting her fingers on her arms. He hesitated for a few seconds but couldn't contain the feeling.

"And our marriage sucks," he said bluntly.

Jeff's candid assertiveness was double-edged. Sam admired that he took charge and spoke his mind, but it often got him in trouble. In third grade, an "unspoken social mores" discussion went south when his civics teacher called on Jeff for an example. He blurted, "Like how you look like Ms. Piggy?" He was suspended for one day. Sam would always tease him about having "no filter."

When Sam heard that "sucks" was her husband's opinion of their marriage, she winced. But she feared to admit that it did suck. And it haunted her thoughts when life wasn't offering a distraction.

Jeff carried on, "It's almost Thanksgiving and we've had sex twice this year. And you haven't called me 'RyRy' in two years."

RyRy was the nickname Sam had given her husband in college because he reminded her of Ryan Reynolds, except with flowing locks of hair and four inches taller. RyRy was an endearment that Sam would quip throughout their dating history and early in their marriage. Whenever Sam voiced his nickname, it was code for friskiness, the kind of frisky that usually ended up with clothes on the floor.

Sam's eyes teared as she silently held Jeff's gaze. He knew mentioning RyRy would stir her heart because it represented a time when they were in love. Not that she needed much help in the tears department. She was the penultimate "easy crier." Jeff once smashed a grasshopper who insisted on chirping during his Cubs game. When the guts splattered, Sam cried bloody murder for an hour.

After she wiped her tears and gathered herself, she spoke plainly. "We had sex after Scott's New Year's party." Scott was Jeff's coworker and sports buddy, a walking encyclopedia of all stuff baseball. If you'd asked Scott about the starting lineup for any random World Series Champion, he'd tell you—right down to the year, game, and inning.

Jeff continued his interrogation. "And after that, you know where?"

Sam glanced at her pregnancy bump but said nothing, wiping another emerging tear with her sleeve. "Yes, exactly. The Ritz Carlton, that little staycation we went on. It was the last time we had any fun, and I'm not just talking about getting naked."

She sniffled and tried to compose herself, bitter that her husband seemed to be more interested in naked time than their marriage. She remarked sarcastically, "Tell you what, let's name the baby Ritz or Carlton. That way you won't forget such a rare sexual escapade."

Jeff chewed on her words for a minute, then jested, "Well it's a good thing we didn't stay at Motel 6." His humor always made Sam smile. They stared hard at each other as if engaged in a mental tug of war. But her seriousness drained away as Jeff tried to restrain a weak smile. When he sensed the calm in the storm, he placed his hands on her knees. He said, "Look, I understand we don't see each other a lot, so that's partly to blame, but we've got to do better. When the baby is born, things are going to get tougher. We have to work on our marriage. Do you want your daughter to have the kind of childhood you had?"

Born in a small town outside of Twin Falls, Idaho, Sam's childhood was a mystery she rarely discussed. But Jeff knew it was bad. When he tried to crack that shell of Sam's past, which was often, she'd deny him of any details other than that she claimed her parents were heartless religious nuts. When Sam refused to go to her father's funeral while they were in college, Jeff just assumed his wife's trauma was child neglect. The mystery deepened when Sam's newly widowed mother didn't show at their wedding. "Revenge because I blew off my dead father," is how Sam explained her absence. Sam's side of the wedding party featured no family but three cousins and an aunt and uncle. About two dozen of her sorority sisters filled the void and spared them the awkwardness. Their marriage, which was consummated three years ago in San Diego at the Coronado, was a blast as the party lasted well past midnight. Unfortunately, with no support from the bride's family, to this day, part of the $30,000 wedding tab still festered on their credit cards.

Sam tried to remain stoic after her husband mentioned her childhood, but her nose twitched and her eyebrows furrowed almost imperceptibly. Not allowing her to answer, Jeff continued, "Neither one of us would have got married if we knew this was how it was going to be."

After another moment, Sam finally broke her silence and conceded, "I know things aren't good, but I don't want it to stress the pregnancy. I figured we could address it after the baby is born."

"I don't see this conversation getting any easier after we become parents," Jeff said dimly. "We should address this now."

Sam sighed. "It's hard to be happy when we rarely see each other, and when we do, we're both spent." She paused and rubbed her forehead. Continuing, she said, "After we graduated, we took road trips on your Harley, we played softball, we went to jazz clubs, and we had date night every Saturday." She paused, reflecting. Then, "You used to serenade me with sultry sax before every date, remember?"

Jeff answered, "Yes, and then the student loans came due. And then the mortgage, and then your overnight shift began." He huffed angrily and added, "And then we stopped eating out when you went on your vegan diet."

Sam sighed and shook her head in disgust. She corrected, "Again, Jeff, for the nth time, it's not a diet; it's a lifestyle." She twisted in her chair and looked away from him, her voice dry. "You knew I was vegetarian when I met you *and* before you married me. I don't want to hear it."

Jeff snapped, "But now you're vegan, not vegetarian!" He loved his pizza, the meat-lovers special at Lou Malnati's specifically. When Sam graduated from vegetarian to vegan, their regular pizza visits ended. Ever since, Jeff had grudged her decision even though he was free to eat whatever he wanted.

Sam ignored his factual retort.

Tartly, she stated, "Well, food is a lot cheaper without us going to the steakhouse every week, isn't it?" She didn't let him answer. "We should start being mindful about money moving forward if we're going to be responsible parents." She glared, her wide-set eyes narrowing. "And I don't want to work in a hospital for the rest of my life."

Jeff crossed his arms. "And what about college for the baby? How much do you think that's gonna cost in eighteen years?" He huffed hard. "Our lives seem to be nothing more than an insufferable amount of work that will never end."

Sam feigned a half-smile, but Jeff knew how to read her. Whenever she sucked in her cheeks as if she was smoking a cigar, it was a concession that Jeff was right. She said flatly, "This is our life and we need to make the most of it. Be happy, in a few months we'll have a daughter, and everything will change."

"Actually, it won't." He snuffed. "It will just be more of the same: more work, more bills, and more stress."

She placed her palm on his wrist and nodded at her belly.

"Someday, after your daughter is born, we can take some chances." She paused and raised her head to think. "Tell you what, why don't we go to Vegas at the end of the month? One last hurrah before we clamp down. We can go for a weekend to relax and recharge." She winked and threw him a coy smile. "We can grab you a meaty pizza and I'll even let you place a few bets on the Bears game."

"You will let me?" Disbelief filled his voice. "Since when do I need permission to manage our money?"

She crooked an eyebrow and looked at him pointedly. She motioned to her belly again.

Jeff understood and tried to think about Las Vegas. He needed an exciting weekend. Gambling, fine dining, betting on NFL games... his brain instinctively lapped up the idea and issued a comforting smile to his face.

His wife smiled back and stood up, walking away. "Great," she said. "I'll book it next week."

Jeff remained in his seat quietly, but his stomach groaned in pain. Not because he was hungry, nor because his wife had an authoritarian streak likened to Stalin, but because he knew he was pliant to the bribe. Little did he know a new type of pain awaited in the new year.

THE COMFORTABLE PAIN PRINCIPLE

Mediocre Comfort Is a Silent Disease that Poisons Dreams

3

In my early twenties, I bought a sports car I couldn't afford: a black Mitsubishi 3000GT. At the time, I had a job that paid more than I had ever earned before. I was so proud of myself, not realizing I was being a dumbass. Instead of saving my paycheck or investing it in my business ideas, I spent it on a car which incidentally, I parked on my Mom's driveway. I wanted to fake outer success while my inner battle was one blizzard away from suicide. The gambit failed miserably. The car sacked me with debt and hindered my choices, but worse, it made me comfortable in my pain. The illusion of fake success marred my motivation to work for real success.

The Comfortable Pain Principle: *Give a man a tolerable job that pays just enough to provide mediocre comfort and I'll show you a man who won't change a damn thing.* New words might appear in his head, but those words won't write a new story[S2]. Make no mistake: if you're moderately comfortable in your pain, you're feeding the beast that is mediocrity. And that beast slowly suffocates your dream. Your willingness to turn off the TV, switch jobs, take risks, or do whatever is necessary dissipates. When dreams can be faked in a six-minute event, or in my case, however long it took to sign the auto loan, my desire to actually work for the real thing evaporated.

Mediocre comfort, just enough to lull you into complacency, is designed to cement you into the same rut week after week, year after year. The regular paycheck and its buying bribes: the college basketball games, the four days in Las Vegas, and the bet on the Chicago Bears—all of it keeps you at the desk with the same pen, the same words, and the same plot. In the end, time passes, but the story remains the same.

This scheme, orchestrated nearly a century ago, is how our slavery is sealed, and our dream bribed. In 1926, in an interview published by the *World's Work* magazine, industrial titan Henry Ford admitted why he reduced his workers' labor load from six days and forty-eight hours to five days and forty hours, all while keeping pay the same. He said:

It is the influence of leisure on consumption which makes the [five-day] workweek so necessary. The people who consume the bulk of goods are the people who make them. That is a fact we must never forget, that is the secret of our prosperity.

He continued:

The people with a 5-day week will consume more goods than the people with a 6-day week. People who have more leisure must have more clothes. They must have a greater variety of food. They must have more transportation facilities. They naturally must have more service of various kinds. This increased consumption will require greater production than we now have. Instead of business being slowed up because the people are 'off work', it will be speeded up... This will lead to more work. And this to more profits.

A six-day workweek makes our slavery (and its discomfort) too obvious, so we're gifted an extra day of comfort and consumption to engorge our complacency. Truth is, the modern five-day forty-hour workweek is a scheme that would make the devil smile. Shrouded in busyness, the presumptive work week keeps you moderately sheltered, diabetically fed, and addictively entertained—just enough to keep you obediently passive and ignorant to this system. And as long as we're comfortable in our busyness, our weekend bribe (and its distraction) continues while change becomes nothing more than a dead dream and an empty political slogan. Suddenly Instagram likes from strangers are more important than the only like that matters... *a like from you.*

Another fact: Most people will never escape mediocrity and its economic cult unless it triggers an FTE or a "fuck this event." A "fuck this event" is a traumatic incident that takes you over the edge. It is the ultimate disrupter of comfort, a pejorative "punch the wall" episode usually accompanied by such phrases as: "F-this!" or "I can't live like this anymore!"

My FTE slapped me upside the head when I silently endured a blizzard on the side of the road. Your FTE could come from an airport bench, your new plastic bed for the evening, as you're stranded by weather thousands of miles from home, a revelation that once again, your child lacks a father and your wife lacks a husband. Other times, your FTE is shared by many like a worldwide pandemic that causes you to lose your job, your savings, and your sanity. If mediocrity feeds on comfort through a feeding tube, the FTE rips it out. It sears your brain with a new reality: the pain of the status quo (and comfort's diminishing medicinal effect) finally exceeds the anticipated pain of its escape. Congratulations, the first step in escaping a soul-suffocating religion is to realize you're in one.

- A person who lives in moderate comfort will rarely find the motivation to fight the status quo.

- Comfort fuels mediocrity and a life mired in tediousness.

- The modern five-day work week is a Scripted tool for obedience and complacency.

- A "fuck this event" (FTE) is a traumatic event where the pain of the status quo is perceived to be worse than the pain of escaping it.

THE SOMEDAY PRINCIPLE

Regard Someday as a Liar Who Really Means Never

A few months ago, I attended a funeral for a family member who by most measures died too young. If you ever want some urgent life perspective, spend some time in a cemetery. As I walked around the cemetery examining the headstones of the dead, many of whom also died young, I was struck with an incredible sense of regret. Not for myself, but for the lost souls who didn't live the life they dreamed. Dreams which most likely died in the world of *someday*—someday I'll do this, someday I'll do that, someday after the pregnancy, someday when the debts are gone… someday.

And yet, someday never came.

Someday needs to be removed from your vocabulary. It is a distant sunrise in the theater of your mind, an excuse for inaction, a mental bribe to dismiss today for an unknown future that never arrives. The problem with someday is it's a liar. Like a mathematical fractal, someday is a reiterative and recursive function that continues infinitely. When one precondition is resolved, another appears. And as old preconditions are met, new ones arrive and someday remains.

"I'm waiting for the new year…"
"I'm waiting to finish school…"
"I'm waiting for my wife to get a job…"
"I'm waiting for a better job…"
"I'm waiting for a promotion…"
"I'm waiting for my kids to be older…"
"I'm waiting for the pandemic to be over…"
"I'm waiting for a new President to be in office…"
"I'm waiting for the economy to get better…"
"I'm waiting until I fix the hot-water heater…"
"I'm waiting until my vacation…"
"I'm waiting to retire…"

The common thread is always the same . . . "I'm waiting." Someday is a bribe to pacify your soul into believing a future possibility. And it's a big fat lie that's birthed in Latersville that dies in Neversville. Stop trusting "someday" because your tomorrow knows it's a liar.

The Someday Principle regards *someday as never.* The timing will never be perfect. Someday must come today. Now. Seven "todays" is a week and 365 make a year. Fail to transform someday into today, and expect a new excuse: "well, I'm just too old to start." The next thing you know, there's a funeral. And you end up dead in a cemetery, your dreams buried with you.

☑ KEY CONCEPTS

- Someday is a lie, code for never.
- Someday is an excuse for inaction, a mental bribe to dismiss today for a tomorrow that never comes.
- Someday is like betting on a fractal to end.
- Someday must become today.

THE HONEYPOT
SUNDAY, SEPTEMBER 26TH, 2010 - 5:31 PM
(Two years later)

S amantha would never book that trip to Las Vegas.

Just days after Jeff spoke to his wife about their marriage and their lives, the stock market crashed. Then a few weeks later, the market crashed again. Neither had investments, but by the time the smoke cleared, Jeff had lost his job.

With no emergency savings and Sam's paycheck their only income, they triaged their bills. First, they defaulted on their cars. When it was over, the 3-Series Beemer and the Navigator were replaced by a Civic and a Corolla. Worse, the Corolla was a stinking cigarette beater owned by Seth, Jeff's older brother, who loved Newport 100s more than life itself. Not that Seth didn't drive, but he was doing ten months in Cook County jail for armed robbery after trying to steal ten cartons of said cigarettes from a 7-Eleven. Don't ask.

Of course, while the markets were free-falling, the financial pundits pleaded "Don't panic!" and "Don't sell at the bottom!" but for Jeff and his wife, they had no choice. Sam had a recession-proof job as a nurse, but she was also pregnant. After giving birth to their daughter Madison, Sam used all her maternity leave as well as her vacation days. Because the recession lasted nearly two years, her job alone wasn't enough to keep the creditors away.

To survive Jeff's unemployment and the recession's masterful haircut of housing prices, they dug into what little they saved in their 401(k)s. When the recovery slunk in, it was too late. They would lose their home to foreclosure. The 401(k)s—gone. All signs of affluence—gone.

Forced to downsize, they rented a two-bedroom townhome in Palatine, which Jeff considered sacrilege. Their landlord was Dave Bliss, Sam's old college boyfriend. Jeff insisted Dave still had eyes for his leggy wife who, after a MAC Makeup hour, could stunt for Cameron Diaz. And because Bella was built like a horse (and ate like one), they struggled to find a rental that would allow large dogs. In Sam's words, "Dave owed me a courtesy."

When Jeff questioned the details of Dave's mysterious "courtesy," a cross-fire erupted. After a few minutes, Sam finally waved off Jeff's insecurities. Nonplussed, she said, "I'm sorry, Jeff, but I told him we had a foreclosure. I told him you lost your job. I told him no one will rent to us because of our Bella. I told him our sob story, and he was sympathetic. And because we're still cordial on Facebook, he did me a favor."

Jeff deadpanned, "Well, I hope that's the only thing he did."

To make matters worse, their two-story townhouse was, in Jeff's words, "a shit-hole," a big downgrade from the house they'd just lost. The main living area was on the second floor and only accessible by a long narrow staircase abutted with a downstairs garage. The floors were a grimy mustard linoleum and the kitchen cabinetry was a flaky matte white made of pressed board, the kind you'd find in a mid-century asylum. Worse, the townhouse overlooked Northwest Highway, one of the busier roads in Palatine. Quiet was scarce, swallowed by emergency sirens, growling traffic, and Harleys with dual pipes. Still, Sam didn't complain. Her childhood home in Twin Falls was a double-wide trailer on sixty acres that looked more like a junkyard than a farm. For her, a fourteen-hundred square foot townhome was still an upgrade. As long as she had a gas stove to feed her culinary hobbies, she was good.

Now parents of a two-year-old daughter, Jeff, 29, and his wife, 28, found themselves in a position worse than before. The recession quickly stifled the marital conversation they'd had before the birth of their daughter. Instead of trying to improve their marriage, they were now working to survive it. The recession ushered in a "new normal" of tedium, but it also cracked their egg of ignorance; their daughter's birth fried it. They had another human to care for, feed, nurture, and educate. When their daughter turned 18, college tuition would be in the six-figure realm. Life couldn't remain business as usual. Something had to change.

Once they settled into their "shit-hole" townhouse, they agreed to seek guidance.

Jeff tuned into CNBC frequently and listened to a variety of financial experts. They all parroted the same talking points, despite reports of many investors losing their life savings. And their jobs. The central theme seemed to be a combination of disciplined saving, frugal living, and patience. As Jeff sat and watched another financial sermon from his bed, his blood pressure rose, and his head throbbed. The last straw was when a Wall Street money manager, who just happened to manage $600 million in assets, pleaded for everyone to "invest more," followed by "be patient." He flipped the TV off and slammed the remote control against the night stand. He turned angrily to his wife, whose back was to him while she rifled through the dresser.

"These fuckers. It's easy to sell patience from a yacht when those buying it are the ones stuck on the Titanic."

Sam glanced up and looked at him in the mirrored reflection. "We can talk about it after dinner," she said, shoving the drawer closed.

After Jeff washed the dishes and Sam put Madison to sleep, they met at the kitchen table. Sam sighed and gazed at the ceiling, eyeballing a small spider web dangling from the corner. Or maybe it was dust. She wondered if there was a spider to catch and toss outside as Jeff didn't share her benevolence for saving anything that crawled. With Jeff's new job starting tomorrow, it was time he stopped playing Mr. Mom. The status quo for the last two years was a treading-water story. She supported the family, and credit cards bridged the gap. Meanwhile, Jeff changed diapers and pushed resumes anywhere they could be pushed. They both knew the recession had exposed them, and they wanted a new plan with a new direction. It was time to make some decisions.

After an uncomfortable silence, Sam opened. "Going forward," she said, flicking a pencil, "we've got to save every penny." She nodded to her husband's old iPhone. "No more upgrading things we don't really need. No more eating out. We won't buy a new car until we need to. HBO and your MLB Season Pass, sorry, that will have to go too." Neutered by a stretch of financial struggles and a wife who had carried the load since shit hit the fan, he protested weakly. "Wait a sec, you were actually listening to those CNBC fools? Is that where this is coming from?"

Sam replied, "Partly. I've been listening to a radio show on the way to work, this guy named Dave. He says we need to have an emergency fund. And if we pay off all our debts and start saving at least a hundred dollars a month, he says we'll have millions by the time we're sixty-five. Millions!"

Jeff barked, his eyes pried wide, "Sixty-five? I'm struggling to get to thirty!"

Sam rambled on. "So, after listening to a few shows, I read his website. And then I found other websites that said similar things." She paused and looked at Jeff pointedly. "Did you know if you stopped going to Starbucks and we saved that money, we'd have thousands of dollars in forty years? And all that money you waste going to Cubs games, how much will that be worth years from now?"

Jeff gestured to Bella, sleeping near their feet. Snippy, he exclaimed, "How wonderful, Samantha, why don't we just dump Bella off at the pound? You know how much money we can save on dog food?" His face tensed as he bit his lips, giving his wife a hard stare. Whenever Jeff called her "Samantha," she knew he wanted her attention.

She dismissed him and continued. "Anyway, here's how it works. We're going to pay off all our debts and save everything we can. Then we invest it. Something called an indexed fund. Starting now, Jeff"—she lifted a finger in the air—"every dime must be accounted for." She paused and flicked him on the wrist with the same finger. "Accounting, Jeff, you're the numbers guy!" She smiled pleadingly. "We can do this!" Bella looked up from her nap, hoping Sam's exuberance signaled a forthcoming cookie.

Jeff sized her up. "Says who? Do I have any say in this? Why are you suddenly going Feminazi on me and dictating our finances? I like my pizza and my Cubs game." Then he yelled. "And my coffee!" He flashed her a look of contempt.

Whoops.

Sam took a deliberate slow-motion sip of her coffee—time for Plan B.

"Jeff," she stated measuredly, "we tried it your way for the first five years of our marriage. What did that get us? A pile of debt, I'm stuck doing graveyard at the hospital, and you lose your damn job. I've supported us for the last two years, so now we're going to do it my way. We haven't even paid off our wedding yet!"

Jeff's voice now boomed. "You wanted that wedding!" He mimicked the memory of his wife's plea in singsong, "*Oh Jeff, wouldn't it be great if we can get married at Coronado?* And then it just blew up into some big party you could throw with your sorority sisters." He shook his head, disgusted.

Sam nervously repositioned herself in the chair and lowered her voice, trying to appear reasonable. "Look, we're both culpable for our situation. I admit that. When you gave me my Louis Vuitton purse for my birthday, I loved you for it and didn't complain. When you surprised me with a big SUV, I didn't object. I was good with it because you knew I was tired of rolling around in junk cars my whole life."

"Oh?" Jeff says, surprised, "The Grand Am or the Accord?"

"Both," she paused. "If we're going to provide for our family"—she gestured to the closed bedroom door—"which is now three people, we have to start being smart about the future, from our retirement to Madison's college. This is how everyone says it's done."

Jeff clenched his jaw. "Everyone?" He scoffed hard and slammed his hand on the table. "What the fuck do they know? Everyone is in the same shitty situation."

THE ECONOMIC RELIGION PRINCIPLE

The Rat Race Is the World's Economic Religion, and Culture Is Its Church

In 2020, a viral video surfaced of a young man receiving his first paycheck. As he tore open the envelope, his wide-eyed smile and joyful gaiety were immediately replaced by a frown. He'd expected the entirety of his earnings and was utterly disappointed when he discovered taxes took a big chunk of it. In his angry words, "They finessed me!"

Like this youngster, you too were "finessed" to partake in this insanity, the world's economic religion, or what's commonly called the rat race. And the Script is its gospel, and media and culture are its church. Behold the Economic Religion Principle: *the rat race is an economic theology for existence where your participation is conscripted, and then expected.* At birth, you inherited this religion from your parents. With your first breath, you were immediately stamped with a barcode, a Social Security number. From then on, it is presumed that you will willfully partake in the rat race paradigm as one of two players:

> 1) *the shopping-rat*, someone who is promised happiness, respect, and fulfillment as a function of conspicuous consumption, i.e., Neiman Marcus over Walmart, Mercedes over Honda.

> or

> 2) *the savings-rat*, someone who believes that saving a hundred bucks a month from her job while penny-pinching will make her rich, provided she patiently invests it in a Wall Street-sponsored indexed-fund for many decades.

The shopping-rat enjoys his cheese every weekend. He scurries around the rat race seeking to improve his cheese, and as fast as possible. Meanwhile, the Wall Street savings-rat minimizes his cheese consumption. He doesn't *spend* his money on rat race bread-and-circuses, no, he *invests his money* in corporations who *provide* the bread-and-circuses. It's completely diabolical!

No matter which role you play, you're groomed for one purpose: *Free-range economic slavery.*

Unbeknownst to most, we're wards of the state. Yes, property. Collateralized by our labor, debt, and consumption, we're owned by our respective country. While this fact sounds like a radical conspiracy theory, it isn't. Try leaving your Fatherland without a visa or a passport. Try buying food or gas without paying the sales tax. Don't renew your driver's license, or worse, stop paying your property taxes and see what you really own. You are biological chattel securitized by a lifetime of taxation. Free? Ha, no, barcoded and enslaved.

In return for our compliance, culture has made rotten cheese seem palatable. If you play the game as a shopping-rat, your cheese is Friday night, Saturday, and a dreadful Sunday that fears Monday. If you're a savings-rat, your rotten cheese is an elderly retirement promised decades later. Regardless of the role played, your indoctrination began young. Consecrated by our parents who are devout believers, we're told to follow the rules and listen to authority. Advancement of the agreement is then reinforced by an inescapable, omnipotent church. From education, to media, entertainment, and government, the dogma is the same: *Success comes from a good education at a good college, followed by a good job and a good house in a good neighborhood, eclipsing with a good investment portfolio grown over a good 40 years.* Despite all those "goods," nowhere in this implied social contract is freedom and soulful happiness. Of course, none of this happens with your knowledge, much less your consent. *The best way to keep slaves obedient is to make sure they don't know they're slaves.*

As with all religious dogma, deviation has consequences. Just ask any teenager who forgoes college and wants to learn how to install HVAC systems, fix cars, or unclog toilets. Ask any college graduate who doesn't interview for a job and instead starts a business. Altogether, this cultural superstructure is the most potent deception ever foisted on humanity: an economic cult known as the rat race.

Here is the script behind the Script, the gospel that powers the scheme:

1. [S]CHOOLING
2. [C]ONSUMERISM
3. [R]ESPONSIBILITY
4. [I]GNORANCE
5. [P]ROMISES
6. [T]AXATION

SCHOOLING

It's no mistake that you are schooled Monday through Friday for eighteen years just so you can work Monday through Friday for the next fifty. All levels of education, from elementary to university, normalize you into the Monday-through-Friday work scheme. Formal schooling tells us that intelligence is correlated to rote memory and repetition, and that such behavior is rewardable. School tells us that truth comes from authority. School teaches us how to be an obedient rat in the system, a good employee in the hive-minded, media-fed citizenry. With critical thinking abandoned, we've become smart enough to *do the work*, but not smart enough to question those who tell us *how to work*.

For example, every so often, I get stuck listening to financial talk radio. On one particular show, a caller complained that he and his wife owned nearly one million dollars in college loans and credit card debt. And yet, both of them had advanced degrees that cost them nearly $300,000. So, over a quarter of a million dollars spent in "schooling" and they're about as advanced in managing money as a chimpanzee. Score two more rats for the Script.

CONSUMERISM

As a child, we're taught to associate happiness with toys—dolls, Lego sets, Tonka trucks. As a teen, this association grows, as do the prices: XBOXs, electric guitars, bicycles. By the time we hit adulthood, this association continues, except now the toys require financing: entertainment systems, cars, boats, houses. As they say, insanity is financing a house for thirty years so you can enjoy it only on the weekend because you're too busy paying for it. While your home might be lovely, its three-decade mortgage isn't just a lien on the property; it's a lien on your labor, not to mention the lifetime lien from the state, commonly known as a property tax.

RESPONSIBILITY (AND SURVIVAL)

The more responsibility undertaken, mortgages, student loans, car payments, children, the stronger the Script's grip becomes. Existence, such as food, housing, healthcare, baby shoes, is damn expensive. Deviously, the Script snags you young. With six-figures in student loans and a crappy job that can't move the needle, what better way to imprison yourself? The yoke of responsibility is the Script's MVP because it forces labor and consumption. In America, a college degree can cost six figures or more. The cost of raising a child can eclipse a quarter-million dollars. Weddings now can cost an upwards of $50,000. Worse, you can't get sick. Your health insurance is about as useful as a chain-link fence is at stopping mosquitos. Oh, the joy of paying $700 for an ibuprofen pill just because the hospital dispensed it. Few escape this cruel joke and its avalanche of debt. It strips you of choice, putting a Scripted pen[S2] in charge. The *work/pay bills/die* scheme is now operative. You're forced into labor, or you live in a trailer, or in today's culture, you live with your parents.

IGNORANCE

Ever wonder why no school or university taught you how to win your freedom? How to get rich? How to build a legacy while tapping into happiness and soulful fulfillment? How to think outside the box created by our thought-policers? Ever notice most information on wealth involves jobs, saving, and stock market patience? Why is the only version of financial freedom sanctioned by the *Script* the "save and invest" narrative? Ignorance is a Scripted goal. Authority pushes it, and consensus seals the deal.

In 1961, the Milgram Experiment revealed a troubling truth. When given orders by an authority figure, the average person will follow them. Without question. Even when those orders are harmful, even fatal, to innocent participants. Obedience to authority starts with our parents and is enforced during schooling. As long as the authority is recognized as legal and legitimate, people will obey. And there is no shortage of Scripted apostles preaching the gospel of the rat race: Yahoo Finance, Marketwatch, CNBC, Forbes, Reddit, and a multitude of rat race approved books from best-selling authors. When the crowd says, "this is how it's done," then it must be the truth. Omission of the truth by authority leads to consensus.

PROMISES

The Script survives on lofty (and often distant) promises. The promise that the six-figure degree you just earned will score you the job of your choosing. The promise of lofty stock market returns, a vibrant economy, low inflation, and a growing job market. The promise that if you buy this car or that tech gadget, you'll be happy. And the dazzling promise that tops them all: invest all your savings with Wall Street (funding companies that support the Script) for thirty, forty, or fifty years, and then one distant day, you'll retire rich and win your freedom. Meanwhile, the central bank just printed another $3 trillion in fiat money, your alma mater just signed a new football coach for $20 million, and that hedge-fund billionaire wrote another book on how indexed-funds are the greatest invention since electricity.

TAXATION

The rat race's primary purpose: Taxation and the confiscation of your labor, your risks, and your consumption. When you get your paycheck, you're taxed (payroll tax). When you buy food and life's necessities, you're taxed (sales tax). When you take investment risks that pay off, you're taxed (capital gains tax) but get no benefit when they don't. When you buy a home, you're taxed indefinitely (property tax). When the Federal Reserve prints more funny money, you're taxed (inflation). And finally, death—up to half of whatever pittance remains after all these insane taxes—is taxed again (inheritance tax). If confiscating 100 percent of your economic output makes slavery, at what point does it stop being slavery? 80 percent? 50 percent? 39.6 percent? No matter the number, we've become human collateral to keep the sovereign debt printers churning.

Once the Script snags you into its web and the walls of the rat race grow taller, mediocre comforts[P3] bribe you with its Pavlovian rewards: an addictive HBO series, a sporting event, a financed Audi that impresses the impressionable. Life slowly deteriorates from our childhood objective, happiness maximization, to nearly every adult's reality, misery minimization. Truth: your lifetime role has been Scripted for an uninspiring, tax-paying performance compliments of a Machiavellian system engineered for debt and dependence, not dreams. Niccolò Machiavelli would be impressed. Once you understand the religion and its priestly operatives, you can plot an escape.

☑ KEY CONCEPTS

- Regard the rat race like an economic religion, a cult of unwitting participants.
- You participate in the rat race in one of two roles: a shopping-rat or a savings-rat.
- A shopping-rat is a slave to consumption (of goods and media), a savings-rat is a slave to his savings and portfolio.
- When a shopping-rat questions the rat race, culture promotes the other rat race role, a savings-rat.
- The Script, or rat race dogma, has six components: [S]chooling [C]onsumption, [R]esponsibility [I]gnorance [P]romises, and [T]axation.

THE HONEYPOT PRINCIPLE

Living Patiently Poor to Die Foolishly Rich Is Patently Stupid

When driving into my neighborhood, there's a sign you wouldn't expect to see in a subdivision filled with seven-figures homes. It reads, *Warning: Bait Cars May Be Present.* If you're not familiar with computer terminology, a *honeypot* is a security measure designed to deflect and counteract unauthorized access to computer systems. The police also deploy honeypots in the form of sting operations, or in my case, parking bait cars in areas where thieves may troll for opportunity. In effect, the Honeypot Principle *is a scheme that tempts divergent behavior—but it still is part of the system.*

The rat race is equally clever and has its own honeypot. Its default orthodoxy is consumption: unconstrained materialism with the illusion that such consumption will make you hotter, healthier, and happier. Work, buy, pay taxes, repeat. But if you're smart enough to expose that scam and attempt divergent behavior, the Script ushers you into its fail-safe honeypot—becoming a fanatical savings-rat who will invest every dime into the stock market.

Open any best-selling finance book, a financial website, or a money magazine. Honeypot dogma is everywhere.

- *If you save 10% of your paycheck every month and invest it into the stock market, it will be worth millions in fifty years! You can retire rich!*

- *If you stop drinking Starbucks and invest your savings in an indexed-fund, you'll have six figures by the time your 65!*

Behind the honeypot scheme is another rat race conspirator: *compound interest,* or what I call the *Slowlane.* The Slowlane is the financial plan of optimizing mediocrity, a stale creed that if you live poorly today, depriving yourself of daily lattes, new cars, nice restaurants, and regular vacations, you can live richly later. Then, such magical futures are backed by magical charts, which undoubtedly show your financial empire magically ascending into the stratosphere after four or five magical decades. Great in theory, not so much in application. Fact is, the capital markets were never designed to make you rich. According to Investopedia, a capital market is "a medium to channel savings and investment between suppliers of capital such as retail and institutional investors, and users of capital, like businesses, government and individuals." The definition says nothing about getting rich as the financial zealots promise.

Simply put, compound interest is a dormant mathematical calculation with little to no impact on small numbers. The only thing that weaponizes compound interest is a large number. And people stuck in the rat race have no access to large numbers. Consider the following chart which shows the compound-interest payday for various lump sums at a five percent yield.

5% INTEREST	MONTHLY INCOME
$500	$2.08
$5,000	$20.83
$50,000	$208.33
$500,000	$2,083.33
$5,000,000	$20,833.33

Five percent interest on $5 million dollars is a decent chunk of change. Problem is, most rat racers will never get there, and those who do, will need forty, or fifty years. You're not going to escape the rat race turning nickels into dimes while waiting for a geriatric ward—for compound interest to truly invoke its power, you'll need millions, *and you'll need it fast.*

To make matters worse, pushing the Slowlane honeypot as a career is terribly lucrative. For example, I once came across a video from *Forbes*, a magazine featuring entrepreneurs and self-made business hotshots. This video, aptly titled "How to Get Rich," pushed the "save for fifty years" narrative. After watching the video, I could only chuckle at the unspoken hypocrisy that escapes critique. So I did a little research into *Forbes* cover models. You know how many *Forbes* millionaires and billionaires actually followed this advice as recommended in the video?

None.

Subtract the entrepreneurs, the inheritors, the sports and entertainment titans, the corporate insiders, and those that serve the financial industry over investing in it, and you'll find exactly what I found: the stock market isn't making investors wealthy. *It makes its sycophants wealthy.* As expected, not one *Forbes* cover model got rich from the Slowlane honeypot. But a massive basket of them got rich pushing the advice.

Champagne hypocrites preach rat race constructs (jobs, stocks, frugality, patience) while they get rich with leveraged entrepreneurship (book sales, money management fees, seminars, financial products). For some reason, I don't think that money guru who lives in Fiji and has houses spread around the world is depriving himself of coffee, nice restaurants, and Swedish massages. In other words, stop drinking $5 coffee so we can buy our $5000 champagne. Beware of champagne hypocrites—propagandists who get rich selling you a "get rich" strategy that didn't make them rich. Sounds like a mouthful, but if what your money guru *sells* and what your money guru *does* are two different things, you need a new guru.

Unfortunately, the consumption and compound interest doctrines are symbiotic to the rat race regime, two sides of the same rigged coin. It's infallibly devious. Two doors, same slaughterhouse. No matter which side you play, you're being conned. Instead of consuming and shopping for happiness, you're saving and waiting for freedom. Adding to the irony, all your excess labor (savings) is invested into the stock market to help grow the companies facilitating the consumption paradigm.

While compound interest is a powerful mathematical truth (I do have a finance degree), in the context of economic realities it's the Script's biggest lie. Not because the math doesn't work (it does) but because its application is never put into a realistic context. In effect, compound interest is the financial world's version of the Drake Equation; it's dependent on variable savings rates, variable jobs, variable returns, variable market instruments, variable inflation, variable political and economic climates, and finally, a variable life expectancy.

True, compound interest via market investments might build a portfolio over the decades. But compound interest's evil twin—inflation—is also gnawing away at your real purchasing power. If you start saving at twenty-five in the year 2021 and end with millions by your sixty-fifth birthday (year 2061) your millions won't be worth what it is today. A million today gets you a decent house. A million in 2061 might only snag a decent car.

Second, compound interest assumes a lot of "constants." Constant employment, constant health, constant saving, constant economic booms, and constant controlled inflation. With all those stars in an unlikely alignment, you're better off rolling dice in Las Vegas. Reality kills dreams. And it kills compound interest calculations on that stupid index card.

Empirically, ask yourself this. If compound interest was so effective, where are all the sixty-five-year-old multi-millionaires? Why aren't at least half of the retired, rich? Are your grandparents multimillionaires?

According to a 2018 study by Northwestern Mutual, a third of Baby Boomers in retirement, or approaching it, have less than $25,000 saved, or worse, nothing. It begs the question: If 33 percent can barely scrape up and invest 25Gs, how much do the other 66 percent have? According to 2019 data from the Federal Reserve's Survey of Consumer Finances, a retiree in the 65-74 age range has a retirement account of a paltry $164,000. Where are all those millionaires? This data unmasks the scientist. Multi-millionaire survivors of compound interest and its ridiculous demands on savings and frugality are probably less than one percent—and that one percent gets the front page of Yahoo Finance and Marketwatch.

The truth is, Wall Street won't make you rich—*unless you work on Wall Street*. Market operators are the scientists, and they're not in the business of funding your posh retirement. They're in the business of funding their posh Hampton estates, their yachts, and their Italian villas. Metaphorically, if the world's economic religion had a heaven, compound interest would be the sacrament. Its preacher—the financial industry (and their media benefactors)—collects the tithes.

So when that radio host who is on 500 radio stations and lives in a mega ten-million-dollar mansion encourages you to scream on the phone because you haven't dined at a restaurant for three years, all in the name of being debt free, ask yourself this: Is this person financially free because that's precisely what they did? Or is he wealthy from selling books and preferred provider endorsements on a nationally syndicated radio/TV show?

In the same way a prison doesn't give their inmates instructions on how to escape, don't expect the rat race to advertise its escape. A financial guru likely lives a spectacular life not because of their advice, but because they've sold it to enough fools who believe the lie. Don't consent to be imprisoned for the first sixty-five years of your life so you can enjoy the last ten. Hope, patience, and deprivation are not a financial plan. It's bondage.

☑ KEY CONCEPTS

- Compound interest, or the Slowlane, is the idea that one dollar saved today will be worth millions in the distant future.

- The spending- and savings-rat are symbiotic, two sides to the same rigged coin.

- Inflation, time, and many lofty assumptions neuters compound interest.

- Data supports that compound interest, when applied in real life with real life circumstances, is grossly ineffective.

- The stock market isn't making investors wealthy; it makes its sycophants wealthy.

- Via mass marketing, champagne hypocrites get rich selling a "get rich" strategy that didn't make them rich.

- In the same way a prison doesn't give its inmates directions for escape, the rat race doesn't either.

DEATH BY A THOUSAND PENNIES
SATURDAY, SEPTEMBER 26TH, 2015 - 2:00 PM
(5 years later)

Jeff peered out the second-floor window, his back to the kitchen table while his wife sat next to him. The sky was mostly overcast. One sunbeam tried to escape, but the gray cumulous quickly swallowed it. He glimpsed down to the backyard and watched his daughter Madison, now seven, playing fetch with Bella. He sipped his whiskey, his second of the day. It burned his throat, but he didn't care. Alcohol was his truth serum, and it pulled no punches today.

As he watched Maddy, it struck him that he didn't recognize her. It seemed just months ago she was crawling. Now she was almost five feet tall and fast-growing into his wife's mini-me. He was saddened that he had little memory of his daughter growing up. She was a spark for his spirit, the light that made his mundane day tolerable, but he didn't spend nearly enough time with her. His heart stung as he remembered that he and his wife have been promising Maddy a Disneyland trip for three years. After failing her again and again, Maddy just stopped asking. Jeff continued his forlorn gaze.

Maddy's long blond hair swirled in the wind as she won a tug-of-war with Bella. It reminded Jeff of riding on his Harley with Sam saddled behind him. Of course, that motorcycle had to be sold after the 2008 economic crash. And today, under Sam's oppressive savings and investment scheme, a motorbike was deemed a "non-essential" item. Worse, Sam had insisted that he sell his saxophone so they could pay off credit cards. He'd vetoed but was overruled. His saxophone was his last refuge of sanity, and now it sat on sale in the window at Saul's Tire and Pawn.

After a victorious tug with Bella, Madison threw the chew toy across the yard. Bella leisurely plodded after it.

Even Bella had changed.

She never used to lose a tug and could typically out-pull a Ford 150. And she could outrun a bullet. But something happened in the past five years... something Jeff couldn't quite explain. Bella went from spry to slog in a blink of an eye. It was like years of pages were added to his story, but the pages were blank—his memories sparse and vague. As the thought marinated in

41

the whiskey, it occurred to him that "sparse and vague" embodied his life. Joy, love, thrill, passion—sparse. His marriage, his life's purpose, his relationship with his daughter—too vague.

He turned from the window and faced his wife, who was swiping through her phone. They were still stuck in their "shit-hole" townhome. Jeff, now 34, and Samantha, 33, were five years into Sam's autocratic financial strategy, a strategy she'd insisted on and enforced while Jeff ambivalently obliged. He couldn't contain the resentment that suffused his face as he glared at his wife. Feeling Jeff's piercing eyes, Sam looked up from her phone.

"Drinking again?"

He mumbled something she couldn't hear. She managed a dismissive nod and returned to her phone.

Jeff wondered why she continued the charade. He knew her better than she did. A lot had changed in five years, but nothing good. A faulty water heater stole Sam's regular hot meditative baths. A loud neighbor who played afternoon *Call of Duty* stole her peaceful sleep. And their hellacious work schedule stole what remained of their listless marriage. He knew she couldn't be happy, but she was hiding it. Or maybe it was denial?

Jeff opened his journal flamboyantly, a journal he'd toted around for his entire life. Named "Neve" (after the actress Neve Campbell, whom he'd crushed on in his teens), the notebook contained various confessions, doodles, calculations, and vision boards. A faded Chicago Cubs decal smudged the cover, its pages frayed and wrinkled. Sam glanced at him as he flicked his pen on one of the pages filled with numbers.

He placidly reported, "Unless we hit the lottery or I start throwing 100 mph fastballs for the Cubs, we're going to be working for the rest of our lives."

Sam gave him a furtive look, ending her phone scroll.

Jeff continued clearing his throat. "I've done the numbers. Even if the stock market kept rising for another ten years, we're still screwed."

Typically dismissive of her husband's overly dramatic situational reports, Sam, for once, was listening. For the last five years, they'd done as all the pundits preached. They saved, they lived frugally, and they invested their excess savings in indexed funds. In exchange for their obedience, their life became increasingly mundane and dispirited. Their reward? An investment account that wasn't growing fast enough because they couldn't save fast enough.

Jeff pointed to Neve, a chart scribed on a page, "This market has been on a tear in the last five years and all we have to show for it is $33,000. For your plan to work, we'll need decades to make this happen, and that's assuming the market continues going higher for the next twenty years!"

Sam placed her phone aside and admonished him, "Well that's $33,000 more than we had five years ago." She glared at him sternly. "We're making progress—they said it wouldn't happen overnight."

Jeff rolled his eyes and then angled into his wife, whispering as if he were speaking near eavesdroppers, "Samantha, let me ask you a serious question, and I want you to be honest. How many great memories can you remember in the last five years?" He glanced out the window at Maddy. "Our trip to Disney with Maddy? How about our Harley road trips in October, you know, when we used to go up to Wisconsin and admire the changing leaves?"

She glared at him with confusion as if he'd just told her they lived on the moon. "Exactly." He slammed Neve shut. "Because there aren't any great memories. We haven't done any of that stuff. And we never will because every dime we earn, we save." His voice grew louder. "It's the same crap. Instead of work, sleep, *spend*, pay bills, repeat, it's work, sleep, *save*, pay bills, repeat. We've replaced the *spend* with the *save*. It's the same god damn rat race."

He furrowed his brow and took another sip of his whiskey.

Sam shifted in her seat, angling away from him. After the silence lingered for an uncomfortable moment, she grabbed his whiskey. She chugged what remained and then exclaimed exasperatedly, "Maybe you're right."

She swallowed hard and scratched her eye, her mind wrangling with the confession. When her lips said nothing, Jeff flashed her an *I'm waiting* expression. She relented. "To be honest with you, I don't know how to feel joy anymore. I don't send my daughter off to school in the morning, and when I do see her, I'm resting in bed trying to sleep off the night shift. I feel like Maddy is my only joy, and if it weren't for her, I'd probably be strung-out on anti-depressants. We don't even see each other anymore, so it's not your fault."

Samantha's nursing career was a grind and had only worsened in recent years. Reality erased her childhood visions of being a thoughtful and loving caregiver who starred in a Nicholas Sparks novel. Healthcare was corporatized and hence, profit optimized. Salaries, benefits, perks, and worse, patient care were all slashed. What wasn't slashed were expectations and patient load. She'd often complain, "If I didn't know better, you'd think I worked at McDonald's. But instead of pushing fries, we're pushing pills while pushing to get to the next patient."

After going second shift for three years, she'd returned to the graveyard shift because it paid an extra $3 per hour. When they discussed—or more like argued—about the move last year, Sam would contend, "We have to save more!" Jeff objected because he knew what the late shift did to her and their relationship. San would rebut, "We need the extra money if we're going to pay off all our debts. I know you hate this townhouse, and we'd like our own place." She continued the spin, "I heard on the news that interest rates are at all-time lows. And I watch the stock market every day. It keeps going up. If we follow the rule of 72, our $30,000 will turn into $60,000 in just six years!" But her face betrayed the confidence in her voice.

Jeff laughed, "Yeah, and then what?" He nodded toward the garage and argued, "By then a new Corolla will cost $40,000. And a 3-bedroom house $1,000,000. And I'm tired of twilight-crosses!"

Their nightly "twilight-cross" was their rendezvous of the workdays. When Jeff got home from work, usually at six or seven at night, Sam readied for work at 11 PM. It was the few hours they had together. But by the time Jeff slugged home, he craved silence, not communication.

Worse, the graveyard shift meant their weekend was mostly ruined. A Friday 11 PM start could have repercussions well into Saturday evening. The return to the graveyard shift drained what little optimism that remained in their marriage—it was death by a thousand pennies, of course, all saved.

Back at the kitchen table, she continued the spin. "Jeff, we've just got to be patient."

But, in reality, she was trying to convince herself. Pointing to her phone, she remarked, her voice still shallow in conviction, "That's what Warren Buffett says, and he's a billionaire."

Jeff stood up from the kitchen table, the chair making a screeching noise as it dragged against the yellowed floor. He ignored whatever was on her phone and walked away. Stopping abruptly, he glared back at his wife, sneering, "I don't think Warren Buffett is a billionaire because he saved five bucks on coffee and diddled with a job he hated for forty years." He slapped Neve on the counter and stomped into the bedroom, the door slamming behind him.

THE SCIENTIST STRATEGY

Don't Play the Rat, Play the Scientist

7

As I walked into my bedroom with my laundry, a small movement at the rear window caught my eye. A fly banged against the windowsill, trying to escape to the world outside. While I reunited my clean socks, I noticed the fly's persistence. Over and over, he smashed himself into the glass, hoping the effort would yield a different result. I paused and watched the fly repeatedly struggle to free himself. With each crash into the window, the insect expected a different outcome from its prior attempts. Clearly the fly's issue wasn't motivation or a shabby work ethic. Regrettably, "trying harder" or "hustle and grind" won't give the fly his freedom… and he will die trying.

Like the trapped fly, our predicament within the rat race superstructure is similar. In scientific experiments, a rat race is a maze defined by predetermined corridors. Within those corridors an occasional reward appears. The rat noses a button, and cheese pops out. The rats appear to make choices, but their choices are bound to a self-contained system. Once the rats resign themselves to the system, they're given the illusion of choice. Some choices are rewarded, but most of them are "walled-in," or scripted, by the maze itself.

As comedienne Lily Tomlin once said, "The trouble with the rat race is that even if you win, you're still a rat." To wit, *only rats win rat races*. Winning the cheese at the end of the week, or in our case, a paycheck and a weekend, changes nothing. The victory is transient and inconsequential. Because next week, we're at it again.

Worse, if you recognize the foolishness of the shopping-rat and its happiness illusion, the Script will usher you into an alternative grind: becoming a mediocrity optimizing savings-rat[P6]. Now instead of working for a weekend that arrives in five days, you're working for a retirement that arrives in five decades. Winners (what few there are) get to retire old at seventy on 40 percent of their normal income while hoping inflation hasn't whittled away their purchasing power. Of course, all this assumes you maintain a high-paying job while being frugal as a Scrooge, as disciplined as a monk, and as patient as a snail.

The answer to this purposeful entrapment isn't a strategy for winning, much less playing. Instead of playing either rat role, consuming for happiness or patiently saving for retirement, refuse to be cast for either. Instead, *take the position of the scientist.*

You probably work a lot harder than me, yet I get paid more. The problem isn't your work ethic. The problem is that you've accepted your role as the fly, a player in the rat race. Your effort is handicapped by an inefficient system—the rat maze, or *rat race economics.* Sit Usain Bolt on a child's tricycle and someone who hasn't raced 100 meters in his life could suddenly beat him. It's not that Bolt lost his speed, it's that he's been burdened by an inefficient system. Is this insanity any different than the fly?

Trying harder doesn't change the system.

The harsh truth is, this "ineffective" system is very effective at maintaining containment. Like a religion that promises heaven behind a comet after drinking the Kool-Aid, the only winning move is not to play. Excommunicate yourself from the church and renounce your role as a rat race participant. Stop banging your head against the window and hoping for a different outcome. Reject the rat race paradigm. Instead, resolve to learn the methods and the means of the laboratory—become the scientist.

☑ KEY CONCEPTS

- The rat race is similar to an actual laboratory rat race, complete with pre-determined corridors and cheese, or rewards.

- Only rats win rat races where victory is a weekend or a distant retirement.

- Hard work in an inefficient system is rendered impotent, sometimes worthless.

- Forsake the two rat race roles and refuse casting for either. Instead, take the position of the scientist.

THE "LOST PRINCIPLE" PRINCIPLE

A Rat Race Investment Pays Negative Returns and Lost Principle

Your friend offers you a $500 investment with the promise to pay you back a week later. Because he's your friend, you accept. After the week passes, he gives you $200 and says, "Thanks, buddy!"

Confused, you ask, "Wow, is this $200 my return?"

Your friend laughs. "Sorry, no, that's what's left of your investment. It didn't work out, and the $300 we lost is gone for good. Would you like to invest again?" After slapping your friend across the face, you tell him to get lost.

Behind this story, you know there is a scam. Your "investment" earned a negative 60 percent. And if your friend ever offered such an investment again, fists might fly. But when it comes to the rat race, we willingly accept this horrible investment. No, not with our money, but with our time. You see, anytime you trade Monday through Friday to earn Saturday and Sunday, you're earning a negative 60 percent. That's spending five to earn two. And unlike money which can be created over and over, time cannot. Once those five days are spent, they're gone. Forever. The Lost Principle Principle states that *a standard rat race investment is subject to a negative 60% return.* Just like your friend's bad investment.

So why wouldn't you hold your time to the same standard? The Script has fantastically convinced you that time is a commodity worth trading, no more valuable than an old rusty wagon at a flea market. If you exchange five days of work for two days of weekend freedom, you're transacting at a negative 60 percent ROI—and it is an expressway to bankruptcy. No wonder no one has time. We're conditioned to repeatedly invest our precious time at negative rates of returns.

Each of us is gifted with 86,400 seconds a day. No one gets more, no one gets less. It is the great equalizer because no one can make more time. Imagine that: you, me, Jeff and Sam Trotman, Taylor Swift, Jeff Bezos, Chairman Kim Jong-un; we all have something in common: We each get 24 hours a day. While most of the world spends those hours leveling up on the latest hot video game or medicating their drab existence in mindless television dramas, others invest those hours in a life with meaning, purpose, and freedom.

Instead of tolerating a negative 60 percent return on your time because that's what your masters told you to tolerate, why not work to shift the balance to a positive return? Is it possible to reverse the deal? Work two days and get five in return? How about working for ten years so you can earn the next forty?

Yes, it is possible. I've done it.

And you can too.

The first step is to prioritize time like you would the king on a chess board. To win at this game, protect the king! Money is the queen: super-important, powerful, and flexible. But time determines the victor. In typical rat race "retire early" circle-jerks, time is marginalized like a commodity, no better than a sacrificial pawn. Protect your king as if it were life or death… because it is.

☑ KEY CONCEPTS

- An investment in the rat race earns a negative 60 percent: you sacrifice Monday through Friday for Saturday and Sunday.

- Unlike money, time cannot be reclaimed once lost—it is always lost principle.

- Time is the great equalizer; all humans possess the same quantity per day.

- Treat time as you would the king in a game of chess, and money as the queen.

THE "FTE"

What's wrong?" It was Friday evening before Sam was to leave for the hospital. After walking upstairs from the garage, Jeff immediately noticed something was amiss. While she was dressed in her burgundy scrubs, her hair was wild and her elbows were planted on the table, her head wrapped in her hands. More concerning, Pinky the Lamb, a tattered stuffed animal Samantha had had since childhood, rested in her lap. The stuffed animal's presence alarmed Jeff. Whenever Pinky came off the shelf, he knew his wife was grappling some intense emotions.

Jeff glanced at the bedroom. "Is Maddy okay?"

She looked up from the kitchen table, eyes glossy. She said flatly, "She's fine. In her room." Jeff spied a torn envelope and a letter in her hand.

"What's that?" Jeff gestured, moving forward, anxiety now chiseling his face. She folded it quickly and placed it atop Pinky, avoiding eye contact.

After a moment, she muttered, "It's my test results."

Jeff gasped, and his mouth dropped, his face draining pale. A week earlier, he remembered Sam mentioning a mammogram appointment. Before he could speak, Sam waved him off. "I'm okay, I'm okay. I just had a scare. Nothing to worry about."

Jeff's face softened as relief washed over him. He loosed a "Whew!" His wife forced a labored smile while she maintained a dead stare on the floor. He dropped his work bag next to the chair still standing over her. "Then why all the gloom? When I saw you pulled out Pinky I got worried."

Sam smiled weakly but her gaze remained locked on the floor. She spoke softly. "Before I opened the envelope, I got Pinky out of the closet. You know she's my good luck charm, and she came through for me again."

Jeff nodded but his wife remained frozen. Voice louder, Jeff said, "Well, we should celebrate your clean bill of health! Let's go grab some margaritas at Pancho's—" he stopped mid-sentence and dropped into the chair like a sack of potatoes, startling Sam out of her trance. He continued sardonically, "Oh wait, that's right… we can't go to Pancho's because we have to save every dime. I'd like to sax you a happy song of health, but you know, seeing you sold the one joy I have left in this world, I can't."

He jerked away in his chair as it creaked and wobbled. They'd needed a new dining set, but their spending celibacy put that expenditure into the 'never' column.

Sam's face painted horror and she leered at him flabbergasted. She finally blustered, "Did you hear anything I said? I just said I had a cancer scare and your first thought is about your sax? Can't you even fucking fake it and act like you care anymore? About me? About our marriage?"

Tears welled from Sam's eyes. *Just like clockwork*, he thought. Her crying always made Jeff uncomfortable, but it softened him and always put him into a reality check. Deep down, he knew his wife was the kindest soul on the planet, and it was something he loved her for. Recognizing his selfishness and how he knee-jerked the situation, he took a deep breath. "Of course, I care. I care that you couldn't even tell me. I care that you went through it all alone." He grabbed her hand and pleaded for forgiveness. "I'm so sorry for being an inconsiderate asshole, you want to tell me about the test?"

Sam's head fell to her chest, and she mumbled, "No."

A healthy lab report shouldn't be tearing her apart. Puzzled, Jeff let the silence linger. Then, "Is there something else?"

More silence. She gripped Pinky tighter, and Jeff noticed it.

The low growl of freeway traffic outside was consumed by a clicking hum from the ceiling fan. As she held back the tears, her eyes turned red. She wiggled herself in the chair and turned, facing her husband. She seized a large breath of air and finally spoke.

"I can't do this anymore."

Fear melted into Jeff's face and his heart sunk. He quickly dropped her hand as if it were a molten pipe. The big "D" word usually followed the phrase "I can't do this anymore." Instantly he thought of divorce lawyers, custody battles, and visitation rights for his daughter. Then his marriage flashed in front of his face—not the daily monotonies, but the moments that deepened his love for Sam. In his thirty years of life, he'd known nobody more kinder or trusting. His wife was a stunner physically, but she had a kind-hearted soul that would give Mother Teresa a run for her money. Jeff's eyes got glassy and he swallowed hard. Sam noticed and placed her palm on his knee, clarifying, "No, not us." She eyeballed the room, surveying the townhouse appraisingly.

"I'm talking about what we've been doing for the last five years. We've been living like zombies, sacrificing the best years of our lives, for what? Some type of retirement fantasy thirty years from now? What the hell are we doing?" She turned away from Jeff and collapsed her head back into her hands. She muttered, "I've never been so unhappy in my life. Everything sucks the life out of me. We haven't been on vacation in years, our jobs are killing us, our financial plan is like slavery, and our marriage is on a respirator." The tears finally broke. Sniffling, she muttered, "And I don't know how to fix our marriage if we never see each other."

She quickly sleeved off the tears now soaking her face. Collecting herself, she pulled out her phone and pointed to the stocks app. It was all red. She said, "You see what happened in the stock market today? I watched two years of savings disappear in a matter of hours." She shook her head, her face disgusted as if she'd just stepped in dog poo. "We went from $36,000 to $27,000 in a matter of hours. You know how long it takes us to save $9,000? It reminded me of 2008 when we watched our 401(k)s disappear week after week."

Jeff sat silent, his voice stolen with relief that her issue wasn't the big "D"ivorce or worse, the big "C"ancer. She continued and sucked in her cheeks, her trusty tell that she was about to admit Jeff was right about something. "Remember what you said last year? About how we replaced the spending with saving? And that it's all the same rat race?"

Jeff nodded yes, maintaining his silence.

After two years of graveyard shifts, Sam had finally appeared to buy what Jeff had tried selling eight months ago. The nighttime hours at the hospital were consuming his wife. Subtle wrinkles angled into her cheeks while crow's feet taunted her eyes. Her sleep was shallow and non-restorative. Always pulled into a ponytail, her blond mane was thin and frayed, suffering constant duress under the fluorescent lights of Northwestern Hospital. Occasional gym visits turned into no visits. After a long night at the hospital pumping stomachs in the ER, the last thing she wanted to do was pump iron in the gym. Sam knew aging would arrive in some year, just not this one. All this for an extra $3 per hour or an extra $352 a month—the going rate of selling your soul to the overnight shift for some future retirement fantasy.

She continued, "And if I'm watching the stock market every day and worrying about every move, how is that going to give us financial independence?" She scoffed. "It's more like dependence. If it crashes again, we're screwed. Just like in 2008. Nothing has changed except now our life revolves around everything we can't do until some future moment. We're wasting our life working at jobs we hate so we can finally live, what, after we retire? And who says we even get old?" She hesitated then eyeballed her test results. "I feel like I'm sixty, and this, right here, woke me up." She tottered in her seat, a nervous energy freeing itself. "Last year you said you blinked and Maddy grew up, like you missed it." She sighed, the disgust still painting her face. "And you were right. We did. Life is too short for this. I don't want to take a passive role in Maddy's life. I don't want to live my life waiting, hoping, and saving

51

for some unknown date and in an unknown future that we might not even see. I'm tired of doing work that means nothing."

"You're a nurse, what you do is important," Jim commented.

She laughed. "You have no idea how bad healthcare has gotten. I can't make a difference because I'm not allowed to make a difference. My profession doesn't allow for heartfelt discussions or the kind of personal care that inspires my soul—it's on to the next patient now or get fired." Her eyes flared fear as if she were on a sinking boat. "Jeff, we have to do something. I can't live like this anymore."

Jeff sat quietly and only nodded.

It was then that the curtain fell, and the unspoken truth crystallized.

The system the Trotmans trusted wasn't designed to provide freedom and purpose. It was designed to enslave them—either as a slave to their lifestyle or a slave to their investment portfolio. Hard work wasn't going to make a difference. They already worked hard, and it had no impact and rewarded little joy. The "system" was a life sentence for meaningless work with a distant retirement parole that was more illusion than reality.

Suddenly they knew the challenge they faced. And as long as they continued playing by culture's rules, the game would remain unwinnable. It was time to do something different, or suffer the same existence, *till death do us part.*

THE UNSCRIPTED STRATEGY

Rewrite the Rat Race Script and Make Life Your Adventure

9

Kurt Searvogel is an ultra-distance competitor who set a goal to bike every day, an accumulated trek of over 75,000 miles. In 2016, he went further and broke the world record for miles biked in one year. As Kurt's story grabbed attention, readers begged to know: How does he afford it? And find time? The rat race has a systematic way of destroying audacious goals. His answer was as I expected: *He's an entrepreneur.*

Kurt's experience as an entrepreneur might seem unusual. I assure you, it's not. A new economic class has emerged in the world. I call it *The Unscripted 1%.* It is a growing class of entrepreneurs who built businesses from nothing but sweat, an open mind, and a willingness to learn. But these businesses aren't typical enterprises like a corner coffee shop or an eBay store. They're businesses that allow their owners to take charge of their life in all meaningful capacities: life purpose, financial freedom, the pursuit of passions (often unrelated to business) and more importantly, free time. Entrepreneurs dabbling within the Unscripted 1% usually enter the Economic 1%.

If you're not familiar with the Economic 1%, it represents wealthy individuals, usually $10 million (USD) in net worth or more. Conversely, the "99 percent" represents the working class. Professions like truck drivers, teachers, even your neighborhood dentist. While I'm part of the Economic 1%, I'm much happier to be a part of the Unscripted 1%. Why? Unscriptees prioritize time as their king in life's chess game.

There are three types of Unscripted Entrepreneurs. Each graduate to the next, and you should aspire to move through them all. They are:

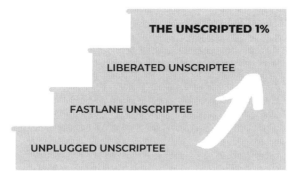

TYPE 1: THE UNPLUGGED UNSCRIPTEE

Have you had your FTE[P3]? Congratulations. The moment you become aware of the rat race system and commit to its escape, you become an Unplugged Unscriptee. Everyone starts as a Type 1, and it is the point of no return. In Hollywood parlance, it's when Andy Dufraine starts to dig his way out of Shawshank prison. If you need another movie, it's Neo swallowing the red pill in *The Matrix*. You wake up. And there's no going back.

TYPE 2: THE FASTLANE UNSCRIPTEE

A Fastlane Unscriptee is someone who has graduated from awareness to execution. At his point, you are someone who is succeeding at entrepreneurship using the Fastlane's CENTS Framework (later in this book). For instance, a 29-year-old entrepreneur on my forum owns a couple of duplexes and an eCommerce website. He recently purchased his second Lamborghini which in his words, "has been my dream since I was 16." While this young man might not be in the Economic 1%, he's in the Unscripted 1%. He authors his schedule and can do (and buy) what matters to him, all without sacrificing his youth, or his future.

The move from Type 1 to Type 2 could involve many failures and take years. It begins when your business starts to change your lifestyle. It begins when you can start exercising authority over your free time while having the means to pursue things that matter. While that's different for everyone, an Unscripted business as engineered in this book can earn you this elusive power.

TYPE 3: THE LIBERATED UNSCRIPTEE

Once a Fastlane Unscriptee accumulates enough wealth to cover their living expenses for the rest of their life—their Escape Number—they become

Liberated Unscriptees. Retired. Free from the rat race with total financial independence. Work—optional.

Still, Liberated Unscriptees often start other businesses or passion projects. Then profit isn't a priority, but contribution, purpose, and charity. And just like a Fastlane Unscriptee, we work flexible hours, make money 24/7, and continue to write the rules to our life. There are no bosses, no vacation limits, and more importantly, no debt burdens. Moreover, we can pursue ventures without the confirmation of money or cultural validation.

In my case, I started a business forum and a publishing company that allowed me to pursue my passion for writing. This book (and the ones before it) are examples of that effort. I don't have to follow a script put forth by an editor or a publisher. In other examples, some of the most famous entrepreneurs in the world are Liberated Unscriptees. They zealously pursue philanthropy, venture capital financing, wild passions, and other outrageous ideas. For instance, Bill Gates suddenly is a vaccine expert, and Elon Musk is fiddling with rockets. Derek Severs, a Liberated Unscriptee himself, wrote the following on his blog in 2012:

> *Some might say I'm retired, because I haven't earned (hardly) any money since 2008. And in some sense it's true: I don't want any more money than I've already got. And I don't want more fame, recognition, or anything external. So in that sense, I'm done. Retired. No longer working for money. Now my ambitions are entirely intrinsic and intellectual. I work as hard as ever, but just for my own learning, creating, and giving.*[1]

As you can imagine, Liberated Unscriptees like Derek and I are not dependent on macroeconomics. For instance, a market crash and a ten-year depression wouldn't change my life. Yes, I still leverage and invest in the capital markets, but I'm not held hostage by them. During the 2020 COVID-19 pandemic, I had no panic. In fact, my income and net worth increased. Yes, increased. If you have to update your resume if the stock market crashes or after a four-year recession, you aren't financially independent, but financially dependent.

Fact: If your financial freedom is dependent on something you can't control, you're not free. Don't confuse a Liberated Unscriptee with the financial world's newest retirement buzzword, FIRE. If you're not familiar with the "financial independence, retire early" movement, here it is in a nutshell:

---

1 - https://sive.rs/about

Supposedly you can retire early by leveraging extreme frugality, regimented saving, and regular stock market investments. Then after you quit your job, you live off your stock market returns. In effect, it's a Wall Street savings-rat who decides to swap their dependency from an employer to the stock market. One dependence is replaced for another. And still a rat. Right neighborhood, wrong house.

Your idea of financial freedom should not be about optimizing mediocrity, stock market returns, withdrawal rates, and a whole host of other uncontrollable variables. Liberated Unscriptees have no co-dependencies. The only threat to our existence is a global financial apocalypse or an extinction event. At which point we're all in deep trouble; the new currency would be guns, ammo, and food.

The beauty of Unscription is that its three tiers can happen to anyone and at any age. You don't need to be a notable Silicon Valley entrepreneur, or someone with money. You don't need a college degree or access to venture capitalists. You don't need a breakthrough idea. You only need the knowledge of what works, and what doesn't. To win an unconventional 1% existence you can't think like the conventional 99%[P1]. Remember, a new story needs new pens to write new words[S2]. Let's find them.

☑ KEY CONCEPTS

- The Unscripted 1% is a new economic class that leverages Fastlane, CENTS-based entrepreneurship.
- There are three levels of Unscription, each graduating to more freedom.
- Type 1: An Unplugged Unscriptee is aware of the rat race, like a red pill.
- Type 2: A Fastlane Unscriptee owns a profitable business that affords schedules to be malleable, offering more freedom.
- Type 3: A Liberated Unscriptee is liberated from the rat race and never has to work again, usually through a large income, or one or many exit events.
- FIRE swaps dependency from a job to the stock market.
- A Liberated Unscriptee is immune from most economic events.

THE DISCOUNTED TIME PRINCIPLE

Trading Good Time for Bad is a Terrible Life Strategy

When I was at college earning a finance degree, one concept was repeatedly drilled home: Money today is better than money tomorrow. This concept, the *discounted time value of money*, is universally taught worldwide, no matter the university. The concept is simple: Given a choice, *rational investors prefer X dollars NOW over X dollars LATER*. One million dollars today is light-years better than one million dollars fifty years from now. If you ever played the lottery, you'll recognize this phenomenon: the winner doesn't get the $10M prize immediately but over 30 years. If they want all of the money now, they'll only receive about half. When time is involved, future money is discounted by an arbitrary interest rate. Back to our first example, one million dollars received fifty years later and discounted at a mere five percent interest is worth only $87,000 in today's money. If there was any evidence proving that TIME is a horrific partner for wealth, look no further than the prior sentence.

Yet when it comes to time itself, a more valuable resource than money, it enjoys no such discounting. No school teaches the Discounted Time Principle: *future "elderly" time is not as valuable as today's youthful time*. No author would dare discount time like money, but I will. Think of it this way. If a genie granted you a lifetime of financial freedom, would you want it at thirty years old? Or at seventy? Isn't freedom better while you're young and vibrant and not in life's twilight when health and energy might be precarious?

The truth is, the rat race has branded time as a trivial commodity. Money's time value is beholden by every rational investor, but freedom isn't. One poison pen[S2] that needs swapping is the prioritization of life's resources: Time first, money second. You can always earn more money, but you can't make more time. It's time to stop trading our time just for money, our time needs to earn both money AND time.

Whenever some rat race media outlet is preaching about financial freedom decades from now, be warned. You're getting propagandized and numbed into believing freedom at twenty-five is exactly the same as freedom at seventy-five. If every school taught the *discounted time value of time* like they did money, Wall Street's "live poor die rich" honeypot[P6] wouldn't survive. Entire industries and economies would go bankrupt because the rats would finally figure out that their time is too valuable for trading. Yes, youth isn't wasted on youth. It's wasted on cultural norms that celebrate the exchange of youthful time for elderly time. Trading good time for bad time is a terrible life strategy. Demand different, work different or live the same.

☑ KEY CONCEPTS

- The time value of money states that money today is always more valuable than money later.

- The time value of money is a universal concept taught at every university on the planet, while the discounted time value of time isn't taught anywhere.

- Freedom young is always more valuable than freedom old.

- Whenever the rat race marginalizes time and treats it as a mathematical variable for financial freedom, you're being propagandized.

THE FINANCIAL FANATICISM PRINCIPLE

Financial Asceticism Is Not Financial Freedom

In early 2021, I got sucked into reading a financial news article featuring the newest form of honeypot dogma; the "retire early" orthodoxy. In this particular story, it profiled a young childless couple who claimed to be financially independent. To achieve this nebulous financial independence, they had to downsize their entire life. The husband, who self-admittedly enjoyed fast cars and daily restaurant visits, had to sell the vehicles and stop visiting his favorite eateries, to the point only one visit was allowed per month. Other downsizing included selling the house and moving into a ten-year-old trailer. As I read, it was clear that this young couple had micromanaged every dollar in and out of their daily existence. Everything had a budget—food, entertainment, gas—in fact, the financial asceticism was so extreme that the husband proudly confessed that he and his wife no longer exchanged gifts.

Folks, this is not financial freedom. This is financial fanaticism.

The definition of "freedom" is without restraint. If your daily existence is ruled by money, defined by money, budgeted by money, sorry, you're not financially free. And I don't care how you define it. Like an authoritarian dictator who owns his serfs, this couple is not free of money, *they are owned by money.*

Do not confuse time freedom with financial freedom. An unemployed college graduate living at home with his parents has time freedom. So does a homeless beggar living on skid row in a tent. These people might own their day, but money owns their choices.

One of my favorite stores is Costco. When I walk in, I have the financial resources to fill my cart with whatever I want. Sometimes I leave with just a few items; sometimes I leave having spent thousands. The point is, "budget" is not in my vocabulary.

Unscription is about both time freedom and financial freedom. You can dine at a different restaurant five days a week. You can buy that fast car. You can live in a luxury house and eliminate the word "budget" from your life. You can walk into a store and buy whatever you want.

If you meet the following five guidelines, congratulations, you are financially independent. If not, you're likely lying to yourself and redefining words to become the next newest coach pushing honeypot dogma.

1. **Lifestyle Freedom**: You can live freely in your desired lifestyle without needing a regular income from a job or a business.
2. **Budget Freedom:** The word "budget" isn't in your vocabulary for daily existence—trips to the store, filling up the gas tank, nights on the town.
3. **Experiential Freedom**: You don't need to "downsize" your lifestyle and sell things that you enjoy; the motorcycle, the saxophone, or the Corvette.
4. **Mobile Freedom**: You can travel for months and not have it impact your financial situation.
5. **Economic Freedom**: Your lifestyle wouldn't change in a stock market crash and an ensuing three-, five- or ten-year economic recession.

While our young "retired" couple should be commended for their saving prowess and having won time freedom, don't fall for the spiel. Time freedom without financial freedom is like visiting Disneyland but you can't ride the amusements. You can smell the goodies but you can't eat them.

When you have financial freedom, you know it.

You feel it.

You live it.

And believe me, you will love it.

☑ KEY CONCEPTS

- Financial freedom means living how you want to live without restraint.
- Financial freedom means the word "budget" is not part of your vocabulary for daily living.
- Time freedom is not the same as financial freedom.
- Financial freedom has lifestyle, travel, economic, and experiential freedom.
- Disneyworld is no fun if you can't eat the goodies or ride the amusements.

LEAVE IT TO BEAVER...
SUNDAY, JUNE 26TH, 2016 - 2:16 PM
(2 days later)

O ur ten-year wedding anniversary is next Sunday." Sam smiled in her dingy pajama outfit. Having just finished dinner and with no late shift that night, the family was at the kitchen table eating dessert, a mango sorbet.

Jeff raised an eyebrow and chuckled, "I know, I didn't forget." He eyed her up and down and then laughed. "Maybe I can get you some new PJs? You know, something a bit sexier?" He spooned a mouthful. Sam pursed her lips and delicately gestured to Maddy who was buried in her sorbet. She didn't hear the quip.

After finishing their sorbet, Jeff retrieved a box of colored Expo markers and a whiteboard from the downstairs garage. It was their first spending extravagance in years. He placed it on the table and uncapped the red marker.

Maddy's face lit up and asked, "What are we drawing?"

"Your Mommy and I are doing some planning," Jeff answered.

Maddy looked suspiciously at her parents and asked, "Is it going to be fun?"

"Probably not pumpkin," Jeff said, "but you're welcome to stay and help us with the drawings."

"What kind of drawings?"

Jeff pondered the question a second and then answered, "We're going to draw the future, things like when you're a big girl and going to college. Mommy and Daddy want you to be happy."

"Yuck," she frowned shaking her head. "College? That doesn't sound fun." She quickly got up from her seat and spoke plainly, "I'm going to practice." Jeff yielded into a warm smile and kissed her on the forehead before she retreated into her room.

"So," Jeff asked returning back to Sam, "where do you want to be in ten years?" He wrote *TEN YEARS* on the whiteboard. "If you could snap your fingers like a genie and make it happen, what would your life look like?"

Since their wedding, life's comforts distracted the Trotmans. Any kind of planning, financial or otherwise, just wasn't necessary. But when a recession spawned a downward spiral, comfort shifted into discomfort. They went from a strategy of deceptive affluence to a strategy of sacrifice and suffocating mediocrity. Little did they know that their saving and investing scheme was just a different demise from the same death camp. After six years of neurotic saving, the results were the same. Actually, worse. Instead of working their tails off to *look rich young*, they were working their tails off to *die rich old*. Nothing changed. Not their meaningless work, not their middle-class pay or wealth, and certainly not their relationship. It was time to make a plan, a plan that would help them escape the system they had trusted for their entire lives.

Sam thought for a bit, a smile overtaking her face. Before she could speak, Madison started playing her flute inside her bedroom. Jeff had tried to lure her to study saxophone, but Maddy insisted girls don't play sax. After her dad corrected her with several YouTube videos of Candy Dulfer, one of the best female saxophonists ever, Maddy still vetoed. Jingle Bells melodied through the townhouse, which Jeff thought was odd, considering it was June. Sam motioned for the marker, and Jeff handed it over. She scribbled on the whiteboard as *one horse open sleigh* finished its rhyme. A bunch of boxes with four legs emerged on the board, followed by another box with the number 50 in it. She finished with what looked like a church—except crossed it out with a big black X.

Jeff said, "Your dream is a bunch of tables, 50 million dollars, and a world without religion?"

Sam laughed and then pointed to each of the four boxes with the four legs. "That's a dog, there's a lamb, and that's a cow and a sheep."

"You want to own a zoo?"

"No, an animal rescue."

Jeff nodded, not surprised by his vegan wife's answer. Sam's veganism was more about animals than nutrition, and she'd embarked on that quest long ago when milk didn't need propaganda ads to stay viable.

"And the canceled church?" He pointed to the crossed-out church. "Rebellion against your parents?" She smacked him on the shoulder. "That's not a church, that's a hospital. And that's me not working there ever again. EVER!"

Jeff raised an eyebrow. "You mean done with the *hospital*, or done with *nursing*?"

"Done with nursing," she said resolutely, rubbing her hands together as if she could taste it happening. Jeff nodded, not surprised.

"And that?" He pointed to the box with the 50 in it.

She demurred and blushed.

Another tune belted out of Maddy's bedroom. "The Imperial March" from *The Empire Strikes Back*. They both looked at each other and snickered. "She's getting better," Jeff commented. The song was executed flawlessly, but the flute didn't do the dramatic song any justice and rang more like a theme from *Sesame Street.*

"Well?" Jeff asked, nonplussed. "What's the big FIVE OH?"

Her cheeks still rosy, she laughed sheepishly. "You ever watch *Leave It to Beaver* on television?"

He mushed his mouth at the curveball and then nodded. "Sure, the Cleavers. I saw a few episodes when I was a kid. Wasn't my favorite."

She continued, biting her fingernail. "Then you know it was an old sitcom from the late fifties. About a married couple with two boys. The dad worked while the wife was a stay-at-home mom, did all the stereotypical stuff for a wife in that era, cooking, cleaning, taking care of the boys. When I was in the doghouse with my parents, I'd lock myself in my room and watch TV. Only a few channels came in clear, we didn't have cable—just a big antenna outside. I remember *Hart to Hart* would be on first, then *TJ Hooker,* and then *Beaver* would come on after. Anyhow, I think I've seen every episode five times."

Jeff raised an eyebrow. "Okay and?"

She sighed and then gazed at him, reticence filling her eyes. "I just wish life was that simple again."

Jeff scratched his head. "I don't get it," he says, gesturing to the whiteboard. "What's this got to do with 50?"

"The 1950s," she reported. "I wish I could be a mom from the 1950s. I've always wanted to be a stay-at-home mom, you know walk my children to the bus stop, watch television with them, cook them different meals, do their laundry," she chuckled, "and maybe even light my husband's cigar after his long day at work while he sits in his easy chair."

Jeff erupted in laughter and slapped the table loudly. "My liberal wife wants to be a domestic housewife? Who will not only light my cigar, but let me smoke it in the house?" He laughed again, slapping his knees. Flashing her an incredulous look, he spouted, "Are you serious?"

"No joke," she assured, her face restraining apprehension. "You know my parents were tyrants. Six seasons of *Leave it to Beaver* was like my pacifier to distract me from my own childhood."

Jeff interjected, "I thought that your filthy stuffed animal was your pacifier?"

Sam gave him a scornful look and corrected him. "Shut-up, Pinky isn't filthy." She shook it off and continued, "Anyhow, I dreamed I had loving parents like the Cleavers, and I knew it was something I wanted when I had kids." Her tone went gentle. "I'm guessing it made me idealistically traditional about motherhood and how I wanted to raise my own children."

Jeff's smirk faded as his stomach started to groan. He forgot about Sam's apathetic parents and their emotional abuse. He readily forgot that his wife's best childhood memories probably came from the television. Jeff knew little, only that Sam grew up as an only child on a ranch in the middle of nowhere Idaho. Her parents weren't the typical backwoods couple; they were worse. As Sam told the story, her father was a failed farmer turned truck driver who was rarely home. Based on the arguments she overheard, Sam suspected a lot more than truck-driving was going on. Except at church when beguiling a role, Sam couldn't remember a time when she saw her parents smile. Sam said her Pops wanted a boy and got her. It was the best guess she had for her father's stableboy treatment of her, not to mention the name "Sam". "Samantha" was a reserved word rarely spoken by her father— it was only yelled in the midst of an angry tirade. Verbal abuse was normal in the household, and Jeff never dared to ask if there was something more. Sam once revealed that her father backhanded her boyfriend in the face after he gave her playful tap to the butt. After kicking him off the front porch, Sam's father called her a whore. Not only did Sam's mom permit it, but her silence defended it, as if she sought approval from her coldhearted husband.

After a lingering silence, Sam cleared her throat. "So where are you in ten years?"

Sam's husband grabbed the marker and drew a curly shape in front of what looked like an audience. Sam nodded, knowing it represented him playing saxophone to a crowd. He then drew a triangle atop a rectangle with a crossed-out dollar sign at its door. "That's our dream house without a mortgage," he volunteered. "And that little box with the wrench is a huge workshop, filled with tools—rich man tools like lathes, planners, and drill presses!" He drew two stick figures holding hands and a palm tree. "That's us on vacation for as long as we want."

She snickered and pointed to the stick figure. "Looks like you lost some weight."

"Funny," he said, continuing. "And these"—he drew what looked like a stack of rectangles—"are my best-selling books. I'd love to write fantasy novels, give Mr. George Martin a run for his money."

Curtly, Sam stated, "I don't think Mr. Martin would be aware that he was in a competition with you."

Jeff shook her off, but his eyes sparkled as he gawked at the drawings.

Ten minutes later, they had their ten-year vision.

Surprisingly, it mostly centered around freedom—freedom to watch their daughter's flute recitals, freedom to travel, freedom to direct their day, and the freedom to do work that mattered. They weren't seeking mansions and Mercedes, and they weren't seeking to "retire early" to a golf course. They wanted expansive financial options free of debt, the kind reserved for the one percent of society. If Jeff wanted to spend three years writing fantasies about unicorns and ogres, he could. If he wanted to buy a Tesla, he could. If Sam wanted to adopt twelve dogs, she could.

Jeff stood up and held the whiteboard in front of him. They both marveled at their potential future, optimistic and invigorated by the new plan, but ultimately confused. After disappearing into the garage, Jeff returned with a hammer and hung the whiteboard on the wall.

The loud noise brought a curious Madison out of her room, flute in tow. She studied the board, which intruded partially into the hallway. "What's that?" she asked.

Jeff smiled at her mother, then back at his beautiful seven-year-old daughter. "That's the future Mommy and Daddy mapped out for our family."

Sam chimed in, "I don't want to throw a wrench into our plans, but how on earth are we going to do all that?"

Jeff shrugged. "I don't know...." He picked up his daughter and seated her on his arms. Looking at Madison, he said, "But we have every reason to find out. And $36,000 to help us get started."

Sam corrected, "No, $27,000."

THE 1/5/10 STRATEGY

Engineer a 1/5/10 Planasy to Direct Decision-Making

12

The last time I packed for a move, I found an old crate crammed on a shelf in the back of the garage. Inside was forgotten memories; stuff from college, old awards, past art projects, and an ancient relic of my youth: my journal. Intrigued, I sat down and read it in a torrential sweat (it was over 100 degrees that day). Inside was mostly frustration and anxiety with few victories. And between all the angst, I found something that lit a smile on my face: My *1/5/10 Planasy*.

A big goal envisioned ten years from now is a fantasy.

That same goal reverse-engineered down into multiple time sequences is a Planasy—a detailed plan to actually do it.

So many people wander through life clueless to where their programming is taking them. We act on expectation and tradition, not what's in the best interest of our happiness. If you don't take the lead in engineering your future, your story will be ghostwritten by the rat race. And you aren't going to like that future.

As an Unscriptee, your future can be whatever you want. We're not stuck wandering within the rat race walls, we're dangling the cheese. As for visualizing your optimal life and how to get there, the 1/5/10 Planasy is your weapon. And it's something I've been using for decades.

It works like this. Envision your dream goals in ten years, but then break it down into its five-year, one-year, and one-month components. First, buy a poster board, a hardback notebook, or a journal, something durable that can withstand time. Today I use a piece of paper which I seal in a plastic sheet cover. No digital devices! Second, transport yourself ten years into the future and visualize your dream life as a Type-3, Liberated Unscriptee[P9]. If everything went as well as it could, what would your life look like? What kind of work would you be doing, if at all? Where do you live and how? What do you drive, or maybe, fly? What kind of people are in your life—and not in your life? How is your health? Write it all down. Draw, clip pictures, do whatever crafts the vision. And be specific and bold about what's essential in your life. Ten years is a lot of time for radical accomplishment.

Now, underneath your Unscripted ten-year vision, draw a line and write *five years.* In this space, repeat what you just did except craft your goals as a Type-2 Fastlane Unscriptee. What personal and business goals do you need to get HALFWAY to your ten-year vision? In both time frames, keep your goals and visions challenging, exciting, yet achievable within the scope of your current circumstances. If you're broke with zero skills and living with your parents, your five-year picture shouldn't be a Malibu mansion on the Pacific Coast. A better forecast might be six figures in investments and a growing business with significant profits.

Next, repeat the process for ONE YEAR. What goals would you need to hit to have the groundwork laid for your five-year vision? Your first customer? Your first software coded? What do you need to learn? How much do you need to earn?

And finally, repeat the process for ONE MONTH. In the next 30 days, what actions do you need take? What actions have to stop, like video gaming or eating highly refined sugar? How do you need to reorganize your day? What education and skills must you start honing to get you moving toward that one year vision?

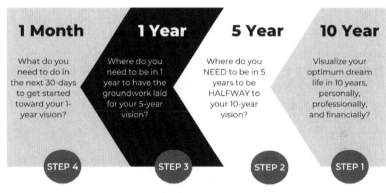

THE 1/5/10 PLANASY

After laying out all four goals and visions, congratulations. You just accomplished what most people never do... *You've created a decision-making framework for your life, a guiding light for all future actions.* It will answer all your "whats." Namely, does this action get me closer to my one month goal? What must you do tomorrow? Next week? What decisions oppose your one-month goal and its future? From this point, everything you do should get you closer to the one-month and one-year future, which brings you closer to the five- and ten-year versions.

For example, my five-year vision (as I wrote two years ago) consisted of a beautiful timber cabin overlooking Sedona's red rocks. Today (as of early 2021), I own the land and am in the architecture phase. Within the one-year vision, I'll be interviewing builders. The following year, construction. Altogether, the 1/5/10 Planasy helps me make decisions today that put me closer to the five-year reality. The 1/5/10 Planasy is the decisional roadmap. But be warned: A ten-year vision without its one-month and yearly subsets is not a Planasy, but a fantasy.

Back to that hot garage and my ten-year vision as I wrote many decades ago... I wanted to wake up when I want to wake up. Lamborghinis. Nice house, pool, no mortgage, no debt, and the ability to do meaningful work without worrying about money. Sound like a pipe dream? The plan was written eight years before it happened, and that's the point. Mostly everything came true, while other things disappeared as I changed and no longer wanted them.

Your 1/5/10 Planasy should be flexible and shifting. As the years pass, your goals will change. If you're doing life right, your goals will meander and morph as you progress, as you discover new things about yourself, and as you expand your awareness. Consider your 1/5/10 Planasy as a living document.

Keep your visions updated and keep the 1/5/10 decision framework at the forefront of your life. Do that, and I guarantee this: you won't recognize your life in ten years, much less a year from now.

☑ KEY CONCEPTS

- The 1/5/10 Planasy envisions your optimum life in ten years, reverse engineered in five-year, one-year, and one-month increments.

- Your 1/5/10 Planasy is a living document and will change as you change.

- The 1/5/10 Planasy acts as a decision framework for your life.

THE OFFENSE/DEFENSE PRINCIPLE

Offense Wins, Defense Preserves

13

The first time I ever profited $10,000 a month was paradigm-shifting but not shocking. Then $50,000 a month, then $100,000, then $200,000. When the acceleration happened, it became clear that my theories about wealth were true: wealth accumulation was mostly about the quality of the numbers attached to your life. It is these numbers that determine if you ever have a chance to become a part of the Unscripted 1%[S9].

The Offense/Defense Principle mandates that *real financial freedom*[P11] *not subject to devout frugality or minimalism only happens with a potent offense.* Offense is income and/or asset explosion. Instead of earning $50,000 a year, you start making $50,000 a month. This is how the wild future you envisioned in your 1/5/10 Planasy[S12] can happen. Unless you plan on becoming the next Brad Pitt or Lebron James, this only occurs in control of a business.

Defense, on the other hand, is about expense reduction and buzz-killing frugality. Oddly, a defensive player somewhat perceives his role in the rat race and opts to live life in the cheap seats, limiting their cheese. Cheap unhealthy eating, cheap airline tickets on Southwest, cheap shoebox apartment, cheap vacations (if any), cheap this, cheap that. Then the game becomes about moral victories. If you can't do, eat, watch, travel, or buy what you want, do you really have freedom? Don't let the rat race's honeypot[P6] convince you this is a winning strategy. It's a tool in the toolbox, but it won't build the house.

A popular phrase in personal finance circle-jerks is "live within your means." True with one nuance: *Live within your means with the intent to expand your means.* Two people earning $35,000 and $350,000 a year respectively can both be living within their means. Yet one lives extravagantly with champagne and caviar while the other medicates their survival with bread and water. When Elon Musk boards his private jet, he's "living within his means."

Unfortunately, the offensive/defensive relationship is a one-way street. A porous fiscal defense can ravage a strong offense. Yet a strong offense can do little to temper a bad defense. Poor money management can't be medicated with more money. It's like throwing deck chairs off a sinking Titanic. Eventually, the boat sinks. This is why many lottery winners and athletes go broke just years after acquiring millions. A strong offense is suddenly shut

69

out, combined with a reckless defense, and wham, bankruptcy follows. A potent offense can cover your ass, but as they say, when the tide retreats, you eventually see who's been swimming naked.

Defense is squeezing nickels from dimes. And because our working life spans roughly a short fifty years, saving nickels doesn't work. Dollars are needed. That's earning a life-altering income or building a multimillion dollar asset. Then, and only then, will defense take its sacred role: wealth accumulation for Unscripted purposes followed by wealth preservation. Yes, both are important: Offense wins the game in ten years or less, defense preserves it for the next fifty.

☑ KEY CONCEPTS

- Financial freedom is won on offense (income/asset), not defense (expense/debt reduction).
- "Live within your means" with the intent to expand your means.
- You can live a luxurious life and still live within your means.
- A poor defense can destroy a strong offense, as in the case of famous athletes, lottery winners, and celebrities who go bankrupt.

THE MONEY-SYSTEM STRATEGY

Don't Use Market Investments for Wealth, Use Them for Income

When I was a child, my great-grandmother would give me a five-dollar bill every time I saw her. I would deposit those bills at the bank in a passbook savings account. In between deposits, I noticed that the bank added more money to my account. This "free money" that mysteriously appeared in my savings account was an interest payment. While it was only a few cents (which is a lot to a ten-year-old), it fired a few neurons. I then understood that old money gave birth to new money. And with no effort or work, other than waiting for next month. This childhood memory was a profound moment for me. It crystallized that I could receive a lifetime paycheck without working.

As I got older and earned a bachelor's degree in finance, I soon learned there was a big problem with this strategy: to earn a large regular paycheck, it required a ton of cash, like millions. And if I wanted a luxury lifestyle immune from economic recessions? More millions. A four percent yield on $10,000 is only $33 a month. That wouldn't pay my electric bill for one week. On the other hand, four percent on $10,000,000 is a whopping $33,000 a month. That would pay for a lot, and with some leftover. Looking back, my free money realization was my first encounter with investment income—not the business of products or services, but the business of money—or a *money-system*.

A money-system is an investment portfolio that pays you for renting or investing capital. In return for your rental, you get paid monthly interest, capital gains, profits, or dividends. And the payment is entirely passive, like my first "free money" experience. Such capital investments could be a bond, a dividend-paying company, a public partnership, an investment fund, or a real estate investment trust found on the world's various stock markets.

Fast forward about forty years. Every month for the last fifteen years, my money-system pays me a big paycheck, or what I call my *paycheck-pot*. I purposely have this payment mailed to my home in the form of a paper check. Better, I will receive this paycheck for the rest of my life. They say that money *won* always feels better than money *earned*. I can attest to this truth. Except I've never won any money, but I feel the rush of "free money" every month when I get my money-system paycheck. The payment varies monthly, but every year it adds up to a nice chunk of change, about the average salary for a C-Suite executive at a mid-sized corporation.

For example, a lot of my cash is invested in bonds: tax-free municipals, corporate, emerging-markets, and closed-end funds. Other investments are in dividend stocks, like Abbie Vie (a healthcare company) and a nice allocation of real estate trusts. This capital allocation gives me diversification where my money isn't parked at one place and solely denominated in cash. For example, one of my favorite money-system investments is Southern Company. This electric utility powers many southern American states. I own thousands of shares. Its yield hovers around five percent, and as of this writing, the dividend is about $2.50 per share a year. The company hasn't cut its dividend in nearly 70 years. Seventy years! Ten thousand shares equal $30,000 a year, completely "sit on your ass" income. Yes, the "free money" fantasy my great-grandmother sparked with her five-dollar gifts has been my reality for years.

Here is a chart that shows the monthly returns for a money-system at varying interest rates—and this is theoretically without touching the principle.

Return	$2,500,000	$5,000,000	$10,000,000
3%	$6,250/mo.	$12,500/mo.	$25,000/mo.
4%	$8,333/mo.	$16,666/mo.	$33,333/mo.
5%	$10,416/mo.	$20,833/mo.	$41,666/mo.
6%	$12,500/mo.	$25,000/mo.	$50,000/mo.

But wait, didn't I say stock market investments are part of the Slowlane honeypot? And that compound interest, the concept behind the rat race's "live poor die rich model"[P6] is an inefficient wealth creator? Yes, but the difference is in its purpose and application. As scientists, *we're not using the stock market for wealth creation, we're using it for income, liquidity, and inflation protection.* We're not trying to turn a hundred bucks into $10 million over forty years, we're trying to turn $10 million dollars into a $30,000 paycheck every month. Specifically, don't use the capital markets to *make* you rich, use it to *keep* you rich.

My money-system is only a small portion of my net worth. At any given time, I don't have more than 25 percent invested in the stock market. As this book asserts, the stock market is risky place for your life savings. Should the markets crash, my life wouldn't change. I'm not dependent on Wall Street. Remember, we're scientists looking to serve the rat race, not be held hostage to it. The money-system's purpose is to beat inflation, to keep money liquid, and to grab an income doing it. Escaping the rat race is a job for our business, not the stock market.

☑ KEY CONCEPTS

- Old money, or savings, gives birth to new money, often completely passive.

- A money-system is the business of renting capital, a considerable cash sum invested in income-producing assets (dividends, bonds, real estate trusts) that produce regular monthly or quarterly income.

- For compound interest to be effective, you need to start with a large sum.

- A boring four percent return on $5,000,000 is more than $16,000 monthly, without touching the principle.

- Your money-system should only represent a small portion of your net worth.

- Your business is for *creating* wealth; the capital markets are for *renting* your wealth which pays you passively.

THE ESCAPE NUMBER STRATEGY

Turn Freedom Into a Real Number,
Not a Forty-Year Pipe Dream

$62,050.

Excluding travel, clothes, and toys, that's the carrying cost for my Liberated Unscripted lifestyle[59] per year. If you think $62K isn't much, let me add some details. I live well and pay cash for everything. That means I have no debt, including every vehicle I own. I own property but carry no mortgages. My home has everything you could imagine. Things like a pool, basketball court, sauna, ten-car garage, even an orchard. This number doesn't include a multi-million-dollar timber cabin under construction in Sedona. Although I have no biological children, I have two teens living in the house who eat as much as two gorillas. Despite the money pit I'm building in Sedona, I have more money between my businesses and investments than I know what to do with.

Still, even without life's three biggest expenses (children, mortgage debt/rent, auto financing), $62,000 is still a chunk of change. It represents pure "existence expenses" mandated by breathing. Things like real estate taxes, licenses, medical services, food, gas, utilities, a litany of insurance and trust products, maintenance and repair services, and other miscellaneous life overhead.

If you want to escape the rat race as a Liberated Unscriptee like myself, you're going to need a ton of money. In that case, you need at least $1.2 million, earning at least five percent yearly to pay for the annual overhead. You'll also need to come up with several million dollars to buy the houses and cars on top of that. And you'll need a safety net. Add another few million there. I'm not saying all this to brag, but to shed light on what many refuse to accept. *Freedom is not free, but damn expensive.* Existence costs a ton of money. And if you desire a luxury lifestyle (cars, dream house, vacation place, etc.), we're now in the mid-seven to the eight-figure realm. As the popular meme posits, yes, "The rent is too damn high!"

So, how much money do you need to enjoy your optimum lifestyle as designed in your 1/5/10 Planasy? This answer is widely different for everyone. Countless entrepreneurs on my forum are not motivated Mercedes Benzes and mansions, but freedom.

In truth, I think everyone is motivated by freedom. For some, a Mercedes S-Class parked in front of a 10,000 square foot house reflects that freedom.

Either way, it doesn't matter. To make that freedom a reality, you need money—and lots of it. But how much exactly? Have you ever taken the time to figure it out?

Now you can and it's called your Escape Number. An Escape Number is the dominant goal that represents the amount of pretax money you need to earn to escape the rat race in the desired lifestyle specified in your 1/5/10 Planasy. Here is the equation:

Escape Number = PTEA + Money-System + POM

The variables are as follows:

- **PTEA** = The pre-tax income you need to EARN to purchase the assets specified at your ten-year vision.

- **Money-System** = The pre-tax earnings you must earn which must be SAVED in a lump sum investment which pays the yearly carrying costs of the assets plus the yearly lifestyle and existence expenses.

- **POM** = The "Peace of Mind" variable is an arbitrary percentage of your money-system which represents liquid, surplus cash providing you with insurance from lengthy economic recessions and/or stock market crashes. This is also calculated on a pre-tax basis (Divided by [1 - TaxRate]). In Unscripted Book One, I called this the "fuck you" pot—money you can use to pursue passion projects or hobbies.

Because these numbers are based on pretax figures, the escape number can seem quite sizable. Taxes are a reality, ignoring them is not. Here is how you solve for the equation:

STEP 1: CALCULATE THE PTEA

Reviewing your 1/5/10 Planasy, calculate the pre-tax earnings needed to purchase the assets you envisioned at your 10 year vision. To calculate the tax rate, divide the asset cost by top tax rate in your country subtracted by 1. At 40%, you would divide by .6, or 60%. Example:

Nice house   = $2,250,000
Vacation condo = $500,000
Four cars   = $250,000

After-Tax Cost of Assets = 2,250,000 + 500,000 + 250,000 = $3,000,000
Pre-Tax Cost of Assets = 3,000,000 / .6 = $5,000,000

Translation: To purchase $3,000,000 in assets, you will need to earn $5,000,000 before taxes.

STEP 2: CALCULATE THE PTEA CARRYING COST

Looking at your ten year vision again, now calculate your yearly carrying cost for the assets described above by multiplying by 1.5%. This covers insurance, utilities, property taxes, and miscellaneous repairs. Next, add your carrying costs for your lifestyle and existence costs. These are costs like health insurance, food, clothing, and entertainment. If you plan to have children, add $15,000 to the carry cost for each child. And finally, to calculate the after tax carry cost, divide total cost by the respective tax rate on passive investments in your country subtracted by 1. At 40%, this is again a division by .60, or 60%.

Asset Carry Cost (1.5% x $3M)   = $45,000
Health Insurance: = $10,000
Lifestyle/entertainment: = $10,000
Existence expenses: = $10,000
Three Children (C):   = $45,000
For each child you plan to have, add $15,000.

Annual Carry Cost   = $120,000
Pre-Tax Carry Cost   = $200,000

Translation: You need to earn $200,000 a year before taxes to support your the 10-year lifestyle outlined in your 1/5/10 Planasy.

STEP 3: CALCULATE THE MONEY-SYSTEM THAT FUNDS THE ASSET'S CARRYING COST

Now it's time to calculate your money-system, or the paycheck pot, the after-tax lump sum savings needed to generate $200,000 in yearly investment income. This is accomplished by dividing the net carry cost ($200,000) by .05, or 5%, the expected yield on safe, non-volatile investments, divided by the expected tax rate minus one.

Paycheck pot = [Carry Cost ($200k) / Expected yield (5%)] = $4,000,000
Pre-tax: $4,000,000 / [1 - 40%) = $6,666,666

Translation: You need to earn $6,666,666 to save $4,000,000 earning 5% to generate $200,000 in yearly passive income which then again is taxed down to $120,000.

STEP 4: CALCULATE THE POM

Finally, multiply your yearly carrying cost investment by your "Peace of Mind" percentage. Because Liberated Unscriptees are not dependent on investment returns, this metric is your insurance policy and immunity from economic recessions. The smaller the percentage you use, the more risk you undertake with stock market calamities and other uncontrollable market events. At least 50% is recommended. I use more than 200%.

POM = Paycheck Pot x 50%   = $2,000,000
Pre-tax: $2,000,000 / [1 - 40%]   = $3,333,333

Translation: $2,000,000 represents your "peace of mind" cushion which is obtained by earning $3,333,333.

STEP 5: CALCULATE THE ESCAPE NUMBER

The last step is to calculate your exact Escape Number by adding the net asset cost (PTEA) to your money-system number.

PTEA + Money-system + POM = Escape Number
$5,000,000 + $6,666,666 + $3,333,333 = $15,000,000

Translation: To escape the rat race and enjoy your dream vision in your 1/5/10 Planasy, you'll need to earn roughly $15,000,000 before taxes. This assumes $4,000,000 is invested in passive income investments, you saved a $2,000,000 "POM" cushion, and you own all your homes and cars without loans or mortgages.

As you can see, freedom enjoyed luxuriously, is ridiculously expensive, especially if you want children. If you want to feel better about your Escape Number, you can transform it into an after-tax savings number. To do so, simply divide your Escape Number by [1 - TaxRate]. In our example above, $15,000,000 adjusted by a 40% tax rate is $9,000,000. Translation? *Save $9,000,000 and you'll hit your escape number and make your 1/5/10 Planasy a reality.*

Review Appendix A to see just how expensive freedom costs—even if it involves frugality and living in a trailer park. Any other expectation will be a lit wick to disappointment. But don't get frustrated: This book will light the dots… all you need to do is connect them.

☑ KEY CONCEPTS

- Basic existence expenses are terribly expensive, even in a mini-malistic living situation.

- Expect a life of unrestricted freedom and relative affluence to cost millions.

- The Escape Number is the sum of the pre-tax earnings needed to purchase the assets specified at your ten-year vision, plus the pre-tax investment sum which funds the carry-cost for your dream lifestyle, plus additional pre-tax funds for economic immunity.

- When calculated on a pre-tax basis, the Escape Number can seem incredibly large.

IGNORANCE IS BLIND

MONDAY, SEPTEMBER 5, 2016 - 4:43 PM

(71 days later)

*T*hump!

Sam dropped four books on the kitchen table.

"They all pretty much say the same thing," she reported to Jeff.

He looked up from his cereal, still chewing his Raisin Bran.

"Apparently the whole world thinks not drinking coffee is the key to getting rich," Sam said flatly. Jeff lifted an eyebrow. Sam started with the Starbucks trope. "If we stop drinking coffee and save—"

Jeff held his hand up and interrupted. "Stop. I don't need to hear the same bullshit, the old *live like a monk for forty years so I can retire rich as an old geezer.*" He paused, then continued, "Am I right?"

Sam nodded, frowning.

Determined to change their lives and finances, the Trotman family spent their Labor Day reading. They agreed: Their current trajectory was unacceptable. Identifying the status quo as the problem, Jeff and Sam became voracious readers. Sam focused on finance books; Jeff gravitated to books on career advancement. They had an audacious dream, and they wanted it done within the next ten years. Great in theory, but it felt like they were searching for a leprechaun in Alaska. So they sought the advice of best-selling authors.

Sam read (and then skimmed) three personal finance books. The first was from a tall cheeky guy with pearly white teeth who made a fortune selling motivational seminars. Then another by a hedge fund billionaire, and then another from a nationally syndicated television personality with orange skin and an annoying voice. After reading the same stale argument over and over, she told Jeff the bad news. "Living poor so we can die rich old seems to be the central theme of all of them."

Jeff laughed. "Yeah, and all of those authors aren't rich because they cheap-skated and saved for four decades. What bunch of fucking hypocrites," Jeff barked as Sam walked away with the books. "Been there, done that. History repeats, and when it does, we won't be in its way. There has to be a better way, something that doesn't involve risking our entire life savings in the stock market just so we can just give it to a nursing home forty years later. Maybe Forex trading? Or wait, Bitcoin! I've been hearing a lot about that lately."

"You're right," Sam sighed, dropping the books in the trash. "I'm tired of the penny pinching, and I'm tired of killing myself at the hospital."

She studied her husband. "Maybe you can rob a bank."

He bounced back, "Or maybe you can work at a gentleman's club."

She raised a curious brow and then said, "Funny… notice how anything with 'gentleman' in it is code for douchebag?"

"Huh?" Jeff asked, confused.

"A gentleman's club?" she asked rhetorically. "It's a place where disgusting men ogle women. And a 'gentlemen's ranch' is a piece of land where a bunch of dickless men hunt defenseless animals with high-powered rifles." She scoffed, "How fair is that? If you want to show your brave masculinity, why the gun? Just go kill 'em with your bare hands. As far as I'm concerned, 'gentleman' is code for a pussy who can't get no pussy."

Jeff gaped at his wife, shocked, but not. Her tangent wasn't unusual, but he knew whenever she spoke vulgarities, she was passionate. Flatly he said, "Well, I guess that's a NO on the strip club." He paused and then snickered, "Which leaves me to rob a bank."

Sam huffed. "I'll head back to Amazon and search for a different answer."

He nodded, then opened his laptop. "I'll look into this Bitcoin thing. In the meantime, you should probably dig those books out of the trash. You could probably sell them on Craigslist or donate them."

Sam feigned a smile, feeling no more confident than ten minutes ago.

Nearly a month would pass, but their financial ignorance would remain the same. Sam couldn't sell those finance books on Craigslist as there were no buyers, not even at a buck apiece. She guessed ubiquitous advice is, well, ubiquitously cheap. She ended up donating the books to Goodwill.

It was now the first Saturday of October and Sam was returning from a walk with Bella.

"Whew, it's getting cold out," Sam reported as she rubbed her hands to warm up. She removed the leash, and the Labrador rushed Jeff at the kitchen table and sidled up to his leg. Bella begged on her haunches expecting a post-walk cookie. Jeff glanced at her but did nothing. The begging continued until Sam intervened. "You just going to ignore her? She wants her treat."

Jeff gestured to the pantry. "I'm busy."

Sam glared at him. "Fine."

After tossing Bella a treat, Sam loomed over her husband, her hands on her hips. Her cheeks were flushed from the cold. "You and Bella have the same personality. Stubborn, transparent, impulsive… easy to fluster…" He looked up, unfazed. She continued, "What's got you pissy on the computer?"

"About five million dollars," Jeff reported, crossing his arms. He nodded at the whiteboard. "Our cute little plan we designed a few months ago. That's how much money we need to make that happen. And that's being conservative."

Sam stood back. "Jesus, five million dollars?"

"Yeah," Jeff scoffed. "We're coming up about four million short, and that's assuming we work until we're eighty years old." He snuffed in disbelief. "I already feel eighty. I imagine if I live that long, I will feel ancient." He corn-hole-tossed a dishtowel onto the chair and shook his head, grimacing. "Not sure how I can make any more money. My company isn't promoting anyone. Hell, they're not even hiring. And my salary is more than I'd earn if I quit and started somewhere else."

He looked up at his wife, fingering his temple. "Maybe I should go back to school and get my MBA. The senior VP in my division has one and he makes almost a $90K a year. With the year-end bonus, he probably makes more."

Sam scoffed, "MBA?! We're still paying our student loans, and you want to take more? And waste two years studying for it? For what, $20,000 more than you're making now? No way."

He paused, processing her passion. "You're right. We've already circled these wagons for five years." He thought about his dream workshop and pointed to the vision board. "So I'm still lost on how we're going to do that. At the rate we get paid, in won't happen in thirty years, much less ten."

Sam sat down where they both sat in silence for several moments.

The television murmured behind Maddy's closed bedroom door.

Bella snored.

A throaty muscle car growled as it drove by on the street below.

Disgusted, Jeff said, "I just don't know our next step and I feel..." His voice trailed off.

Sam leaned toward him. "Helpless?"

"Not really, maybe, I can't explain it." He ran his hands through his hair, pondering the emotion. "I feel blind even though I have eyes. I can hear the world, taste it, smell it, that there's this beautiful universe out there, but no matter how hard I look, it remains hollow and one-dimensional." He chewed his lip, giving the unremarkable wall a hard stare.

She unenthusiastically offered, "I can take on a second job bartending. I already work nights, so it wouldn't be too disruptive to my real job."

Snapping out of his trance, Jeff blew a raspberry. "You can't be serious; didn't we just end that insanity? You already work four ten-hour shifts, and now you want to sling bottles at some dive bar on the other three?" Jeff huffed, "Heck, Maddy and I barely see you now. We're not doing that again."

She curled a strand of hair behind her ear, her jaw clenching in frustration.

"I just don't know what the answer is besides spending our every waking hour working for more money." She sighed as she felt her stomach roil.

"Did you look into that Bitcoin thing?"

Jeff gave her a disappointed nod. "It's way too complicated. I felt like I needed a computer degree to understand it."

Sam commented, "I think I understand what you meant about being stuck in the darkness no matter how hard you look. It just doesn't seem fair."

Jeff laughed, "Fair? The media is bought and controlled by either Wall Street, the politicians, or the mega-corporations. You were expecting them to give you some golden truth into paradise?"

Sam didn't answer. After a long silence, she jested, "Well, which will it be? Chase or Wells Fargo?"

Jeff shot her a puzzled look.

"The bank we're robbing." She stood up and faced their ten-year vision on the wall. "Because there's no way I'm giving up on this." She turned and peered at her husband.

Jeff shrugged and then winked. "You tell me, Mrs. Cleaver."

THE PROFIT LOCUS STRATEGY

Change Your Locus, Or Stay Blind

The first sports car I bought was a Corvette. After a few days of driving it, I started seeing Corvettes everywhere. Turns out, the car wasn't as unique as I thought. Of course, more Corvettes weren't on the road— the only thing that changed was my perception. Namely, *awareness*—my brain was no longer blinded to this visual stimulus. This is why the car you own seems more common than it actually is.

Every day, your brain is flooded with billions of bits of data. To survive the chaos, your mind has to ignore most of it. Put another way, you're blind to what hides in plain sight. This phenomena, known as your reticular activating system, simply means that once you're made of aware of X, you brain no longer filters for X and X becomes highly visible. Think of it like a radio— while there are hundreds of frequencies, you only hear the one you're tuned to.

In much the same way, the rat race has trained your brain to perceive the frequency it wants you to hear. Your brain is blinded to the solution it needs to hear, even though it is right in front of your face. In the Trotmans' case, their brains are trained to see Toyotas and Hondas when they need to be looking for Corvettes.

Each of us possesses a *locus of money,* and it presages how you attack money problems. When more income is needed, what is the plan? Better job? Better wage or salary? Your money locus is like your reticular activating system for wealth—if it is tuned only to see cars owned by the rat race, that's what it will see. Further, your money locus also gives you a default identity for operating within the rat race. This rat race identity gives you the golden ticket to escape, or the golden handcuffs to remain. Namely, you can't go from a rat to a scientist[57] until you hone the right locus, giving sight to where there was once blindness. Here are the three loci...

THE WAGE LOCUS

Rat Race Identity: The Worker
Rat Race Reality: The Unskilled Job Hopper
Monetization: Wages for Unspecialized Labor

With a wage-locus, you identify as a *worker* in the rat race, an unskilled job-hopper paid by the hour. If you earn $15 an hour and trade ten hours of your life to your job, you get $150 in return. Money is always a function of time traded at a job, jobs which are often paid poorly. Retail clerks, delivery drivers, cashiers, construction laborers, and fast-food cooks—all jobs where your boss views you as a disposable body, an easily replaceable cog in a system. And likewise, the employee returns the favor by viewing the job as equally disposable—jobs come and go based on who pays the most. With a wage-locus, financial distress is attacked by looking for a new job with better wages. Carry a wage-locus through life, and your likely rat race outcome will be poverty.

THE SALARY LOCUS

Rat Race Identity: The Professional
Rat Race Reality: The Skilled Salary Optimizer
Monetization: Salary for Specialized-Skill

Rats with a salary-locus identify as *professionals*. They link money to a profession, a skilled labor mindset which no longer commands cash by the *hour*, but by the *year*. Money is framed as a function of the specialized-skill and the salary commanded by the craft, specialized fields such as dentistry, engineering, pharmacology, or software development. Upward mobility is linked to specialized-skills and the company that employs them. Folks with a salary-locus often go to graduate school to seek expanded skills and/or credentials. With any skill that commands a salary, a salary-locus tends to lock that person into a career for life. While some change careers mid-life, few do. Unlike their unskilled job-hopping counterpart, a skilled salary-optimizer seeks to maximize their pay by the year, not by the hour. Money problems are narrowly attacked by existing skills and experience, and hence, narrow solutions are found. Case in point: the Trotman family. The likely outcome for those carrying a salary-locus is mediocrity.

THE PROFIT LOCUS

Rat Race Identity: The Entrepreneur
Rat Race Reality: The Value-Creator
Monetization: Profit for Net Perceived-Value

View the world with a profit-locus, and money won't be an esoteric concept linked to your time. It will be seen as a function of *profit* earned as an *entrepreneur.* While this might seem obvious, it isn't because profit has become a politically incorrect piñata. So, let's examine that word…profit.

Profit is net perceived-value (NPV)—the margin between the value you create and the value you sell it for. If you invent a gadget that sells for $50, but it costs $20 to get to market, your net perceived-value, or profit, is $30. If you sold 500,000 over ten years, your profit is $15,000,000. Sadly, profit (or NPV) is a double-edged sword. If you sell ten gadgets in ten years, you make three hundred bucks while losing valuable time.

Net perceived-value by way of net profit also represents enterprise value. If you sold 500,000 widgets, your company might be worth $3,000,000. If you do sell that many, $3 million becomes realized net perceived-value or profit.

With a profit-locus, you identify within the system as an entrepreneur who creates value. Income is not linked to jobs, your skills, or your experience, but profit, which is a function of value delivered. Carry a lifetime profit-locus, and wealth and freedom will be your prize.

To identify your locus, ask this: If you needed to earn an extra $25,000 by next year, how would you do it? Here are how the different loci react to this question.

The Wage Locus:

I need a better job that pays more per hour! Anyone hiring? Can I get more hours at work?

The Salary Locus:

I need to go back to school and learn a new skill, one that pays a better salary! Time to call the head-hunter!

The Profit Locus:

I need a better product that is more valuable to more people!

Locus determines focus. It unblinds and gives sight to possible solutions. The Trotmans aren't struggling because they're lazy. They struggle because their loci is still owned by rat race. And hence, the Trotmans are stuck dithering as they discuss advanced degrees and second jobs. As the old saying goes, when you're the hammer, everything looks like a nail. Better jobs or better careers isn't the answer, seek a better profit through a better product with better value.

- Awareness, or your reticular activating system, gives you sight to things that normally would remain hidden.

- Your locus of money is how you tackle money problems.

- A wage-locus sees money as a function of unskilled labor earned by an hourly wage.

- A salary-locus sees money as a function of specialized-skills earned by yearly salary.

- A profit-locus sees money as a function of profit from units of net perceived-value and unlocks the door to a rat race escape.

- Your locus determines focus.

THE BAD MATH PRINCIPLE

No Leverage, No Chance

Tell me what you do for work, and with near certainty, I'll predict if you'll ever escape the rat race. How? I simply look at the type of personal leverage you have, if any. The Bad Math Principle reveals that *every person stuck in the rat race is subject to unscalable and uncontrollable math, namely, no leverage.* Truth is, every Unscriptee who's successfully freed themselves did so through some type of mathematical leverage. And no, I'm not referring to business leverage such as investment margin or real estate loans. These are three *rat race anchors* that keep the Bad Math Principle active in your life.

ANCHOR ONE: INCOME AND WEALTH ARE CORRELATED TO TIME.

Carry a wage- or a salary-locus and the rat race will convince you that the only way to make money is to trade your time for it, either by the hour or the year. When I had a job stocking shelves at Sears, I only made money if I clocked in. No work, no progress. My income was limited by the hours I traded and the hours available, both uncontrolled and unleveraged. Similarly, a respectable profession, say a manager, wouldn't be paid by the hour, but by the year. Wealth creation is directly correlated to how much time you trade. If more money is needed, more time must be traded.

ANCHOR TWO: TIME CANNOT BE SCALED.

When you have a wage-paying job, your income is limited by the number of hours you work. Theoretically, the upper limit per day is twenty-four, but realistically, it is about eight to twelve. Likewise, if you are paid by a yearly salary, the same constraint exists: the theoretical maximum number of years you can work is just fifty or sixty. Realistically, it's about forty years. Forty hours and/or forty years is what I call, bad math.

40 hours a week @ 20/hour = $800 a week
40 years of work @ $50,000 a year = $2,000,000 lifetime earnings

If time was scalable...

400 hours a week @ 20/hour = $8,000 a week
400 years of work @ $50,000 a year = $20,000,000 lifetime earnings

No matter how energetic you are, you can't work 400 hours a day, or 400 years. Time cannot be scaled.

ANCHOR THREE: RAT RACE ECONOMICS CANNOT BE SCALED.

The rat racer's reaction to these punitive problems is to seek a higher wage or a bigger salary. In doing so, they will switch jobs, seek new careers, or even go back to college and blow a fortune on an advanced degree. Now, problem three stands in their way. Instead of being constrained by time, now the rat racer is constrained by rat race economics. Namely, excess supply, weak demand. When a gazillion people can do what you do, you have no leverage. You won't make $20/hour one day as a short-order cook, and next week, you're paid $1,000/hour because suddenly short-order cooks are in high demand and short supply. If you earn a yearly salary, the same economics apply: if you make $60,000 this year as a transaction auditor for a drug company, you'll never make $600,000 next year because suddenly no one can do your job. Thousands of college graduates would be standing in line waiting to take your job. In both instances, you cannot control or scale dollars.

For example, let's simplify our financial journey and assume your Escape Number is **$5 million**. In this scenario, you can safely save your money under a mattress, and there are no taxes or inflation. If it takes you 30 years to save **$5 million**, it will be just as valuable as it is today.

Let's examine the math and see how poor leverage plays out in various careers and jobs. Keep in mind, these figures are BEFORE any taxes and presumes a generous 10% savings rate.

Career / Profession	Average Pay	Years to Earn $5M	Years to Save $5M
Architect	87,130	57 yrs	574 yrs
Auto Mechanic	46,760	107 yrs	1069 yrs
Carpenter	54,200	92 yrs	923 yrs
Chef / Head Cook	58,740	85 yrs	851 yrs
General Medicine MD	211,000	24 yrs	237 yrs
Dentist (Employed)	180,000	28 yrs	278 yrs
Elementary School Teacher	65,300	77 yrs	766 yrs
Insurance/Claims Adjuster	70,650	71 yrs	708 yrs
Loan Officer	76930	65 yrs	650 yrs
Retail Salesperson	31,200	160 yrs	1603 yrs
Commercial Pilot	110,830	45 yrs	451 yrs
Software Developer	109,950	45 yrs	455 yrs

Source: https://www.bls.gov/oes/current/oes_nat.htm (May 2020 Figures)

As you can see, if you make $31,200/year as a retail salesperson, expect to trade 160 years of your life to gross $5,000,000. That's 41,666 eight-hour shifts every single day. Add life overhead (taxes, inflation, basic necessities), and saving $5,000,000 at a ten percent savings rate, you'll need a cosmic 1603 years. In other words, to amass a freedom-making fortune today, you'll need a early fifth-century start, a time when Attila the Hun ruled. As you can see, driving the rat race with a wage-locus is a death sentence.

The news isn't better with a salary locus. Suppose you have a respectable job as an architect. In that case, you'll need 574 years to save $5,000,000, assuming a generous ten percent savings rate. Perhaps the experts who push this method of getting rich consulted the Old Testament first—those Biblical folks supposedly lived to 900. With a $87,000 salary, your best-case scenario is hardwired in the rat race system—and that scenario is mediocrity. Wage- and salaried-rats are stuck with what I call *Uncontrollable Limited Leverage* or ULL. And "ULL" means you'll never escape.

Professional athletes and celebrities are one of the few professions that can disrupt ULL. When there's only one person on the planet with Lebron James' skills, and everyone wants him for basketball or endorsements (low supply/high demand), Lebron James is not subject to Uncontrollable Limited Leverage. As such, he gets paid a leveraged amount. This is why most people desire fame but don't know why. Fame equals leverage and favorable economics. Who doesn't want to make $5 million per movie, $500K per speech, or $50K per game? The human talent itself is the system of leverage, usually as an outlier skill, like pitching a baseball over 100 mph. When it comes to average Joes like us, we have no such option. I'll never sing, act, or play baseball. If you want any chance of a rat race escape, bad math, or Uncontrollable Limited Leverage cannot be part of your existence.

The truth is, the Bad Math Principle isn't taught at university. It would never be revealed in some financial "stop drinking coffee" best-seller. Most educational sources promote bad math strategies: save a hundred dollars a month, invest for forty years, hope for eight percent returns, blah blah blah. Numbers like 100, 40, and 8% doesn't create wealth fast, it creates wealth old, or never. Bad math handicaps wealth and becomes a bad offense[P13]. A motivational quip might inspire you for a day or two, but if your numbers aren't right, it doesn't matter. As they say, running enthusiastically in the wrong direction is, well, the wrong direction.

☑ KEY CONCEPTS

- There are three anchors to bad math: 1) Income is correlated to time, 2) Time (hours/years) cannot be scaled, and 3) Rat race economics (wages/salary) cannot be scaled.

- Even in respectable, good paying professions, saving $5 million dollars at a 10% savings rate would take centuries.

- Celebrities and athletes are not subject to ULL, or bad math.

- Financial gurus or universities do not teach Uncontrollable Limited Leverage.

THE SPECIALIZED-UNIT STRATEGY

Put Leverage into Your Life: More Money, Less Time

For most of my early twenties, I struggled with money, paying debts, and building wealth. While I had a profit-locus[S16], I wasn't offering perceived-value. The fancy car didn't help either. But everything changed when I taught myself a specialized-skill, web development, and then transformed it into a specialized-unit. It was my first significant step at fielding a powerful, life-changing offense[P13]. How? Anytime you transform a specialized-skill into a specialized-unit, you weaken the rat race's anchors and its bad math[P17]. There are two types of specialized-units—one weakens time's grip on your income, the other fires it.

1. The second-order specialized-unit
2. The first-order specialized-unit

THE SECOND-ORDER SPECIALIZED-UNIT

After I taught myself a specialized-skill, web design, I sought to sell that skill. I sold websites to clients who needed them. Through a second-order specialized-unit, I multiplied my return on time. Here's how: With a wage-locus, I could take my specialized-skill in web design and seek a part-time job designing websites. The outcome is $15/hour. With a salary-locus, I might seek a full-time position with benefits. The outcome is $42,000/year or about $22/hour—an improvement over the wage-locus but costing much more time.

However, if I charged an average of $2,500 per website and spent an average of ten hours delivering it, I would 10X my return on time. I'd go from $22/hour to $250/hour. More money earned; less time spent to earn it.

Despite this nice 10X pay bump, a second-order specialized-unit is still subservient to time. If I can't find and sell clients who need websites, I'd earn nothing. The second-order specialized-unit is also limited by time since I can't code 24 hours a day, and many of those hours are needed for the sales process.

Similarly, tools can also create second-order specialized-units either through ownership or competence. Think sewing machines, welders, scissor lifts, or lawn mowers. An entrepreneur on my forum mows lawns for $150/mo. Seems cheap eh? Maybe, but he's smart and has done the numbers: With his crew, it takes him 15 minutes, 20 times a year, for $1,800 in revenue. Total time spent is just five hours to earn $1,800 or $360/hour. He admitted that few people would hire his company if they worked out the numbers—$150/mo. is reasonable, $360/hour is not—that's the power of a specialized-unit. A second-order specialized-unit is a decent start to breaking rat race economics.

THE FIRST-ORDER SPECIALIZED-UNIT

A first-order specialized-unit can be anything with a demand as long as this product/service can eventually survive disconnected from your time. Think software, franchises, physical products including food, games, information, books, clothing, gadgets, inventions—anything that exists separate from you, the entrepreneur.

This book offers a good example. If I carry a salary-locus and my specialized-skill is writing, I could seek a writing job and make $30,000 a year. Or, with a profit-locus and a second-order specialized-unit, I could charge 100 clients $500 per project and earn $50,000 a year as a freelancer. Problem is, I can't work 50,000 hours or freelance 50,000 jobs—time remains in control. Or I could make $500,000 a year selling my specialized-skill 50,000 times packed as a first-order specialized-unit, a book.

Ultimately, the specialized-unit is a three-pronged attack against the rat race anchors. Unlike time and rat race economics, specialized-units possess scaling power. From foodstuffs to software subscriptions to grooming products, your creation must have the theoretical power to be sold in massive quantities, which transforms bad math into good math. The right first-order specialized-unit can be replicated, used, consumed, or sold repeatedly. This fact puts rat race economics on notice: more dollars, less time.

☑ KEY CONCEPTS

- There are two types of specialized-units which can help you 10X your return on time: first- and second-order.
- A second-order specialized-unit transforms your specialized-skill into a finished product or service, like a website, a copywriting service, or a freelance project.
- A second-order specialized-unit is usually subordinated by time.
- A first-order specialized-unit is a product/service severed from your time and can be sold in big quantities, and often repeatedly.

THE BUSINESS SYSTEM STRATEGY

Fire Time: Make Profit Timeless and Unending

My stepson is a great writer of fantasy. Like, *Game of Thrones* material. And as the owner of a publishing company, I'm dying to publish his work. The more he endures college (which he hates), the more he writes. He senses a job isn't in his future. Surely that has nothing to do with his stepdad. :-)

Anyway, by itself, a book is worthless. So is a video game, a mobile application, a food product, or an invention.

Ultimately, a specialized-unit[S18] needs to get into the hands of buyers who need it. If a specialized-unit weakens the rat race, the business system kills it. A business system is responsible for getting your specialized-unit into the hands of the right audience.

For my publishing company, the business system consists of my forum, my customer list, my eCommerce website, my social media accounts, and all the business channels that sell my books like Amazon, Ingram, and Baker & Taylor, including several dozen foreign publishers outside the USA. My stepson could write the best book ever written, but without a business system to sell it, it's untapped potential. If you owned a food product, your business system would be your eCommerce website, your marketing initiatives, as well as the wholesale distributors and retail channels like Target, Kroger, or Safeway. Here are some examples of specialized-units and their business systems.

Specialized-Unit	Business System
A mobile app	Apple store, Google play, your website, your mailing list
A book	Amazon, Audible, Ingram, bookstores, your blog, your mailing list
An invention	Your website, retail stores, distributors, your mailing list
A clothing line	Your website, retail and wholesalers, your mailing list
A movie	Netflix, YouTube, movie theaters, TV networks, syndicators

Like your specialized-unit, a business system is not constrained by time, namely, your time. It dissolves the rat race's first anchor. The systems used to sell this book exist in perpetuity, essentially becoming hundreds, perhaps thousands, of full-time salespersons who never stop working, never go on break, and never need a vacation. My publishing company earned a tiny paycheck the moment you bought this book. Who knows what I was doing at that moment—sleeping, writing, walking the dog?

In effect, the business system puts you "on the clock" 24/7 for the rest of your life. The business system trades *its time* for money, replacing YOU as the method for trade. Whereas a specialized-unit invalidates rat race economics, rendering the last two rat race anchors null and void, a business system gives you power over time. For example, I wrote the book *The Millionaire Fastlane* more than ten years ago, and it still provides me with a six-figure annual income. The writing time I invested in this specialized-unit occurred over a decade ago, but the business system is still working, giving me a positive net return on my time, not the standard negative 60 percent[P8].

Ultimately, I could sell millions of specialized-units, but pushing those sales comes down to driving demand and the business system I employ. For example, there are millions of authors who have tried self-publishing, uploading one book into the Amazon eco-system and waiting. They ultimately sell little to nothing. They have the specialized-unit (the book they wrote) but they don't have the business system. *Publish a book on Amazon and wait* is not a business system, it's a lottery ticket. I spent years building my business system. From advertising mediums to retail channels, to wholesale distributors, to marketing strategy—the grind doesn't end at the specialized-unit, it begins. A specialized-unit without its business system is like ying without its yang.

☑ **KEY CONCEPTS**

- A business system is an all-encompassing system from sales channels to marketing initiatives and is responsible for getting your specialized-unit into the hands of the right audience.

- A specialized-unit combined with a business system gives you power over time and limited leverage.

- A specialized-unit and a business system are both needed to break the three rat race anchors.

THE KNOWLEDGE GAP STRATEGY

Mind the Knowledge Gap or Fall Behind

You didn't tell me exactly how you did it! Some years ago, a reader griped that my book failed to reveal the "exact" methods I used to grow my business. Clearly, the comment was from someone who had never run a business, much less worked in marketing or sales. The fact is, the business building strategies that I used years ago, even months ago, will no longer help me today. A sales-shattering tactic that worked in 2018 won't work in 2021. In short, *yesterday's beneficial knowledge is today's worthless knowledge.*

Behind this truth is what's called a *knowledge gap.* The knowledge gap is the divide between what you need to know but don't. This could range from a skill you lack, to a poorly executed marketing strategy, to a misinterpreted data point on a cultural trend. The knowledge gap carries a natural expansion bias and is correlated to change. Because technology, economics, societal norms, consumer tastes, and behavior are all dynamic, the knowledge gap is continuously expanding. Jeff looked into bitcoin and relented that it was "too complicated." In the future, this will be a big missed opportunity simply because he wasn't willing to close his knowledge gap. Just because something seems complicated, doesn't mean you can't learn it. Learning anything new always seems complicated!

For example, every success I enjoy today was earned yesterday by minding the gap. I was in constant pursuit of knowledge: I learned how to code, learned new industries, learned marketing, and learned how to adapt. In another example, the 2020 COVID-19 pandemic has blown a massive chasm in the world's collective knowledge gap. Ever hear the phrase "the new normal?" This collectively references the knowledge gap and its rapid expansion.

How do you shrink your knowledge gap? The first step is to acknowledge its ever-expanding existence. The second step is persistent learning. How many books have you read in the last month? If you think about it, anytime you read a book, you're getting a personal one-on-one mentorship with the author. In other words, countless experts, billionaires, scientists, and other leaders are willing to mentor you and help you close your knowledge gap. New education, and therefore, new opportunities are always just a few googled keystrokes away, a bus ride to the library, or just being a keen observer.

Regrettably, Scripted rat racers don't mind the knowledge gaps; they mind the cultural ones: the latest celebrity news, royal weddings, and dumb football games that won't matter a mere week later. In fact, the larger your knowledge gap, the deeper the rut your life will suffer. The origin of a rut relies on the same knowledge that got you there in the first place. Mind the gap or get swallowed by it. *An old education rarely fits a new opportunity.*

☑ KEY CONCEPTS

- What works today doesn't work tomorrow.
- The knowledge gap is the ever-growing space between what you don't know and what you need to know, caused by shifts in tastes, technology, and human behavior.
- Only persistent learning can shrink a knowledge-gap, preceded by acknowledging its existence.
- And old education rarely fits a new opportunity.

A NEW HOPE

Sam sat down in the booth across from her husband. Her hair was wild as if she'd arrived by motorcycle, and her face was pale without its usual makeup. She tore off her jacket. Underneath, she wore one of her preachy vegan T-shirts which read, "INTELLIGENCE DOESN'T GIVE YOU THE RIGHT TO MURDER—DO YOU WANT AN ADVANCED ALIEN SPECIES EATING YOUR CHILDREN?" Jeff glanced at the shirt and tried to remain expressionless as his wife usually kept her militant shirts confined to the house. Between the shirt and her disheveled appearance, it looked like she was ready for household chores, not a night out.

They were at their favorite restaurant, Pancho's Mexican Cantina. After Sam pressed for a "date night," they met for dinner. Jeff arrived straight from the gym on Sam's urgency, his shirt stained with sweat, his hair messy.

"You couldn't wait until I got home and changed?" He sized her up and didn't let her answer. "You look as bad as me."

Sam gleamed, ignoring the dig. "Looks like you had a good workout." He had been on the treadmill when his wife beckoned to meet, and she'd insisted—no drive home to shower, no change of clothes, and no explanation for the urgency.

"Yes," he said, dressing his lap with a napkin. Looking around, he said, "First time we've been here in years. We loved this place, you know, before we became Mr. and Mrs. Scrooge, except without the fortune."

Sam's eyes twinkled, detached from her husband's flippancy. When the waiter came by, she ordered a margarita, a deviation from her usual Cabernet. Jeff ordered his typical whiskey. After the waiter shuffled off, Jeff stared at her pointedly. "Okay, let's have it. What's up? Since we've sat down you've had this shit-eating grin. And you didn't order a glass of wine, which is your chill-out drink. The margarita suggests a celebration."

Sam veered in, her eyes sparkling. She whispered as if discussing national security, "I found it."

"Found what?" Jeff eyed her incredulously, his tone just as hushed. "You

found the floor plans to the bank? You found you're long-lost English roy-
alty?" He chuckled.

"No." She fell back into her booth, "I found the answer to our problem."

"Our problem? Which one? Last I checked we had a few hundred."

"Escaping the rat race," she reported.

Jeff motioned to their drinks, which had just arrived. After the waiter
took their food order, Jeff continued, "Seeing we ordered twenty-dollars in
drinks, I'm guessing it doesn't have to do with living like broke coeds for the
rest of our lives?"

"Right." She licked the salt on her margarita and sipped. "I found the answer
in a couple of business books."

"Business books? Like how to climb your way up the corporate ladder and
get promoted to CEO? I don't—"

Sam held up a hand, interrupting. "No, this is not about working in a
business, but starting one."

Jeff didn't flinch. "What books? Anyone I know?"

"No, probably not. This first book was called *The Millionaire Fastlane*, the
second was called *Unscripted*." Jeff eyed her suspiciously. She continued, "At
first, I dismissed the author because of the cheesy title, but once I dug into
his message, it really made sense. The writing is a bit juvenile for your taste,
but the math made perfect sense and—"

"The millionaire what?" Jeff snapped, "Please don't tell me this is one of
those pyramid things. Everyone in our family hates your cousin because she's
always peddling that skin care crap on anyone who breathes."

Sam shook her head and then smiled. "No, Jeff, *Unscripted* isn't a pyramid.
More like we'll be building our own. According to the author, we need to
start our own business, a particular type of business which can yield asymmetrical returns."

Jeff curiously spiked his eyebrow. In a million years, he never expected his
wife to utter the phrase "asymmetrical returns" and it raised a red flag. *Was
she falling victim to scam?* She continued, her pace increasing. After a twenty-
minute overview followed by their dinner's arrival, she asserted, "Read the
books and you'll see what I mean. We can do this in ten years or less. And it
won't involve the stock market or living like hippie cheapskates." She sipped
her margarita and continued. "We've been approaching this rat race thing
from the wrong angle, blindly following a bunch of strategies suggested by
the scientists who control the lab rats. It's time to turn the tables and be the
ones who make the rules. And the rules are all based on math." She held up
her drink as if she was toasting. "And you're the math guy, not me."

Unconvinced, Jeff's eyes narrowed as he bit into his quesadilla. His wife
and math mixed like chores and a spoiled brat in the middle of video-gaming.

Sam said, measuredly, "I'll give you the books when we get home so you can read for yourself."

Jeff followed with a glare as if he was a child begrudgingly tasked with a week's worth of homework. "Start a business? Rats and scientists in laboratories?" He wiped his mouth with his napkin. "Sounds, ahem"—he cleared his throat exaggeratedly—"interesting."

THE ASYMMETRIC RETURNS STRATEGY

Construct a Leveraged Vehicle: One Unit of Effort, Five Units of Pay

Whenever I drive to the post office, I pass a small fashion boutique in a strip mall. The street is lightly traveled, and the parking lot is always empty. One day after breakfast at an adjacent café, the wife dragged me into the store. While inside, I managed to ask the owner, an older woman, if she sold online or had a website. She admitted she did not and flashed me a sideways grimace as if she expected me to sell her one.

After leaving the store, I could deduce with certainty that this clothing store owner will never set herself free from the rat race. Why? She's stuck in an inefficient business system with bad math[P17]. Suppose the boutique averages 100 customers a week, which is a function of both foot and auto traffic near the store. Because this boutique doesn't sell on the Internet, I can make a foolproof prediction: there's nothing the owner can do to scale those 100 customers into 1000. Or 10,000. Not by next week, next month, or next year. The owner could be a genius marketer and it still doesn't matter. There is a zero probability that this business owner could earn $2,000,000 next year, much less $500,000. This boutique owner has a silent partner, and it's bad personal leverage. While our boutique owner owns a business, she's failed to annul rat race economics[P17].

The fact is, most business owners are struggling like their wage and salaried counterparts. Having a profit locus isn't enough, especially if bad math governs your business model.

Ultimately, you don't want to trade your time selling your skills; you want to invest your skills in a specialized-unit and its business system. Instead of increasing the frequency (more hours) or skilled value (more salary), work to expand the reach (more people) and external value (more impact) of your specialized-unit. This transformation creates the potential for asymmetric returns—one unit of work, five units of pay. The rat race's primary ally, ULL, is replaced CUL, or Controllable Unlimited Leverage.

In a business system, our specialized-unit[S18], could be sold repeatedly and infinitely through time. Create a specialized-unit with $50 of net perceived-value[S16], and you'd earn $50,000 if you sold two to three of them per day. Sell fifty per day and the number explodes to $912,500 and only a short sixty-six months to earn $5 million.

Average Profit Per Unit	Average Units Sold Daily	Years to Earn $5M
$25	50 100 200	11.0 yrs 5.5 yrs 2.7 yrs
$50	50 100 200	5.5 yrs 2.7 yrs 1.4 yrs
$100	50 100 200	2.7 yrs 1.4 yrs 8.5 months
My internet business: $6	900	2.5 yrs

When I owned my internet company, 20,000 people would routinely visit my service daily, and each visitor was worth and average of $6. My conversion rate was around 4.5%. Looking at the chart above, how fast do you think I built wealth and hit my Escape Number[S15]? I had influence over the numbers implicit in my rat race escape. Time was not in control, I was. Math was not limited, it was unlimited.

That same physics exist with my publishing company. First, "units sold" is a variable that scales into the stratosphere. I can theoretically sell millions. I can't sell the hours or years in my life by millions, but I can sell my creative contribution. Second, I can increase unit profit on each book I print by price shopping, changing formats, or producing shorter books. For example, I recently switched book printers, which saved me about 60 cents per book. That might not seem like much, but if you're selling 200,000 units in one year, that's a whopping $120,000— all because I requested one quote from one different printer. One hour of work yielded a $120,000 return and created an leveraged earning event.

And finally, I can expand my leverage by adding more authors and more books to my publishing company's library of offerings. The leverage is continually growing, evolving, and is always pliable to my effort. And it is chock-full of specialized-units[S18]. Not bragging, just illustrating the power of Controllable Unlimited Leverage as it relates to scaling wealth.

Sell a million of anything, and yes, you will earn millions. Impact millions, make millions. These four words are the simple secret. The more people you affect, either in scale (width) or magnitude (depth), the more money you earn. Scale, or width, refers to the volume of sales you can possibly make—ten million phone cases sold at $1 profit on each equal ten million dollars. Your market size and leverage potential is denominated by how many people want phone cases, not by margin. On the other hand, magnitude represents the gravity of the impact and is reflected in a much larger unit profit. One thousand bronze sculptures sold at $10,000 profit on each is also ten million dollars. With magnitude, the potential leverage is both in the market size and the margin. Scale minimally impacts many; magnitude maximizes impact on a few. Both lay the foundation for asymmetric returns.

Here's another way of looking at it. Imagine our rat race as an actual marathon across a vast countryside covering thousands of miles. For your participation, the Scripted gangsters promise you a wonderful "retirement" at the end of this journey, a retirement filled with wealth, freedom, and mobility. Put another way, the number of miles you need to travel is your Escape Number. Have a three-million-dollar Escape Number? Great, your marathon is three-million miles. As you can imagine, this long marathon could take decades. And progress is randomly dependent on weather and road conditions. Plotting a route will be the hardest thing you've ever done. Getting lost is easy—frustration, even easier. Most die during the marathon, their soul crushed and their body broken. Others complete the marathon at the end of their life, arriving old and exhausted, their freedom confined to a nursing home.

When we take to the marathon with a wage-locus, we're walking with sandals. Our progress is unleveraged and symmetrical—one unit of effort, one unit of movement. Going faster, or running, is nearly impossible. If we go to college and earn a degree, we graduate with a salary-locus and upgrade to a pair of nice sneakers. Now we can walk faster, or better run. One time-based unit of effort is still rewarded one unit of movement, just a larger unit. In both cases, constant effort is required and based on time "pounding the pavement." While running longer or faster for a higher wage or salary might be possible, the rat racer is still stuck doing labor. Take a day off, and the movement stops. But more telling is this: Neither method has the capacity for leveraged, asymmetrical movement. You can't run at 40 mph or travel 500 miles in one day. One unit of a time-based effort will always generate one unit of movement.

Moreover, a foot marathon puts you at the mercy of uncontrollable environmental forces like rough roads, steep hills, and stormy weather—unpredictable events like job losses, economic recessions, inflation, and now, pandemics that cause worldwide shutdowns. A bad storm (recession) could halt your trip or a steep road (inflation, cost of living, etc.) can drag movement to a crawl. Altogether, these travel methods lack the speed and control needed to get across the country, at least within five years.

If you want a chance at freedom, you're going to need to ditch the conventional travel methods and upgrade to a faster, more efficient means of movement—*a leveraged vehicle.* Instead of wasting your time running the marathon, invest your time in a system that will leverage your effort, and eventually, run the marathon for you. When you invest your time in a specialized-unit, the engine, and a business system[S19], the vehicle, you're ditching the "time for money" orthodoxy. While your foot-based peers might get off to fast start and seem further ahead on their marathon, eventually you'll overtake them. Soon, one unit of effort can translate into ten units of movement—output goes asymmetrical.

Better, when you build a business system, you can assign an operator to drive it. Or, put it on autopilot. You can make progress on your journey while not at the helm. That's like having someone climb the Stairmaster for two hours while you enjoy the fitness benefits. The point of this marathon analogy is to demonstrate the losing gambits. People don't struggle because they're lazy. Working five days a week for fifty years is not easy. People ultimately struggle because they're stuck in the rat race on foot. Sandals and sneakers aren't solutions—the levered vehicle is. You can't move mountains with your bare hands when moving mountains needs a bulldozer.

☑ KEY CONCEPTS

- A business with bad math is also subject to rat race economics.

- Replace a time trade with a time investment in a specialized-unit and its business system and asymmetric returns become possible—one unit of work earns you five units of pay.

- Impact millions of lives, and you will make millions.

- Asymmetric returns are possible when Controllable Unlimited Leverage replaces Uncontrollable Limited Leverage.

- Consider a rat race escape like a long-distance marathon across the country.

- With a wage-locus, you walk the marathon in sandals, with a salary-locus, you jog the journey in sneakers, and with a profit-locus, you take the road in a leveraged vehicle.

- An operator can drive a leveraged vehicle, giving you a tool for freedom.

THE POLYMORPHIC PAY PRINCIPLE

Invest in Time, Stop Trading It

Bill Gunton is the actor who played the corrupt warden in the famed classic, *The Shawshank Redemption,* a movie I've seen at least fifty times. Recently, he disclosed to a journalist for the *Wall Street Journal* that he still earns nearly six figures a year for his supporting role. At the time of filming, his acting talent earned a leveraged amount because it was a second-order specialized-unit[S18]. Still, the time he spent acting for the role was considered *monomorphic pay*, a direct trade of time for money. If he wanted to earn more money acting, he needed to invest more time into more movies. Time still was in control.

The good news is the actor also contributed to a first-order specialized-unit—the movie—which could be licensed over and over, the business system. The specialized-unit and its ability for replication and repetition allowed the actor to enjoy a lifetime dividend in the form of royalties. In Unscripted terms, the Polymorphic Pay Principle is *when a past time investment continues to yield future income.* Sometimes indefinitely.

Trillions of dollars are spent every year in finance, from accounting to money-saving techniques to investment research and strategy. If you could turn a buck into a buck-twenty (a 20 percent return) year after year, you'd be considered an investment rockstar. The world has no shortage of resources willing to educate you on how to invest your money.

However, when it comes to investing your time, *your most precious asset,* there are no resources. Absolutely nothing.

What few realize is that you can invest your time just like money. And the yield on a good time investment pays *more time,* namely free time. Money earned while not working is a payment of free time. And this phenomenon only comes from business systems[S19]. If you make $1,000 overnight from a business system (your past time investment), that's $1,000 you don't have to earn in the future. If you value your free time at $50 per hour, you just earned twenty hours of free time: 20 hours X $50 = $1,000. Income earned while not working pays free time—the work time spared from your future. Likewise, money-systems[S14] pay polymorphic pay, just not very well. If you bought one share in a dividend-paying company that pays $2 a year in dividends, a third-party business system, your past time investment pays you polymorphically for life.

Monomorphic pay, on the other hand, is the rat race's default method of payment—trade time, earn money. Culture has easily conditioned us to associate time as a monetary means of barter. Work is rationed by the hour or the year, linked to one sequence of cash. *McDonald's is hiring at $15 per hour, Raytheon is hiring an engineer for $110,000 a* year. Monomorphic pay is the only approved narrative for earning money inside the rat race. Hence, time, as it is culturally sold, is a conspirator against your freedom.

To convert time into an ally, *you need to invest in time, not trade it.* Anytime you invest in a business system through a specialized-unit, whether successful or not, you're an investor of time seeking to get a yield of polymorphic pay... eventually. This multi-payment oddity exists in few professions, and those careers that do possess it rarely achieve it. An inventor can get paid license fees for past inventions. The specialized-unit is the invention and the channels that sell it are the business system. An actor can earn residuals on scenes acted long ago, as in widely syndicated television shows. An author can earn royalties from a book written years ago. My books have been translated into over 25 languages, and I get royalties on all of them. The book is the specialized-unit, the foreign publishers are the business systems... all working around the globe for me, 24/7. When someone buys my book in Thailand or Korea, I'm likely sleeping. But I'm earning polymorphic pay—1) the small profit and 2) the time I don't need to work for it in the future. If you formulate a product that sells in stores nationwide, the same applies. You're earning polymorphic pay because that product can be sold all day, every day.

In "making money" circles, this concept is often romanticized into *passive income,* but don't be fooled. Notwithstanding Warden Norton and his windfall, passive income is anything but passive. Passive income is often put forth by hucksters who sell five-figure coaching programs to a growing tide of wannabe entrepreneurs, or what I call *dreampreneurs.* After dealing with thousands of entrepreneurs over the years, I've come to learn that passive income seekers are also, ironically, quite passive. When dreampreneurs discover that "passive income" can take years to foment, they often quit, seeking easier pastures. All my business systems that pay polymorphically took years to build—a period where the pay was poor and the work long. *Passive income is for amateurs, polymorphic pay is for the professionals.*

☑ KEY CONCEPTS

- Monomorphic pay is income earned for a direct trade of time for money, either by the hour, by the year, or by the unit.

- Polymorphic pay is income earned from a past time investment.

- Like money, you can invest "time."

- Anytime you invest in a a specialized-unit, whether successful or not, you're a time investor seeking polymorphic pay.

- Polymorphic pay is romanticized into its popular twin, passive income.

- Polymorphic pay isn't as easily obtained as its "passive income" hucksters would advertise.

THE CONSUMER / PRODUCER PRINCIPLE

Math Doesn't Lie, and Neither Will Your Annual Report

23

Math doesn't lie, but people do. This was proven during the 2008 housing crisis when most foreclosures weren't from people on the fringes of poverty, but affluent and well-educated buyers, according to a study by the St. Louis Federal Reserve.[1] The crisis was less about predatory lending and more about buyers overreaching for appreciation and affluence with "liar loans." Without the numbers to verify the truth, the fiscal "health" of any buyer was relegated to their honesty, or I should say, dishonesty.

When you want to investigate the health of a corporation or assess an investment, you look at its annual report—the math: cash flows, income statements, balance sheets, margins, profits, revenues, debt, rate of return—all data points which offer an unassailable look underneath the hood. By law, corporations need to report the truth, or it's fraud. The bigger question is, if you had to tell the truth about the numbers in your life, what would they say about the team you're playing for?

The Consumer / Producer Principle states that *your annual report reveals your role in the rat race.* Rats play for Team Consumer, scientists play for Team Producer. Whatever team you profess, your rat race role—as it stands now—has a definitive, foolproof lie detector test. It's called math, and math doesn't lie.

Despite our corporate status as human chattel barcoded with a Social Security number (SSN), we simply don't examine the mathematics hitched to our life. But we should. If you had to organize a personal annual report exposing the numbers in your life, what would it look like? What would the numbers say concerning how you generate revenue, spend money, and invest in your future? If your personal financial situation, *You Inc.*, traded like a stock on the stock market, would an investor buy it? Hell, would *you* buy it? Or would *You Inc.* have already filed bankruptcy and gone the way of Blockbuster, Enron, or Leeman Brothers?

The fact is every human on the planet is backpacking an invisible annual

---

1 - https://www.stlouisfed.org/~/media/files/pdfs/publications/pub_assets/pdf/re/2011/c/foreclosure.pdf

report which bears our numbers. But unlike a corporate report with hundreds of numerical variables, there are only five you need to worry about. And they will reveal your role as either a rat on Team Consumer, or a scientist in Team Producer. They are:

1. Gross Annual Production (GAP)
2. Gross Annual Consumption (GAC)
3. Annual Net Existence (ANE)
4. Net Worth (NW)
5. Research and Development (R&D)

GROSS ANNUAL PRODUCTION (GAP)

Your gross annual production (GAP) represents the total production value you and your assets generate in the year. This could be your job salary, investment returns, business profits (and its corresponding valuation), a real estate holding, anything that has sellable value. Altogether, the GAP represents your offense in the offense/defense pair[P13]. In the past, I've interchangeably referred to Gross Annual Production as a Wealth Creation Equation.

For example, let's say you're a stonemason with a salary-locus[S16] derived from a specialized-skill. Last year you earned, net of taxes, $50K, and your home appreciated $10K. Your GAP on that prior year's annual report would simply be:

GAP = After tax salary ($50,000) + Net Investment Gains ($10,000)
GAP = $60,000

GROSS ANNUAL CONSUMPTION (GAC)

The second variable is your gross annual consumption (GAC), or total expenses, such as food, cars, housing, healthcare, and entertainment. This number also includes any liabilities incurred. Going back to your hypothetical job as a stonemason, if you spent $40,000 that year and financed $30,000 for a new truck, your gross annual consumption is $70,000.

GAC = Living expenses ($40,000) + New Truck Loan ($30,000)
GAC = $70,000

ANNUAL NET EXISTENCE (ANE)

The third variable is your annual net existence (ANE). This number reveals your net production or consumption for the year. A negative ANE means you consumed more than you produced for the year. A positive number means you have produced more than you consume. Here's the equation:

ANE = Gross Annual Production - Gross Annual Consumption

Here it is for our stonemason:

ANE = $60,000 (GAP) - $70,000 (GAC) = -$10,000

For that year as a stonemason, you were a net consumer, or a shopping-rat.

NET WORTH (NW)

Your net worth is the infallible lie detector test, the definitive truth serum for outing rats and scientists. Technically your net worth is the cumulative sum (Σ) of every ANE figure since you were old enough to work. Or it is simply your assets minus liabilities. If your net worth is positive, congratulations, you're a producer—you're playing the game as a scientist. Negative? Sorry, that means you're a consumer and navigating the game as a rat.

Net Worth = $\sum (ANE)_{Years}$ or
Net Worth = Total Assets - Total Liabilities

ANNUAL R&D (R&D)

The final number is the annual sum of hours you spend developing yourself—namely, the knowledge and skills for excelling in a scientist's world. Remember, culture automatically drafts you to play as a rat for Team Consumer. As a shopping-rat, your cheese is the weekend, for the savings-rat, an elderly retirement. In both cases, you're consuming either material goods or investment products.

However, when you defect from Team Consumer to Team Producer, it's like learning a new language. Studying how scientists play the game will require a constant education in resources not easily found. Yes, they exist, but they must be doggedly sought. This means becoming a lifetime student of production, the language of scientists. For instance, when you read an advertising message that persuades you to buy, examine it from the producer's perspective. What specific reason made you buy? A label? Price? A benefit? A good story? Why didn't you buy the competition's offer? How does this company make money? What psychological tactics are used in its marketing? What kind of operational processes are involved in offering this product or service? Is this company making a profit? What is the revenue model? Is this product manufactured overseas or locally?

Once you take on a scientific role of production, suddenly you won't be buying products on Amazon, you're selling them. Instead of chasing the trend, you're serving the trend. Instead of taking a class, you're giving a class. Instead of investing in a hedge-fund, you're the one managing it. Instead of consuming investment research, you're offering it.

Additionally, R&D could be self-improvement, from learning how to write or speak better to learning code to getting yourself in tip-top shape. In the business world, *companies* who invest nothing in R&D die. Likewise, *people* who invest nothing in R&D die in the rat race. No corporation can survive without a purpose and, ultimately, a profit. Look at yourself in the same manner! Altogether, these five variables reveal your financial life. Moreover, they expose (and then prove) your current rat race status.

Are you a rat? Or a scientist? And are you progressing or regressing?

Like math, your net worth won't lie.

☑ KEY CONCEPTS

- Math doesn't lie, people do.
- Rats play for Team Consumer, scientists for Team Producer.
- Your annual report represents the numbers in your financial life and determines your chances of a rat race escape.
- The five key numbers in your annual report are Gross Annual Production (GAP), Gross Annual Consumption (GAC), Annual Net Existence (ANE), Net Worth (NW), and Annual Research & Development (R&D).
- The rat race automatically drafts you to be on Team Consumer.
- To succeed on Team Producer, focus on your R&D and aim to learn the language of scientists... business, finance, marketing, management, etc.
- Your Annual Net Existence determines if you are a net producer or a net consumer for the year.
- Your net worth, the sum of ANE, indicates your current role in the rat race; positive = scientist, negative = rat.

THE MONEY CHASE

WEDNESDAY, NOVEMBER 16TH, 2016 - 6:15 PM

(4 days later)

"I'm boiling water for tea, you want some?"

Jeff sat quietly rubbing his chin while staring blankly at his notebook, Neve. Today's twilight cross was unusual. Instead of retreating to the bedroom from the day's work, Jeff sat at the table and started doodling in his journal. Sam had seen the expression before, the last time he attempted his taxes.

"Hello?" She walked to the table and pulled out a chair next to him. "If this is about Thanksgiving, I said I'd take care of it, cooking, cleaning, all of it."

"No, not about Thanksgiving." He shrugged. "You said we should start a business, so I was just trying to figure out what we can start that will make us some quick money." He opened Neve and pointed to a bulleted list. "I've been reading up on hustles. Everyone on the Internet talks about following your passion. So I'm thinking you could start a blog about organic gardening or vegan diets. Or maybe I can start a podcast about the Chicago Cubs, or do YouTube videos on playing saxophone." He scratched his head. "I just don't see how any of that's going to make us money. And enough that we can retire early and afford to send Maddy to DePaul." He closed his notebook. "I mean, do I just throw some videos up on YouTube? And they pay me? It's all pretty foreign to me."

Sam chuckled, "DePaul? You're already making college decisions for Maddy and she's not even out of elementary school yet?"

"I know, but with this business thing we're planning, I thought we'd axe one thing off the to-do list." He chuckled, "You have a problem with our alma mater?"

They'd both attended and met at DePaul University in Chicago. Coming from the Idaho tundra, Sam wanted a city experience, complete with the cold. Jeff tried to avoid the cold and wanted to attend the University of Texas. When he was 17, he'd spent some time in Austin and loved it. Surely South Padre Island and the spring break that followed days later had nothing to do with his college preferences. His parents vehemently vetoed the choice, and DePaul was the compromise.

Jeff didn't wait for her to answer about college and carried on. "You love gardening, and the amount of food that we get from a tiny patch of land is amazing. Between the tomatoes and carrots, you've saved us a fortune. Your garden know-how certainly has to be worth something. Or maybe we start selling at the farmer's market?"

His wife swallowed hard. She strayed over to the window.

Now gibbering at her back, Jeff added, "Or wait a sec, how about we sell custom mirrors? Didn't you say your nurse friend worked for a manufacturer in L.A.? Mirrors can be pretty expensive—I'm sure there's got to be some good profit margin there."

Sam gazed through the glass from their second-story window. It was already dark, and flurries had started to fall. The oak trees surrounding their neighborhood were already bare, their naked branches weaving up into the dark sky like tentacles. She could feel the cold night touching her through the window. She stood silent as her husband rambled on for another minute. Tuning his voice out into a muffled mess of nothingness, Sam's gut churned with anger. Her husband meant well, but he didn't like being told what to do. Clearly, he had no clue. Sam had given him the DeMarco books, literally dropped them in his lap as he lay in bed. But if the empty coffee mug that sat atop them for four days was any tell, she doubted he'd read them. She sighed and turned back to him, trying to hide her disappointment. "Jeff, you're not going about this business thing the right way."

He looked at her as if she'd just told him to jump into a lake in mid-January. "What's the right way? We need to start a business and make money. You said it yourself." His eyes narrowed. "My new boss has been a complete asshole. Ever since the last audit underperformed process review, he's been hell at work." Jeff crinkled up his napkin and threw it at his empty dinner plate. "I can't take it anymore."

"It's not that simple."

"Sure it is." He leered at his wife, tone forceful. "We find something and sell it. T-shirts, some trinkets from China, I don't give a shit. We can put it on eBay or something. You wouldn't believe some of the crap people buy nowadays." He paused and then cracked the evening's first smile. "And then I can march into my boss's office and tell him to take his job and shove it."

Whiiiiiiieeeeeeeeeeeeeeeee!

He motioned to the whistling kettle. "Oh yes, and I'll take some tea."

She frowned at him, a dubious look painted her face. "Get it yourself."

THE POLARITY STRATEGY

Reverse Your Polarity to Attract Money

24

Ptolemy, famed second-century Greco Roman astronomer, is best known for his "Earth-centered" or geocentric cosmology. He postulated that the earth was not only stationary, but it was at the center of the universe. His model, however, wasn't entirely conjecture as it contain numerous mathematical models to account for the erratic paths of the celestial bodies. In hindsight, it was a theory made of human hubris.

Unfortunately in today's entrepreneurial culture, that hubris remains. Countless aspiring entrepreneurs remain aspiring because of their own selfish preoccupations—they are operating as if they were the center of the universe. Whenever you enter a market selfishly, you risk becoming a Ptolemy money-chaser.

Many years ago, when I sat on the shoulder of the road contemplating suicide, I didn't know I was a Ptolemy money-chaser. My reasons for starting a business were purely selfish.

> *I want be my own boss.*
> *I don't want to wear a suit and ride a train downtown.*
> *I'd like to help my mother retire early.*

Whatever motives you have for starting a business, I've have sad news. *No one gives a shit.* Well, except maybe for your mom or your wife.

Ptolemy money-chasing is a poison-pen[52] and is *a business mindset guided by me-centered introspection instead of a market-centered extrospection.* This poison pen framed my early entrepreneurial days, from "following my passion," to wanting to own a Lamborghini, every business I failed was centered on my selfish desires and needs. I never paused and considered market needs because I was too busy considering my own.

As an owner of a business forum with nearly 1,000,000 posts, I read a lot from aspiring entrepreneurs. It only takes me a few words to know if they are Ptolemy money-chasers. How? If their words reflect a *positive charge* toward money, then I'm betting they bust. Take, for example, the following statements, typical money-chasing:

How can I make money starting a business?
What hustle can I start with $500 and still make $5K per month?
I have a friend who makes widgets; you think I can make money selling them?
How can I make passive income?
What's a good product to import so I can sell on Amazon?
What's the best business to start on a shoestring?
I knit a damn good sock; how can I sell them?

All these questions reflect a positive charge toward money—Ptolemy money-chasing— as if money were something to be captured, like a lost dog or a feral cat. Sadly, money is also positively charged. And what happens if you take two magnets of the same charge? *They repel.*

A rat race isn't a rat race without its cheese. When a scientist arrives at his laboratory on Monday morning and drops a rat into the maze for the day's study, he needs a way to motivate the rat. Give it a reason to run. A reason to work. Instinctually, rats are hungry for cheese. In the real world, this cheese is money. As humans, we have an instinctual, positive charge toward money-chasing, no different than that rat seeking cheese. And it doesn't matter who holds the cash—the broke college student or the billionaire philanthropist—cash always carries a positive charge.

If you want to attract money instead of repelling it, deploy The Polarity Strategy and *reverse your polarity*. Instead of accepting culture's positive charge and its failing instincts, become negatively charged. How? Drape yourself in value like you would a golden cloak. Value is negatively charged, giving its owner gravity. Think of it like a drug-dealer without the illegality.

While humans are positively charged to money, money is positively charged to value. So if you or your business offers perceived-value, the money will pour into your life. Namely, what do you have that other people want? What solutions, conveniences, or hungers are you filling? How many lives have you impacted, even if minimally?

Think of it this way. Attacking money with a positive charge is akin to chasing a finicky cat around the neighborhood who outwits you in every pursuit, up the tree, behind the bushes, under the car. This is how most people attack the rat race, but it's the wrong way to win the chase. Instead, *grab the cat's attention*. Offer the feline something he wants. A can of tuna? Catnip? With a polarity reversal, suddenly, the cat scampers right into your lap. Chase not required.

When you carry rat race loci into the game of entrepreneurship, you also bring with it its positive charge. Instead of being need-focused, solution-oriented, and value-driven, you're "me" focused. *Oh, it's always been my dream to own a sports bar, so I'm going to open one!* Sorry but no one gives a fuck. You're chasing cats.

The harder you try to earn cash with me-centered fantasies, the more it will elude you. You can't win this game if you can't oust your selfishness. *If you're too busy focusing on what you want, you'll never see what other people want.* The marketplace is a hungry, self-centered brat. And one hungry brat doesn't need another brat to join him. He needs an adult to fill his needs. Be the adult. Feed the brats, and they'll stop crying while paying you for the privilege. The world simply demands its mediocre comfort[P3]—provide it, and you will enjoy magnificent comfort.

☑ KEY CONCEPTS

- Nobody gives a shit.
- Ptolemy money-chasing is a poison pen marked by selfish internal motives, not external market gaps.
- People are positively charged to seek money, like a rat would cheese.
- Money is also positively charged, and two positive charges repel, not attract.
- Value, which is negatively charged, reverses your polarity and attracts money.
- If you're too focused on what you want, you won't see what others want.

THE PASSION PRINCIPLE

Winning Guarantees Passion, But Passion Doesn't Guarantee Winning

I walked into the bank, my guitar case strapped to my back. The security guard eyed me suspiciously, and deservedly so. I walked up to the teller and handed her three coupons from my mortgage payment. "I'm behind on my mortgage, I need to catch up," I said.

The teller nervously glanced at the guitar case on my back and then grabbed the voucher. She entered my account number into the computer and, after a few clicks, said, "With late fees and interest you owe $5,253. How would you like to pay?"

Without answering, I whipped around my guitar case and flipped its latches. The teller's eyes widened as she lurched back in her chair. The security guard jumped off his stool and darted toward me. Expecting to see a rifle in the guitar case, the mortified teller threw her hands up. But instead of a gun, it held a banjo. I whipped it out and started strumming Dixie.

The teller lowered her hands slowly and said, "What on earth are you doing?"

I said, "You asked how I wanted to pay my mortgage. This is my answer: I'm paying with passion."

Okay, this story is not true.

I don't play the banjo, but worthy to note: Beware of self-help nobodies preaching passion as something to be followed. The Passion Principle states that *passion is a horrible business model.* Please, for the love of God, stop following your passion. Because more than likely, that passion won't pay well, or it won't pay at all. Trust me, there's no passion when you can't pay the electric bill or hit the Olive Garden once a month. Worse, you can ruin your passion by lynching it to money, responsibility, and mortgages.

When I was young, I loved driving as it represented freedom. As such, many of my early jobs were behind the wheel, from delivery driver to a limousine chauffeur. In a few short years, my love for driving turned into a hate. And decades later, it remains a hate.

The first problem with passion is that the markets represented by passion are jam-packed. A glut of supply means three things, all seeding a bad opportunity: 1) Increased competition due to everyone chasing the same passion,

2) Depressed margins due to commoditization and limited differentiation opportunities, and 3) Diminished leverage and poor probabilities.

First, the idea of getting paid to do passionate things is juvenile and idealistic hooey. How many teenagers would love a fat paycheck for playing hoops, riding horses, or strumming guitar? Step in line behind the other gazillion. When there are thousands, perhaps millions who are and want to be doing precisely what you do, you have no leverage[P17] and rat race economics are in play. Remember, a crying infant doesn't need another whiny infant in his crib. He needs an adult.

Second, commoditization risk. When value is ubiquitous and undifferentiated, the lowest price often wins. Think gas stations, air travel, T-shirts, data storage, even personal training. For a small business, a race to the bottom is a race to poverty.

Third, wherever there is high competition, low margins, and commoditization, your probabilities for success plummet, as well as leverage. Remember, your annual report and the math you put into it plays a huge role in your success. If there are 70 million other "digital marketing" companies you're bidding against, expect leverage to be thin and probabilities to be poor.

Adults are value-focused, and they don't follow passion. They follow needs, wants, desires, and solutions with a production focus. They understand that passion doesn't come from *doing*, but from *accomplishing*. It comes from being better today than yesterday. It comes from self-development, overcoming fears, learning something new, and solving the world's problems one person at a time.

Jobe Stevens followed his passion for 12 years and now works at Walmart as an assistant manager. Never heard of Jobe? Well, that's because he failed, and his passion couldn't pay the bills. His passion, abstract finger painting, then became a hate because he no longer did it from the depths of his soul but from the urgency of his bills. Don't expect Jobe Stevens' failure to be featured on the front page of *Yahoo Finance* where he shares his secrets to success, one being, "follow your passion."

Don't let the publicized few (the survivors of the ill-famed survivor bias) convince you otherwise. But what about Steve Jobs, MJ?! He said, *love what you do*! Of course, he did. But he was also a billionaire who created massive value worldwide. Would you be passionate if half the planet found value in your creative contribution? And what if in a parallel universe, Steve Jobs is actually Jobe Stevens? Someone who followed his passion but couldn't sell a damn thing and pay his bills? Is there passion for losing? For failing? For someone telling you that your product sucks? Think Steve Jobs would be on a stage at Stanford University inadvertently immortalizing the horrific business advice, "follow your passion?"

Conventional wisdom is wrong again, and like many things, has it backward.

Enduring determination *doesn't come from passion but from purpose.* Your effort itself must induce passion. When you win or exceed your expectations—winning a game, acing a final exam, or completing a grueling exercise routine—the passion flows. Specifically, winning and self-growth generate passion; losing and marinating in comfort does not. Stop following passion; have passion follow your effort.

☑ **KEY CONCEPTS**

- Passion is a horrible business model.

- Passionate pursuits likely have increased competition due to surplus supply, depressed margins due to commoditization, limited differentiation, diminished leverage, and poorer probabilities.

- Lasting, enduring determination comes from purpose, not passion.

- There are no passionate losers who get the stage and the spotlight.

- Passion should follow your effort and its favorable results from self-improvement and character building.

THE VALUE MARRIAGE STRATEGY

Partner Relative- and Perceived-Value to Make Money Magnetic

26

Do you know who Wolfgang Druckenheimer is? You should... he cured cancer[1].

His formula had the potential to save millions of lives.

But it didn't. Why?

Wolfgang failed at understanding the confusing world of value. And that failure prevented him from being the most revered person ever to live. Wolfgang and his cure died together.

The fact is, you can wildly succeed at "creating value" but fail at delivering it.

I've read hundreds of business books over the years, including college textbooks required for two business degrees. In all of them, I never read about perceived- or relative-value. And it's criminal. To succeed in any business, you must combine these two variants of value. Or take your value to the grave.

When I wrote my first book more than ten years ago, the generic phrase "creating value" was a novel concept. Fast forward, and today it's now regurgitated by every twenty-year-old YouTube guru with an iPhone. Still, entrepreneurs repeatedly get "creating value" wrong. They think value is monolithic when in fact, it's nebulously varied. How you deal with these variants will mark the difference between attracting money ethically, chasing or stealing it, or worse, suffering the same fate as Wolfgang.

The five variants of value are:

1. True-value
2. Utility-value
3. Surplus-value
4. Relative-value
5. Perceived-value

---

1 - Wolfgang and his cancer cure are fiction. But it's quite possible a person like him exists, or once did.

The first and simplest is *true-value.*

True-value is the total value that your product delivers when used as intended. The true-value of a cancer cure is just that; cancer is eradicated. With software, it's when all of its functionality is used as designed to affect a solution. If it's a bottle of water, it's thirst solved plus the bottle. With any book, it's every chapter and all its concepts in full comprehension and deployment. If someone quits reading after ten chapters, true-value—the book's solution—is never realized. In this case, true-value degrades to utility-value.

Utility-value is the customer experience after using your product. As such, it is the most uncertain variant and often subjective. If you used Wolfgang's cancer formula and were cured, the utility-value is a clean bill of health. If you used his formula but didn't get cured because you failed to follow the precise instructions, utility-value fails true-value. In another example, when I owned my marketing company, some customers underutilized my software. Some didn't use certain features, others ignored customer leads. Utility-value didn't measure up to true-value. Suppose someone stops reading this book at page fifty. In that case, utility-value degrades from true-value, a value gap caused by their skepticisms, biases, and expectations—not because I delivered a book with three hundred blank pages. Conversely, for someone who fully comprehends this book and escapes the rat race, utility-value equals true-value.

Next, *relative-value* is the matriarch of value variants. It is the true-value of your product as compared to other products in the marketplace. Does your true-value have relative worth when compared to what already exists? Or is it exactly the same? Or worse? If Wolfgang's cancer cure was one among one million others, relative-value doesn't exist. Likewise, suppose you start a business selling T-shirts. In that case, you fail relative-value because the world already has four million entrepreneurs offering the same thing. Does the world need another business selling T-shirts on Facebook? It doesn't. Instead, you create another value variant: *surplus-value*—the dog in the value family.

Surplus-value is found in commoditized fields where typically the best price wins. Surplus-value always struggles to find a bid because there are hundreds, perhaps thousands of alternatives.

The final value class is *perceived-value*, the patriarch. Perceived-value is your product as advertised and viewed in the marketplace. Optimally, it is your best demonstration of true- and relative-value. This is your website, product labeling, marketing, advertising, and messaging. When a customer buys from your company, they always act from perceived-value, hoping that what you advertise and boast is what you deliver.

Perceived-value is the only value variant that can polarize your charge from positive to negative[S24]. Yes, a profit-locus with a specialized-unit is a start[S18]. But the circuit only closes when relative- and perceived-value are partnered.

This is where Wolfgang failed. His cancer cure, while truly valuable, failed at delivering perceived-value. The truth is, no one believed his marketing campaigns. No one believed his messaging or his delivery. He couldn't secure a hearing with the Food and Drug Administration, much less get approval for the cure. True- and relative-value remained hidden in the marketplace.

Perceived-value is king. And as such, it is often abused by shady marketers and wannabe entrepreneurs. When companies struggle with true- and relative-value, perceived-value becomes their hustle. Overpromising and underdelivering, they often use deceptive marketing, questionable claims, and shady behavior. A perceived-value scam always rings "too good to be true."

The 2017 Fyre Festival is a great example of a perceived-value scam that didn't deliver relative- or true-value. Using a combination of influencer and social media marketing featuring beer, beaches, and bikinis, a *bro-marketer* ("bro" = boiler room operation—a huckster who operates a perceived-value scheme) successfully sold millions of dollars in tickets to a defunct festival on a tiny Bahamian island. When festival goers arrived, they were met with a barren wasteland with no stage, no beach, and no Instagram-worthy selfies. Instead, they got processed cheese sandwiches served in a FEMA crisis tent. Festival experience? Ha, more like a prison experience. Perceived-value gets the fish to bite. It's negatively charged to money, and the scammers know it. Great marketing, garbage product.

Still, perceived-value can transform surplus-value into relative-value. If you're the best marketer in the fitness industry, putting a unique spin on a stale concept, suddenly your blog (surplus-value) might be perceived differently, hence creating relative-value.

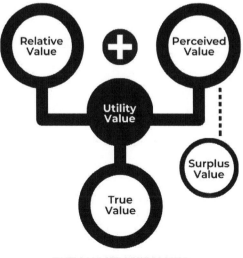

THE VALUE VARIANTS

As entrepreneurs, our perfect scenario is the marriage of relative-value, which is perfectly perceived (communicated) and then used. If the marketing is inadequate or the product is not used properly, utility-value sinks below true- and relative-value. And then customers start asking for refunds or calling you a scammer. If this happens, it could signal issues in marketing, customer support, and/or onboarding.

Likewise, if you offer incredible relative- and true-value but have no sales, you've got a problem with marketing and messaging—the marketplace doesn't discern value. And finally, if you're rolling in cash but have 200 employees dedicated to chargebacks, complaints, and lawsuits, you have serious issues. True-value being one of them. Don't be a scammy "bro-marketing" shyster: Provide relative- and true-value, and then communicate it effectively. You will make a killing. Better, you won't have to worry about the FBI knocking on your door.

☑ KEY CONCEPTS

- Value has five variants, true-value, utility-value, surplus-value, relative-value, perceived-value.

- Perceived-value is the king value variant as it exposes your relative-value to the right audience.

- Marry relative- and perceived-value to become a money magnet.

- Perceived-value that doesn't deliver relative- or true-value exposes operational deficiencies, or is a scam.

- The greatest entrepreneurial tragedy is to create relative-value but fail at perceived-value.

THE JOB PROXY PRINCIPLE

Job Proxies Are A Loaded Gun: Kill or Be Killed

27

In 2018, Amazon stopped paying commissions on rogue authors gaming the Kindle Unlimited program. Within a few days, entire author libraries were deleted along with their author accounts. Revenue streams to the tune of millions disappeared overnight. Not surprising, not just for the sketchy tactics, but because these money-chasers chose to build a job proxy.

The Job Proxy Principle is when *your company's entire revenue stream is sourced from one patriarchal company and subject to instant ruin.* If you make thousands a month as a network marketer and your paycheck comes from one company, you have a job proxy. If Amazon represents 100 percent of your business revenue, you have a job proxy. If you have the #1 ranking on Google for widgets, and all your revenue comes from that favorable search result, you have a job proxy. If you're an inventor, and Walmart is your only customer, again, you have a job proxy.

Job proxies are no different than having a job. Instead of a human boss, you have a corporate boss. That boss determines everything: your rate of pay, the rules and regulations, and more importantly, your relationship. When the boss decides to change commissions, procedures, or terms, you're stuck with the outcome. Usually with little to no recourse. Worse, they can fire you altogether. That's not why you wanted to own your own business, is it?

Imagine the horror of growing a business (and supporting a family) built solely on the Amazon platform. Then one day, the dreaded email arrives: *Your Amazon account has been terminated.* Within seconds, years of work is lost, and your income goes from hero to zero. To add insult to injury, your ability to reinstate your account and resurrect your business lies in the hands of some low-level employee in Mumbai.

Search the internet for entrepreneurial horror stories, and you'll find job proxies as a common cause. *Google changed their algorithm and my search traffic dropped to zero! Facebook changed the rules on API calls! Our MLM founder was indicted for fraud! T-Shirt Emporium terminated my account for supporting Alex Jones! My YouTube channel was cancelled!*

As an Unscripted entrepreneur, you should be innovating and creating value. Hitchhiking aboard another company that is actually doing the innovation and value-adding is a risk. Turn-key opportunities are turn-key for a reason: *You're either the product, or you're the cog.* Yup, more rat race illusions.

When one person in one company can instantly kill your business with one decision, you're playing Russian Roulette. Sure, job proxies can be lucrative. A big YouTube channel is a great asset and it can thrive for years unblemished. Just be aware, you're dancing to the bank with a loaded gun. One day, it might kill you.

☑ **KEY CONCEPTS**

- A job-proxy is a business that is subject to a patriarchal corporation that can essentially disrupt or end your business with one decision.

- Job-proxies expose you to catastrophic risk but can run profitably for years.

WILD PITCH

*K*ading!
   Sam's phone chimed. Then again.
   Kading-ding!

She opened her eyes, and once she saw the early afternoon sun peeking through the blinds, her anger seethed. It was after another graveyard shift and another lousy sleep. She confronted the phone for the time—1:49 PM—eleven minutes before the alarm would strike. Her rage sharpened to a target once she unlocked the phone and saw the text message was from Chase Bank. She cursed, "Damn bank robbed me of eleven minutes."

After tossing the phone on the bed, not caring to read whatever the bank thought so urgent as to wake her, she closed her eyes and groaned heavily. The fatigue she'd felt six hours ago still nagged. Nightmares of Gertrude, her last patient, haunted her sleep. She'd walked into the emergency room with a migraine; three hours later, she was in the morgue. In between was an aneurysm, and Sam had witnessed it all. The aftermath was worse. When the family was told the news in the waiting room, anguished children and great-grandchildren cried inconsolably. Gertrude's husband of forty-seven years collapsed on the hospital floor. He was rushed into the ER, his fate unknown to Sam.

She tried to quarantine the thoughts. Her mind quickly argued for eleven more minutes of sleep, but she disagreed. A short slumber wouldn't do her any good; she needed eleven hours. Then she snickered, remembering the struggle Jeff had once had with eleven minutes. She now knew what he was talking about. It was eight years ago, but it felt like twenty. And her life had been nothing but a suck-fest for the whole time.

   Kading-ding!
   "Ugh!" She slammed her hand on the bedsheet near her phone.
   "Fucking leave me alone!"

She sat up and glanced at the phone, still taunting her. The text from Chase Bank read: A $499 charge was just made on your VISA credit card from Tee-Shirt Emporium. Sam fumed. The bank didn't instigate the text, it was her husband and he knew not to disturb her after a graveyard shift. Sam dropped back to the bed and dialed him. He should have been at the end of his lunch hour.

"Hey," Jeff answered, "why are you awake?"

Sam huffed, unable to be tactful. "You don't know, asshole? Is this what you woke me up for? A five-hundred-dollar charge from some T-shirt place?"

There was silence on the line as Jeff realized that his credit card purchase woke up his wife. "Yes!" he tried to report excitedly, hoping to dispel her anger. He forgot that his wife wasn't to be disturbed in the afternoon after a night shift. He continued, "It's an internet company that prints and drop-ships T-shirts; all we have to do is sell them! We'll make as much as $7 per T-shirt. If we can sell a million, that's $7 million dollars!"

Sam jerked the phone away from her ear and tilted her head to the ceiling. The dizzying fan offered more intrigue than Jeff's venture. Phone back to her face, voice stern, she said, "Our business? I'm sorry Jeff, did I miss something? When did we decide to sell T-shirts? Or did the other zillion T-shirt companies suddenly go out of business?"

Jeff wasn't sure why Sam sounded upset. He thought she'd appreciate his initiative and even his use of math. His wife, never fond of math, had suddenly started talking about it, gross annual production, wealth equations, probabilities, and other terms she usually wouldn't utter. "I signed up while at work. My boss left early, and I figured I'd work on our business."

"Our business?" She let loose a disgusted sigh that could swell the seas. Jeff dared to say nothing. His wife urged, "Can you get a refund for the five hundred-dollar lottery ticket you just bought? Because clearly you haven't read a damn thing I asked you to read."

"Read?" Jeff asked quizzically.

"Exactly. You don't even fucking remember." After a silence, Sam clarified, "Hello? The DeMarco books I asked you to read?"

He offered several lame excuses—something about not being a "bookworm," Donald Trump's surprise Presidential victory, and even a lousy bean burrito. Sam challenged him on all of it, and they quarreled for what seemed like an eternity. But it wasn't. When Sam's alarm started to scream for her scheduled awakening, interrupting their argument, she knew exactly how long they'd argued. Eleven minutes.

THE THIRSTY RAT PRINCIPLE

You Can Lead a Rat to Water, But You Can't Make Him Drink

28

W hat was the last book you read and when?"
You'd be amazed at what people ask when you drive a car that costs more than a house. It's as if an expensive car turns you into an instant life coach or career counselor. Whenever this happened to me (and often), I would gift the asker a book… my book. After a few years of this, I stopped. Not because I was cheap or short on books, but because I realized it was a waste of paper. When I asked curious bystanders about the last book they read, most couldn't recall or admitted they didn't read.

The fact is, if I had a buck for every time I heard, "Hey, I gave your book to my friend, but he didn't read it," I'd be a billionaire, not a multimillion-aire. The Thirsty Rat Principle is as it's been said, you *can lead a rat to water, but you can't get him to drink.* Your friend/colleague/family member just isn't thirsty enough. Of course, this has nothing to do with my book or any book, for that matter. No amount of begging, cajoling, or bargaining can make someone read something they don't want to read. Even if you have a solution to their problem. A book that challenges their identity, or worse, challenges their excuses will not be read. In short, mediocre comfort[P3] and/ or the promise of freedom half a century later[P6] has made them docile and compliant—the perfect rat.

There's only three ways to get someone to read a book they haven't selected themselves: *timing, curiosity,* and *bribery.*

The first is timing, namely, after an FTE[P3]. When your friend loses his job because the government decided to close all "non-essential" businesses due to a pandemic, that's the best time to drop a book. Teachers appear when the time is right because the best time is a post-FTE.

The second is to snare your target in a curiosity play. Unfortunately, you can't do this until you've succeeded in whatever you're peddling.

"Damn Greg, how'd you afford this gorgeous estate? It's freaking amazing!"
"Yes, I paid cash."
"Oh my God, how? Is business that good?"
"Yes, you remember that book I recommended four years ago?"

Think your friend would read it now? Of course he would.

"Damn Greg, you look great!"
"Yeah, I lost one-hundred pounds."
"Wow, I've been trying to lose weight for twenty years."
"Remember that book I recommended a few months ago?"

And the final method that helps spur someone to read a book they've been gifted? *Bribery*. Sex, food, money, whatever it takes. If your husband doesn't read a gifted book, keep your clothes on. Likewise, if the wife is giving you problems, stop massaging her toes or rubbing her back. Of course, I'm partly joking, which means I'm partly not.

Stop giving books away to comfortable, satisfied people. Give them to uncomfortable, dissatisfied people who have endured the pain of an FTE.

☑ KEY CONCEPTS

- You can gift or recommend a book to a rat, but you can't make him read it.

- *Timing, curiosity, and bribery* are three ways to get someone to read a book they don't want to read.

THE PROCESS PRINCIPLE

Sweat the Process, and You'll Win the Stage

When Michael Phelps won his twenty-third Olympic gold medal, the world record, he was celebrated on a winner's podium and then around the world on television, in magazines, and on websites. Millions in endorsement deals followed. Fame, fortune, respect, and more.

The secret to Phelps's success and that of other high achievers is no secret. It hides in plain sight, and if you train your Unscripted[59] senses, you can always find it buried in a paragraph or a footnote. The Process Principle denotes that *every success story started with a big goal followed by a disciplined process of many trials, repetitions, unseen failures, and adjustments.* The disciplined grind is the ordinary drudgery that never makes headlines.

In Phelps's story, we see the events (gold medals, fame, endorsements), but we aren't told about the process, the hardship, that created them. The daily training in place of sleep or video games. The post-swim ice baths. The regimented diet. The missed parties and social hours. The dolphin kicks in the pool with a 10-pound weight strapped to his chest.

As I write, Michael Phelps's Wikipedia page is over 19,000 words. Yet only 27 of them reveal the process details like the ice baths. Twenty-seven freaking words! That's one-tenth of a percent (.001) for the entire Phelps story, the lonely 27 words that made the other 18,973 words possible. In other words, his private story[52] is not the public story being showcased.

Like anything in life, there are no shortcuts to a masterpiece. Especially when it comes to starting a business. If it takes you five minutes to start your business, you don't have a business. You have a commoditization grind, or worse, you're just a cog in someone else's business.

Newsflash: Here's another divergence between the 1% and the 99%—one-percenters are *process-oriented*, while ninety-nine percenters are *event-driven*. Namely, the 99% focus on the results, the desired goal and potential shortcuts for its achievement, while the 1% focus on the process, the activities that derive the outcome.

Everything significant starts insignificantly: with one solitary action, one small win, and one move forward. My forum started with just one user, one post, and in one thread. Now it has nearly a million messages. *War and Peace* by Tolstoy? A single word breathed life into a 587,287-word novel. No matter your goal, success is hundreds of good but small choices that compound into a big picture. The little things done *daily*? They cause the big things *yearly*. Many pixels create the photo.

The same can be said about starting a business that grows into a strong offense[P13], one anchored by a specialized-unit with polymorphic[P22] components. If creating and then communicating net perceived-value was one event—just one choice—everyone would do it. This is why drop-shipping, affiliate market-ing, and "click and you're in business" businesses are weak pursuits. Creating specialized-units of relative-value[S26] is a process that cannot be bought. *Your effort will need to be consistently ordinary to produce something extraordinary.*

The event/process relationship is like the difference between a wedding and a marriage. The wedding is an evening, the exciting event. The marriage is lifelong, the compromising process. Events are like a supermodel who gets the spotlight and the headlines while Miss Process is underneath the stage grinding as a seamstress, a personal trainer, a dietician, a publicist, and a makeup artist all rolled into one. The event shines on stage, the process sweats.

For example, losing weight is simple: *Eat right and exercise.* And then make it a habit. Process equals disciplined persistence, which becomes a life-style. That's the ordinary process. Straightforward and succinct. There are no shortcuts. The struggle is the struggle, but it works. It's shamefully comical: *the secret to success is no secret, it just never finds a headline.*

☑ KEY CONCEPTS

- The event is a short, visible, and celebratory accomplishment; the process is the enduring sweat and grind that made it happen it.
- Culture is event-oriented, often derelict or neglecting process.
- The secret to success is no secret, it just never finds a headline.

THE PROBLEMOLOGY PRINCIPLE

30

Problemology: The New
Career for the New 1%

After I sold my company for the second time, I reflected on the journey and concluded I was no entrepreneur—I was a *problemologist*. From idea to launch, the entire process from management to growth was just one problem after another. How do I implement this feature? What are the best advertising mediums and the best converting message? Should I hire someone, and if so, how do I deal with the nightmarish human resource complexities such as payroll, taxes, and employment law? How this, how that?

The day the problems ended was the day I sold it. (Well, maybe not—the tax bill was a fortune.) Later, I started a publishing company and a business forum. And then the problems started again.

The Problemology Principle asserts that *the moment you decide to be an entrepreneur is the moment you decide to be a lifetime problem solver*. A problemologist studies problems and learns how to solve them. Entrepreneurs solve big problems and offer their solutions for profit. In solving those problems, you'll encounter dozens, perhaps hundreds of smaller problems. Each micro-problem solved brings you closer to solving the macro-problem.

The first moon landing is a classic example of micro/macro problem solving. The macro-problem "How do we land a dude on the moon?" embodied hundreds of micro-problems. From inadequate rocketry to freezing hydraulics to even the seemingly banal, like what if moon dust is flammable? Thousands of tiny problems had to be fixed so one big problem could be solved.

Entrepreneurship is the same way. A business is dozens, perhaps hundreds of solved problems which aggregate into solving a larger problem. The problems can be both external (can someone manufacture this?) to internal (how do I learn how to manufacture this?). Altogether, this solution represents many things: your relative-value[S26], your specialized-unit[S18] and your medium for polymorphic pay[P21]. Unscripted Entrepreneurs are problem solvers. It's another piece of the hidden process[P29] that is never advertised or mentioned in those guru seminars that sell for an arm and leg. The choice is clear: you get a self-taught Ph.D. in problem-solving or update the resume and pray to the Wall Street gods.

- Entrepreneurs are problemologists.
- An entrepreneur solves one macro-problem, their relative-value, by solving dozens, perhaps hundreds of smaller micro-problems.

THE SHORTCUT PRINCIPLE

Stop Working Hard to Find a Shortcut, and Start Working Hard on the Process

I graduated from college jobless. Despite having no job (and no business), I went on a shopping spree compliments of my Chase credit card. No, my shopping spree wasn't spent on beer, clothes, or stereo equipment. I blew it on shortcuts; get rich quick infomercials, seminars, and anything that promised an easy path to wealth. Waving a "quick start video" in my face was like offering an alcoholic an all-you-can-drink pass to a distillery. In any event, my lenders and the seminar hustlers got rich. I got poor.

Take a guess at the biggest multi-trillion-dollar industry on the planet? Is it oil? Healthcare? Finance? Nope, the largest industry in the world is the business of *shortcuts*. From pharmaceutical companies who pill our ailments to banks who finance our saving impatience to gurus who promise wealth without the risk to the diets that pledge results without sacrifice (you can eat your favorites!) to self-development books that tickle our fantasies, trillions are spent yearly looking for a shortcut, a hack, or a super-duper secret that will shorten (or eliminate) the process. The Shortcut Principle reveals that *anytime you search for a shortcut, you'll likely go on a detour and get unsatisfactory results.* Shortcuts are events looking for the results of a process. And it's the easiest sell in the world.

Wouldn't it be great if you could just pop a pill once a day and get the body you want? What if you could just write a few plot lines and get a full-length novel? The fact is we all want the same thing, we just don't want to endure the same processes that get there. Everyone wants to rock the six-pack abs, but few want to sweat the cardio. We want health but we also want pizza for dinner and ice cream for dessert. We want a successful business, but we also want a comfortable weekly paycheck. It's a pickle that doesn't compute.

Sadly, because society and its media accomplices are event-driven and process-blind, achievement and rewards get the spotlight, but not the processes that birth them. Remember Michael Phelps's Wikipedia page only had 27 words dedicated to the process[P29]. As such, our minds become attracted to sexy events, often causing a misdirected focus on shortcuts or "hacks" that claim to soften (or skip) the process. As a result, we operate from an event-modality, seeking quick fixes and solutions to things that have no quick fixes or solutions. Here are just a few examples of how an event-modality tries to shortcut the process:

- *Cheating* on the exam is an event; *studying* for it is the process.
- *Planning* a wedding is an event; *enduring* a marriage is a process.
- *Financing* a car is an event; *saving* for the car is the process.
- *Swallowing* a pill to lower your cholesterol is the event; *changing* your diet to lower your cholesterol is the process.
- Posting your New Year's *resolution* on Instagram is an event; posting your New Year's Resolution *results* is the process.

When we perpetually search for a shortcut that doesn't exist, we go on a detour. Real achievement and their processes are stymied. Expectations are not met, and frustrations boil. My infomercial spending spree funded my poison-pen[52] and put me on the road to suicide, delaying my personal growth. *I was working hard to find a shortcut but not working hard to build a process.*

☑ KEY CONCEPTS

- The largest industry on the planet is the business of shortcuts, anything that is marketed as an aversion to the process, for example, weight loss drugs.
- Seeking shortcuts, or event-driven actions, are detours—an ineffective event looking for the result of a process.

THE STORM
FRIDAY, DECEMBER 2ND, 2016 - 7:37 PM
(12 days later)

"We need to talk," Jeff said out of breath, rain dripping from his hat. Bella greeted him, tail wagging hard, but Jeff ignored her. He tossed his hat on the kitchen table and plunked into the chair, his wet jacket dripping on the floor. Sam sliced cucumbers at the cutting board in the kitchen. She had a few hours before her late shift and was already in her black scrubs. With Jeff's arrival from work, their twilight-cross began.

She tightened her grip on the knife and stared at her husband, eyes wide, worried and waiting. The last time Jeff said, "We need to talk," he'd confessed to getting laid off—a week after the fact. Sam felt a tear well in her eye and her gut wrench as if expecting the worst. For the last week, Jeff had returned home late from work, including today. And then he'd recently bought new underwear, not the ugly white ones, but the kind that should raise the suspicions of any sexless marriage.

A rolling thunderclap boomed, and Jeff waited for it to finish. Stormy weather was forecasted, and their home on Ridgeway Court was in the path. In the bedroom, Madison started fluting a cheery melody. Perfect timing as Jeff hoped it would ease the mood.

Avoiding eye contact, Jeff let it rip. "I lost $1,400."

Sam firmed up from her slouch, eyes flaring. "What? How? Like, stolen? Where?!"

Jeff eyeballed the knife still locked in her hand, which was now trembling. "Uh, no," Jeff apologized sheepishly, "it wasn't stolen, but I feel like it was. I lost $1,400 advertising our T-shirts on Facebook." He quickly corrected, "*My* T-shirt business I signed up for. That's why I've been late all week. I've been running this side business after work. I thought I'd surprise you with some good news, but after fifteen hundred dollars and six thousand clicks, it was clear I made a big mistake."

Sam's eyes flared, and she slammed the knife on the counter. She threw her husband a disgusted glare as if he'd just picked his nose. No words were needed.

135

Jeff continued groveling, "You know I'm a political junkie, so when I kept hearing authors say I should 'follow my passion,' I was really stoked about selling T-shirts." He opened his satchel and held up an ugly chartreuse T-shirt with "Trump Sucks" on it. "I thought I'd sell T-shirts with political memes, but as soon as people started commenting on how stupid and unfunny my designs were, I got scared." He paused then, carefully selected his words knowing his wife liked President Trump as much as a teenager loved a zit on prom night, "You know, a lot more people like Trump than we thought."

Sam tilted her head. "You think? Only 66 million people voted for him." Neither Sam nor Jeff voted for Trump, but neither voted for the criminal cartel known as The Clintons. Between Bill's friendly travels to Epstein Island and Hillary's penchant for destroying innocent iPhones used solely for discussing the day's yoga plans, they both passed on the election circus.

"Anyhow," Jeff maintained, "the ad money just started to disappear. They asked what my budget was, and I didn't know, so I just typed $100. Within minutes, it was mostly gone. So, I tried again, next time $200. Same thing. Nothing but hate mail, no sales. It was miserable. I kept staying late after work trying to dig myself out of it. Different designs, different ad targeting options, nothing worked."

"So you didn't sell anything."

"Actually, I sold two T-shirts." He laughed satirically. "But thanks to my expensive finance degree, the one I'm still paying for, I figured out that spending $1,400 to make $9 isn't a path to success. And then I knew I had to break the bad news to you."

Lightning flashed outside, and silence consumed the townhouse.

Seconds later, the thunder boomed.

The storm was here. And Sam spoke not another word.

THE VALUE SKEW STRATEGY

Outperform The Competition: One Improvement Makes A Business, Several Make an Empire

The other day I bought a bag of tortilla chips. I know, not interesting. But what is interesting is *why* I bought them.

Whenever you have a buying decision, your mind undergoes a *value competition* to determine where the better value lies. The *value threshold*—the point at which you pick one product over another—is determined by one attribute or many. Sometimes that attribute is "the best price" or "the best ingredient," but most consumers judge based on many factors, both primary and secondary. Whatever weighs strongly with your value hierarchy wins the race.

That bag of tortilla chips? Here is a list of attributes that filled my decision process:

- One bag of chips was $.89 cheaper. (Primary attribute)
- One used biodegradable packing, the other did not. (Secondary attribute)
- One used canola oil, the other avocado. (Primary)
- One used corn as their main ingredient, the other cassava (Primary)
- One had a funny story on their packaging. (Secondary)
- One had a more visually appealing package design. (Secondary)
- One had a NON-GMO label on their package, the other did not. (Primary)

The bag I chose was more expensive and didn't have the best packaging. But I bought it because it specified NON-GMO ingredients. Specifically, one attribute took me from shopper to buyer.

Add another item to the *I wish I knew this when I was 20* list. To succeed at entrepreneurship, you don't need to reinvent the wheel. You don't need to launch the next Facebook, invent the electric car, or find the cure for cancer. The secret is simple: Relative- true-value[S26] is engineered through a *value-skew*.

A value-skew is any attribute in your specialized-unit[S18] perceived better than the competition. More positively skewed attributes—the more runners in the race who can cross the finish line first—equals more sales.

Each of the attributes listed above, including every ingredient, is a potential value attribute. Because health is strongly held in my value hierarchy, I buy the chips boasting the NON-GMO label. On the other hand, environmentally conscious people might pick the chips with the social mission and biodegradable packaging. The point is this variable value competition is highly subjective and different for everyone. You never know what attributes are running the race and which one(s) will cross the finish line. Your goal is to *have as many runners in the race* as possible. Yes, *you can't be everything to everyone, but you have to be something for someone.*

THE VALUE-SKEW

To add runners, skew value, and win sales, identify all the potential value attributes for your offer and industry. No matter how insignificant. Start with primary attributes: your product deconstructed down to its core components. Is there any component or ingredient that you can improve vis-a-vis competitors? Better features, better user interface (UI), better price, better color options, better craftsmanship, better raw materials? Every component is a skewing opportunity.

Next, attack secondary attributes, which consist of the product's marketing and delivery to the customer. Marketing is the most important secondary attribute because it is the tiebreaker between identical (or similar) value-skews. He who wins eyeballs wins sales. Other secondary attributes include your website's order process, photos, shipping/return policy, your company's story, customer service, sales copy, Yelp reviews, and social media posts. Anything comparable to the competition that isn't a primary attribute is secondary![1] Where can you be better in the eyes of the consumer? Remember, every customer has a different value hierarchy. So it's best to brainstorm them all.

While having the "best price" is a powerful runner in the race for sales, it isn't as preferential as you think. "Best price" is an analytical metric, whereas most decisions are based on emotional appeals. A strongly skewed emotional attribute can justify significant price premiums. Think Apple, Nordstrom, Audi, Ferrari, or Louis Vuitton.

In a commoditized industry, value-skew is the only way to differentiate and create relative-value. For example, the low-market beer is commoditized. It's fascinating to watch these mega-beer manufacturers attempt to create skew. Coors has a specialized can with a mountain that turns blue when the beer is sufficiently cooled. During the 2019 Super Bowl, Budweiser advertised its beer free of corn syrup in an attempt to create skew.

Bottom line: Skew two or three value attributes favorably, and you have a business that will win a few races. Skew four or more value attributes and you might head to the Olympics with an empire. Even better? Value-skew isn't taught in business school. Advantage: YOU!

☑ KEY CONCEPTS

- To win sales, you must take your customers over a value-threshold.

- Many value attributes are evaluated in a consumer's buying decision, all weighted differently.

- Primary value attributes relate to the product itself; secondary attributes relate to its presentation, distribution, and delivery.

- When you "skew" a value attribute, you do something better than your competitor which is discernible, and sometimes obvious to your potential client.

- You never know what skewed attribute will draw your customer over the value threshold.

- The more attributes you skew, the more runners you have in the race for sales across the value threshold.

---

1 - In my first book, *The Millionaire Fastlane*, I mentioned that you should "ignore the competition." While this is true in some respect, it isn't true when exploiting value-skew.

THE COMMODITY PRINCIPLE

Compete for Profit, Not Poverty

In the late 2000s, I had a forum friend who sold rubberized cell phone cases. While he made a decent profit in the first months of operation (he was early to the market), he eventually quit selling them. I asked what happened. He reported that within a year, his margins got squeezed so tight by competitors (many from China and Indonesia) that, suddenly, he would have been better off working at Taco Bell. For him, the only value-skew[S32] he had was price—cheaper, cheaper, cheaper... out of business.

The Commodity Principle affirms that if you *sell a commoditized product, you ultimately won't compete for profit but for poverty.* A commoditized product or service appears homogeneous among providers. Think data storage, a ream of paper, insurance, taxi service, gas. Value-skew is thin, and as such, the only skew is the price. *To win sales, I have to be the cheapest!*

I recently switched insurance because my provider raised my rates for no reason. I left a six-year relationship for a new company with the same benefits for a mere $500 bucks. Air travel is another example: Most people aren't loyal to any airline; they're loyal to the best price. An economy fare on Southwest Airlines and United Airlines both gets you to Chicago in identical discomfort—so lowest price wins. Loyalty is easily bribed for a few bucks.

Hitching your wagon to a commoditized product is a race to poverty because the price is the only value-skew. This one-dimensional attack puts entrepreneurs into recursive bidding wars, marginalizing their offers with one goal in mind: to be the cheapest. Competing in a commoditized climate is a race to the bottom as margins deteriorate with each player deciding, "How small of a profit am I willing to accept to survive?"

I'd guess that half the crap on Alibaba (and then sold on Amazon) is commodified goods, patiently waiting for another wannabe entrepreneur to join the flooded ranks of commodity pushers hoping to win the "Cheapest Price of the Day" award. Winners win poverty with ever-weakening margins and an eventual self-extinguishing profit. Worse, when a commodity pusher finally decides to exit the market rationalizing, "Enough is enough!" they are quickly replaced by another entrepreneur yet to discover the same insanity.

As Peter Drucker said, "In a commodity market, you can only be as good as your dumbest competitor." As an entrepreneur, ask yourself: Why do you exist in the marketplace? What value are you skewing? And who will yearn for your company should you close up shop? Or would your sudden market absence be met with eerie silence? When dreampreneurs ask dumb questions like, "What's a good product to sell on Amazon?" they're begging to become commodity pushers. Think you'll be the only one selling it? Nope, you'll be one amongst a mob. Leave the circular firing-squad to the unfortunate folks who aren't reading this book.

☑ KEY CONCEPTS

- A product that has limited skew potential is ripe to be commoditized to the "best price."

- Selling a commoditized product is a race to determine who is willing to accept the least amount of profit, or worse, losses.

THE EASY GOES HARD PRINCIPLE

Accept Easy Now, Suffer Hard Later
While Hoping for Luck Along the Way

When I was going through my failing years, I spent some time selling at flea markets. Chicago had several import wholesalers. During the week, I'd visit them and buy an assortment of random items. "Random items" = junk. Then I'd try to sell these goods at the weekend swap meet. Few people stopped at my booth. Fewer bought. The return on my time was less than the minimum wage. However, an older merchant several booths away from me was killing it. His booth was always crowded. Moreover, I saw cold hard cash being exchanged often. Back then, a $100 bill was quite a lot.

The difference between myself and this other entrepreneur? *I was chasing money.* The goods I was selling were a commodity, cheap framed art, knick-knacks, stuff easily found elsewhere. Worse, other merchants at the market were selling the same commoditized junk[P33]. That other guy who was making money hand over fist at his booth? He was offering relative-value. Specifically, he was selling hand-crafted furniture and other wood-carved statues. What he sold was unique and couldn't be bought on the cheap at some warehouse in Chicago.

Looking back, I wish I'd known the Easy Goes Hard Principle—*the easier it is to start your venture, the harder it will be to succeed at it.* First, if anyone can compete with your company because they invested a few hours or a few dollars, like visiting a Chicago wholesaler, then you're not starting a business. Any Joe Blow could have done what I was doing. I was joining a crowd filled with positively charged rat racers[P24]. If there is no difficulty in starting your business, you probably aren't solving any problems or skewing value[S32]. And if you aren't doing either, the market won't perceive relative-value[S26]. You're just another fish in a barrel hoping to get lucky.

As problemologists[P30], our problem-solving careers as an entrepreneurs should be a process[S29]. A business that provides genuine relative-value can take weeks, months, or years to build—not hours. "Sign and drive" opportunities are cattle calls, often selling commoditized surplus-value[S26]. And surplus-value is bought on the bid, not the ask. If half the ladies on your block are selling the same essential oils, you've put yourself in a saturated position with zero skew. Sales is like a single-number bet at the roulette wheel.

Second, the easier it is NOW to enter a business, the harder it will be LATER to make money. An "easy" startup process has a high price. More competition. Depressed margins. Saturated marketing noise and elevated advertising costs. More stress and less pay. For example, I started my business forum over ten years ago. It was easy to start: Pay for the software and hosting, and voila, it's up and running. Yet getting it off the ground, growing it, and keeping it active was (and still is) extremely difficult. Like blogs, most forums are graveyards. Worse, my competition is Facebook groups which are even easier to start. One of the toughest things I've ever done was to start a forum; I talked to myself for months[1].

Anytime a process[P29] is potentially "easy" or "fun" (including the syrupy platitudes like "follow your passion" and "do what you love"), expect to be exceptional if you want to free yourself from it. Not the top half, not the top ten percent, not the top five percent... We're talking about the top one percent, or *exceptionalism*. Why? Once again, it comes down to the math, namely, probability. Go on to YouTube and look for piano players. You'll find hundreds of highly skilled pianists, but only a few of them will hit the big-time and get to play to a sold-out theater.

Think about it from the viewpoint of a professional athlete. All sports are offshoots of the "do what you love" and "follow your passion" platitudes. Anyone, rich or poor, can shoot a basketball. The field for that profession is flooded worldwide, perhaps hundreds of millions. Anyone who plays the game would love to make millions playing professionally. I know I would. Yet you know how many basketball players are in the NBA, the pinnacle of the profession? A trifling 494.

If one percent of the world loves hooping (a conservative estimate), that means only .0007 percent of the world gets to play on the big stage. The entirety of the world's exceptional basketball players on any given day could fit into a small hotel ballroom. To succeed in a crowded market like basketball, you need to be exceptional.

Exceptionalism is being the best at what you do among millions. And it's the only way to shine in a crowded market with zero entry barriers. To wit, be so good they can't ignore you. My flea market neighbor did great work and couldn't be ignored. My cheap imported picture frames? I was ignored.

Easy is hard because easy is crowded. And likely a job-proxy[P27].

Easy might be easy to enter, but exceptionalism is a probability nightmare. Anyone can sell dropshipped T-shirts. Anyone with ten grand can start trading foreign currencies. Anyone with an internet connection can

---

1 - I do not recommend forums as a primary business, but they could work as part of a business system.

install WordPress or toss some gadget on Amazon. Simple, easy, with zero entry barriers like picking up a basketball. Yet, thousands of entrepreneurs make less than minimum wage doing it. Only a few make the fortunes. Why? Exceptionalism is the process. Claiming your new CEO title with a fresh WordPress install is the event.

Carry the right expectations. Starting a business (solving problems, improving products, and skewing value) is like losing thirty pounds—think weeks or months, not hours or days.

☑ KEY CONCEPTS

- The easier it is to start your business, the more likely it is that it doesn't solve problems or skew value, and the harder it will be to profit.

- "Turn-key" or "sign and drive" businesses are likely commoditization grinds offering surplus-value.

- Exceptionalism is being great at what you do in a crowded market which improves probability.

- Starting your business should be a process that takes weeks or months, not minutes or hours.

THE MOAT STRATEGY

Create with Difficulty, Replicate with Ease

35

A friend of mine owns Hemingway Accoutrements and Barberry Coast Shave Company, which sells proprietary shave creams and colognes. I'm an avid user, not because he's my friend, but because he's created—pardon the barstool expression—"panty-dropping" scents and aromas. His formulas are difficult to reproduce and took him months of experimentation. Still, if demand warrants 1,000,000 orders, he could make it happen. His specialized-unit is *hard to copy competitively, easy to replicate internally.*

Tell me how easily and how many times you can replicate your specialized-unit or how many people can use it, and I'll tell you how rich (and free) you'll become. I can print this book a million times without much effort. My forum, same thing: it can handle an exponential increase in eyeballs before bandwidth and resources become an issue. Likewise, my business service enjoyed the same structure: more users equaled more money. The mathematics are unlimitedly scalable while zero leverage and zero probability[P17] are eliminated.

Optimally, your specialized-unit[S18] should be hard to create but easy to replicate or use. This is also a function of problemology[P30] and the inverse correlation between startup ease and execution difficulty[P34]. After enduring your creative build process, its replication (or use) should possess nearly unlimited mathematics within the scope of your niche. If you're targeting guitarists, every guitarist might find value in your offer. That's millions. Please note: ease of replication is not about scaling customers or sales (which is always difficult) but about scaling potential demand.

This simple relationship ensures not only leverage[P17], but protected leverage. You want your product/service hard to copy competitively but easy to replicate internally. New competitors must endure a process, not an event.

☑ KEY CONCEPTS

- Your specialized-unit should be hard to create and get to market, but easy to replicate.
- "Hard to build; Easy to replicate" offers protected leverage.

THE NEGATIVE SKEW STRATEGY

Minimize Negative Skew to Maximize Buying Probabilities

Imagine being single and dating a successful, tall, dark, and handsome man. After a date or two, you think you're in love. But by the third date, you notice a pattern: He's rude and belittling to anyone he doesn't know. Waitstaff, doormen, valet parkers, even the grocery cashier. For you, this negative attribute is an immediate deal-breaker. All his positive features—hotness, richness, style—are invalidated.

One negative value attribute can destroy ten positive ones. While positive attributes frame the house, negative attributes are the lit match that burns it down.

The same cognitive gymnastics happen with buying decisions.

When a customer uncovers negative attributes associated with your company, positive skew is weakened, and sales are lost. Instead of entering runners in the sales race, they join the opposing team. Yes, you send sales to your competition. Worse, most negative attributes are asymmetrically forceful, creating "deal-breakers" and immediately giving victory to your opponent. Just like our hot guy who is rude, one negative trait can kill dozens of positive ones. Like positive skew, you never know which negative skew will trigger your potential customer and send their money elsewhere.

In business, some examples of negative skew could be inadequate product labeling, a questionable ingredient, lackluster customer service, a polarizing political position, such as endorsing or condemning the right to own guns, or even a spelling error on a website. All are negative attributes that endanger the positive ones, giving a client more reason to say, "Meh, I'll pass."

For instance, let's say Bill recommends my first book, *The Millionaire Fastlane*, to his co-workers, Sandy and Tyler. Tyler nods and says he will check it out. But in his mind, he's already dismissed it. For Tyler, the title *The Millionaire Fastlane* sounds cheesy and like a "get rich quick" scam. He ignores Bill's recommendation based on his judgment of the title, which, whether I like it or not, is a negative value attribute to Tyler.

On the other hand, Sandy finds the title intriguing. She investigates and finds the book's website and reads it over. In her reading, she spots two spelling errors. For Sandy, this oversight is a monster negative attribute, and she weighs it heavily, opting not to buy. Despite Bill's recommendation, I lose Sandy and Tyler as new customers due to negative skew.

The politicizing of your company is also a dangerous form of skew. In 2017, Nike hired Colin Kaepernick to endorse a new line. The hiring created immediate skew, both positive and negative. For Nike's disapproving market, it created immediate negative value-skew, causing many to burn their Nike gear. Some said they'd never shop Nike again.

Conversely, many customers rallied to Nike's defense and loved the decision, hopefully compelling more sales. Either the marketing execs at Nike are forecasting this action as a net positive, or they're derelict in their knowledge of skew. Either way, politicizing is a dangerous skew unless your company is politically based or if you're hoping the politicizing could generate billions in publicity.

Here are some deal-breaking negative skews that sent my money to competitors:

- The product had an undesirable ingredient: Red 40, Aspartame, Maltodextrin, GMO corn, milk powder, animal products.

- The product was packaged in thick jailhouse plastic.

- The company was actively engaged in political activism against my beliefs.

- The product had too many negative reviews.

Again, all skew[S32], both positive and negative, is subjective and unique to each customer. Every attribute skewed positively while eliminating the negative ones improves your unseen probability for crossing customers over the value-threshold[S32] while expanding your total buying audience. And boom, the advantage goes to you.

☑ KEY CONCEPTS

- A negative-attribute is something about your product or offer that strikes someone unfavorably.

- One negative-attribute can invalidate dozens of positive ones.

- Eliminating negative-attributes can help you get more customers over the value-threshold leading to more sales.

THE IMPERFECTION PRINCIPLE

Imperfection Is the Seed of Skew (And a New Business)

There's a huge shortage of T-shirts in the world, said no one ever. And if no one ever said it, that means starting a T-shirt business is a money-chasing grind reflective of a positive charge.

Every day I see opportunities worthy of a money-making fortune simply because I know opportunities are a function of imperfection. And imperfection is ubiquitous. Unless you found Utopia, it is everywhere. From the shitty health insurance you begrudgingly bought, to the bland Mexican food you ate at lunch, to the lack of reliable babysitters, imperfection is perfectly pervasive. If you defected from Team Consumer to Team Producer[P23], this truth isn't upsetting but insanely exciting. The Imperfection Principle asserts that *anything that can be improved is a business opportunity.*

If you visit my forum, you will notice a shared struggle amongst aspiring entrepreneurs—namely, finding business ideas.

What business should I pursue?
I don't know where to start!
Everything is already being done!

Such statements reflect entrepreneurial ignorance. Entrepreneurship isn't about inventing the light bulb or engineering the next iPhone. Anywhere imperfection lives, relative-value[S26] opportunities await. That's complaints, inconvenience, problems, wishes, hates—all of it is relative-value's language of opportunity. Learn this language, and suddenly, opportunities are everywhere.

Even similar products that solve identical problems with comparable prices can be skewed[S32] through their secondary attribute pool. Offer a better website, a better story, a better label design, a better user interface, a better customer service experience, a better return policy, a better this, a better that, and you'll win sales. Again, you never know what value-skew will compel your potential customer to buy—the more positive skew you create, the better your probabilities become.

- Imperfection is the scent of a skewing opportunity.

- Identical products can be skewed by way of their secondary attribute pool, things like better design, UI, story, return policy, customer service, or an owner who isn't a billionaire tyrant.

The Imperfection Principle

THE STAKEHOLDER PRINCIPLE

Adulterous Corporations Have Unhappy Customers Wanting Divorce

38

Many years ago, I was a customer for a mid-sized hosting firm that managed my web presence. Their prices were reasonable, their customer service exemplary. Foremost, a human answered calls to their support line. Second, technical issues were solved fast. I felt this company was a trusted partner. Then one day, something seemingly innocuous happened. I received an email from this company, headlined something to the likes of "Exciting news!" Inside wasn't exciting news, but bad news: A larger corporation had acquired them. Indeed, the bonanza was exciting for the corporate owners, but not for their customers.

Within months, everything changed. Inbound calls suddenly were met with a voicemail or long wait times. Support requests went from answered in minutes, to hours, to days. My inbox blew up with "Upgrade Opportunities!" and every support call seemed like a sales pitch. The relationship ended when my website went down for more than two days while "we're working on it" was the de facto response. Clearly, I was no longer important.

I'm betting you have a similar story because this scenario is common. The Stakeholder Principle *is when a business abandons its customer as a top priority in the stakeholder chain.* Practically every company traded on the stock exchange is an *adulterous corporation.* Adulterous corporations are one of many market imperfections[P37] ripe for opportunity as they cheat their customers in favor of other mistresses: shareholders, employees, C-Suite Executives, investors, and Wall Street analysts. For privately held companies, priority stakeholders could be partners, VC investors, private equity firms, banks, or even spouses.

If your favorite company goes public—be warned. Expect higher prices and lower value—new, external stakeholders must be appeased. As soon as a corporation looks to allay anyone other than the customer, they become adulterous. This is the exact moment when the platitudinal mission statement on the CEO's wall goes from stretched truth to absolute bullshit. The value-driven, customer-centric policies that precipitated exponential growth is suddenly abandoned after the banker's claws bite into management. Ever do business with a private company, and after they go public or attract millions in investment, suddenly everything changes for the worse? Sonos, the wireless stereo company, is one such example. After they went public, they quickly abandoned their customer-centered philosophy. In an email to customers, they informed them that their old Sonos equipment would soon need to be upgraded or suffer the consequences. Bluntly speaking, if you spent $6,000 as I did a few years ago, you're fucked. And you'll need to spend thousands all over again—planned obsolescence. Worse, when they informed their customers of this snake-oil scam, they insulted them with a cute email that was received as well as a sledgehammer to the ankles. Good thing Kathy Bates lives in Los Angeles.

This phenomenon is called *the squeeze*. The customer is squeezed off the value throne, replaced by everyone else who demands a return on their investment... namely Wall Street. From there, you can expect a systematic extraction of money through increased prices and fees, cost-cutting, reduced product quality/quantity (the old cereal trick: same price, smaller box), and diminished relative-value. This is what happened with Sonos and my web hosting company. Customer service went to hell (cost-cutting), and the sales prodding (we need more sales!) jetted to the sky.

Of course, not everyone will agree. Some "thought-leaders" say that employees should be top-stakeholder. Ridiculous. What happens when you have 100 happy employees and 0 satisfied customers? The happy employees become unhappy—because they'll soon be out of a job. If a business was an organism, your customers are its heart and your employees, the brain. An organism can survive while brain dead but can't without a heart.

The billion-dollar natural-food business is a direct consequence of such squeezes. Fed up with processed laboratory food, consumers now consider natural sources or local artisans. The industry is rife with small companies disrupting the space because BIG-agriculture is too busy zombifying ingredients while appeasing shareholders. Of course, stakeholder demotions aren't just found in food and agriculture, they are anywhere entrenched corporations have lost sight of their purpose. Rejoice. If your competition has lost its allegiance to the customer, its stakeholder demotion and an instant value-skew[S32] for you. You cannot serve two masters at once.

☑ KEY CONCEPTS

- When a business abandons its customer as a top priority in favor of investors or shareholders, it is stakeholder demotion.

- Stakeholder demotion is likely with most public companies and is a skew opportunity.
- "The squeeze" is when a corporation tries to squeeze its customers for more profit through increased prices, reduced services and value, and other measures designed to appease higher stakeholders.

THE SUCKS TO BUCKS STRATEGY

Transform "Sucks" to "SUCS" for Bucks

39

Thank you for calling Evil Banking Corporation. Your call is important to us, so much so that we outsourced your call to a minimum wage employee halfway around the world. Press [1] to speak to a guy who hates his job, press [2] to speak to a person who can barely speak English, or press [3] to speak to a rep who will read you a scripted corporate policy. No matter what you press, your current wait time is 42 minutes.

Sound familiar? It should. When a major corporation disowns you as their primary stakeholder[P38], "sucks" is the result. So, when I called Chase Bank recently, something happened that shocked me silly. On the first ring, my call was promptly answered by a cogent human being. It left me speechless. Such an event is what I call, SUCS—or *sudden unexpected customer service.*

When your company provides SUCS, you'll turn SUCKS into BUCKS. As you know, customer service in the modern world is frustratingly terrible. But don't fret. This repeating world history is your advantage because you're in the know… crappy customer service is a huge skewing opportunity[S32]. In fact, I'd argue that customer service is the most critical skew in the secondary attribute pool.

No one wants to be treated as an ambiguous number on a computer screen, and yet this is normal for most corporations. When two identical products face off, the company that provides better customer service will win. Excellent customer service is a value-skew and makes relative-value[S26] more likely. Moreover, it entitles you to higher prices.

Exceptional customer service is one of the skews that helps me in business. My first company was known in our industry for super-fast customer service—phones answered and emails addressed within minutes. Some customers called us just to test our speed. Even today, I use this technique. My forum stays active because I am there every single day, contributing and interacting with my readers.

The formula for transforming SUCKS into SUCS is simple:

Identify your client's customer service expectation profile and then violate it. First, your customer's customer service *expectation profile* is simply the industry standard for service. My Chase Bank interaction was such a breath of fresh air; it violated my expectations. Before I dialed the bank, I immediately identified expectations for the call. Here was my "expectation profile":

- I expected to hear a recorded message or an automated attendant.
- I expected to press a never-ending menu of buttons: press [1] for this, press [2] for that, press [3] for something else.
- I expected to be shuttled from one person to the next.
- I expected to speak with someone in broken English.

These are my low expectations. Corporate monoliths get away with crappy service because it is the expectation profile. But when Chase violated that profile, including a resolution within minutes, the end result was wow-worthy. I entered the call with pure dread and left with sheer satisfaction.

It needs to be said: Beware of syrupy mission statements. They mean nothing. The loaded weapon for customer service is your employees. Great customer service only happens on the frontlines with first and final contact with the customer. A great example of this is the West Coast hamburger chain In-And-Out Burger. Every employee greets you cheerfully and asks you how you're doing, food is delivered with a smile, and you're left with "Have a great day." The mission statement on the wall is executed downstream to the frontline.

Violate customer expectations, and you'll amass repeat loyal buyers, and ultimately, disciples for your business. That's like getting free advertising. Morph SUCKS into SUCS and you'll get BUCKS. One skew, but one step closer to grabbing the sale.

☑ KEY CONCEPTS

- Sudden unexpected customer service (SUCS) is when your company provides service that exceeds industry expectations.
- SUCS is a value-skew.
- To execute SUCS, identify your customers' expectation profile as evaluated by industry standards, and then violate it.
- SUCS must be more than a mission statement on the wall, it must be executed downstream by employees.

THE RED PILL

Madison lay on the floor with Bella near the Christmas tree, the Labrador staring at her human sister as she nibbled on a tortilla chip. Jeff smiled, thankful for the appearance of normalcy. But his wife was a different story. More like a story of Queen Cersei. Or maybe Marie Antoinette.

After Jeff lost $1,400 on a failed T-shirt venture, his wife's personality took an icy turn. Conversations were curt, eye contact was cutting, and doors slammed harder. If given a chance, he wasn't sure his wife wouldn't throw him off a building or bend him over a guillotine.

Jeff found the motivation to read between his wife's recent transformation and the VISA bill yet to arrive. He treated the books his wife suggested like a make-or-break final exam before graduation. At this point, he didn't expect the DeMarco books to help other than removing the curse that besieged his wife.

With the fire at his ass, he only needed a few days to complete the books. Left behind was a confusing tapestry of feelings that didn't blend. It was anger with hope. Regret with relief. Fear with excitement. Sureness with unpredictability. While he didn't have a word to express the emotion, he knew it was a net positive. He felt lighter. And the thought of Cersei Antoinette no longer tortured him.

That night on their twilight-cross, Jeff pulled out a chair with his dinner and positioned it next to his wife. As usual, the chair screeched as it dragged the linoleum floor. Sam jumped, startled from her Instagram feed. She glared at him expectantly. Below her furrowed brow, upshifted pupils were black holes, her lips tight. *Shame!* echoed in Jeff's mind.

He tapped her on the knee and smiled. "I finished the books you wanted me to read."

Sam's expression didn't flinch.

"The books you recommended," Jeff clarified. He stirred his soup, still steaming hot. She nodded dismissively but said nothing. Before her hair could turn into live serpents, he conceded. "I'm an idiot. Had I read this stuff weeks ago when you asked, you wouldn't be eyeballing daggers at me."

She returned her gaze back to her phone, swiping away. After several photos of scenic gardens rolled by, she deadpanned, "Is that so?" She continued swiping, her focus on the phone too intense for Jeff's comfort. After the Royal Botanic garden flew by, she finally looked at Jeff, head cocked. Not expecting much, she asked, "And what have you concluded?"

Unsure if it was a trick question, Jeff exhaled deeply. He muttered, "I think if I had read them when you asked, it would have saved us $1,400 dollars." He took a guarded slurp of his soup and waited until Samantha's face surrendered its hardness. When she curled her lip in a near smile, he continued, "Everything makes sense, including why you yelled at me for the T-shirt thing."

"Would have saved you," Sam corrected, now with a smile, placing her phone on the table. "I'm not paying that off. Your Visa, your mistake." She turned her body in the chair and faced him with a self-satisfied grin.

Jeff nodded, relieved at her demeanor shift. *Ding-dong the witch is dead!* Now he knew what Dorothy felt like standing over a freshly melted puddle. She remarked, "I didn't yell at you to steal your enthusiasm. I had to slow you down and redirect it." She laughed then pinched his thigh with her fingers. After Jeff yelled a juicy *Ouch!* she winked, leaving the table to fetch her toast.

While Sam chewed into her evening breakfast, Jeff slurped at his dinner. He wanted to talk about the DeMarco books, but his wife's soup had a hypnotizing effect. Asian Tofu Udon. Might sound nasty, but it was one of Jeff's favorites. Tofu? Leeks? Udon? The idea that he could like something as much as sirloin or pizza seemed ridiculous. But here he was, buried in his bowl as if he were a starved prisoner. Despite his wife's hectic schedule, Sam always found time to cook the most delicious meals. Jeff felt fortunate for his epicurean luck considering Sam refused to cook anything that had animal products in it. His delight with Sam's vegan lifestyle was on par with his pleasure for pulling weeds or unclogging a toilet. He loved meat as much as any red-blooded American with a poor lipid panel. The thing is, his wife's meals might have been dairy- and meat-free, but they never lacked for flavor. He wasn't sure how she transformed kale, quinoa, and tofu into something he'd gulp down with glee.

He drank his last drop and clanked the spoon in the bowl, pushing it away. Reclining back in his chair, he rubbed his chin with an unsettling grimace.

Sam glanced at the empty bowl, and then at him, one eyebrow spiked. "Didn't like the soup?"

He shook his head as if to awake from a trance. "Oh no," he snuffed, "it was delicious as ever." Wrestling with his thoughts, he piano pecked his fingers on the table. Still eyeballing his finger dance, he said, "I was just thinking how sad it is that we don't question everything. How we just assume the system has our best interests." His restless fingers continued. "From news and Netflix to education and sports." He shook his head in disgust. "I mean seriously, why the fuck do I care about the Chicago Cubs?" He finally looked up at his wife. "Samantha, I've spent months, probably years of my life caring about something that means absolutely nothing in the grand scheme of things." He straightened up. "I mean seriously, what do I get when the Cubs win? Money? Vacation? A free month of Hulu? Nope, I get nothing but a dopamine high that helps me numb the miserable life I've accepted." He tapped the spoon against the bowl. "I would have sent Maddy to DePaul no matter the cost." Madison glanced up from her art project inquisitively. Jeff glanced at her fondly and continued. "Didn't even think about it, just accepted it blindly." He loosened his tie and pulled it half off. "And marijuana, don't you love how they vilified that shit for years? I've always dismissed your cousin and thought she was just a pothead, but she always said weed cured her depression." He paused. "She was serious?"

Sam looked at him pointedly and spoke singsongy. "You mean my cousin Jaime who 'everyone hates' and sells 'that skin care crap'? Yes, she was serious."

Jeff cracked his neck, deaf to the comment. He gazed down at his hands on the table, his fingers fiddling again. He carried on, pace faster and louder. "And the thing about Saturday and Sunday being the paycheck for Monday through Friday, I never thought about time that way. How we spend our days. If I lost half my money in an investment every week, I'd say, 'Fuck no,' and yet, here we are, pissing our time away and not thinking twice about it. And for what? Some stock market bullshit that pays off at the end of our life?" He flicked the spoon in his bowl, giving it another clank. Sam watched him intently but she let him continue his monologue. "Misery is the business model of the human race, and we live it like marionettes on puppet strings. *They* got us enslaved or addicted to something: fast food, TV, video games, social media, and just like good little rats, we go along with it, medicating our misery with whatever salvation they produce. And if we get fat or depressed medicating our emptiness?" He laughed, "Well, the drug companies have a product to sell you too."

He shook his head in disbelief and carried on. "But what really pisses me off is that the escape to this insanity boils down to math." He turned to his wife. "Freaking math. I'm a finance guy, and I didn't even bother to analyze the mathematics of life. Of existence. It's a literal equation, like a formula for cracking the code to wealth. And time is nowhere in it."

He turned and grabbed his wife's wrist, a little firmer than she'd like. He yammered on, bug-eyed, "It's like we're dropped into this world and told that we're free. But we aren't free and it's just a lie." His caramel eyes swelled wider. "Because the world itself is just a brilliant scheme to keep you working, spending, and saving. And when you're smart enough to figure that out, the scam advertises a way to escape, but it doesn't help you escape. It keeps you in it. Grows tighter the harder you try." He leaned in closer to Sam, wild-eyed. "Like one of those Chinese finger traps!"

Sam coiled back in her chair as Jeff bellowed on.

He went on for another minute and finally concluded with a snicker, "Thank you for coming to my Ted Talk."

Sam blew out a roomful of air as if emerging from a pool and then snickered. "Jeff, are you high?"

"No!" he asserted. "But the whole fucking system is so clever, so deviously orchestrated, so meticulously devised that it had to be invented by someone who was." He flopped his head back, now facing the ceiling, mouth open. Exasperation rushed out. "We've been living our entire lives based on a Script."

Sam laughed, now confirming her suspicions. He was pontificating over the DeMarco books. "Well, you called it. You're an idiot. I told you to read the books, but you thought selling *Trump Sucks* T-shirts on Facebook was a better business." She shook her head, still chuckling, and covered his fiddling fingers with her palm. He glanced down at his wife's smothering hand and back at her. "Great to have you on the team, Jeff. Now let's talk business. Something that makes sense."

Jeff corrected, "You mean CENTS?"

THE "FORCE DOESN'T AWAKEN" PRINCIPLE

Talent and Skill is Earned, Not Born or Awakened

40

I'm not good at writing.

I once mentored a young man who said this. To which I replied, "Of course you aren't good at writing, you never studied it. You never tried it, and you never practiced it. Did you expect to be 'good' at something without ever trying?"

My reply was not about exposing laziness; it was about exposing his external locus of control. He expected talent to be genetic. *I told him to expect talent to be earned.*

In psychology, the locus of control is the degree to which you think you can influence life's outcomes and circumstances. It also dictates your view on skills and talent. With an internal locus, you control the pen writing your story[S2]. New skills, talents, and successes are possible in the right system, combined with hard work and good decision-making. Moreover, health, happiness, and hope are also associated with an internal locus.

Conversely, if you have an external locus, you see life's situations as static. Decision-making has little effect. You're merely a victim of the system. The pen writing your story is ordained from luck, fate, genetics, or environmental changes. Caught drunk driving? If you blame your arrest on the police or your dad who bought you the car, you have an external locus. Or maybe the blame rests on that hot guy who bought you five Cosmopolitans at the club?

The Force Doesn't Awaken Principle mandates that *talent and skill doesn't emerge or awaken, it is earned.* The birth of Wolfgang Mozart did not include a piano. Tom Brady did not pop out of Mom with a football. Jerry Seinfeld didn't say hello to the world with a joke. In all cases of future excellence, it was earned in the past through a disciplined process[P29] in pursuit of exceptionalism[P34].

Regrettably, most people believe talent is genetic or born. They wait for talent to strike them like lightning. Ever hear someone say, "That's not my thing?" Of course, it's not your thing; you gave up after two tries! If you falsely believe talent is coded into your DNA and you're waiting for its emergence, you'll wait forever. Worse, you'll never work hard to get talented. Likewise, if the competition was born with talent, but you weren't, why bother? The only uneven playing field exists in your head.

Hollywood promotes this pervasive myth. And it is a Trojan horse that kills dreams. For example, in *Star Wars: The Force Awakens*, within hours, Rey wields a lightsaber as if she trained for years. But she didn't. She grabbed the weapon and wham—instant skill. If only life was so forgivingly accurate. Sadly, most people go through life with this expectation—they hope some mysterious talent "awakens" within them so they can skirt the disciplined process. Thanks, Hollywood!

With this hereditary view of talent, you are likely to live your life talentless. Why? Because you aren't interested in *earning* talent; you're interested in *discovering* it.

The fact is, you can succeed and learn how to build a specialized-unit[S18] as much as you can learn how to play piano, knit blankets, or plant flowers. Unlike hitting a baseball or singing to a sold-out crowd at Madison Square Garden, there are no physical limitations. You don't need the right voice, the right height, the right strength, or the right genetics. None of that matters. Simply put, nothing is stopping you from learning the skills you need to become a talented entrepreneur.

Nothing.

I wasn't born an entrepreneur. Or a writer. Likewise, doctors, lawyers, athletes, engineers, teachers, cooks, dishwashers—no one is born anything. While you might have a physical attribute better suited to a particular profession, we're all born in complete ignorance. Even the infant who giftedly grows up to be seven feet tall still has to learn how to put the ball in the hoop.

Fact: Entrepreneurship is entirely learnable, as are the skills within its practice. In fact, every skill and talent which helped me Unscript and become financially free I learned after college graduation. My education didn't end at graduation; it started. My true skill-building and learning began when I leaped into the world of entrepreneurship. While most of my early business ventures failed, my skills and knowledge accumulated: programming, Excel, Photoshop, wordsmithing.

Regardless of your business venture or its industry, there are two core skills you need to target:

DECISION-MAKING AND PROBLEM-SOLVING

The willingness to become a scientist, the ability to analyze data and situations, and set a course of action.

COMMUNICATION

The ability to sell, from customers, to investors, to employees, to partners. The selling never ends.

Once again, the secret to success is there is no secret. No shortcut. No unique DNA or special genetic code will get you what you want. You might not have been born the sharpest pencil in the box, but you're surrounded by pencil sharpeners. The world is already yours, but only if you seize it. Accept what is and just do the damned work. Pursue talent and skill as if your life depended on it. Because it does.

☑ KEY CONCEPTS

- Individuals with an external locus believe life's circumstances cannot be influenced, that circumstances arise from luck, fate, genes, or environmental randomness.

- Individuals with an internal locus believe life's circumstances can be influenced through good choices and hard work in an efficient system.

- Talent is earned, not birthed—no one is born with any particular expertise.

- You can learn entrepreneurship.

- Education doesn't end at graduation; it starts.

- You will probably need to learn new skills to escape the rat race.

THE HOT STOVE PRINCIPLE

The Big-Ed Swindle: Handle College Like You Would a Hot Stove

41

Here's some food for thought: The most lavishly expensive real estate on the planet all enjoy massive profits, but only one of them is treated like a business. I'll let you guess which one that is. They are:

1. Government buildings
2. University campuses
3. Churches of all religions
4. Casinos

When you walk into a casino, you know there's a target on your back. They are designed to extract every dollar out of your wallet. There are no clocks on the wall, sandalwood scented air is pumped into the gambling hall, and the floor is laid out like a maze. Heck, some still offer free drinks. The point is you know you've walked into the belly of the beast, and the odds of you leaving with more than you came with are unlikely.

Deviously, the same can be said about "Big-Ed," or formal university education.

Like casinos, they too want your money, and they want you to spend it just as frivolously and void of critical thought, just as if you were rolling the halls of the MGM Grand.

If the rat race was a prison (and in many ways it is), Big-Ed would be the bus that got you there. Worse, your parents are the ones who perp-walked you to the bus-stop. Big-Ed is the educational industrial complex that has essentially become an indoctrination camp. This human assembly line is charged with the mass manufacturing of obedient rats[P5], rats who are educated just enough to earn their cheese in the five-for-two slave system[P8] but not educated enough to question it.

The sad reality is that there's only one degree that might be worth the high cost of college, and that's a degree in relative-value[S26]. Everything else is worthless and merely a debt scheme that irreversibly commits you to rat race superstructure, no better than a big bet at one of those casinos.

Never heard of a relative-value degree? Don't worry; every university offers them. The problem is most universities are diabolically pushing their alternatives: lottery and greater-fool degrees. More on that later...

A *relative-value degree* is any degree that is based on a skill or expertise that has marketplace demand. Relative-value in business and relative-value in job hunts are no different. Your education must give you skills that are relatively valuable in the marketplace. Otherwise, your degree is worthless. Think science, technology, engineering, medicine, robotics, AI, or anything that requires specialized knowledge for practice AND has a vibrant job market. Obviously, if you want to be a great medical researcher or a civil engineer, you're going to need college.

Regrettably, the Big-Ed racket has marginalized relative-value degrees to favor *lottery degrees*, which feature more leisurely and passionate pursuits. A lottery degree entails a specialized-skill in a narrow field with an existential job market, and the competition for such jobs is likened to winning a lottery. Degrees in oceanography, anthropology, archeology, astronomy, and fashion design might sound like passionate pursuits. Still, just like all followed passions[P25], you're joining a stampede trying to thread a needle. Sure, your sports management degree might help you manage a professional baseball team, but how many baseball teams are hiring? In short, you're rolling the dice and betting that you can be "the chosen one." If there are two million psychology graduates but only one hundred jobs nationally, you're rolling dice with a five-figure price tag. Utility-value exists; relative-value does not. Lottery degrees are low probability career bets with high probabilities for debt and underemployment; bartending, cashier, or any other low-skilled job.

While relative-value degrees are the good and lottery degrees are the bad, *greater-fool* degrees are the ugly.

A greater-fool degree is any study, usually liberal arts, that denies both economic reality and relative-value. Not only is the degree lacking useful value, but some would also argue that the field has no job market at all! Philosophy, art history, gender studies, critical theory on 19th-century feminism, renaissance poetry—all topics that might win you a debate in a sociological discussion over a beer, but they won't win you a thriving career. Students pursuing greater-fool degrees deny the reality outside of the cloistered bubble of academia. In contrast, their university denies them the truth while taking their money with a smile and a promise worthy of Wonderland. Worse than a lottery degree, the only market for greater-fool degrees is in fact, the greater fool market: teaching the field to other greater-fool degree seekers. Graduates exit college debt-ridden and jobless, looking for a job that simply does not exist.

As an employer, I don't care about degrees. I care about the value your skills can offer my company. Show me a great web application you coded and boom, you're hired. I don't care if you skipped college. Likewise, Elon Musk said in a 2014 interview, "There's no need to have a college degree... at all[1]" Tech giant Google has even started to shift away from the ideology of college degrees. When they analyzed job performance, they found no relationship between GPA or college affiliation within the first years on the job. In fact, Google's senior vice president echoed a similar sentiment, saying, "GPAs are worthless as a criteria for hiring, and test scores are worthless.[2]"

Sadly, we're indebting an entire generation of kids with college degrees they can't use for jobs they can't get. Meanwhile, student-loan debt tops a trillion, and thousands of well-educated youngsters are lined up at the job fair competing for jobs they could have snagged out of high school. A college degree doesn't produce jobs out of thin air. It entitles you to nothing. Nada!

If you're going to college, don't roll dice and don't deny reality of the Hot Stove Principle: *handle college as if it were a hot stove—it can cook you something good, but it can also burn you.* Don't get burned, get educated on something that makes you relatively valuable.

☑ KEY CONCEPTS

- Casinos and universities enjoy massive profits and own the most expensive real estate on the planet.

- The only degree worth pursuing is a degree in relative-value; skills that have a strong demand in the marketplace, usually STEM related.

- A lottery-degree is a skill or profession that has excess supply with little to no demand which makes a job in the field like a casino bet.

- A greater-fool degree is a skill or professional that has little market value other than teaching it to others, creating a "greater fool" market.

- Approach university like a hot stove, or worse, a walk into the casino.

1 - https://www.youtube.com/watch?v=vqcdF1oWaD0

2 - https://www.cnet.com/news/google-gpas-are-worthless/

THE DUAL CHANGE STRATEGY

Embrace the Two Sides of Change and Put Luck in Your Life

I once had the misfortune of tripping over someone's opinion. I didn't seek it; I was tagged on social media. Somebody opined that my success was entirely attributed to luck. Namely, "MJ was lucky to be 'there' when the Internet was just starting to get popular." *There* meaning I was alive during the late nineties. As if I was the only person alive in the late nineties, not one of six billion. Ladies and gentlemen, these idiots vote. And they breed more idiots who vote.

Anyhow, the real luck in my story and its continued evolution has nothing to do with luck. It has to do with how I interact with the thing that causes luck: *change*. Notice anything in common with the following statements?

- *Sarah got lucky when the Internet was just starting to get popular...*
- *Joe got lucky when blogging was just starting to get popular...*
- *Craig got lucky when self-publishing was just starting to get popular...*
- *Lucy got lucky when Amazon was just starting to get popular...*
- *Harry got lucky when vlogging on YouTube was just starting to get popular...*
- *Michele got lucky when bitcoin was just starting to get popular...*

The common theme in all these appearances of luck is the entrepreneur took advantage of an emerging change in the environment. They weren't the late adopters in the business cycle; they were the innovators and early adopters. Moreover, change, and the luck that comes from it, is constant. If you can ride the change, you also can get lucky.

Think of it like a coin flip. If a coin rests tails-up on a table, there's a 100 percent certainty it will remain tails. Only change—picking up the coin and flipping it—can change the probability and the potential outcome. If you have the wherewithal to recognize when (and where) the coins are flipping, you give yourself a chance to call the outcome correctly. And get lucky. That said, taking advantage of change is a complementary system, like yin and yang. Both are needed to conjure luck.

The first is yin, or *extrinsic changes* in the environmental such as shifts in tastes, culture, and technology, all of which cause the knowledge gap's[S19] natural expansion. All the statements above sprung from extrinsic changes where emerging sweet-spots turned into fortunes. And yes, such changes existed in the '90s, as they did in the '00s, the '10s, and now the '20s. Behind every millionaire and billionaire, you'll find one constant: they built a business system[S18] that took advantage of an extrinsic change, or they were the catalyst behind the change. And because change is constant, guess what: so is opportunity!

As humans, we're wired to prioritize comfort and efficiency[P3]. This cognitive shortcut makes us naturally averse to extrinsic changes, keeping us pliant to convention[P1]. When our favorite website is changed and redesigned, we feel anxiety, even if it is beneficial. Are you sending Instagram hate mail because they changed their newsfeed? Are you hoping that Fortran jobs will suddenly make a remarkable corporate comeback? If so, you're covering your eyes and not seeing the coins flip around you. Change adversity is why we take the same route to work, drink the same coffee, read the same genre of books, and watch the same television shows.

To take advantage of change and the ever growing knowledge gap, the best tool I've found is a PESTLE analysis. PESTLE is a textbook strategic model that can help you identify changes, opportunities, or threats to any business.

- **Political:** What political factors are likely to affect the business?
- **Economic** - What supply and demand considerations will likely affect the business?
- **Sociological**: What cultural shifts and/or tastes are likely to affect the business?
- **Technological**: What technological changes (or disruptions) might affect the business?
- **Legal:** What current or future legislation could affect the business?
- **Environmental:** Will environmental shifts or trends might affect the business?

Answer these questions and external changes won't be a threat, they will be an opportunity.

The yang of the dyad is *intrinsic change*— how much have you changed lately? When you perceive extrinsic changes, how does your mind react? Do

166

you notice the difference and adapt? Resist? Analyze it? Are you closing the knowledge gap as change modulates around you?

Here's a question that needs answering: *How different are you today than five years ago?* Your answer exposes the truth with how reactant (or non-reactant) you are to change. For instance, TODAY ME is different from the OLD ME of five years ago, ten years ago, and so forth. When I reread my first book (written in 2009), I felt like I didn't write it. While I stand behind every concept, I didn't like my "voice." What changed? Not the book, but myself. Remember, the R&D numbers in your annual report[P23] reflect your disposition toward change.

Ignore change's yin and yang and I guaranteed you will be the same person year after year. As such, I can predict that your life, including your financial situation, will also stay the same. Master martial artist Bruce Lee once said:

Empty your mind, be formless, shapeless, like water. If you put water into a cup, it becomes the cup. You put water into a bottle, it becomes the bottle.

If change isn't changing you every couple of years, you stand to star in a stale television rerun, repeating the same job with the same salary, the same skills, and the same routine, all with the same two-week vacation. Un-fucking-watchable.

If you need an easy reminder, remember *Change equals Cha-ching!* There's always some "hot" cultural shift that can make you a fortune: from plastics, to fax machines, cell phones, to blockchain, to Amazon, to cannabis, to whatever else soon arrives and is labeled the next new thing "so-and-so" got lucky with. When I saw the culture coins flipping, I learned new skills[P40], spotted imperfection[P37], skewed value[S32], and offered relative-value[S26]. I took a stake in the outcomes. You should too.

☑ KEY CONCEPTS

- Change is dual system and the impetus for conjuring luck.

- Extrinsic changes are environmental and/or cultural shifts, the force behind the knowledge gap.

- A PESTLE analysis can help you identify extrinsic changes.

- Intrinsic change is your annual report's R&D number, self-development, new skills, knowledge, and perspectives.

- Change, and adaptation to it, is what creates millionaires and billionaires.

THE HARDLINE STRATEGY

Consider Harder Hardlines as They Are Riper

I get dozens of reader emails per day. Some of these are just words of thanks, some success stories, and some questions. At least one or two of these emails always seem to come to an errant conclusion regarding my books. That conclusion? *Start an Internet business!*

The core message in my books isn't about starting an Internet business. The Internet is a business channel, and a necessary one. It is a medium that fixes bad math[P17]. In other words, leverage. Sadly, as the Internet has grown, so have the money-chasers, and now I see better business opportunities in hardlines—physical products that might sit on a store shelf. Hardlines also include local brick and mortar businesses where scale would require multiple locations, franchising, or chaining. Yes, hardlines pose more scaling challenges than their Internet counterparts, but the competition is less intense. When everyone is chasing after the low-hanging fruit found on the Internet, better opportunities exist higher up the tree.

Stop ignoring the real world over the digital world.

If you profit ten million dollars from a physical product over a digital product, the money spends exactly the same.

☑ KEY CONCEPTS

- Don't ignore physical products or businesses that sell from a storefront simply because they aren't digitally delivered.

THE FASTLANE STRATEGY

Make it CENTS, and Your Business Will Make Sense

44

One of the greatest challenges I had as a young entrepreneur was not knowing which ideas to pursue. Would my idea be worth the effort, especially if you have to work seven days a week to get it off the ground? I'm guessing your objective for starting a business isn't to just pay bills. It is to set yourself free. Regrettably, most businesses are no better than a rat race job. In fact, they could be worse if the owner remains lynched to time while having no leverage[P17]. This is why I created the Fastlane Strategy, a business framework designed to change your life and set yourself free. Powering the Fastlane Strategy is the CENTS Framework, a set of five commandments that evaluates business ideas and their veracity for Unscripted outcomes. Each commandment represents several strategies and principles. If your business idea meets all five commandments, congratulations. Your idea packs potential for a 1% outcome. The commandment definitions and their constituents are as follows:

THE COMMANDMENT OF CONTROL

No one should rule over your business. If one decision from one person or company can instantaneously destroy your business, you're violating The Commandment of Control. Optimally, you want your entire operation insulated or diversified from disruption. From product development to marketing to distribution, no third-party should be able to incite a catastrophic incident. If Amazon cancels your account and you lose 99 percent of your revenue, you're violating Control. This commandment is about risk mitigation, effectively giving you black-swan insurance. The Commandment of Control lets you sleep well as a scientist[57]. The following strategies frame the Commandment of Control.

- The Scientist Strategy
- The Specialized-Unit Strategy
- The Job Proxy Principle

- The Shortcut Principle
- The Commodity Principle
- The Easy Goes Hard Principle
- The Moat Strategy

THE COMMANDMENT OF ENTRY

The Entry Commandment provides insight into where real opportunities hide. As the entry barriers to any business weaken, so does the opportunity. Simply put, the easier the opportunity appears, the worse the opportunity is. Conversely, as difficulty increases, so does the opportunity. The following strategies frame the Commandment of Entry.

- The Specialized-Unit Strategy
- The Process Principle
- The Problemology Principle
- The Shortcut Principle
- The Commodity Principle
- The Easy Goes Hard Principle
- The Moat Strategy

THE COMMANDMENT OF NEED

The Commandment of Need states that if you provide relative-value through a specialized-unit, satisfying needs or wants, money magnetizes toward you. Growth, profits, and an explosive offense are likely to follow. The following strategies frame the Commandment of Need.

- The Profit Locus Strategy
- The Specialized-Unit Strategy
- The Consumer/Producer Principle
- The Polarity Principle
- The Passion Principle
- The Value Marriage Strategy
- The Problemology Principle
- The Value Skew Strategy
- The Negative Skew Strategy

- The Imperfection Principle
- The Stakeholder Principle
- The SUCS to Bucks Strategy
- The Dual Change Strategy
- The Hardline Strategy

THE COMMANDMENT OF TIME

With the Commandment of Time, you commit to a mid- to long-term vision of having your income and wealth detached from time. This is done through *physicality*—your specialized-unit sells on its own through a business system[S19], eventually detached from your labor. The following strategies frame the Commandment of Time.

- The Lost Principle Principle
- The Specialized-Unit Strategy
- The Business System Strategy
- The Discounted Time Principle
- The Bad Math Principle
- The Polymorphic Pay Principle

THE COMMANDMENT OF SCALE

The Scale Commandment holds that your specialized-unit must be replicated in a significant quantity and profitably. The following strategies frame the Commandment of Scale.

- The Offense/Defense Principle
- The Bad Math Principle
- The Specialized-Unit Strategy
- The Business System Strategy
- The Consumer/Producer Principle
- The Asymmetric Returns Strategy
- The Moat Strategy

The fewer commandments met, the worse the idea, and hence, the worse your business potential. While a CENTSless business might pay bills or provide some great experience, it becomes probability challenged. Meet more commandments, and chances improve, either for that business or the one that follows. That said, you could violate one or several commandments with the goal of eventually solving them. For example, a restaurant could meet four commandments (CENT) but lack (S)CALE. As such, your vision should be many restaurants, accomplished either through franchising, chaining, or duplication.

When you combine CENTS with your 1/5/10 Planasy, something remarkable happens… you install a dual decision framework. The 1/5/10 Planasy guides your life; CENTS guides your business. So if it makes CENTS, it makes sense[1].

☑ KEY CONCEPTS

- CENTS is a business framework that can help you improve your probability for building a business that creates massive wealth with Unscripted outcomes.

- CENTS is a blend of twenty plus strategies and principles.

- The Commandment of Control says that no entity should hold a patriarchal position in your business with the power to shut it down.

- The Commandment of Entry says that your business should be a process to start which offers a moat, or barriers to new competition.

- The Commandment of Need says that you need to skew value, solve problems, and fill needs.

- The Commandment of Time says that eventually your business needs to operate disparate from you and your time.

- The Commandment of Scale says that your core offer should be hard to create, but easy to replicate among millions, if not, thousands.

- Opportunities improve as the commandments are met.

---

1 - To evaluate any idea you have, visit GradeMyBusinessIdea.com for a full CENTS business analysis. And yes, it is FREE— no email address required.

FROM FANTASY TO PLANASY

THURSDAY, DECEMBER 15, 2016 - 9:13 PM

(3 hours later)

Jeff didn't move from his seat at the kitchen table. For the next thirty-minutes, his mouth did all the moving. Even when Sam retreated into Madison's bedroom to kiss her good night, Jeff simply raised his voice and carried on. He recited all flavors of the red pill, from the hot stove of college to the role of mathematics to the futility of time.

When Sam returned to the kitchen, she finally interrupted. "Sounds like you're 100 percent sold." He wistfully looked at her as if she just offered him an hour-long massage.

"Yes," he said. He then gestured to the vision board on the wall and continued, "We need to fix that mess."

Sam nodded. "Well, it was a nice start."

Jeff stood from his chair and walked to the vision board, pulling it down. He laid it on the kitchen table. "We need to nail this down to next month and this year, then five. Otherwise, it's just wishful thinking."

"Agreed," Sam said, sitting next to him, a black marker between her fingers. When they originally mapped out their ten-year dream, they'd failed to dissect the plan into its five- and one-year milestones. Now they were no longer focused on some nebulous future decades away but next year. Jeff spied his wife dressed in her mint-green hospital scrubs. "How long until you leave for work?" She glanced at her watch. "Little over an hour."

Jeff nodded. "Well I'll start and say by this time next year, we should have a business that meets, or will meet, all of the CENTS commandments."

Sam furrowed her brow. "All of them? I can see that maybe at three or five years, but just getting started? It might be hard to pull off, especially since we've never done this. And we don't have a lot of money."

Jeff thought about it. "You're probably right. But our product has to be good, it has to be scalable in the millions, and we have to own it. I don't want our business copied in a few days by some punk living in his mom's basement."

Sam chuckled because he'd just described CENTS. She intervened. "So how do we know we've met this milestone? A product or a prototype? A finished website? Our first inquiry?" She paused. "We should be specific, something that demonstrates legitimate progress. Owning a business that loses money is not progress. For example, your T-shirt business."

Jeff pointed at her. "There you go. In a year from now, we will own a business that enjoys a profit."

"How much profit? Thousands? Millions?"

"A few bucks, it doesn't matter. Let's just build the foundation, a springboard so to speak."

Sam rubbed her forehead. "Okay, so in one year we will own a business, and that business will have at least one sale which delivered a profit. Right?"

Jeff nodded. "Yes. We can worry about the millions after the hundreds. Once our business generates a profitable sale, we can go from there."

He commandeered Sam's marker and started scribbling on the whiteboard, drawing various arrows, symbols, and numbers. His voice buzzed with enthusiasm as he spoke, lending him an unusual cadence as if he were already free of the rat race. His wife gazed at him, impressed at his newly found initiative. "Wow, where's this confidence coming from?" she asked. He smiled and revealed that he'd consumed hours of information at several entrepreneur forums. Between Facebook groups, the Fastlane Forum and Hacker News, he suddenly felt dangerously competent.

As he continued drawing on the whiteboard, the thick black marker squeaked. Its odor wafted through the room and reminded Sam of college, when she'd met Jeff in a communications class. Stuck in a group project, Sam had been instantly impressed by Jeff's leadership, outspokenness, and confidence. He'd volunteered to lead the group, kept them focused, and acted like he knew the outcome would be an "A." And when a group member slacked, Jeff called him on it. The slacker fell in line, and ultimately, they did get that "A."

Jeff finished writing on the board and stood back to review his handiwork. He barked, "We nail it, and then we scale it!"

The whiteboard now clarified near-term goals. In the next year, they weren't looking to become millionaires with a million-dollar business. They wanted to create and control a great product that could be sold at a decent profit. In the next thirty-days, they would need to define an idea and a problem.

Jeff was still studying the whiteboard with a wry smile, rocking back and forth on his heels as if besieged by a nervous frenzy. He glanced at his wife, who seemed to be drinking him in. Her wide-set eyes sparkled as she gleamed at her husband with as if in a trance.

Jeff felt like a child the day before Christmas. And it made him realize that his spirit had been dead for the last ten years. This wasn't like the misplaced optimism of their first plan. This was a real plan, a plan they could direct and control. The road was visibly difficult, but visible nonetheless. Instead of relying on time, jobs, and stock market returns for their dream life, they now would depend on themselves. He and his wife would become entrepreneurs.

As a kid, Jeff had concrete dreams, dreams that seemed doable. He'd pictured himself in a jazz band, blowing away at the saxophone. He saw himself fabricating impressive pieces of furniture in a huge woodworking shop. Now he dreamed of something esoteric: freedom and the liberty to make those concrete dreams possible—without the crucible of money.

He took the marker back to the whiteboard and loudly proclaimed each mono-syllabic word while underlining it.

"Nail. It. And. Then. Scale. It."

Sam gazed at her husband, biting her lip fondly. It intensified the memory back to the classroom when Jeff was a force of nature: the resoluteness, the unshaken fervor, the vigor. The smell of marker waxed as it squeaked on the whiteboard, the memory growing more vivid. Jeff's faced glowed with passion. He suddenly looked thinner, his long flowing locks of hair messy, but still dapper in a cover-model way, complemented by a dark evening shadow. He grinned at her with reverence, a look she hated to admit she hadn't seen since their wedding vows. It reminded Sam of when life had hope and promise. A time when the rat race hadn't chewed them up and spit them out. Fearlessness oozed from her husband. And it melted something in her.

Sam had a mask, just like culture and all its façades. Just as all humans do. Cognizant of her shift in less than one hour, she glanced at her watch and then flashed Jeff a cocked eyebrow. The thought ran free in her brain like a fenced puppy who finally saw the open gate. She let it fly. "So, RyRy... is there anything else you want to nail?"

THE RULES AND RISKS STRATEGY

Break Rules to Break Through the Noise

Yikes. Did MJ just mean what I think he meant? I did.

I know you're not reading this book to hear about a married couple's flirtatious foreplay, but it segues perfectly into the next strategy. *Rules are meant to be broken.* They're part of the Script, and that exists to keep you contained in the rat race.

Of course, this isn't about breaking laws. It's not against the law to encourage your kid to be a plumber. It's not against the law to drive your Lamborghini to Costco. It's not against the law to go to an empty movie theatre on a Monday morning. I'm talking about the rules of culture and business that define the Script's prevailing wisdom and keep you obediently confined in a bubble. Are the rules you're following based on cultural inertia and tradition, or are they evidence-based?

The interesting thing about bubbles is this: They have shape and appear structured, but they're easy to break out of. From diet bubbles to political bubbles, to religious bubbles, few bubbles are self-developing but self-hindering.

I believe the world would be a much better place if people knew the theology they followed and *why* they followed it. Know why most people follow a particular religion? Is it because they studied the world's religions in an exhaustive search for truth? Or is it because they just happened to be born in a particular region on a particular planetary landmass? In America, Christian; in Utah, Mormon; Latin America, Catholic; the Middle East, Muslim; East Asia, Taoism or Buddhist. Particularly, *Mom and Dad say X, so X it is.* There is no search for truth, just blind faith and a random chance that God put you on the planet exactly where the absolute truth equals your spiritual truth. No, I'm not an atheist nor do I have a religious axe to grind, but I've had my share of ignorant evangelists who don't know a damn thing about the religion they endorse except what's preached from the pulpit.

The point is, I've broken countless rules in this book.

The last paragraph on religion was one.

Putting a fictional story in this book is another, not to mention an outspoken vegan who asks her husband about getting "nailed." Equating humans to rats in a maze—yes, risky. Using a new distribution and production methodology to bring this book to market, another risk (Yes, I'm doing that!). The cover, as always, anything that I touch cover-wise is risky. The lengthy subtitle, yes, risky. I'm willing to break the rules because I know rule-breaking has a better chance of breaking out.

A great example of this is in my industry, the book trade: I recently strolled into a bookstore, one of the few remaining in my area, and couldn't help but notice the self-help section. Books titled with curse words littered the shelves. *How to Unfuck Your Life, The Subtle Art of Fucking Your Spouse, The Fucking Book on Kick-Ass Book Titles, Fuck This, Fuck That...* I found it funny and a bit ironic. You see, someone discovered that using "fuck" in a book title broke the rules and killed it doing so. Now that that rule has been broken, it becomes part of the Script. A convention. A path already traveled. Simply put, rule-breaking slowly degraded into rule-following. Sorry, but I believe the use of swear words in book titles is a coin that has flipped and landed. Do that, and you're not being novel or edgy; you're being seduced by a new set of rules. Rules are for rats. Change is for scientists.

☑ KEY CONCEPTS

- Rules are like flimsy bubbles.
- Know why you follow certain rules... tradition, culture, or evidence based?
- Rule-breaking gives you a better chance at standing out from the crowd.

THE SMALL WINS STRATEGY

Aim for Minor Improvement: The Little Things Cause the Big Things

46

Over the years I've read thousands of messages from aspiring entrepreneurs. A common thread I read follows the following format:

I have 3 ideas, X, Y, and Z.
None of them meet all of the CENTS Commandments.
X is missing entry, Y is missing scale, and Z is missing a mix of both.
I don't know what to do.

The end result is the person does nothing.

The problem with this mentality is that it causes you not to engage the market. And market engagement is what causes you to grow, gain skills, and uncover better opportunities—opportunities that abide by the CENTS Framework. Just because an opportunity isn't CENTS initially doesn't mean you should ignore it. CENTS can come into play after years of engagement, not in your first week.

If you're new to entrepreneurship, much less working at a job, set your expectations for small wins. A small win is any entrepreneurial endeavor that yields you a profit. Buy something old at the thrift store, clean and polish it up, and sell it for a $50 profit… small win. Paint a picture and sell it at Etsy for $30… small win. Ring a doorbell and offer to clean your neighbor's garbage bins for $15… small win.

Don't complicate this. CENTS is a guiding framework for entrepreneurs who are looking to do things bigger than they've ever done. But if you've never done *done* before, don't set yourself up for failure. Attempting to start the next billion dollar social media company simply because it complies with CENTS is a zero probability endeavor.

Do something. Anything. Small wins, small profits. Take swings at the plate, learn how to make contact. Once you're ready to go into the deep end of the water, let CENTS be your insurance policy so that your effort pays life-changing wealth versus bill-paying profits.

- Market engagement is what causes you to grow, gain skills, and uncover opportunities.

- If you're new to business, it might be best to target small wins before a full fledged CENTS opportunity.

FROM ZERO TO ONE
SATURDAY, DECEMBER 24, 2016 - 9:11 AM
(9 days later)

It was Saturday morning, the day before Christmas. Melted snow flurries speckled the windows. A white Christmas it would not be. Loud hissing from an air compressor echoed throughout the townhouse. Family photos rattled on the walls. In her "off day" pajamas, Sam lay on the family room floor with Madison under the Christmas tree. Nuzzled next to them was Bella, trembling and ears spiked like antennas. The noise from the garage had her unnerved.

Unlike years past, the Christmas tree was not real and didn't tower to the ceiling with lavish decorations. Two strands of white string lights and a fraying gold garland garnished its plastic branches. Some years ago, Sam had sold her collection of handcrafted ornaments, some of them heirloom memorials of past holidays with friends. At the time, she believed that every surplus dollar in her life should be saved and then invested. She took that advice to the extreme, going as far as selling things that no family should sell. Now the tree stood nakedly.

Adding to the tree's bare was the lack of gifts under the tree for Maddy. When Sam was a child, Christmas was a day for chores. Her memories consisted of scrubbing floors and pitchforking chilled hay while her father stood sentry. And it wasn't like her parents didn't celebrate Christmas. No, they were devout parishioners to a small Pentecostal church where everyone was into everyone's business. Still, Sam couldn't ever recall seeing a Bible in the house. It's almost as if they used their church attendance to justify their awful parenting and sinful life.

On the other hand, Jeff reported much happier holidays. He wasn't spoiled by any measure, but it was a holiday where his parents let him know that he was heard. The things that sparked his interest throughout the year would mysteriously show up underneath the tree. When Jeff marveled about a new woodworking tool, it had a way of showing up at Christmas. Like Jeff's parents, Sam wanted to encourage Madison's interests. But she couldn't. First, they were broke. Second, the last several years had been ruled by cheapskate insanity. They didn't manage money; money managed them. She grimaced at the memory as it deadened her heart with regret. Madison deserved more.

"You can't fix it?" Madison whimpered, examining her dollhouse. Sam jerked out of her memory, studying Maddy and her concern. "I'm sorry. Maybe Daddy can fix it." She knew they couldn't afford a new dollhouse. Sam picked up the structure to examine it. She muttered under her breath as she saw the tiny sticker under the floor: *Made in China.*

The loud banging and hissing from the garage continued, adding torment to her Christmas anxieties. She stood up and marched downstairs to the garage door. With a nail gun in his hand, Jeff was stapling carpet onto a sheet of plywood.

Hiss bang! Hiss bang!

Sam stared a few moments and then interrupted, "What the hell are you doing? You're going to wake the neighbors!"

After blasting several more nails into the wood, he paused, still facing his project. "I'm making one of those cat condos," he said flatly. He pulled the trigger again.

Hiss bang! Hiss bang! Hiss bang!

Sensing the death stare from his wife, he slammed the gun down and threw her a menacing look. "It's nine in the morning; the neighbors should be awake." He turned back to the carpeted wood and jacked another nail into the shag. *Hiss bang!*

After two more nails, he straightened up and examined his workmanship. Sam jumped at the silence and snarked, "Uh, are we adding a kitty to the family for Christmas? I hope not because we can't afford it. And Bella won't like it."

"Nope, not adding a cat," Jeff stated matter-of-factly, his eyes locked on the feline fortress. Without looking at his wife, he added, "I'm trying to add some money to the family. So we *can* afford stuff. I can sell this on Craigslist and make some quick bucks."

Remembering Jeff's last unilateral business venture involving T-shirts, Sam blasted him with a salty look. *Not again,* she thought. But before she could go vocal, Jeff held up his hand as if to signal a "stop." He clarified, "I know what you're thinking, so sit tight. We need all the money we can get if we're going to start a business. Starting a business is risky. And expensive. So I thought I'd run a little experiment to see if I could create something of value and sell it." He fawned over his creation. "This didn't cost me anything to build but a few hours, so we have nothing to lose."

Sam nodded, but the silence lingered as Jeff waited for her to respond. It took Sam a minute to process the situation. Her husband was taking the initiative. He was being proactive and thinking long-game for the family, and here she stood, subjecting him to a bitchy interrogation. She'd let the broken dollhouse, the pawned heirlooms, and the gift deficit sour her mood. And her interaction with Jeff. Her husband wasn't a dolt. He had creativity with periodic streaks of analytical brilliance. She wasn't giving him the benefit of the doubt. Sam moved closer and smirked, reverentially holding up her hand for a high-five. "Glad to see you want this badly."

He sized her up, his face chiseled with seriousness, her arm still hanging. Jeff eyed her palm and finally slapped it, but kept his grip in her hand, pulling her closer. His face was serious. "Yeah, I want it bad," he said firmly.

Unsure if this was a continuation of their reinvigorated sex life, Sam playfully grabbed his shirt and asked quizzically, "Oh? How bad?"

Jeff snickered, shaking his head. His wife was either hot or cold, and she could change temperatures like a faucet. He had a project to finish, and he had to turn down the heat. He answered, "So bad I'd crawl through a *Shawshank* shit-pipe for it."

Sam's face lurched back, disgusted. "Gross," she said as she turned on her heel. "But I'm glad to hear you're all in."

Two days later after Christmas, they were back at the kitchen table, ready to resume their strategy for escaping the rat race. It was their first "board meeting," a weekly conference to discuss progress and their objectives for next week. To keep each other accountable, they'd agreed to meet every Saturday. Alone. While Maddy wasn't a child who needed constant supervision, they knew their best thinking would be done in a controlled environment.

They'd also decided that their weekly board meeting could occur at a restaurant, if not their home. Sam suggested it. But Jeff guessed she was scheming for more visits to Kabuki, her favorite Japanese restaurant with an extensive vegan menu. In truth, they both knew it without saying—it gave them an excuse to spend time with each other. Since Madison's birth more than seven years ago, date night had gone from a monthly event to a yearly one. They hoped their weekly meeting would not only launch a business, it would relaunch their marriage. Sparks had already fired.

Luckily for them, the day after Christmas is the best day to get an eight-year-old girl to disappear into her bedroom for hours. A new tablet pre-loaded with musical apps did the trick.

Up until this point, there wasn't a lot of action, but a lot of thinking. Back on the wall was their newly modified 1/5/10 Planasy. Each was armed with a pencil, and Jeff had Neve open to a blank page. Time to brainstorm. Their goal was to find an idea that had skewing opportunities, an idea that could be transformed into relative-value and sold at scale. It seemed awfully simple.

"I can't believe it sold that quick. And at full price," Jeff reported, smiling as if he'd just stolen a cookie out of the jar. Sam's lips pursed in satisfaction.

"Well, you didn't build a cat condo; you built a towering palace fit for the Lion King. Did you make sure the person who bought it had at least 12-foot ceilings?"

"Yes, I made it clear about the size, weight, the whole thing. They pick it up tomorrow afternoon."

"So you don't have the $300 dollars yet?"

"No." He started to unwrap a protein bar. "They'll pay me tomorrow after they load it."

"Well, let's not celebrate too soon. Wait until you get the money."

Jeff took a small bite of his protein bar. He was used to his delinquent brother shrugging off his accomplishments, but his wife?

He finished chewing and swallowed. "Everyone loved it and said it was the coolest cat tree they'd ever seen. After reading about value-skew, I just didn't want to build a boring old cat tree. I wanted something unique that could command a bigger price." Another fast bite and a swallow. "I had seven inquiries on it. And it was during a holiday. If the guy doesn't show up tomorrow, I got six people waiting in the wings." After a brief silence, he suddenly jabbed the half-eaten protein bar in the air as if it were a magic wand and said, "It feels great to be appreciated. To have your work praised and demanded." He chomped another forceful bite and leered at his wife. Before she could defuse his verbal affront, he continued, "The Cat Mahal took me only four hours. That's $75 an hour."

Sensing he was throwing her another pitch she could hit and not miss, she remarked, "You should be proud of yourself. You've always been good with your hands." She raised her eyebrows. "Seventy-five dollars an hour is more than we both make at our jobs." She snickered. "It's too bad we can't crank out thousands of them. We'd hit our goal pretty quickly."

He raised his forehead. "Yeah, you know I love woodworking, but if I had to build those day-in and day-out, I'd hate woodworking in a few weeks. I'll build a few more as a side-hustle but that's all it will be—you know, a nice way to grab a few bucks." He crinkled up the protein bar wrapper and put it in his pocket. "And if I might say, it feels great to kill your own meal." He lobbed his wife a mischievous wink.

Sam shook her head and flung him a pooh-pooh look. She let the poorly placed vegan joke wash through her. "Okay, so no cat condo business. How about a book sampling service?" Sam asked. Jeff said nothing but lowered his gaze. She continued, "I'm so sick of buying books that I never finish. It would be nice to read more than a few chapters before buying."

Jeff said, "Don't all the big online retailers already let you do that? I know I always read the sample before I buy."

"I was thinking more than just a few chapters, like half the book."

"If the book is bad, why not just return it?"

183

She fiddled with a pencil, thinking. Then, "I guess you're right. Amazon can set their preview settings at whatever they want and just like that our skew would be gone. And it never occurred to me that I could just return a bad book." She slowly tucked a blond lock of hair behind her ear and then scratched her forehead. "Bad idea, never mind."

"Not at all. There are no bad ideas when brainstorming." Jeff wrote the idea on his notepad then turned to her, tapping his pencil. He paused in thought and then said hesitantly, "The other day I found myself cursing while cutting through a piece of salami and then—"

Sam interrupted, "—because you knew I'd hate you for eating it?"

He scoffed at his vegan wife. "Sorry, no…. You have your diet, I have mine."

"Damnit, Jeff! For the tenth time, it's not a diet!" She playfully jammed her heel on his foot under the table.

"Ow!" he yelped. He grabbed the wrapper out of his pocket and threw it at his wife. She swerved, and the wrapper landed on the floor. Bella raised her head from her slumber but wasn't pressed to get up.

After composing himself, Jeff spoke measuredly. "Anyway Samantha, as I was saying, the other day... well... I was cutting a huge block of *meat,* and the knife sucked ass. Dull as a doorknob. Like a damn butter knife. And then I thought *God, I hate sharpening knives!* The noise, the little metal shavings that always get under my skin, it's a royal pain in the ass." He paused for effect. "But in that moment, I wished there would be a service that would come to our house and sharpen our knives."

Sam nodded her head, perhaps too exaggeratedly. "That's actually not a bad idea. We might be able to work with that."

Pencil back in his hand, Jeff wrote the idea down in Neve and said, "Oh my dear Samantha, what little faith ye have in me."

"Don't get your hopes up. I'm sure there's a business like that, we just don't know about it."

"Marketing is a skew. If we don't know about it, or have never heard of it, then there's an opportunity."

"True. Or we can spin it entirely. Maybe a mail order service? Send the knives away dull and get them back sharp? Or how about a subscription service of some type! Those are really popular nowadays."

They talked for another ten minutes about dull knives.

By the end of the hour, they had eleven more business ideas brainstormed, thirteen total. By next week's kitchen table conference, they hoped to have it narrowed down to one. They weren't getting any younger, and it was time to jump into the deep end of the pool.

THE FEEDBACK LOOP STRATEGY

Connect Your Feedback Loop to Spark Passion

The first time I had to speak to a large audience was the scariest thing I ever faced. As an introvert, public speaking ranks up there with colonoscopy minus sedation. I spent hours preparing and practiced in an empty room. I stumbled on words, crisscrossed ideas, and quickly lost my train of thought. But I worked through it. And when it came time to speak, I did just fine.

But what happened afterward was interesting. As I left the podium amongst applause, I was intoxicated with a high that I imagine rivaled heroin. Power. Relief. And then jubilation. Altogether, this particular "high" is called *transformative passion*. And it fuels the Unscripted process.

Think of the last time you accomplished something, the last time you conquered a fear or exceeded your expectations. After it was over, remember how you felt? I'm betting you felt incredible, like jumping up-and-down incredible. That's transformative passion. Cognitively, it's fired from a *positive feedback loop*—when your effort is connected with a positive result.

Here's another example that might be familiar. Jill worked her butt off for four weeks eating right and exercising. While she lost eight pounds, she could barely see it in the mirror. Jill was ready to quit until she met Rose, a friend who hasn't seen her in two months. When Rose regarded Jill, she beamed, "OMG Jill you look great, how much weight have you lost?" Instantly Jill felt inspired, passionate, and motivated. So she continued working out. A few weeks later, Jill fit into a pair of jeans she'd last worn years ago. Again, she grinned, her heart warmed, and the passion flowed. Compliments of a rewarding feedback loop, first from Rose (externally) and later from herself (internally), Jill continued to exercise and eat right. Weeks later, the action turned into a habit. Months later, it became a lifestyle. Altogether, the *transformative passion pushed Jill from action to habit to lifestyle.*

The reality of personal transformation lies within a connected (or disconnected) feedback loop. When you fail to lose weight, gain a sale, or win a game, your feedback loop is severed. Passion does not fire. And the only way to connect your feedback loop circles back to that ugly word we all hate: *process*.

Process[S29] holds that anything worthwhile comes attached to habitual action. And that process will test your mettle. After you've conquered a challenge, becoming someone new and improved, the transformative passion arrives. Ironically, passion is process's event. That's solving a problem that took you weeks to solve. That's getting your first sale, your first "your book changed my life" review or your first million saved. That zinger you feel zipping up your spine is freaking passion. Congrats, you did it.

The other type of transformative passion is winning. Whether it's a scholarship, a sporting competition, or an Academy Award, winning inspires passion. Losing does not. Ever see an athlete grimace in misery after winning a championship? There are no miserable winners.

And yet, the process for winning is anything but passionate. In the case of professional athletes, that's endless hours of training, early mornings, restrictive diets, injuries and rehab, and of course, losing games. Their passion doesn't come from the art; it comes from the art's event—improvement, draining buckets, hitting home runs, winning, and being better than the competition.

But once again, culture has it backward: *passion doesn't lead your effort; it follows it.* If you insist on "following your passion" or "doing what you love," you will avoid the transformative pain that forces growth. Yes, the key to success isn't "doing what you love" but doing what's uncomfortable, and yes, sometimes hated.

For instance, I'm a mechanical idiot. From changing a filter to a faucet, I'm about as skilled at household chores as Queen Elizabeth is at walking amongst the plebs at Wembley during a football match.

Recently, I made a daring purchase: I bought four bidets for my four bathrooms. The purchase itself wasn't gutsy. It was that I aimed to install them myself. As a practitioner of my own advice, I recognized an opportunity to grow and spark a positive feedback loop. The first install took me nearly an hour. The second, thirty minutes. By the time I completed the fourth, it was just minutes. After finishing, I won more than a clean butt. I won increased confidence, personal growth, and identity recalibration. Maybe I'm not so mechanically challenged, eh? Like my loathed public speaking gig, I transformed hate—plumbing—into passion.

The truth is, the more you're willing to suffer, willing to endure, persevere, and challenge yourself, the more you will succeed. I can "do what I love" for the next fifty years and not worry about money confirming that love. How? *I was willing to do what I hate.*

Transformative passion is like nitrous oxide in a sportscar. Or rocket boosters. And in cases where motivation starts to wane, it is a jump-start to a dying battery. Don't mistake this for *intrinsic motivation*, which must come internally from a purpose. For example, Jill's intrinsic motivation for losing weight might not be vanity, but about health—a wish to grow old and have grandkids.

Once you understand the cognitive mechanics behind *superficial passion* (I want to race cars!) and transformative passion (I'm going to fight until I get one small victory, connecting my feedback loop) you'll win more battles. Achievement and self-development sparks passion—wallowing within comfort, an agent of mediocrity, does not. Master your mind, and the right passion will serve you for life.

☑ KEY CONCEPTS

- Transformative passion fuels the Unscripted process.

- Transformative passion fires from a connected positive feedback loop when your effort yields a good outcome.

- A severed feedback loop blocks transformative passion and stunts motivation.

- The more you're willing to endure and challenge yourself, the more you will succeed.

- If you're willing to "do what you hate," you'll be able to "do what you love" without a fiscal or cultural confirmation.

- Superficial passion is about activities that bring you joy, like playing the violin or skiing.

THE MACGYVERISM STRATEGY

Combine Low Value to Create High Value

48

One of my favorite shows from the 1980s was *MacGyver*. *MacGyver* was American television drama featuring a scientist who had a knack for assembling common household items to get an uncommon result. Lock MacGyver in a cluttered basement, and within hours he'll build you a rocket to the moon.

MacGyverism is the key to innovation and creating value where there is seemingly none. In many ways, entrepreneurship is the same. It's scientific and all about discovery. You have to look at ordinary things so you can "MacGyver" them and make extraordinary solutions.

Consider this an experiment in value and sales. Before you dive into entrepreneurship intending to compete with Uber, try MacGyverism. Innovatively combine low-value items to create high-value. For instance, remnant carpet and scrap wood could become a cat condo. Old tree stumps could be fashioned into furniture or coffee table legs. Old wooden skids, the raw materials for a decorative accent wall. Old denim, insulation; old tires, landscape mulch; old CD covers, killer wallpaper for a teen or an old guy like me looking to stay young. Heck, some dude in Oregon is selling tumbleweeds. Because my home is in the Arizona desert, I just saw at least $200 roll by.

The purpose of this exercise is simple: Impact one stranger's life, and you will impact your own. Further, you can't impact millions of lives until you learn how to impact one. Remember, small wins[S46] creates big wins. If you can create value—something self-made, self-procured, or self-engineered—and sell it just once to someone, congratulations. You will fire transformative passion[S47].

MacGyverism usually involves products that don't scale easily. Assembling a cat condo in your garage is time intensive. Scaling is one major problem to solve. But if not, it's a great side hustle and an exercise in becoming value-focused. Many years ago, I learned how to code HTML, CSS, SQL, and a wee bit of JavaScript. Those individual skills "MacGyvered" into a specialized-skill[S18] that I could sell at a healthy hourly rate. While MacGyverism might not put you into a bungalow on the beach, it might reorient your compass that way. You can earn hustle cash and score some small wins, and more importantly, fire transformative passion[S47].

- Before you can impact millions, you have to learn how to impact one.

- MacGyverism is the transformation of low-value items into something higher value.

- MacGyverism can help you spark transformative passion with some small wins.

THE MARKETING TIE-BREAKER PRINCIPLE

Treat Marketing Like a MEGA-Skew

49

Congratulations. You've just invented an awesome gadget that will make you millions. Perhaps billions. Unfortunately, three other people also invented the same exact gadget, and at the same exact time. And get this—you all have the same amount of money to spend on your invention.

If there could only be "one winner" in this competition, what would determine the victor? Since our four inventors have created an identical gadget and have the same amount of money, the winner can be determined with one variable... *marketing*. In other words, the best marketer wins—it is the tiebreaker.

The Marketing Tie-breaker Principle asserts that *marketing represents a basket of value skewing opportunities.* Furthermore, marketing creates perceived-value[S26], the value variant responsible for magnetizing[P24] money. Marketing, by itself, is a value-skew[S32], perhaps the biggest one in the attribute pool. In my first book, *The Millionaire Fastlane*, I equated business success to the game of chess. Marketing is the queen. If you're playing without your queen, winning is difficult. Why? Because marketing itself encompasses many variables for value-skew.

Attractive product labels
Persuasive copy
An emotional story tied to your company's mission
Attention-grabbing headlines
Solid testimonials

Each of these variables can be skewed positively. Your product could have a more attractive label or packaging, it could be sold with better ad copy, better headlines, and so forth. Marketing is just one word, but it represents dozens, perhaps hundreds of potential skews.

If there is ONE discipline to master, it is marketing. If you can't master it, hire someone who has. Marketing can turn surplus-value[S26] into relative-value. Put a spin on something old and commoditized, and it suddenly could be perceived differently. Marketing can make your one blog of amongst 4,000,000 others stand out.

Ultimately, you can have the best product in the world, but if you can't sell it, you will have problems. Remember Wolfgang Druckenheimer hypothetically cured cancer but couldn't sell the cure. Initial momentum needs sales. Buyers need convincing. All things held equal, the best marketer will win, and not just sales. Customers always need to be sold, but so do secondary stakeholders.

- Potential investors
- Potential employees
- Potential suppliers
- Potential acquirers
- Potential lenders
- Potential contractors

At the end of the day, your career as an entrepreneur also needs to be a career in marketing. Focus on the marketing discipline, and you expose yourself to multiple skew opportunities, even in crowded fields.

☑ KEY CONCEPTS

- All things held equal, the best marketer wins.

- Marketing generates perceived-value, and perceived-value is what magnetizes money.

- Marketing consists of many value attributes with skewing potential: product labels, website design, corporate mission, etc.

- Marketing also has a big impact on secondary stakeholders: investors, employees, suppliers, etc.

MY BROTHER ONCE STARTED A BUSINESS...
TUESDAY, JANUARY 3, 2017 - 3:30 AM
(9 days later)

As Sam microwaved her 3 AM morning lunch in the hospital's employee cafeteria, she gazed vacantly through the microwave's glass door. She looked haggard and drawn. She hadn't slept well, and the early morning hours were when fatigue would strike. The bright fluorescent lights of the hospital showered on her like acid rain. A pop from the microwave and the smell of black beans jolted her out of her trance. Before she could open the door to the microwave, its reflection mirrored her co-worker approaching from behind.

Janice was Dr. Middleton's PA and a convicted gossiper. A nice woman and a good worker but a typical representation of many people in healthcare: duly charged with the health of others, but oddly couldn't maintain their own. Janice was two Butterfingers away from type-II diabetes. At the tender age of 34, she was already waddling like a penguin who hit the all-you-can-eat buffet too often. As Sam removed her beans, Janice spoke over her shoulder. She whispered, "Hey, Sam, what do you think about the buyout?"

Janice was referring to the new management that had recently assumed hospital administration. The transition was anything but smooth, and there were rumblings that Dr. Lantzman, one of Northwestern's most respected surgeons, had quit abruptly over corporate gerrymandering and quota-pushing.

Sam answered, "I honestly don't care as I plan to get out of this racket." She carefully plated her beans and then swiveled to face Janice. She continued, "Jeff and I are starting a business."

Janice shot Sam a dumbfounded look, eyes weary and narrow, lips contorted as if she was eating something sour.

Sam remembered the last time Janice had flared that expression. It was when Sam had admitted that she didn't eat meat. Janice's shocked response was, "Oh my God, no bacon?" Then she'd jested, "Who can live without bacon?" Sam had quickly rebutted with a smile and affirmed, "Me, Janice. Last I checked bacon comes from a dead pig. And pigs are equally as smart as your Bessie." Bessie was Janice's dog, a great Pyrenees. Janice's dissonance filter had been operating efficiently and quickly severed the connection. She had retorted unabashed, as if she was reporting the day of the week, "Well, I can't live without my bacon." Sam had smiled facetiously. "Well, it's a good thing that McDonald's isn't serving any fried Pyrenees sandwiches. We certainly wouldn't want to ruin your lunch."

Back at the microwave, Sam smiled weakly and spooned her beans onto a plate with some chips. Puzzled, Janice said, "A business? Like Avon or something?"

"No, a real business. We haven't decided quite yet what we'll be doing."

Sam waited for a glib response from her co-worker, but Janice stood silent. Sam volunteered more, "Jeff and I plan on retiring by the time we're 40."

Janice eyeballed Sam's black beans as if she were eating dirt. Then she smirked whimsically, a "bless your heart" bemusement, as if Sam just confessed believing in Santa Claus. Janice offered, "My brother tried to start a business for nearly ten years. Was always talking about some nonsense. First, it was some hocus-pocus about attraction and positive thinking, then one of those pyramid things, then he started talking about some rich dad. After losing a bunch of money in real estate, he just stopped working altogether." Janice paused, lost in thought, then shook her head. "He was always looking for some fastlane to success and yet he was convinced he could do it only working four hours a week." She sighed exasperatedly, looming over Sam, careful to make sure she heard her. Loudly, she muttered, "He ended up going bankrupt and now works down at the mall. A janitor." She paused for effect. "You got to be pretty lucky to start a business, much less get rich from it. You know they say that most new businesses fail after a few years. My brother—"

Sam interrupted, "—I know the odds," she said, looking up from her beans. "We have a plan to beat them."

Janice's lips pursed, and she shrugged. As if to console Sam, she gently patted her on the shoulder twice and then said dismissively, "Well, good luck." She pirouetted and tottered away but spoke over her shoulder, audibly singsonging, "You'll need it!"

THE "DONE KILLS DOUBT" PRINCIPLE

Stop Talking, Start Doing

My business was exploding, and I needed a new employee. In the meantime, my mother helped. Her job was accounts receivable. Backstory: Mom always doubted me, but justifiably so. She'd witnessed too many of my harebrained schemes fail, so let's just say she was supportive but jaded. As she compiled vendor invoices and receivables ramped beyond $100,000, she asked, "You're owed all this money?" I nodded, and her eyes lit up. In an instant, all doubt she held for my entrepreneurial visions vanished. Several years later, I paid off my mother's mortgage with one check. The Done Kills Doubt Principle asserts that *visible success kills doubt and nails it in a coffin.*

The point is, save your breath.

And don't bother with that social media post.

The unsettling truth is this: not only does no one care[S24], but no one believes you. Even if they support you, congratulate you, like your post, or say nothing, they're skeptical and as doubtful as aliens wandering Earth. And they're expecting you to crash and burn.

I'm talking about the announcement of your lofty goals, your business ideas, your Unscripted visions, and your dreams to be financially free within ten years. Yes, everyone will think you're delusional. Announce a promotion or a new job on Facebook, and you'll get hit with a pile of likes and comments. Say something about quitting your job to start a business, and you'll get crickets. Worse, your family, spouse, or parents will try to talk you out of it. Some go as far as making threats: divorce, eviction, denied financial support. You see, whenever you defy conventional wisdom, the rat racers cursed by convention[P1] will try to knock some sense into you.

Get rich quick is a scam!
Nobody really retires in their 30s with millions!
95 percent of all new businesses fail!
You never started a business!
MJ DeMarco exemplifies a survivor bias and is selling lottery tickets!

This reaction is entirely justified. And it will always be justified because talk is cheap. Advertising your lofty goals is an event; accomplishing it is a process[P29]. You can't make unbelievers believe with chitter-chatter. You can throw this book in their face and expect them to read it. The only way to eliminate *doubt* from doubters is to transform it into *done*.

Done shows up on your parents' driveway with a brand-new Ferrari without the loan. *Done* is hiring your uncle because you're growing too fast. *Done* is doing. *Done* is an achievement. *Done* kills doubt. Never live within the parameters of someone else's opinion unless you want to live within the parameters of their existence.

☑ KEY CONCEPTS

- Expect no one to believe your lofty goals, and expect some to dissuade you.

- Advertising your goals or aspirations is an event; achieving them is a process.

- If you want to convert doubters, achieve visible results.

THE EXECUTION PRINCIPLE

Your Idea Sucks Until Execution Says It Doesn't

A round 2007 I made a big mistake. That mistake? Oh, I lost a few million dollars, perhaps billions. At the time, I was having a conversation with a female friend about online dating. We both were on a dating service, and she complained about the number of inquiries she was getting. It was overwhelming—to the point where she would have missed Brad Pitt's message mixed in the "hey baby" and "yo" garbage. Because I recognized her complaint as an opportunity[S37], I immediately thought of the idea for a dating service where only the women could instigate a conversation. Fast forward seven years and Bumble was founded, a dating service where men cannot make first contact, saving millions of female inboxes worldwide. Today Bumble is worth billions. I had the idea seven years earlier and now it's worth nothing but a regretful paragraph in a book.

The Execution Principle asserts that *all ideas suck unless brought to life by execution.* Yes, even that CENTS idea is worthless. No, not because it won't work, but because right now, you haven't done a damn thing about it. After my conversation with my lady-friend, I did nothing with that idea. Ideas with zero execution behind it are worth exactly that: zero.

Sadly, all ideas are still events[P29], even well-researched ones with business plans attached. Once you've adopted an Unscripted production[P23] mindset, ideas start popping up everywhere. They become easy. Too easy. The worst mistake you can make is thinking that your ideas mean anything. They don't. As such, no one will give you capital for it. No bank will loan on it. And no, you can't swap 900 programming hours from a coding genius in lieu of 50 percent of your business, which at this point, is just a neurological Christmas tree in your head.

In a blog posted many years ago, Unscripted entrepreneur Derek Sivers[1] perfectly highlighted the relationship between ideas and execution. Execution

---

1 - https://sive.rs/

is where the asymmetrical meat is, while the strength of your idea is just a multiplier.

Idea Value		Execution Multiplier		Potential Value
Great idea =	$100	Poor Execution =	$1	$100
Good idea =	$75	Fair Execution =	$10,000	$75,000
Okay idea =	$50	Average Execution =	$100,000	$5,000,000
Fair idea =	$25	Good Execution =	$500,000	$12,5000,000
Poor idea =	$1	Great Execution =	$1,000,000	$1,000,000

As you can see, a great idea with poor execution is worth little: $100 (100 X 1) while an okay idea (think surplus-value) with astounding execution is worth $50,000,000 (50 X 1,000,000).

The idea is nothing; its execution is everything. Remember, done kills doubt[P49]. Talk is cheap. If you want anyone to pay attention, demonstrate a talent for executing.

Show sales.

Show a prototype.

Show a website mockup and ten pre-orders.

For the love of God, show something!

☑ KEY CONCEPTS

- Your great idea is absolutely worthless until execution says it isn't.
- Your idea is like a multiplier, while execution is where the money goes asymmetrical.
- A mediocre idea with great execution could be worth tens of millions.

THE KNIFE AT THE GUNFIGHT
SATURDAY, JANUARY 21ST, 2017 - 6:51 PM
(18 days later)

Tell me lies, tell me sweet little lies...

As Fleetwood Mac sang overhead, Jeff's friend and co-worker, Scott was yapping away. They were at O'Boyles Gastropub, a crowded bar with live music, cheap beer, and cute waitresses dressed in sexy Irish kilts. Jeff and his wife scheduled their weekly business meeting at the pub. Jeff arrived first while his wife ran an errand prior. Scott was at the bar and joined Jeff when he spotted him alone. After Scott sat down and ordered a beer, he went on an agonizing diatribe. Mostly about how everything sucked: his job, their boss and their employer, his pay, his love life, and his lack of television time. It appeared that Scott's most pressing problems were Showtime canceling some political drama and the Chicago Bulls' losing preseason bleeding into the regular season.

Jeff's chest tightened with anxiety.

After telling Scott about his business goals weeks ago, Scott never inquired how it was going. Never asked about Sam either. Instead, Scott dragged on about how he had to wait six hours outside of Best Buy for the new *Call of Duty* release. That's when Jeff knew. He'd finally had enough. He interrupted Scott's latest rant about how his four-year-old Chevy Malibu was cramping his style as if he saw himself as the next incarnation of 007.

"Scott, let me ask you something." He paused, taking a swig of his beer. "Where do you see yourself in five years?"

Scott's face drew a blank as if he were just asked to solve a differential equation. After a crooning David Coverdale chorused, *Is This Love?* Scott straightened up from his slouch and said, "I don't know really." He sipped his Bud Light and continued, "I guess I'm hoping to move up the ranks at work. Get one those corner offices with a window. And a Mercedes G-Wagon, the kind the pro athletes drive!" He paused and smiled as if he were a child reciting a Christmas list to Santa. Jeff said nothing, face flat. Scott slapped the table and continued, "And courtside tickets to the Bulls next to Bill Murray! Did you see the trailer for his new movie? It looks pretty bad ass!"

Jeff failed to mask his annoyance and crimped his lips. Scott's smile disappeared, clearly upset Jeff was unable to ratify his idyllic life fantasy.

"Scott, do you remember anything I said last time we talked?"

He hesitated in thought. Then, "You mean at work when you said you wanted to quit and start a business?"

"Yes."

"What of it?" Scott asked, looking irritated.

"Well, since you've been sitting here, you've done nothing but complain. Your job sucks. Your pay sucks. Your car sucks. Your dating life sucks. Sucks, sucks, sucks, and yet, your idea for the future is to double-down on the same shit that is making your life suck? It makes no fucking sense. Do you have any goals? A dream? Something better than an office with a window?"

His expression dulled. After a moment, he sneered, "Dude, what's with the attitude?"

"I'm serious. What do you want to do with your life?"

"I don't know." He shook his head. "I'm just trying to survive and have a little fun along the way."

Jeff folded his arms and snapped, "Well, I don't want to just survive, I want to live, like *really live.* I want to be free of the BS, free of the bills and the job, and yeah, free of the stupid basketball games that mean absolutely nothing to me. I'm not gonna wait until some godforsaken age to retire and then finally live."

Scott's face reddened in anger, but he sat quiet.

"Let me ask you something, Scott. What benefit do you get knowing every baseball statistic since 1970?" Jeff didn't let him reply and continued, "What benefit do you get if the Bulls win the next ten world championships? A huge payday? Respect? A hot wife? Vacation time? Seriously, I want to know."

He gave Jeff a befuddled look. "I get bragging rights. And it'd be hella fun to watch."

"Bragging rights?" Jeff huffed. "Over who? Over some other bumpkin in another part of the country who is sitting on a couch like you? Do you hear yourself?"

His tone changed into a stern whisper, "Do I hear myself? Do you hear yourself? You're dissing me because I know baseball stats and like basketball, but suddenly you don't? Because you read some damn business book?" He looked around, fearful as if someone would overhear. "Look Jeff, this is life. You get up, you go to work, you pay your bills, save a little money, and maybe you get ahead at some point. Your fantasy about building this big business and getting rich is a pipedream. If you ask me, you've been watching too many internet videos with that Ty Dopez guy."

Jeff shook his head in disgust and retorted, "This isn't about stupid cars and tickets to some dumb game that will be forgotten a week later. It's about living a life that I won't regret when I'm seventy years old. Culture and tradition ain't gonna write my story; I'm gonna write it." Jeff gestured at him and continued, "You? You've given up. You have no dream other than some overpriced car that looks like a toaster on wheels. It's sad because you don't even realize you're already dead—you just aren't buried."

Scott shuffled back and twisted his face as if Jeff had just told him he'd cheated on him with his wife. He then angled in, snarling, "Are you fucking done? Because I am." Scott stood up and threw a ten-dollar bill on the table. "That's for my beer, and you can keep the change and put it toward your business." Before marching away, he sneered. "I'll see ya Monday morning, champ."

By the time Sam arrived, Jeff had finished his Guinness. He smiled weakly as his wife slithered into the seat next to him. Her hair was freshly salon styled, and her lips painted a candy apple red. Her face was dolled up and glowing. She was wearing dress pants and an oversized turtleneck sweater with a smiling lamb embroidered on the front. The bulky sweater transformed her leggy frame into a beefy presence, but Jeff thought it was cute. Silver earrings dangled from her ears, not shoulder dusters, but Jeff was surprised by the impression. It made him forget about the terse conversation with Scott.

Sam sized up the bar's patrons, and Jeff saw her scrunch her nose. The place was packed and stank of stale beer and cabbage. Jeff loved it, but his wife considered the odor as offensive as a porta-potty at a traveling carnival.

Jeff gestured to her. "Why you made up to the nines?"

She looked at him curiously. "What, a girl can't look fabulous once in a while?"

Jeff laughed, "Here? It's an Irish dive bar that plays music from the last century."

Sam studied her husband. His hair was pulled back in a ponytail, his eyes darker than usual, a sign he was into his second or third beer. She nudged into him and slapped him on the knee. "Wow, it's like we're dating again. Did you order me a margarita?"

"You sure you want to drink? Remember New Year's Eve." Jeff stated it like a suggestion, not a command. He had had to carry Sam home from a neighbor's party. But not before she puked on the street, her vomit splattering on a parked Prius.

"I'll be careful." She winked. "Promise."

Once they settled in and the waiter delivered their water, they started talking business.

"I can't believe how easy it is to spot ideas," Jeff volunteered. "Ever since I started thinking like an entrepreneur, I get a business idea practically every day." He considered his wife and then asked, "You sure you're not hungry?"

Before they left, Sam said she would only order a drink. "Yea sure," she said, surveying the restaurant. "There isn't a plant-based meal to be found in this place."

Jeff smiled at the memories of when she'd curl up next to him in a booth no matter the restaurant. It was a time when she would listen to his every dream, and she would cheer him on. A simpler time without the mortgage, the jobs, and the pressures. Sitting next to each other in a booth for the first time in eight years set a positive tone for the night.

After a thorough review of their ideas over several drinks, it was decided.

They were going into the knife sharpening business. There was a need, one that every household in the country could use. They reasoned that, like Jeff, people don't want to be bothered with this household task, from the inconvenience to the noise to the equipment hassles. They didn't bother with a business plan. But Jeff scribed a CENTS analysis into Neve, which he now carried with him at all times. It read:

- *[C]ONTROL... No major dependencies*
- *[E]NTRY ... Sharpening knives requires special tools and is a bit of a skill*
- *[N]EED... Sharpening knives is inconvenient, and they always go dull and offer a repeat customer component (re-orders, yah!)*
- *[T]IME ... Big unknown, must address this later once we learned more about the industry*
- *[S]CALE... The most potent commandment: every household has knives, and they repeatedly go dull. Maybe franchise this nationally?*

When clarifying the size of the market, Jeff riffed an impersonation of the newly elected US President, "Billions and billions." His wife grimaced. Jeff loved playing the Trump card; it was a button he could push to rile Sam. But he stopped short, careful to not ruin the productive tenor. Once the knife business was decided, they identified multiple value-attributes to potentially skew, from mail-order services to pick up and drop off concierge to good customer service. They just couldn't decide which. Nonetheless, they were stoked.

"How the hell do we start?" Jeff questioned.

Sam toasted her half-empty margarita into the air, her third in the last hour. "Got to hand it to you, baby, I feel like this idea is worth millions."

"Well, I guess we're officially problemologists now." Jeff snuffed a half-hearted giggle, "Because I don't know a damn thing about sharpening knives."

THE OLD FRIENDS, OLD WAYS PRINCIPLE

Beware of Old Relationships as You Fight for a New You

52

I once had a friend who laughed at me because I wanted to start a business. In his words, "You're wasting your college degrees," and "You should grow up and get a job." Then I had another friend. His best idea for wealth was to join one pyramid scheme after another. Each conversation was about some hot ground floor opportunity. BTW, if you ever hear the phrase "ground floor opportunity"—run the other way. Anyways, these folks are no longer my friends.

The Old Friends, Old Ways Principle explains that *as you grow and morph into a NEW you, old relationships will fight for the OLD you.* Anytime you arm yourself with new pens for a new story[S2], the stagnate relationships in your life will resist. They will fight you, question you, and tease you. Dead weight is people who belittle your dreams. They don't support your growth or success, They encourage the status quo. They don't want you losing fifty pounds or becoming financially free. Leaving the rat race plantation is a threat to their self-worth and forces them to confront their own mediocrity. As the old saying goes, *misery loves company.*

Dead weight could be co-workers, childhood friends, and even family. And you never know who dead weight is until they catch wind of your ambitious goals. Worse, if you go from done to doubt[P50], old relationships can set you back into old ways. Ever read the headlines of professional athletes who always get in trouble after the off-season, or in retirement? As the athlete advances in life, they hold on to old troublesome relationships, old relationships which keeps him mired in the old ways.

Once you take to the road to escape the rat race, and let it be known, pay attention, the dead weight will emerge from the shadows to set you straight. *You're wasting your time! Dropping out of college is a mistake!* Yes, big dreams will have big doubters. That's normal. Playing devil's advocate is a good exercise, and doubters can serve that purpose. However, when doubters cross the line into dead weight, you have to cut the anchor loose. Hanging out with losers will likely keep you a loser.

- Dead weight, people who belittle your dreams or don't support you, should be left behind.

- Hanging on to dead weight can cause you to regress into old ways.

- Dead weight surfaces when you make your dreams known or when your dreams start gaining traction.

To impact millions, you must reach millions. And have something they want. The key to asymmetrical-returns[S21] is to hunt where there are plenty of biting rats. Okay, perhaps the rat analogy is too crude. Let's be politically correct: *consumers*.

The volume of consumers who can use (or want) your product is demonstrated by your market's size for your specialized-unit. In business terms, this is called your *total addressable market*, or TAM. If the target audience for your business is harp musicians who are seven feet tall, you're fishing in a pond the size of a thimble. The market is poor, if not non-existent. While your product might solve a desperate need for towering harp players, its TAM muzzles leverage[P17].

TAM is like fishing in a body of water. The larger the watering hole, the more fish can be caught. The four bodies of water that lend to larger TAM sizes are as follows:

1. The pond (your customers are in the city/county/community)
2. The lake (your customers are in the state or region)
3. The sea (your customers are in the country)
4. The ocean (your customers are in the world)

There are three questions to ask in estimating your specialized-unit's TAM.

ONE: If geography or proximity was no issue, how many people would find value in your specialized-unit? This determines your *total unreachable market*, or TUM. For example, if you owned an Indian restaurant, your TUM is everyone on the planet who enjoys Indian food. Your TAM, however, is only the local city.

To estimate TAM/TUM figures, you will need to do some research from a top-down approach. Start with industry sources or marketing research companies like Gartner or Forrester. Then narrow the whole into its relative subset. For example, if your product served owners of poodles, all dog owners are the whole, all poodle owners are the subset. A couple of internet searches should give you a good idea if your idea is worth pursuing.

TWO: If TUM does not equal TAM, what needs to be done to transform TUM into more TAM? Franchises? Chains? Internet orders? Change business models? Remember that fashion boutique in my small town? I asked the owner if she sold on the internet and she replied, "NO." TAM was not siphoning from TUM so I could mathematically deduce the venture was making little profit, if any.

THREE: Can you effectively reach your TAM? If your relative-value offer can't reach your market through marketing, the size doesn't matter. Even if you had an excellent product for seven-foot-tall harp players, how would you get your message or product in front of them?

Unfortunately, TAM and TUM figures are wildly variable and speculative. There are two best practices: Target markets large enough to make your estimates inconsequential. For instance, my books target people who want financial freedom. I'm also writing a mystery. A friend of mine sells dog accessories. These markets are large enough that our TAM estimates don't matter. There are millions, perhaps billions of fish in this ocean. Put another way, if you're dropping a nuclear bomb, you don't need a bullseye.

Second, larger bodies of water will always have better TAMS. And inaccurate estimates are easily forgiven. Given a choice, it's easier to start in a larger body than to graduate from a smaller one.

Going back to our Indian restaurant, to increase your TAM from TUM, you would have to open several restaurants. Or start selling franchises. Instead of starting in the pond (city), perhaps there are better opportunities in the ocean? Selling your secret Indian herbs and spices on the internet with worldwide distribution? An Indian cookbook? An Indian food product that could be sold worldwide?

With my publishing company, I sell licenses to foreign publishers for non-English speakers who want to become entrepreneurs. With over thirty around the world, this transforms TUM into TAM.

The Trotmans decided to start a knife sharpening business. Their initial TAM will be dependent on how they structure their business model. Their TAM could be the entire country, or it could be their city. Yes, big decisions are ahead.

A significant TAM is a key to asymmetric returns, which is the key to leverage and large expected values. This is how your income can go from $42,000 a year (my one Indian restaurant) to $42,000 a month (my line of Indian spices). If you want to catch more fish, you'll need to put yourself in a bigger body of water.

- Your total addressable market (TAM) is the total audience who has an interest in your product or service.

- Your total unreachable market (TUM) is people who might have an interest in your product, but don't have access to it due to logistics or geography.

- Typically, the larger the TAM, the more potential for asymmetric returns.

- Chains, franchises, distribution, units, and licenses can transform TUM to TAM.

THE DRAKE EQUATION PRINCIPLE

A Business Plan is Entrepreneurship's Drake Equation

54

Suppose Frank Drake, the mind behind the astronomical Drake Equation, started a business. In which case, he'd no doubt spend considerable time preparing and researching. Probably too much time. That's because entrepreneurship has its own Drake Equation. It's called a business plan.

If you're not familiar with the Drake Equation, it's a mathematical equation with many immeasurable variables. Its purpose is to speculate on the number of intelligent civilizations in the universe that exist. The equation is:

$$N = R^* \bullet fp \bullet ne \bullet fl \bullet fi \bullet fc \bullet L$$

Each variable represents a wild guess, like the fraction of stars with planets and the galaxy's average star formation. As such, the "N" or the hypothesized answer also varies wildly. The Drake Equation Principle affirms that *a business plan is like a modern-day Drake Equation with so many immeasurable variables that such a plan is practically useless.*

The market represents millions of minds, each with different value hierarchies. Individuals buy items based on different value-skews and the perceived-value communicated[S26]. It is an unpredictable and unforecastable body.

No business plan survives first contact with the market. It's like that Mike Tyson quote: *everyone has a plan until they get punched in the face.* And when the market chews up and spits out your business plan, you'll discover another truth... You shouldn't have wasted six months PowerPointing a business plan so perfect it should be in the National Archives.

So unless you're seeking venture capital or investors, I'd skip the business plan. Instead, here are seven things to identify:

1. Does it make CENTS?[S44]
2. Is the TAM large enough to change your life? How can TUM be expanded into TAM?[S53]
3. How many value attributes can you skew? And at what cost?[S32]

4. Can you reach the market? Are there viable mediums and channels? Can you communicate or demonstrate your value-skew?
5. How easy is it to replicate your solution once created?[S35]
6. Does this potential business align with your decisional framework established in your 1/5/10 Planasy?[S12]
7. Do you have an exit strategy that can help you hit your Escape Number?[S15] And who would be a potential suitor for that exit?

Spend a few hours on these questions, and you'll have the best business plan you can buy. And you can leave the Drake equations to the cosmologists.

☑ KEY CONCEPTS

- Business plans are as wild and speculative as the Drake Equation.
- As soon as the business plan is executed into the market, it becomes invalid.
- CENTS, TAM, skew, medium, replication, vision, and exit ideas suffice for a sufficient business plan.

THE 3A STRATEGY

Act, Assess, Adjust: Solve Problems
with the Scientific Method

Years ago, I taught myself how to code. It started at the library and then advanced to the internet forums. It was a decision that launched my mini-empire, first through a specialized-skill, then a specialized-unit. Behind my blueprint for success, there was a simple formula that I relied on. This recursive formula should be the foundation for your entire entrepreneurial career, from idea to growth to liquidation. And if you want to succeed, you need to use it too.

It's called the 3A Method. It mimics one of the most widely known procedures for knowledge and skills acquisition: *the scientific method.* Remember, entrepreneurs are problemologists[P30] which are pseudo-scientists[S7]. Except your laboratory isn't a room with test tubes and beakers, but the many marketplaces that offer the rats their cheese. The 3A Method is the experimental process for interacting within this lab, consisting of three steps:

1. Act
2. Assess
3. Adjust

ACT

The first *Act* is the experiment itself.

Anytime you launch action into the marketplace, the rats react, or they don't. This reaction creates your "problem," which needs to be analyzed and then solved. For instance, let's say you launch a clothing line, and after $500 in advertising, you have zero sales. In rat race parlance, your cheese didn't draw sniffs. It wasn't appealing. The experiment's result is a non-reaction from the marketplace. It's also a problem.

ASSESS

The second tier within the 3A Method is *Assess*. Once you've identified the problem (no sales!), then identify possible causes for the problem. Is your clothing line unappealing to your target market? Did you reach the right target market with your advertising? Is your advertising a compelling message for that audience? Is your website not designed to convert? Is your branding ineffective? The list of potential causes can be quite extensive. Your job as a scientific problemologist is to test these variables.

ADJUST

The final step is *Adjust*.

Once you've identified the problem and its potential causes (there should be many), you adjust one variable in your strategy. For instance, you might hypothesize that your advertising failed because you didn't target the right audience. As such, your adjustment might be to test a new marketing channel.

Make the adjustment, *act* again, and repeat the experimental cycle with the new variable. If changing channels doesn't improve results, you might determine your advertising needs a new headline. Another adjustment is made. Altogether, these strategy tweaks might entail learning new skills, a lot of internet research, or reading books. You could recursively go through this process dozens of times before striking gold.

Once you get your first sale, then the process restarts.

Instead of asking, *Why am I getting no sales?* the 3As narrow into more specific problems. Your new problem could be, *Why is only one percent of our traffic converting? Or Why are we getting a lot of returns and refunds?* Strictly speaking, acting, assessing, and adjusting has no end date.

Some years ago, the word "pivot" became an entrepreneurial buzzword and was bandied around like some phenomenal new concept. The scientific method (similar to the 3A Method) has been around for centuries. *Adjust* is the infamous "pivot" which is derived from the *assess*.

But be warned. If you are *acting, assessing*, and *adjusting*, you will travel in a much different direction than intended. You get into business to sell X and then you end up selling Y. For example, when I started my Internet company, my vision wasn't lead generation, but I ended there. Had I not sold the company, lead generation would have morphed into online reservations and ride-sharing. Likewise, Amazon started solely in the book space. When PayPal first launched, its original intention was payment processing for eBay's top sellers. Instagram started as a check-in location app and then deviated into photo sharing. Countless businesses start with one objective, but the 3As take them elsewhere.

This is why business plans are overrated and like relying on a fair-weather float-plan to get you through a hurricane. You can read countless books on startups, marketing, and business, but nothing will prepare you for the market's volatility. No matter how tight a vehicle you run, your vehicle cannot change the weather and its data. If you're driving to China but the market is signaling you to Spain, stop fighting it. When the experiment gives you clues, the scientist doesn't resist; he adjusts.

THE 3A METHOD

In 2015 on Chinese television, Elon Musk was quoted as saying that ideas are mostly wrong—and that they must be adapted and refined, and that success was basically recursive self-improvement[1]. Namely, the 3A Method. It is that mysterious process[S29] I continue to reiterate. Learn it, and you will succeed at whatever you do. The 3A Method is entrepreneurship, and everything great in my life is because of it. First, it trained me to be a master problemologist, a scientist. Second, with each iterative cycle, I expanded my skills and knowledge base. Soon problems are solved easier, and things progress faster. Past failures shrink knowledge gaps. Don't pivot, experiment. Then *act*, *assess*, and *adjust*.

1- https://www.youtube.com/watch?v=y6909DjNLCM

- The execution process for Unscripted Entrepreneurship is like applying the scientific method indefinitely, not in a laboratory, but a marketplace.

- The 3As mimic the scientific method consisting of Act, Assess, and Adjust.

- Act is the experiment itself—your offer placed in front of the market.

- Assess is the experiment's evaluation.

- Adjust is a minor shift in strategy which retests the original experiment.

- The 3A process is iterative and never ends.

THE EXPECTED VALUE STRATEGY

Maximize Expected-Value: Match Your Potential Skills With the Largest Potential Outcome

56

Before leaving Chicago for Arizona, I had the opportunity to buy a business which also happened to be my employer, a small limousine service. The owner gave me a smoking "no money down" offer, one that I seriously considered. But ultimately, I declined—and without the superpower of hindsight, I know it was the right decision.

How?

Had I bought that limousine service, I would have subjected myself to a business system where asymmetrical returns were nearly impossible. My income ceiling in that business was hampered by geography, hours in the day, and the number of cars I could finance. Even in my early twenties, I knew I wanted to go bigger—and buying a glorified taxi service was akin to me buying a job.

Here's a big secret that no one will ever try explaining to you: *Asymmetrical returns are impossible unless you match your near-term potential skills with the largest potential outcome.* This does two things: First, it ensures that when execution is average or better, your profit is life-changing. Second, a large potential outcome gives you the largest expected-value for your effort, even at low probability, such as less than one-percent

If you're not familiar with expected-value (EV), it is a statistical concept that quantifies the nominal value you can expect from any action, especially if repeated many times. For example, a Las Vegas casino's expected value for gambling is about 5%. The casino stands to win five cents for every dollar you bet. Bet $100,000 over the night in many bets, and you'll likely leave a loser with $95,000 or probably worse. Before I continue, keep this in mind: A 5% expected-value built Las Vegas, a city beautified in luxury and richness. In our case, starting a business is an action—but few entrepreneurs ever consider expected-value in their business opportunity selection process. Here's why you need to.

If you play it safe in a business opportunity with a small TAM, you cheat both asymmetrical returns and expected value. In fact, the expected value could go negative, despite higher probabilities. The totality of your effort is marginalized with weak rewards. In my case, buying a limousine service would have rewarded me with a middle-class existence, and that was if I executed better than average!

Here's another way of looking at it, purely mathematically speaking. When it comes to business, evaluate opportunities like you would various games of chance with different awards and odds based on how well you play. Let's call it a *value game*. In our value game, prizes aren't awarded by a single organization but by a global marketplace. And the global market routinely takes ordinary people and makes them millionaires and billionaires.

Let's say you're reviewing two business opportunities, each with a startup cost of $5,000. The following chart outlines the opportunity's ten-year profit outcomes and their theoretical probabilities for execution. After reviewing these two scenarios and approaching it as if this were a game with awards, which "game" would you play?

EXECUTION LEVEL	GAME/BUSINESS "A"		GAME/BUSINESS "B"	
	Reward	Odds	Reward	Odds
Excellent Execution	$1,000,000	.05%	$20,000,000	.025%
Good Execution	$250,000	1%	$10,000,000	.125%
OK Execution	$50,000	3%	$5,000,000	1.85%
Fair Execution	$5,000	5.95%	$50,000	3%
Failed Execution	($5,000 LOSS)	90%	($5,000 LOSS)	95%
All potential outcomes = 100%		100%		100%

At a glance, logic appears to say that Game A or Business A is a good choice. With the given odds, you have a 10% chance of minimally doubling your money, best case, a return of 50X. Additionally, your odds of profit are double (10% vs. 5%). Game/Business B, on the other hand, has a bigger risk of failure (95% vs. 90%) and only gives you a 5% chance of profit.

If you think Game/Business A is the "safer bet" you'd be terribly wrong. When these opportunities and probabilities are analyzed, the expected value clearly says that Game/Business B is the best bet, not just marginally but by a staggering amount.

EXPECTED VALUE

Game / Business A: -$1,078 (-21.55%)
Game / Business B: $106,750 (2135%!)

These figures represent the power of asymmetry as it deals with expected outcomes. Despite bad odds and super-low probability, your best bet is always to choose the opportunity with bigger outcomes as it blows up expected value, and the possibilities of your effort. Remember, Las Vegas is built on a 5% EV—Business B has an expected value of 2135%, while Business A is negative. Potentially outsized returns are the key to asymmetrical returns, even when you don't execute exceptionally.

Of course, this analysis requires some self-reflection. If you never started a business and your first business idea is to take your $5,000 and start the next Amazon, you're delusional. Yes, you've attacked a market with huge potential outcomes—but you've failed to match your potential skills with reasonability. Your probability for success in that venture is exactly zero—potential outcomes are irrelevant.

TAKE ON AMAZON!		
Execution Level	Reward	Odds
Excellent Execution	$100,000,000,000	0%
Good Execution	$250,000,000	0%
OK Execution	$50,000,000	0%
Fair Execution	$5,000,000	0%
Failed Execution	($5,000 LOSS)	100%
All potential outcomes = 100%		100%

The optimum decision in both business and this game scenario is a careful balancing act. First, take the opportunity *wherever your maximum potential meets non-zero probability.* For clarity, "maximum potential" is knowledge and talents you can reasonably learn with discipline and practice. Specifically, the business you should start isn't the easiest one— it's the one that you feel gives you the most considerable reward for your effort, even if you execute averagely. Second, you have to be honest with yourself—is your first business a delusional stretch that is forcing your odds of success at zero, and your odds of failure at 100%?

Of course, the entrepreneurial reality isn't as simple as playing a game with a five thousand dollars entry fee. But our analogy isn't much different. Whenever you engage the marketplace with a business venture, you're buying game tickets with tremendous odds that no government organization could ever offer—only the global market can. The question is, are you buying tickets for our value game that appear to have better chances but offer lower rewards? Or are you challenging yourself in a game where excellent execution, or worse, average execution, can change your life? Decent execution in a large TAM opportunity might change your life—decent execution in a small opportunity might pay your bills.

Every company I started cost less than $5K to form, just like this game.

And each one of them had the potential for asymmetrical returns, even if I executed just averagely. Going back to our decision between Business A and Business B, that was the choice I was faced with many years ago. Business A was buying that limousine service; Business B was starting an internet company serving the limousine industry.

	BUY LIMO SERVICE		START WEB SERVICE	
Execution Level	Reward	Odds	Reward	Odds
Excellent Execution	$1,000,000	.05%	$20,000,000	.025%
Good Execution	$250,000	1%	$10,000,000	.125%
OK Execution	$50,000	3%	$5,000,000	1.85%
Fair Execution	$5,000	5.95%	$50,000	3%
Failed Execution	($5,000 LOSS)	90%	($5,000 LOSS)	95%
All potential outcomes = 100%		100%		100%

My execution was good and I was rewarded with a lifetime of financial freedom, instead of a middle-class existence of survival. Don't play the rat race to optimize mediocrity, play to change your life. Asymmetric returns need significant potential outcomes which drive up expected values. If you have no business experience, job or otherwise, you might need to start smaller than you'd like to turn *zero* probability into *a* probability. That's perfectly OK. Overall, we're matching your potential skills, what you can learn, with opportunities that have largest outcomes so "no chance" becomes "a chance". Do so, and success won't be a matter of luck, but of probability and expected value.

☑ KEY CONCEPTS

- Match your skills, or potential skills, with the largest potential outcome to maximize asymmetric returns and expected value.

- Working with a large potential outcome, even at low probability (<1%) gives you the largest *expected-value* on your effort and can make average- to above-average execution worthwhile.

- Avoid opportunities that have zero probability for success when referenced against your near-term potential.

- The expected value of "playing it safe" or dabbling in a small TAM is often negative, despite higher probabilities.

- Expected value requires many attempts (failures or losses) to be valid.

THE DESERT OF DESERTION
SATURDAY, JUNE 17TH, 2017 - 8:03 PM
(148 days later)

It was a Saturday night at the kitchen table, the scheduled date and time of the Trotmans' weekly board meeting. But neither Jeff nor Sam were talking business. Five months had passed since deciding to start a knife sharpening business. But Jeff saw their meeting as progress. The last time they met to discuss their business venture was three weeks ago.

With Madison at a friend's sleepover, Jeff and his wife ate their late dinner alone. Aside from an occasional drooling beg from Bella who stalked their meal, an eerie silence hung over the table. Jeff wondered if he had done something wrong. His wife slurped her pasta while eyeing her phone vacantly; oddly, it was locked with a black screen. Jeff saw no messages displayed and spied his wife's reflection, an empty gaze as if she was hypnotized by the dark abyss.

Enough of this, he thought.

For the last few weeks, his wife had been distant and dour. Melancholy, he speculated, thinking it was the fitting word. He wasn't happy with their business progress either, but he didn't let it affect him. Not like this. Even culinary hygiene was abandoned; red sauce soiled the outside of her mouth.

Her fork clinked and clanked against her dinner plate again and again, its chaotic song disrupting the quiet.

Clank. Clink. Clink.

With each, the weight of what Jeff knew grew heavier.

He felt like quitting the knife venture and feared broaching the subject. His wife's gloom indicated she might have felt the same. Gone was the energy and the enthusiasm they felt about their business venture. Also gone was the excitement of setting themselves free, as the DeMarco books described. It felt as if each week's problems and their challenges were a slap to reality.

Months earlier, they'd agreed that they'd start a subscription knife sharpening business. They weren't sure about the logistics, just that the process had to be seamless for the customer: drop dull knives in the mail, get them back sharp a week later. The first problem they encountered was the high cost of sharpening equipment. Another problem quickly followed: the prohibitive shipping cost and the custom boxes they needed for the task. With all the costs involved, not including the actual time spent to sharpen a knife, Jeff just couldn't get the numbers to work.

A few weeks ago, Sam had joked as she reviewed her 'to do' lists and their associated costs, "There's a ton of issues here, issues which won't be easy to solve."

"Assuming we get that far," Jeff added. Tone snarky, he asked, "And who's sharpening the knives, me in the garage?"

Despite the business problems begging for a solution, life added to the problematic minutia. Sam's nursing group was transferred to Mercy Hospital, which lengthened her commute time twenty-five minutes. With the added stress, dealing with new doctors and procedures, she had little energy left to give to the dream.

They started missing their weekly Saturday meetings. Soon, it was implied that neither had any progress to report. No action, no results. Worse, Madison caught an ear infection, which landed them in a pediatric ER for seven hours, followed by multiple doctor visits. As such, they had to cancel her 9th birthday party. With life in the way, they were closer to Uzbekistan than their Unscripted dream.

Back at the kitchen table, Jeff looked up from his sandwich, still chewing, and broke the silence. "The numbers don't work." She paused from her phone, her eyes shifty and unfocused. He mashed his lips and knocked on the table. "Hello? Our business, this knife thingy?"

Sam slowly nodded as if time had stopped, seemingly calculated, her thoughts miles away. Her face hardened, and her blue eyes grayed as if she was looking through Jeff, not at him. She answered monotone and despondent, "Yes… our business."

Jeff instantly noticed the distress telegraphed by her face. Shock, confusion, sadness, but reserved and controlled, as if resigning to fate. The expression seemed oddly familiar. After a moment, he realized it was from the famous Titanic movie. Sam had the same sullen expression the captain gave to a passenger when asked about the sinking boat's fate.

Sam rubbed the back of her neck and then turned back to her smartphone. She fixated her gaze on the looking glass again, as if betrayed by her own reflection. Jeff put his palm on her wrist but said nothing. He sensed something of gravity, something beyond knives, lathes, and custom mailing boxes.

"Samantha," he asked softly, "what's going on?"

She looked up facing him, eyes withdrawn, tears welling. Gently placing her palms on her husband's knees, she pressed her lips and swallowed hard. Hesitation again as her eyes wandered at the wall. She finally spoke.

"I'm pregnant."

THE DESERTION PRINCIPLE

Beware of Curve Balls Hurled from the Desert of Desertion

In many ways, your first customer as an entrepreneur is like your first kiss or your first love. My first customer was Julie from Melbourne, Florida. I remember her name because as my first customer, Julie helped me escape the Desert of Desertion. It was paid not only in money, but water.

The Desertion Principle is an expectation *that your business process will be difficult, and motivation will wane, to the point of quitting.* When it happens, you're lost in the *Desert of Desertion.* The Gods of Mediocrity are attempting to steal your dream. As the name implies, the Desert of Desertion is a phase of intense struggle. It is when you feel your goals are slipping away, or worse, lost. It's when life gets in the way, from a child with a common cold to a hard day at work, to unexpected bills. There is a lot of work ahead and many problems to be solved. Altogether, motivation is sparse, and the dream has been scarred by life's minutiae.

Be warned.

The Desert of Desertion is a rite of passage. Every Unscripted success story has gone through it. And you must as well. The longer your feedback loop[S47] remains disconnected, the tougher the desert is. Regrettably, most who enter this arid land die with their dreams. The Desert of Desertion is a cemetery of unfilled aspirations, and its hell is a lifetime of weekday horrors. If you "try" to be an Unscripted entrepreneur and fail at business once and quit, the Desert thanks you for adding your dream to its tapestry of quitters. You were at milepost one on a forty-mile journey.

From a hanging curve like a pregnancy to a slider like a job loss, curveballs are the Desert's way of testing your mettle. It wants to know if your purpose is strong and your sacrifice worthy. It wants to know if you want it badly enough. It wants to know if *The Book of You*[S2] is a story fit for newspapers or a story fit for the garbage bin. The Desert of Desertion awaits… defend your dream or have it die in the sand.

☑ **KEY CONCEPTS**

- Expect a period called the Desert of Desertion, a phase where the feedback loop is disconnected, motivation sparse, and quitting seems likely.
- The Desert of Desertion is where all dreams die.

THE BASEBALL PRINCIPLE

One Swing Doesn't Make A Season

In 2013 at the age of 33, David Reichart taught himself to make mobile games while he parked cars as a valet[1]. He worked to close his knowledge gap[S20] and expand his skils[P40]. In six months, he built 40 games and found himself in the Desert of Desertion[P57]. Those games only earned about 40 dollars, and asymmetric returns[S21] were nowhere to be found. Color Switch was his 41st game, a game that eventually would break through the desert. It would be downloaded over 200 million times. Good thing David didn't give up after his 40th at-bat.

If you ever played baseball (or softball), you know that one swing at the plate, one at-bat, or one game does not make a good player. Many seasons make a career for the pros—each filled with many good games and many bad ones.

The Baseball Principle states that *one swing at business, or better, multiple swings, does not make you an entrepreneur.* In one game, you might go 0-for-3, popping out and striking out twice. One try is one action, a solitary swing: you register a domain, read a codebook, or write down an idea. An at-bat is you launching a website, placing a Facebook ad, or making a blog post. A full game is the outcome of that action series and how you react to it. Only a season is meaningful: a business executed to real failure or real success.

Success typically demands several seasons, and the level of success in any season can be classified likewise: a single, double, triple, or a home run. The problem is, some quit after the first swing or one at-bat, but most quit after just one game. And your first game will be lousy.

Like baseball, entrepreneurship has a lot of ups and downs, streaks and slumps, wins and losses: you lost $1000 on a bad marketing channel, your manufacturer botches an order, or you cold-called a great new client. Yes, entrepreneurship is bipolar.

So, if the late Joe DiMaggio was your hitting coach, would you quit on

1 - https://venturebeat.com/2018/03/31/after-40-mobile-games-david-reichelt-hit-gold-with-color-switch/

him after a foul ball or a strikeout? After one bad game? Remember, for the entire mathematical system of expected value[S56], asymmetrical returns[S21] and improved probability are dependent on many occurrences; otherwise, randomness will win a short time series.

For instance, losing two coin flips in a row (25 percent chance) would not be unusual. Remember that outcome is neither lucky nor unlucky. But losing all seven calls, well, that's probability .007815, or seven-tenths of a percent. No, you don't need to fail 1000 businesses. But "one try" rarely works, and it won't test inflated expected-values. It's like taking one blindfolded swing at a piñata and expecting to hit it open. Every game David Reichart built, regardless of success or failure, was another flip of the coin which improved his probability for striking leverage.

In better news, failing seasons are much shorter than successful seasons. In two years, I endured six failing seasons. That means I had six seasons of experience and education, making each subsequent season more probable for success. I had a good seventh season that lasted four years, my eighth season seven years, and my ninth and current season, eight years and still going. I'm three for nine (batting .300), and I'd classify all my hits as just singles and doubles. As reported by entrepreneurs on my forum, the average number of business failures before profit is around eight.

Nothing great ever comes from "one try." One try can't lose two hundred pounds and it can't bake a great soufflé. One try is like a drug, a quick dopamine hit of fleeting-feel-good. If you're shopping for a baseball bat, but deep down, you know you're going to be one-and-done, keep the job and save your time. This Unscripted[S9] stuff is not something you try; it's something you live.

☑ KEY CONCEPTS

- Succeeding at entrepreneurship is like baseball: One or two swings at the plate is not enough practice for success, much less competence.

- Your entrepreneurial career should be segregated into at-bats, games, and seasons.

- To take advantage of big expected values, multiple at-bats and games will likely be required.

- Nothing great or lasting comes from "one try."

THE PROBABILITY HACKING STRATEGY

59

Stop Dreaming for Luck, Start Manipulating Probability

While speaking at the 2020 Fastlane Summit, I asked for a volunteer to come up on stage. I'd guess only 20 percent of the room raised their hand. After picking a volunteer, a man came on stage, and I promptly gave him a crisp $50 bill. I told him, "Thank you, that's yours—you can sit down." The audience laughed but was a bit dumbfounded. I then polled the audience to see why only a few volunteered. The answers varied, but three common ones were "uncertainty," "comfort," and "introversion." And this was in a room full of entrepreneurs!

Behind this exercise is a harsh truth: All the reasons why you aren't succeeding are the same reasons why most people did not volunteer. Yet, after giving this man $50 for doing nothing, can you guess how many hands would have gone up if I'd asked for another volunteer? I'm betting near 100 percent—all because uncertainty disappeared and probabilities became visible. Did the man who got the free $50 get lucky, or did he just manipulate probability by raising his hand?

Here's another way of looking at it. Suppose I offer you $5 million dollars to correctly call a coin flip. And you lose. I'm guessing you'd curse yourself unlucky. This type of missed opportunity would sting for a long, long time. Now let's assume that I give you another chance to call the coin flip. And you win! Except you don't win $50, or $5 million, you win a measly dollar. Now, be honest: Since you won, would you now label yourself as lucky? I'm guessing this pyrrhic victory wouldn't change your unlucky viewpoint of losing the earlier $5 million dollar coin-flip, if anything, it probably salts the wound.

Yet, in both cases, the probability of calling the flip was exactly the same. The only difference between the two flips was the reward and the emotions tied to the outcome. In other words, *despite identical probabilities, luck will be felt when there is a significant outcome.* Put another way, luck is emotional, probability is logical.

In the lottery, one winner won $10 million, and 10 million people lost. Neither the winner nor losers were lucky or unlucky, but mere participants in a probability event. The ten million losers don't curse themselves "unlucky" because they know the probability is one in a gazillion. But undoubtedly, the winner will be cast as lucky. Someone had to win, and the guy who does gets the luck label. As rewards rise for any probabilistic event, so do the emotions. Like emotions, luck is ethereal and only exists as a mental construct, a human fabrication as much as humans invented Monday through Friday as presumptive workdays. For many people, luck is a fancy word that explains a significant result with unknown, often low odds.

The only thing that truly exists is probability. The fact is, if you can influence probability, you can influence outcomes and the appearance of luck.

Think of it this way. Every day you drive, there is a real probability that you will get into an accident and die. Let's say it's 1 in 1,000,000. But today you choose to hack probability and drive drunk. Congrats, you just manipulated probability, which now stands at 1 in 100,000. Further, you choose to drive twice the speed limit. Wham: Probability moves again; now it's 1 in 1000. But that isn't enough. You're a master probability hacker and choose to run every red light you encounter. Suddenly probability is 1 in 3.

Is luck anywhere? Or just probability? Probability is like oxygen or radio waves—it exists but stays hidden. Despite this, you can hack probability. And if you can hack the odds, you can rig the game and summon the appearance of luck.

Here's how: Every choice you make hacks probability, either positively or negatively. When you make the right choices, day after day, probability continually improves. At some point, low probability becomes a fair probability. Make the wrong choices, and you hack probability against you. In either case, luck will be blamed, and emotions will boil.

As an entrepreneur, you have this magnificent power to move probability, including the outcomes that they represent. Think about that for a moment. You can manipulate the variables in this game!

Going back to our hypothetical value game[S56], you can 1) dictate the opportunities you pursue (the potential reward via TAM), and you can 2) dictate your effort as long as you're willing to pay the game fee. Probabilities are improved by playing more. More coin flips! Remember, the entrepreneur who shoots once and gives up does not take advantage of larger expected values or probability manipulation. *I tried the DeMarco CENTS methods, and it doesn't work! He sucks!*

The problem with many entrepreneurs is they're stepping into the batter's box and swinging once for little rewards. Yes, there are many variables you cannot control, which also affect probability. No biggie, that's life. But probability hacking is NOT about controlling the uncontrollable, but controlling what you CAN.

- You can control hard work in a system with potential leverage.
- You can control the industry you work within.
- You can use CENTS as a framework, or not.
- You can control how you spend your time.
- You can control how many "tries" you input into the system.
- You can control consumption-based money-chasing versus value-adding.
- You can control where you live within your country, sometimes outside as well.
- You can control how your mind thinks and how it classifies events.
- You can control working in a system where non-zero probabilities are eliminated, and favorable EV bets are made.
- You can control how you regard luck and its probabilities.
- You can control how many principles in this book you follow.

While you might not see the odds improve like a flashing neon sign, they do. It's freaking mathematical wizardry, and your choices are the magic wand. In the simplest terms, think of it this way: Great business opportunity selection gives you better rewards and outcomes. The marketplace's coin-flip fairy isn't offering $1,000 to win a flip; she's offering $10 million.

- ✔ Great choices give you two chances to call a coin flip.
- ✔ Average work gets you one.
- ✔ Laziness gets you zero.

Make choices that give you the mathematical edge. The only law that matters is mathematics. Pursue opportunities with high EV outcomes[S56], so effort pays asymmetrically[S21], eliminate zero probabilities [P16], and hack probability[S59] by flipping coins more often. You'll change your outcomes. Business is like me standing on stage handing out cash—you know raising your hand pays off. Raise it enough times and luck will call on you.

☑ KEY CONCEPTS

- Every choice you make hacks probability, either for better or for worse.

225

- Luck is emotional and abstract; probability is concrete and logical.
- As rewards rise for any probabilistic event, so do the emotions.
- Probability hacking is about changing the odds regarding things you can control, like how you spend your time, the opportunities chosen, and the friends you keep.
- Probability exists, even though you can't see it.
- Better choices give you better probabilities, and hence, induces luck.

RESOLVE, STEELED
SATURDAY, JUNE 17TH, 2017 - 1:12 AM
(5 hours later)

After hearing Sam's pregnancy confession, Jeff lurched from his seat. Not in shock, but fear. His wife's glum reporting twisted his heart in worry. After Sam reeled back, he hung over her and gently placed his hands on her cheeks. Breathlessly, he huffed, "Oh my God, is the baby okay?"

Sam sat silent, her face telegraphing bewilderment. After she removed her husband's hands from her cheeks, she shook her head and said, "Jeff, I'm not even six weeks in. I haven't seen a doctor yet." She hesitated, her face softening as if a backpack of bricks had left her shoulders. Confused, she swayed her head and looked up at him. "You're not upset I'm pregnant?"

Jeff's face returned the confusion. Then, "So your... depression..."—he waggled his fingers at her—"is because you think I'll be upset?"

She proffered her "red-handed" smirk, a look Jeff had seen many times. Jeff called it red-handed because Sam had the worst poker face on the planet. Whenever she fibbed or had to admit a mistake, Sam's smirk would not only give it away, but her face would flush crimson. When she brought Bella home as a pound-puppy, she insisted it was temporary. In her words, "We're only going to be foster parents until she finds a good home." Insert a red-handed smile, and Jeff knew that Bella was staying.

When Jeff caught her pale skin darken red, his smile faded. He charged, "Wait a second, was this something you planned behind my back? I thought you were still on birth control."

Her eyes flared shock, and she stood. "No, no!" she asserted.

"No, you aren't on birth control!?"

"I meant no, I didn't plan it. And no, I'm not on birth control anymore. When we stopped making love years ago, I didn't renew my prescription. It's only this year that we"—she hesitated—"well, you know. Started going at it like two college kids again."

Jeff sank to the kitchen chair. He peered up and asked, "So what's this all about? You've been walking around here like someone killed your puppy. You should be happy; we've always wanted two children."

227

Sam sat again and explained. Surprisingly, no tears flowed.

Jeff understood, and the mood turned from helplessness to happiness.

Sam admitted that she'd thought another baby would be the death of their dreams. She feared Jeff would insist on playing it safe and revert to the status quo, cowering in fear back to a Scripted existence, the one where lovemaking and flirtation were not, well, part of the script. And it had saddened her for weeks, leaving her pale and without optimism. She thought it was over: their marriage, their business, their dream, and their sanity. Life would once again relapse to a weekday hell punctuated by a weekend bribe. They'd become caretakers of their kids and nothing more, other than hoping their kids would grow up to live boldly different.

Jeff made himself a margarita and gave his wife one—sans tequila, of course. They toasted, and then Jeff reassured her, "I'm in this Unscripted business till death do us part," he said chummily. "Or I die trying."

Turns out, expecting another baby steeled their resolve. Before they got married, they'd agreed on two children. But now, they wanted freedom, the freedom to build a sane existence inside an insane world.

On Sunday morning, they conferenced and reaffirmed their weekly business meeting.

Jeff looked at his wife. She was wearing a pink Bulls jersey and matching pink headband which pulled her blond hair back. She was out of her dingy pajamas, which meant her mood had improved. The summer sunshine glowed through the window and illuminated her face, her bereft cloak melted away.

Jeff opened Neve and presented the business numbers to Sam. After reviewing it, they agreed to drop the knife idea. Even if they solved the logistical issues, the numbers didn't seem to work. And it felt as if they were creating themselves a job. Jeff volunteered, "I say we go back to the drawing board, find a better idea."

Sam massaged her chin deep in thought. Then, "But maybe our idea is fine, we're just giving up too early. Or not solving the problems we're facing. We're supposed to be problemologists, but we haven't solved any problems." She hesitated then remarked, "I was so sure we were on to something—I hate sharpening knives."

Jeff shook his head. "No, you saw the numbers. It just isn't going to work." He lifted up Neve to his face. "I'm going to loop through my notebook again at the ideas we had. In the meantime, let's keep our eyes peeled for anything that might work. Remember," he said, "opportunity hides in language like 'I wish' or 'I want' "

"And 'I hate,'" Sam added.

Jeff nodded. "We've just got to keep our ears peeled."

With a flowery smile, Sam concurred, "It's good to be back in business."

THE NAPKIN STRATEGY

Run the Numbers or Have Them Run You

Recently an inventor visited the forum and unveiled his product. It was an apparatus that stored bath scales on the wall. For folks with small bathrooms, the product appeared to solve a need. It struck up some mixed reviews, some likes, some dislikes. But what the group did agree on was its price point: its relative-value wasn't worth $99, its price point, but more like $19 or $29. Looking back—and this is my personal opinion (I'd love to be wrong)—this inventor probably shouldn't have proceeded with the idea unless the product could be produced at an appealing price point AND provided enough profit for the inventor.

Here are the numbers you should run to determine if any idea is worth pursuing.

- The sales price—the relative- and perceived-value at which the consumer will need to buy. Is this price realistic based on the value received? Or is it an arbitrary price designed to make you a profit, but few sales? The former should set the price, not the latter.

- The manufacturing price—the cost to produce one unit.

- The net profit, per unit. (Sales price - manufacturing cost)

- The customer acquisition cost—the cost to find one customer via marketing.

- Is the TAM large enough to boost expected value?

- What are the initial costs to go from idea to market to your first sale? Is this reasonable with your financial situation?

- The lifetime value of a new customer. Do they buy over and over? Or just once?

- Are there channels/mediums to reach your audience with an offer?

You'd be surprised how many entrepreneurs visit my forum seeking business riches yet never run the numbers. Is your effort worth the potential profit? Enough to pay the bills? Change your life? Does the time you're investing warrant the potential payoff? Or are you just building yourself a job?

In the case of our scale apparatus, the numbers simply don't work well on paper. Yes, the product might solve a need, but it doesn't do so in a meaningful way that BOTH gives the customer value and gives the entrepreneur a significant profit. One must be sacrificed for the other. Worse, once purchased, the customer (currently a family unit) is unlikely to buy more. It's a "one and done" product.

Remember, entrepreneurship is tough, from inventing to CENTS-based enterprises to a pizza joint on the corner. If you're creating a specialized-unit[S18] and a business system, ascertain that the numbers are working for you, not against you.

☑ **KEY CONCEPTS**

- Before pursuing any business, you should run an extensive analysis of the numbers implicit in the business model: sales price, manufacturing and acquisition costs, TAM, ad mediums, etc.

- A great business idea isn't a great idea if the numbers cannot induce leverage and asymmetric returns.

THE OPTIMUM EXPERIENCE STRATEGY

Select a Business Model that Optimizes the Customer Experience

61

In early 2007, Netflix started offering online streaming as it began to "adjust" its business model away from mailing DVDs. As technology and bandwidth improved, it became clear that mailing physical DVDs was an unsustainable business model. Had the company not shifted, Netflix would have failed like Blockbuster. Speaking of failure, did you know in 2000 Netflix offered itself as an acquisition to Blockbuster for a mere $50 million? They declined.

Anyhow, a great business idea strapped with the wrong business model, or soon-to-be wrong, is destined to fail. You're in the right neighborhood, but at the wrong house. And business models can be great in one year, but suck in another. This was the predicament I found in my own business. As consumer expectations changed, I knew I wasn't offering the optimum customer experience— the key to uncovering the optimum business model.

Whenever you're solving problems with your business, start with the customer experience as if you were a "snap-your-fingers" genie. If money and resources were unlimited, what would the best customer experience look like? When you work backward from the best customer experience, it can help you uncover the right business model. Question is, does that business model work with the numbers[S60]? Sometimes it works, sometimes it doesn't.

Let's use the knife sharpening business as an example.

I don't know about you, but I can't see myself packing a bunch of knives in a box and dropping them in the mail. Yes, dull blades are a problem, and I hate sharpening them. That's the right neighborhood. But packing them in a box and waiting a week or so to get them back? That rings like the wrong house.

If we work back from the optimal customer experience, how would that look and feel? What is the most convenient customer experience to have dull knives sharpened? Does it seem logical from a functional perspective for people to send knives in the mail? What knives do you use while they're gone? Sure, these are challenges to solve, but are they worth solving? Would you wait a week for your car's tires to be replaced?

The answer to these "problems" might be a personal home visit and a roving mobile unit. The technician arrives at your home, sharpens the dull knives in his mobile van, and then returns them a mere hour later.

Once you identify the optimal experience, you can then work backward on the problems presented by that experience. Can you sharpen knives in a van? What are the challenges? What is the price point and the cost of performance, from labor to vehicle expenses? How many can you do in a day, and can it be scaled with multiple vans, multiple regions, and multiple states?

The optimal customer experience (and their solved problems) exposes the numbers and will tell you immediately if the numbers work or not. If they do, start solving problems.

☑ **KEY CONCEPTS**

- You can have a great idea based on needs and problems, but the business model for executing that idea can still suck.

- To identify a business model, reverse engineer the solution evolving from the best customer experience and problem solve from there.

- Once a business model is identified from an optimal customer experience, it must also be mathematically feasible to profit and scale.

LOVE WORKS AS WELL AS HATE

THURSDAY, JUNE 22, 2017 - 2:45 PM
(5 days later)

*M*eet tonight instead of Sat???

The text was from Jeff. Moments later, another chime. *We need to chat ASAP.*

Sam texted back. I work at 11. Can't we just wait until Saturday?

Yes, I know. But this can't wait.

Sam texted back a thumbs-up. She wondered about the urgency. Did he lose another $1,400 on some harebrained T-shirt business? For the next three hours, she couldn't relax. Her mind ran wild with all kinds of speculation. She figured Jeff had made another impetuous unilateral decision and was going to lobby some position.

Sam situated herself at the kitchen table and waited for Jeff's arrival. She only had to wait three minutes as he was early. After Jeff galloped to the top of the stairs, he regarded his wife and sat immediately. His tie was still snug on his neck, his suit jacket slung over his shoulder. He dropped his briefcase and immediately sat down next to her—no bathroom break, no refrigerator detour for a snack, no tie loosening, nothing. He smirked, pulling out Neve and a pencil. Frenetically, he started thumbing through its pages.

Relief washed over Sam when she realized her husband was excited, not distressed. She asked, "Well? What couldn't wait until the weekend?"

Jeff shifted to face his wife, nervously tapping the pencil on the table. He said, "Remember DeMarco said opportunities hide in language. Things like 'I hate' or 'I'm tired,' phrases of dissatisfaction. For the last week I've been busting my balls, hoping to hear something, anything. But I heard nothing." He peeked back at Neve then continued, pace quicker. "So then I started thinking about the past year. Was there a hate I missed there? At work, in life, here around the townhouse? My thoughts drifted to Thanksgiving dinner, the one last year when my family was here."

Sam interrupted. "You mean last year's Thanksgiving travesty when you got into a debate with your dad about Trump, then you argued for an hour about the Cubs/White Sox rivalry?"

Jeff laughed. "Yes, but I recall it wasn't just about politics. Or baseball. When my mom forgot you were vegan and you refused to eat the turkey stuffing, you embarrassed me and said food jammed in a dead bird's carcass wasn't appetizing."

She winced. Jeff continued, "Anyway, the tension was so thick you could slice it. And then I remembered something about that night because it was brutally cold out, something that stood out against all the negativity."

He rocked his seat forward and then asked, "What if opportunity isn't just in the language of hate, but in the language of love? And what if that love could solve a hate?" His eyes flickered with anticipation, now expecting Sam to figure out his cryptic story.

"Think, Samantha! Amongst all the family bickering, what was loved at the Thanksgiving we hosted?"

Sam narrowed her brow in thought. She stared at the floor, trying to reflect back on a stressful family night that she wanted forgotten. A moment turned into minutes. And then, like a subtle knock at the door, it occurred to her. As she remembered and put it together, the knock became a pounding. Then, like an avalanche, it broke through. She lifted her head, her eyes now as wide as Jeff's. "Oh my God, you're right. How could I not see it?"

She shifted back in her chair and stared hard at the ceiling in disbelief. She confirmed what Jeff alluded to. "Everyone loved the soup we had before dinner. Your parents, your sister and her family, my cousin, they all wanted the recipe, and heck, they're not even vegan." She scratched at her temple in more thought, then added, "People at the hospital love my soup too, again, people who aren't even vegan."

"You mean Janice?"

"Yes, even Janice." She turned to Jeff swiftly. "And you love my soup and you're as finicky as anyone." She rubbed her mouth, eyes sparkling.

"Yes, but this is more than non-vegans liking your soup," Jeff added. "You know how long you've been complaining about no vegan soups at the store? Years! And then when you want it, you complain about having to make it?"

She affirmed. "True. It's a pain in the ass." Then, "Hey, there's that negative language DeMarco talked about."

They both flashed self-satisfied smiles at each other until Jeff's melted away. Instantly his whole demeanor changed as if he'd just learned his winning lottery ticket was for the wrong week.

"What is it?" Sam asked.

"Maybe it isn't such a good idea." He reflected. "What if plant-based food is just a fad? Hot today, but cold tomorrow?"

Sam vigorously shook her head. "It isn't. I've been vegetarian most of my life and vegan for at least five. I only see it growing. It will be mainstream in a few years."

Jeff mocked, "But you're biased. Of course, you think that." He nodded at her and then continued, "I'm married to a vegan, and I have no intention of giving up my burgers or pizza."

She pursed her lips. "I know, but many people like me go vegan because of the animal atrocities. Then there's climate and environmental reasons, and of course, the health benefits."

"The health aspect is debatable," he said. "There was a Joe Rogan podcast and—"

She interrupted, "I know"—she shrugged—"but the animal and climate issues are stone cold facts." She paused and let him process, his mood lightening. The night-shift nurse continued, "And besides, who's in better shape with a better lipid panel, me or you?" She cinched the two inches of belly fat careening over his belt.

He sneered, "Aw c'mon, that's not fair."

She smiled. "Anyway, half the young girls I work with at the hospital are either vegetarian or vegan. It's a trend being driven by younger generations, and I expect it to continue."

Jeff sighed, "You sure? This is a big decision for us."

"I'd bet my unborn child on it."

"That sure, huh?"

She cast a self-assured smirk. "Absolutely."

Jeff's smile returned. "Well, that decides it. This could be our gold mine. If people who aren't vegans love your soup, can you imagine what your fellow vegans will think? We've found a need, and you have a delicious solution."

Jeff quickly turned to Neve and flipped its pages frantically toward Sam. He confessed, "I didn't sleep last night and got nothing done at work today." Sam saw a colorful menagerie filled with graphs, pictures, addresses, telephone numbers, and other indecipherable scribbles. He grinned slyly and declared, "And I've never been so excited about something vegan in my life."

THE JOCKSTRAP JANE STRATEGY

Don't Wait to be Starving to Feed an Appetite

62

If you don't know Chip Wilson, he's probably the most loved man on the planet. And get this, he's loved by other men. And the rest don't know who he is. You see, Mr. Wilson is Lululemon's founder, the company who pioneered "yoga pants" way back in 1998. I haven't read his recent biography, but I'm going to take a wild guess that Mr. Wilson is not an avid user of his product, stretchy black tights.

In short, you don't have to use your specialized-unit of relative-value; you only have to be sure of its worth to other people. Namely, feeding an appetite doesn't require you to share the same hunger. *One who sells a bottle of water doesn't need to be thirsty himself.*

The world's insatiable appetite for wants, needs, and desires are yours for the filling. To quench others' thirsts, you only need to see and understand their thirst. You don't have to share it. Nowhere in the entrepreneurial rule book states that you have to be an avid user of your product. Yes, you must believe in your product and its worldly value-skew, but you don't necessarily have to be its own customer. It's like an atheist who sells thousands of dollars in Bibles. Toast the champagne glass—true story. The founder of Keurig K-Cups, John Sylvan? He recently reported that he doesn't use them. Me? I spent ten years in the limo business. Know how many times I've rented a limousine? Once. You can sell pet gear and own no pets. Opportunities hold no prejudices.

Relative-value[S26] doesn't care if you love an industry, share a gender, or use the product yourself. Bob can sell brassieres, and Jane can sell jockstraps. Let the market sort it out while you roll in the dough.

☑ KEY CONCEPTS

- You don't have to be an avid or "passionate" user of your product or service.

- You only have to be passionate about the results of your effort: the value you provide to your customers, the difference you make for the world, and your family.

THE ENGAGEMENT STRATEGY

Engage with the World and Opportunities Will Never Be a Problem

Since becoming an author more than a decade ago, I've come up with hundreds of ideas and opportunities in the book publishing space. Many of those ideas would later come to life as other entrepreneurs took advantage of the same voids I saw. Likewise, since adopting a plant-based lifestyle, the same thing happens today: I see dozens of opportunities in the plant-based industry ripe for solutions. In fact, I'm so flush with ideas that I have my own "Neve" notebook filled with them.

If you want an endless book of ideas waiting to be exploited, start engaging the world. Get out of the house. Take on a new hobby, a new job, a new purpose, or a new project. Anytime you engage the world, you set yourself up to spot ideas. Every venture I've undertaken occurred because I was engaged—from jobs to market interactions (with multiple failures) to engagement in specialized and observable knowledge. When people complain about having no ideas, it means they are stuck in their *own* bubble, and not engaging the *real* world. In short, you don't spot ideas sitting on your couch stuffing your face with Pringles while watching Netflix. You don't spot ideas sleeping until noon and watching YouTube videos all afternoon. The Trotmans' discovered several ideas (both of them legitimate opportunities) simply because they observed their own struggles. Dull knives suck. Having no plant-based soups on store shelves sucks. Get out into the world and see what sucks and what needs fixing. As Captain Picard of Star Trek fame says, *Engage!*

☑ KEY CONCEPTS

- New ideas or opportunities are unearthed through any type of engagement, jobs, hobbies, or otherwise.
- You can't spot ideas or opportunities confined in a bubble.

THE CINDERELLA PRINCIPLE

A Business with an Expiration Date Is Not a Good Business

64

What would you say if I told you I was going to start a leg warmer business? How about a business focused on BMX bikes, lava lamps, or blow-up chairs? You'd probably tell me I was crazy. And yet, entrepreneurs chased these fads as they peaked and then later plummeted. Newsflash: If you're selling a fad today, you won't be selling one tomorrow. Fads die, as do their businesses. The Cinderella Principle holds that *a business based on a fad has an expiration date because they have a self-extinguishing demand.* Once the clock strikes midnight, the company turns into a pumpkin.

Starting a business is challenging enough. Handicap yourself with a Cinderella business, and you strap yourself to a TAM[S53] that is naturally designed to shrink and eventually expire. If your total market size is ten million people, by next year it might be half. The next, nearly gone. Think of it as the sands in an hourglass. Would you consider a similar declining industry that exhibited the same type of behavior? Of course not, but fads get a pass.

For example, if you were exclusively selling BMX racing bikes in the eighties (think *E.T.*) you'd be out of business by the nineties. Each year would be worse than the prior. Waiting forty years for its resurgence is not an option. You either reinvent into a different line that might appeal to your customers, or you shut down. Particularly, teenagers who dropped their BMX bikes in favor of the next new thing probably wouldn't be interested in your shop's new line of cruiser and tandem bikes. As with most reinventions, you're starting over with a different audience.

So how do you know if you're targeting a fad or something with longevity? The best method for identifying fads, trends, or mega-trends is to identify the trend's utility-value[S26] and its cultural relativity. Will culture (government/media) support the trend through time? And will that evolution change society? Or is the utility-value static and a function of taste or trend? Think cars over horses. Email over postal mail.

In our fictitious story, plant-based food (or meat replacements) is considered a more environmentally friendly food source. There's an argument that culture (and politicians) will support its evolution. Of course, this is debatable, but what isn't debatable is that better environmental options (as well as better health options) are a value-skew. What isn't debatable is that there is no "humane" way to kill a sentient being that doesn't want to be killed. As more people awaken to this spiritual enlightenment, it's more likely that Sam's assumptions about the trend are correct.

Fashion always falls into the category of static utility-value—if men (or women!) suddenly find long lumberjack beards grotesquely ugly, the beard businesses will find themselves with a fast-shrinking market.

Mood rings, fidget spinners, and fanny packs might have made their original entrepreneurs rich, but those who came later chased fewer buyers with fewer dollars.

An Atkins diet center might seem like a great business opportunity at the apex of its fad, but the clock is ticking, and the pumpkin is ripening. Lock yourself onto a Cinderella business and you'll need to go beyond the change dyad[S42]; you have to reinvent and, most likely, start over. Don't make business harder than it already is by slapping an egg-timer on your business.

☑ KEY CONCEPTS

- Fads, or short-lived trends, are poor business opportunities unless you are the innovator or the instigator of such fads.

- A Cinderella Business is a business that has an expiration date based on the trendiness of the fad.

- A trend's utility-value and its cultural support will determine whether a trend is expiring or a valid consumer shift that is worthy of investment.

IN THE HEAT OF THE NIGHT
THURSDAY, JUNE 29TH, 2017 - 8:41 PM
(7 days later)

W hat are you reading?" Jeff voiced loudly from the kitchen while pour-
ing himself a cold beer.

Three fans buzzed around him, one on the kitchen island, one in the living room on the coffee table, and one in the door of Madison's room, who
now was hopefully asleep. Their air conditioning had stopped working two
days ago, and their townhouse was now an oven. A humid 94 degrees in the
concrete suburbs of Chicago might as well have been 110.

"Yo!" Jeff waved his beer in the air. "What you reading?"

Sam was on the couch, nearly naked. Not because she was in a seductive
mood, but the native Idahoan always ran hot. From behind, Jeff could see the
sweat on her neck. He was surprised she was on the couch, much less reading. For Sam, this kind of oppressive heat was worse than a visit to the rodeo.

It was time for their weekly business meeting, and Jeff was hoping she'd
suggest calling a sitter and leaving for a cooler spot. While a *Top Chef* episode softly played on the TV, Jeff stood up and walked in front of her, seating
himself on the coffee table in front of the fan.

With her airflow blocked, she nodded curiously. "Something wrong with
the couch?"

"I asked you what you were reading. Can't you hear me?"

She glimpsed at the TV, and then at the fan that Jeff was now blocking.
"Sorry, I didn't."

"I figured." He gestured at the book. "Doesn't look like your usual femme
fatale." She held up it up and waved the book as if Jeff knew what it was. He
lifted an eyebrow. "Employer Law for Entrepreneurs?"

She sighed, tossing the book down next to Jeff, still perched on the coffee table. "You should read it. I haven't had this much fun since reading
Deuteronomy in Sunday School."

Jeff smiled in admiration and then regarded the room as if it were a sauna.
"Are we meeting here?"

For the last three twilight-crosses, they'd plotted their new venture: a plant-based soup business. Their hope? Get it on every grocery shelf in the next five years. To Sam's surprise, Jeff had already done a lot of research. His plan made sense to her, and this time, the initial numbers worked out. Moreover, Jeff had an answer for her every question, her every concern. But one still nagged her.

She shifted up from the couch closer to her husband, who still sat on the edge of the table. Sweat dripped from her nose. Sam ignored her husband's question about the meeting location. Her face etched concern, she asked, "As I said, I love the vegan soup idea, but I have to wonder..." She paused to wipe her face. "Do you expect me to slave in a hot kitchen while making big vats of soup?"

Jeff furrowed his forehead. "Kind of like you expected me to slave in the garage sharpening knives?"

She simpered embarrassingly. Jeff put his hand on her knee and reassured, "To answer your question, no, not for long. Only to get us started with the right recipes. Eventually we'll partner with a co-packer. A food processor. They manufacture the soup; we merely give them the recipe. Or I should say, you give them the recipe."

A dead stare didn't soften her face. "Co-packer? What's that?"

"A co-packer manufacturers food on behalf of other companies."

She quickly followed, "But how do I know if canning my soup would work? What about shelf-life? Do I need to know anything about preservatives?"

Jeff answered surely, voice confident as if he had done it a hundred times. "Most co-packers have consultants on staff. And I already found two food chemists that can be hired by the hour just in case our co-packer doesn't have a consultant."

"So you already found one of these co-packers?"

"Actually, I found five. We just need to decide which fit our needs—you know, cost, ingredient selection, minimum order quantities that kind of stuff."

"Five? How on earth did you—"

"Google. Started with searching for 'food processors' but ended up with nothing but Cuisinarts and Vitamixes. After two hours down a rabbit hole I learned a ton. Everything you could possibly want to know is out there. You just need to know how to search for it."

"Okay, so how in the world are we going to sell it? What do we know about soup? Or food merchandising?"

Jeff grabbed his ragged notebook off the coffee table. Sam noticed the iconic Steve Jobs photo with his finger on his chin covered the old Chicago Cubs decal. Her husband flipped to a page and pointed. Sam spotted a bunch of numbered items but couldn't read the text. She shrugged but said nothing.

"That's our marketing plan. There's a ton of ways we can reach our market."

He beamed. "And a ton of money awaits." He rubbed his palms together like a cunning scientist who just found a cure to cancer.

Her stern expression finally melted into a smile.

She thought, *Nice, he did his homework.* Jeff's take-charge attitude rattled lose another fond memory long buried by diapers and late shifts, a memory that memorialized the week when Sam fell in love and knew Jeff was marriage material.

It was 2003.

In a stubborn streak of take-charge spontaneity, Jeff took the reins and surprised her with a spring-break trip to South Padre Island. Not a bad idea in spirit, but a bad idea when you're driving a twelve-year-old Pontiac. Long story short, their car died in Gum Springs, Arkansas, with a ruptured oil pan gasket, and with it, their dreams of beaches and margaritas. Instead, they spent the next three days at a Fairview Motel that doubled as a hair salon, which, mind you, was in the middle of fixing a broken water main. Jackhammers woke them up every morning. Water pressure drizzled like a leaky faucet. To get their car back on the road, an auto mechanic tried to sell Jeff a new transmission. Worse, their motel neighbor in Room 2C... well, let's just say Sam didn't know that two tattooed teardrops meant that they were bunking next to a two-time murderer. Still, Jeff remained in control. Showed no fear and never angered or showed frustration. Despite the situation, Sam felt 100 percent safe. After four days, they were back at DePaul, and Sam knew Jeff was "the one."

Even in the hot townhouse, Jeff's forehead was dry. Once again, calm with no fear. Her husband was finally beating back at life; suddenly, the broken air conditioners, the dreadful Sunday nights, and the old Corolla weren't winning. And for the first time in years, she too felt as if her dream was an actual probability. Indeed, not a sure thing, but better than five or ten percent perhaps? She asked, her voice giddy, "Okay, RyRy, so what's next?"

He fired her a slick grin and then raised his hands as if to signal victory. "The fun part! You get in the kitchen and start making soup. I figured we should start with three recipes. So start there." He gestured to the stove. "Just do what you normally do but record your ingredients and their amounts. We will need several formulas."

She huffed, shaking her head. "I hope you don't expect me to cook until the A/C is fixed. This townhouse is like a sweat lodge."

"The repair guy comes tomorrow."

"Great," she said, standing up, glistening. She slinked over to the bedroom door and looked back at her husband, still planted on the coffee table. "I need a cold shower," she whispered. "Care to join your pregnant wife?"

THE CRITICAL PATH STRATEGY

Identify the Path to Your First Customer and Light the Roadmap for Action

65

Problem: Your car is stranded in the desert with a flat tire, and you don't know how to fix it. If you could instantly download knowledge into your brain (aka The Matrix), what would you download? *How to Bake a Soufflé?* or *How to Fix A Flat?* This flat-tire problem is relevant when it comes to planning and action. Ultimately, entrepreneurs fail because they drip-feed themselves with information that has nothing to do with the problems they're facing. Instead of downloading *How to Fix a Flat*, they're assimilating other knowledge, knowledge that doesn't get them moving. Soufflé knowledge, while perhaps interesting, doesn't solve the immediate problem.

Like our flat tire, if you're led by the need or the problem you are solving, you'll always know what to do next. And you will never get lost. When the tire blows, you assess the problem immediately. Instantly, you go into problem-solving mode, and "What do I do next?" becomes clear: You exit traffic, pull to the shoulder, and change the tire. Or you call Triple-A or your friend for help. You don't sit on the shoulder of the road and google "Is a subscription to AAA worth it?" or "What cars are more reliable than a Chevy Malibu?" *Your problem defines your next course of action.*

Without a defined problem, the solution (and its roadmap) will also remain undefined. This is why aspiring entrepreneurs binge books while never doing anything. They never get started, launch a business, or make a profit. Why? They fail to put themselves in the face of a problem, either externally in the market, or internally with a deficient talent.

Another common question I hear from readers is, "Where do I start?" or "What do I do next?" It leaves me wondering if I've failed as an author or if the reader failed comprehension. When you are a problemologist[P30] looking to solve problems, improve processes, and offer relative-value[S26], what to do next becomes crystal clear.

- I'd like to create a pure, all-natural supplement line that doesn't use artificial colors, sweeteners, or chemicals.
- I'd like to invent a gluten and dairy-free pizza line.

- I want to write a book exposing the charlatanism of Scripted finance.
- I'd like to start a sports bar with an ancient Roman theme.

As soon as you identify your relative-value objectives and their value-skews[S32], the roadmap appears. It is your GPS. And just like any roadmap highlighting how to get from mediocrity to Unscription, it will have many permutations of streets, roads, and freeways. If you're not paying attention to the problem at hand, it's easy to get lost or go on unnecessary detours.

Simply put, the correct course of action is the shortest path to your first customer—*the critical path*. Doing so highlights all the dots that need connecting, and maybe some that do not. Do you really need a Delaware corporation, a richly appointed mahogany desk with a red leather pin cushion chair, and a nice set of letterhead on woven linen stationery?

It is your job to connect each dot that matters while ignoring the rest. One dot might be hiring a CAD designer, another sourcing manufacturing, another learning how to market to your target audience. Because connecting the right dots might take days, weeks, or even months, you must eliminate the ones that aren't on the critical path. Does this action get you closer to your first customer? Identify the relative-value you seek to provide, and you'll identify the roadmap—the critical path—the next steps, and the right steps.

☑ KEY CONCEPTS

- If you're led by the problems you seek to solve, you'll always know what to do next and rarely get lost.
- If you don't know "where to start" then you have already failed.
- The critical path, which is like GPS navigation, is the shortest distance between your idea and your first customer.

THE RIGHT BOOK STRATEGY

Read the Book that Solves Problems, Not the Book that Wastes Time

Guess the most common question at my forum? There are two that stand out. The first is always about finding ideas. The second is about books, namely, "What's the next best book I should read after reading *Unscripted*?" Hopefully, the next two minutes will stop this insanity.

The answer to the "next best book" is "Depends."

As an entrepreneur staring a business, you will face an endless array of problems. If you're using the 3A Method, it will give you a good clue about the book you should read next. When people ask me what book I'm reading, they expect to hear the latest bestseller or the current month's trendy book pushed by the mainstream. That is never my answer because I'm busy solving problems. And problems demand more specific silos of knowledge and action. For instance, the last three books I read had nothing to do with entrepreneurship or finance. They were all fictional thrillers because that's the side project I'm working on. Because I never published a thriller, my problem—how do I write thrillers—started with me reading fiction. Not just for the story, but for the style, structure, and plot.

Instead of mindlessly reading books for the sake of reading them, read them to solve your front-facing problems. *Whatever problem stands in your way—the book with the solution is the book you need to read!* Read the book that moves you up the mountain. You can't climb mile two until you climb mile one. What's the best persuasive language to use in advertising campaigns? How do I leverage sales funnels, onboarding processes, and email marketing? How do I hire good employees? Your answer—your solutions—are found in books and material scattered across the internet.

If you're not facing problems (yet), the same concept applies. Read whatever moves you forward on life's journey. If the book isn't a business builder, make it a character builder. For me, such books are on world history, health and nutrition, and meditation.

What you know today is never enough for the problems of tomorrow. And when you opt to be an entrepreneur, you opt to have a ton of problems. Books solve problems, but it must be the right book. Read the book that fixes the flat tire and advances your 1/5/10 Planasy[S12].

- Stop reading books for the sake of reading books.

- The best book you should read next is the one that will solve the problem that blocks your progress.

- The 3A method exposes the subject matter of next book you should read.

- What you know today is never enough to solve tomorrow's problems.

THE ACTION-FAKING PRINCIPLE

Stop Sharpening Needles, Start Moving Them

67

When I was in my early twenties, I was failing at business often. Interestingly, with each business failure, I had to throw away thousands of newly minted business cards. My pattern back then was simple: get a business idea and then make business cards—even if the business idea didn't need business cards.

The Action-Faking Principle asserts that *any action or expenditure that doesn't move you closer to the critical path is an action-fake.* Namely, you're not moving the needle, you're just sharpening it. When a sewing needle is moving, it's knitting itself closer to a completed quilt. On the other hand, while sharpening the needle might help in some small indiscernible way, it gets you no closer to the quilt.

The fact is most failed entrepreneurs are needle sharpeners. Instead of moving the needle and getting closer to a quilt worthy of sale, they're busy grinding the lathe for a sharper needle.

Instead of focusing on the critical path[S65], they're focused on ancillary activities that serve other purposes: building confidence, sparking motivation, or inflating egos.

Action beats activity. And the only step worth taking is the one that moves the needles found within the critical-path. If it doesn't, it's an *action-fake*. Action-fakes are activities that lie outside of the critical-path. Action-faking can be many things, from trivial busywork to data research to reading books—none of which gets you deeper into the critical-path. Such "action-faking" could also be business plans, investor slide-decks, or even LLC formations. Such activity might make you feel good for two hours, but it gets you no closer to your first customer, much less a salable value-skew[S32].

Sadly, some aspiring entrepreneurs have made book-binging a form of action-faking. They're not reading the best book to solve front-facing problems[S68]. Instead of grinding the difficult critical path, they're fooling themselves with dopamine games no better than a video game or a bag of greasy potato chips. Activity wastes time: action attacks the critical path. At some point, you have to stop reading about swimming and jump in the pool.

☑ **KEY CONCEPTS**

- Any action outside of the critical path is an "action-fake."
- Action-faking gives you a faux sense of accomplishment, often stimulating a dopamine release with ineffective action.

THE ONE PROBLEM STRATEGY

Stop Shopping for Ferraris, Shop for One Solution

68

A common triteness you'll read at my forum is, "What color Ferrari should I buy?" This odd statement is often dropped into a thread whenever an entrepreneur fixates on a distant problem, one predicated on dozens, perhaps hundreds of successful actions prior. Here are just a few examples:

What kind of accounting firm should I hire if my company goes public?
Didn't you say your finished product isn't for sale yet?

What should I know about employment law?
Aren't you months away from hiring your first employee?

Any asset protection strategies I should use to protect the millions I'll make? *Don't you live at home with your parents and work at Taco Bell?*

All these questions are examples of Ferrari shopping. Stop worrying about distant problems when you haven't even made your first buck or found your first customer. Put another way, stop ignoring the elephant in the room while stressing about the others, which are miles away.

The only problem worth worrying about, and thus, worth solving is the one that has stopped the needle from moving[P67]. Attack problem #1 before problem #99. Worrying about a distant unknown, say payroll law, when you are months or years away from hiring your first employee, is a neurological exercise in futility. Worse, some don't focus on the mountaintop and its many problems, but its tantalizing reward: high living and fast cars. When you're focused on rewards that may or may not happen in the distant future, you're Ferrari shopping.

As a problemologist[S30] who seeks to solve a macro-problem, only one problem matters... the one that stops you from advancing on the critical path[S165]. While having a big picture vision as designed in your 1/5/10 Planasy[S12] is essential, focus only on the problems that directly impact the critical path, or advance you to the one-year vision. As they say, the best way to eat an elephant is one bite at a time. Notwithstanding that no one should be eating elephants, looking at the big picture "the elephant" causes paralysis, overwhelming fear, and needless distractions. Fact is, if you wait to have all the answers before starting, you'll never get started. It's like waiting for all the traffic lights to be green before starting a road trip.

Relative-value starts with one. One paragraph starts a novel, one bar a musical piece, one scene a play, one mile a marathon. So stop stressing about how you'll afford new clothes after losing the thirty pounds. Lose one pound first. Stop fretting about how much tax you'll owe on a million bucks in profit. Profit one hundred dollars first. Incremental progress of one problem and action underwrites the process[S29] while connecting your feedback loop and firing transformative passion[S46]. Small wins turn into larger wins. Momentum builds, and before you know it, you're at the mountaintop.

☑ **KEY CONCEPTS**

- "Ferrari Shopping" is focusing on a distant problem instead of the problem in front of you.
- You'll never get started if you require all the answers to the future problems.

THE 1/2/3 MARRIAGE STRATEGY

Execute 1 Hour, 2 Days, 3
Years Before Marrying

69

Y ou are the CEO of *You Inc.*, not just your business. And one of *You Inc.'s* biggest expenses is getting married.

Even bigger is getting divorced.

Even if you never Unscript or start a business, the following piece of advice is worth 1000X this book's cost. Here it is: If you want to get married, follow The Rule of 1 Hour, 2 Days, and 3 Years. It will save you a bad marriage, a lot of emotional turmoil, and perhaps a fortune.

THE RULE OF ONE HOUR

Before getting engaged, spend one hour discussing the five relationship killers of failed marriages. They are:

1. Politics
2. Religion
3. Children
4. Career/money
5. Diet/Fitness/Nutrition

Do your political and religious philosophies align? Does your potential spouse believe your children need to be raised in a strict Catholic tradition while you're agnostically Buddhist? Do you even want children? Are you a purebred capitalist while your partner thinks communism got a raw deal in the last century? Is your partner a carefree spender, but you're a cheapskate? Do you want to take risks as an entrepreneur and live Unscripted[S9] while your partner insists that 50 years of Wall Street[P6] is the better option? Is your partner a vegetarian who is at the gym five times a week while you're sitting on the couch eating hot dogs and pizza?

I'm batting perfect when it comes to predicting failed marriages. Whenever a divergence occurs in the five breakpoints or becomes known, divorce follows. Just some examples I've witnessed on the periphery of my life... 1) the wife suddenly shifts to fitness and nutrition while the husband continues a lifestyle of junk food and laziness. She transforms her body and energy levels. The husband does not… *divorce*… 2) The husband wants to spend discretionary income on entrepreneurial risks while the wife insists on spending every surplus dollar on fashion fads and brands… *divorce*… 3) The wife wants kids. After four years of marriage, the husband finally confesses he does not… *divorce.*

No, I'm not psychic, I've just old enough to have seen it over and over again.

THE RULE OF TWO DAYS

The Rule of Two Days asks that you must spend two days with your partner in hell before getting married. You must endure each other in the worst of conditions and the most trying of circumstances. For example, my wife and I were once stranded in Belize at a small airport. If you have never been to the airport in Belize, it's terribly tiny, hot, and lacking basic amenities—for starters, a clean toilet. For the next 48 hours, we had to endure long lines, humidity, mosquitoes the size of hummingbirds, and a temporary overnight stay at a decrepit Days Inn infested with cockroaches. I thank United Airlines for the nightmare! Bottom line, we saw each other at our worst. If you survive trying times, like being stranded in a small town on spring break, it's a sign she/he may be a keeper.

THE RULE OF THREE YEARS

And finally, The Rule of Three Years asks that you regularly date for at least three years before marriage. And by regular, I mean at least seeing each other several times a week, if not living together. Three years is long enough to witness your partner's habits, idiosyncrasies, and, more importantly, their change-cycle[S42]. If you discussed the five relationship killers in The Rule of One Hour, the three years of dating will prove it. Have you grown together or apart? Are divergences emerging in the discussion from the Rule of One Hour? Moreover, in three years, you will likely experience a situation covering The Rule of Two Days.

Too many young people visit my forum talking about marriage with partners they haven't known but for one lunar cycle. Are you nuts? What's the damn rush? If she's great today, she'll be great the three years from now. If it's meant to be, time won't matter, and neither will a piece of paper from the government. Be patient and be rewarded.

Marriage can be one of the most important decisions of your life. Don't rush what doesn't need to be rushed. Meet the 1-2-3 Rules, and I'll bet your marriage will last a lifetime. Ignore it and pay dearly later.

☑ **KEY CONCEPTS**

- Getting married is one of life's biggest expenses; getting divorced is another.

- Before tying the knot, apply The Rule of 1 Hour, 2 Days, and 3 Years.

- The Rule of 1 Hour is a detailed discussion about "marriage-breaking" topics such as politics, kids, diet, money, and religion.

- The Rule of 2 Days is spending two full days with your future spouse in the most trying of circumstances.

- The Rules of 3 Years means to date a minimum of three years to validate your partner's Rule of One Hour admissions, as well as their change cycle, if any.

THE SEARCH CIPHER STRATEGY

Hunt for Search Ciphers to Unlock Unlimited Knowledge

D o you know what "kiting" is? No, it's not someone who flies a kite. It's the process of assembling a product together before it can be sold. For instance, let's say you invented a talking teddy bear, and there are four central components: The bear suit, its stuffing, its exterior parts (like eyes, nose, paws), and its electronics. The likelihood that this item would roll off an assembly line as a finished product is slim and none. A "kiting" company would likely be responsible for its assembly. How would you know this? You probably wouldn't.

And that's where search ciphers come into play.

A search cipher is an official terminology that unlocks business-advancing knowledge when performed at any search engine. With the right search cipher, the world's knowledge is at your fingertips. In our fictional story, the correct search ciphers for producing results that advance their soup business on the critical path are "food co-packers" or "soup co-packers." Jeff started with "food processors," and it sent him off on a wild-goose chase. Luckily for him, he didn't give up. After a half-dozen more searches, he eventually searched for "food manufacturing processes." This uncovered results, results which lead him to expose the correct search cipher... a food co-packer. That search turned up gold.

Unfortunately, the right search-cipher takes some investigation to uncover. Back to our teddy-bear example, if you do need assembling services, a google search for "assembling services" likely won't produce the right answers. To find the cipher, you probably have to search many variations of what you're seeking. Start with a description of what you need. Then move to the industry itself, prefixed with phrases such as "how are [widgets] made?" or "[widget] manufacturing process." The correct cipher might be buried in an article on page two in your fifth search. It is indeed a rabbit hole. Yet the right search cipher "kiting services" dropped into any search engine would produce the problem-solving answers... immediately.

If that doesn't work, try search operators. Here are some effective ones to deploy.

- "site: [keywords]" - Find and limit results contained to a specific website
- "intitle: [keywords]" -web pages with a certain keyword in the title
- "inurl: [keywords]" -web pages with a certain keyword in the URL
- "filetype: [keywords]" - web pages with a certain file type, useful for finding poorly ranked PDFs.

The challenge as a problemologist[S30] is always figuring out what you don't know. Namely, the official terminology of what we have to learn so we can move forward. Without the correct search terminology, our hunt will not snare the information we need. But it will put you on the scent. Follow it down the rabbit hole. The answers are there.

☑ KEY CONCEPTS

- Unlimited knowledge is accessed with the correct "search cipher" at any search engine.
- Discovering the right search cipher often requires multiple searches and guesswork, like following a scent down a rabbit hole.
- Use search operators for more targeted results.

THE "BRO-MARKETING" ENCOUNTER
WEDNESDAY, JULY 5TH, 2017 - 5:14 PM
(6 days later)

$1,700!?"

Jeff sneered as he stood in the foyer of his townhouse. The townhome's rental agreement specified they were responsible for all repairs, up to a maximum of $2,500— it was why Dave Bliss, their landlord, gave them a break on rent, not to mention his lustful intentions with his wife. Beside Jeff was an HVAC technician from Precision Air Conditioning. Dressed in navy maintenance bibs with "Harvey" stitched on the pocket, the technician looked more like a Wall Street banker than a repairman. Jeff had called Precision Air because they advertised in their weekly advertising mailer, an envelope chock full of coupons from plumbers, pizza joints, and home remodelers. Jeff was also familiar with Precision Air because he heard their radio ads every drive to and from the train station.

Still writing on his clipboard, the technician continued, "You have a bad capacitor. And your coils are dirty; they need to be cleaned. Your unit is about six years old. I doubt they were ever serviced. The seventeen hundred dollars is to replace the capacitor, clean your coils, and give your overall system a tune-up." Still scribbling on his clipboard, he continued, "With your ten percent off coupon, it will get you under $1,600." He finally looked at Jeff and with a simper said, "How would you like to pay?"

Jeff studied Harvey up and down. Without saying a word, he walked three steps to the door, opened it, and fanned his hand outside. The technician stood motionless as the silence hung, but then he nodded in resignation. He walked out, the slam of the door the only thing spoken.

Their air conditioner would remain broken for the next three days. In an act of sweaty desperation, Sam called Dave. Turns out, Mr. Bliss wasn't so bad after all. He recommended a reliable HVAC company, and they were out the next morning. And as Jeff expected, they didn't need a capacitor or a "coil cleaning." Rats had chewed through the feed wires. The bill came to $180.

Later that evening and in her newly air-conditioned space, Sam would begin cooking.

The delightful odor of Italian bistro and beachside seafood brought Jeff to the stove next to his wife. He kissed her on the forehead and nodded to the pots simmering atop the burners. "Right there is our escape. Our freedom. Our ticket out."

Sam elbowed him in the ribs playfully. "Okay, moneybags, why don't you try it first before you make your way to the bank?"

Jeff mouthed a spoonful, spilling some on his loosened tie. "Yum. The Asian Tofu Udon?" Sam nodded. He gestured to another pot. "What's this one?"

"Italian Minestrone." Jeff spooned it in and tasted. He gave an approving grin. "And this?"

"Creamy Potato Kale." Jeff dipped his spoon and sipped it carefully. "Mm, tastes like lobster bisque." After savoring the mouthful, he dipped and sipped another spoonful. Afterward, he looked at Sam, puzzled. "I'm confused. How do you make something so nasty as kale taste this good?"

"Put the damn spoon down," Sam chuckled, "and quit eating my inventory." She leaned on the counter and then winked. "With the right blend of seasonings, I can make your poop taste good."

Jeff's eyes popped, glancing back at the stove. "Well now. In that case, I hope I've flushed the toilet this morning."

Sam grinned, another time machine back when her husband's humor had tickled her heart. "These will be ready tomorrow afternoon. I have to let them sit overnight so they soak in the flavors."

The next night, Jeff arrived from work and found his wife on the couch with Madison. Sam heard him ping-pong up the long narrow stairwell from the garage with something in tow. A large box. Sam and Maddy flipped around to spy on the commotion. They watch him unload three stacks of circular cardboard quarts, the kind you might get at a delicatessen or for food takeout. Names of restaurants decorated the boxes: Sakura Japanese, The Neighborhood Garden, and Romano's Italian Bistro.

Sam asked, "What on earth are those?" Maddy added dryly, "Mommy already made dinner."

He smirked wryly. "This, my wonderful queens of the house, is how we're going to figure out the one soup we'll manufacture." Confused, Sam asked, "One? I thought we were doing three."

He shook his head and then grimaced. "We can't afford to manufacture three, much less two. When I was doing research on co-packers, they all had pretty steep minimum order requirements."

"How steep?"

"Steep enough that it's going to be a stretch for us to produce just one soup." He saw the distress on his wife's face. "Leave the numbers to me. Just worry about the soup."

She raised her voice. "Leave the numbers to you? Like your knife idea, or worse, your 'Trump Sucks' venture?"

Jeff glanced away, but she saw his cheeks tense. Sam caught it, then corrected herself. "I'm sorry." She got up from the couch and walked to him, tousling the hair in front of his eyes. "You've been working your tail off, and I see it. I'm proud of you. And I love getting back the man I fell with. It reminds me of college when we felt the future was whatever we made it." She paused, allowing the moment to absorb. Stepping back, she gestured to the cardboard restaurant cartons. "So what's with these now?"

He smiled cleverly. "I had those made up after work. It's how we'll test our soup and get unbiased feedback."

Sam furrowed her brow, hoping what she was thinking wasn't what he was thinking. "Is this going to be legal?"

Jeff winked. "Perfectly."

THE PRODUCTOCRACY STRATEGY

Aim for a Productocracy: A Pull Prints Money, A Push Advertises for It

S ome years ago, I ran an unofficial experiment as a scientist. Because I listen to the radio often, I get stuck listening to a lot of commercials. For this experiment, I paid close attention to the advertisers. Over the next week, I recorded all the businesses who advertised frequently. I'm talking dozens of times per day, every week. Many advertisers even had radio personalities endorsing their companies. After I created my list, I investigated the public reviews (Yelp/Google) for these advertising behemoths.

What did I find?

The average review for these frequent advertisers was a dismal 1.8 stars out of 5. Some reviewers even accused these companies of being blatant scams. The point? If a company advertises heavily, flooding the market with coupons and other "in your face" activities, more than likely, they're *pushers*. And pushers aren't selling relative-value; they're marketers of perceived-value.

As an Unscripted Entrepreneur, your objective is its holy grail: *the Productocracy*. A Productocracy is achieved with a unique and recognizable value-skew[S32] that isn't offered elsewhere. The value-skew can be one attribute, or a combination of many. Perhaps your HVAC repair company provides free consultations and operates with complete honesty. Maybe your eCommerce company offers a no-questions-asked guarantee and return policy. Or it could be as simple as a good product at a good price. When the market reacts to this favorable skew, your current customers become the primary driver for your business growth through reviews, referrals, and recommendations. In other words, they *pull*, not *push*.

Create relative-value worth recommending, and you'll gain a miraculous ability... *the power to print money*. Suddenly, one happy customer turns into two, three, or more. And disciples (customers who love your product/service) have the best return on investment. No ad campaign or marketing strategy can match it.

While sales and profits are essential, a Productocracy ultimately determines how fast you grow and if that growth is accelerated with improved margins. When one happy customer refers a new customer, miraculous money-making math occurs: your new customer has zero acquisition cost. And the first customer's acquisition cost halves. If your first client cost \$10 to obtain and he recommends you, suddenly his cost drops to \$5. One satisfied customer who creates two additional ones lowers the aggregate acquisition cost by two-thirds. In short, your product contagiously sells itself. Productocracies move probabilities[S59], they magnetize money[P23], and they create to-the-moon leverage[P16].

For instance, if you scan the many reviews for my books, you will find a common theme. Many readers report that someone recommended the book. This is how I sell books year after year: Not slick advertising or big Facebook ad spends—a Productocracy.

Likewise, every podcast and interview I've ever done happened because I was invited. I didn't send a cold email and beg to be interviewed. Translation licenses, same deal: Publishers solicited me, asking to be a part of my book's success. My book did the selling, not me.

Behind this phenomenon is a business dynamic called a *push-pull polarity*—the mechanism determines if your company grows spectacularly, a Productocracy, or struggles to survive. Companies held hostage by advertising yoke themselves to a *push*. Companies that grow like weeds and enrich their founders boast the *pull*.

Not long ago, whoever spent the most on advertising won the sales. If the AC broke, you searched for HVAC firms in the Yellow Pages or phoned the one that had sent you a coupon in the mail. If you found a new food product, it was advertised on television or was slotted favorably in the grocery store. Both required deep pockets. To sell large volumes of products, corporations had to buy large volumes of advertising. Advertising pushes its product to the masses, driving sales.

Conversely, the pull in the push-pull polarity is a Productocracy where your relative-value has recommendation power. Customers come to you. With each new customer, the expansion loop and its network effects strengthen. Your company starts to get gravity. The pull is word of mouth, social proof, and satisfied users. If clients are recommending and sharing your products on social media, congratulations, your product is pulling. And it's proof of a Productocracy.

The most important questions for your business are:

1. Are customers recommending my products?
2. Are people tweeting about it or raving on social media?
3. Are people sending you love emails?
4. If applicable, are people reordering?

If they aren't, get deep into the 3A Method[S55] until they do. Otherwise, you take the risk of becoming an ad-dependent boiler-room. I'm skeptical of any operation that advertises heavily. I'm not suggesting that advertising is negative or evil. Just be leery of massive advertising. The standard I apply is the three Os. If it's *obtrusive* (cold calls, door knocking), *obvious* (OMG I'm sick of this commercial!), or *outrageous* (seems too good to be true!), I avoid it. Heavy advertising reveals you aren't likely dealing with a Productocracy, which is why a scammy $1,700 repair bill follows.

Don't build a business that becomes a churn-and-burn. Replacing old fools with new fools is not a business model; it's a marketing racket.

☑ KEY CONCEPTS

- Pushers are sellers of perceived-value, not relative-value.
- A Productocracy demonstrates a unique and recognizable value-skew not offered elsewhere.
- A Productocracy's value-skew can be one attribute or a combination of many.
- Happy customers, or disciples, earn the best return on your investment, as one customer equals two.
- Productocracies boast a pull which magnetizes money and creates explosive leverage.
- Evidence of a Productocracy is customer recommendations, reorders, fan mail, and favorable social media posts.

THE NO LIST PRINCIPLE

The Road Less Travelled Has No Map, No List, and No Escort

Life's problems are problems for a reason: They're difficult to solve. And as the truth states, there is no fucking list that will help you solve them. Whatever specialized-unit you seek to offer or problem sought to be solved, be warned. *The No List Principle asserts that there is no list, no exacting roadmap, and no mentor who will hold your hand to a successful business.* One-size-fits-all solutions are marketing gimmicks and perceived-value hustles[S26].

Practically every week I see a post from a *list-looker*, an aspiring entrepreneur who has this great idea, and now they are on the hunt for this coveted and mysterious "list" that will show them the exact steps to make it happen. If your idea is some phenomenal invention or a new business with just a few positively skewed attributes[S32], it doesn't matter: There is no blueprint for its execution. If there was, would it be an idea worth pursuing in the first place?

Be happy there is no list telling you what to do, how to do it, and where to do it. This is your moat to stop the drive-by entrepreneurs from entering your space. Remember the Commandment of Entry within the CENTS Framework[S43]: The more difficult it is to start and launch, the more potent the opportunity. If it's easy now, it will be hard later.

For instance, as I write this, selling on Amazon is the current hot business-du-jour. As such, everyone is trolling Alibaba, looking for some hot magical product that will put them into seven figures a year while lounging on a beach in Bali. Except, guess what? Everyone else is on Alibaba looking for the same damn thing.

If someone is selling you "a list," be wary: everyone else is getting the same list, which means everyone else will be your competitor.

Similarly, the most common threads at my forum are book threads. What book do I read next? What book will help me the most? The motive behind these book queries is usually a combination of list-looking and needle sharpening[P67]. While many books are helpful, ultimately, most of them (including this one) are only dots, like signposts in an entrepreneurial wilderness. The chasm between these signposts is your knowledge gap[S20], which can only be closed with engagement: trial and error, adapting, and skill-building. Seeing the dots is one thing; connecting them is another.

- There is no list that will give you the step-by-step plan for success, and if there was, everyone would have it and wouldn't solve problems, or it's a scam.

- Books, such as this one, only offer signposts in an entrepreneurial wilderness.

The No List Principle

THE BREAK-ROOM RUSE
FRIDAY, JULY 7TH, 2017 - 6:55 AM
(2 days later)

Two days later, Friday's ride into work made Jeff terribly uneasy. Outside of his T-shirt gaffe some months ago, his wife generally liked his take-charge attitude. But he had to admit it. The bluster and bravado he'd peacocked to his wife was more illusion than reality.

He swallowed hard as the freeway traffic slowed to a crawl. He mostly took the train to work, but today's experiment called for him to drive. As he remembered, bumper-to-bumper traffic usually started at the Geico billboard. That was at least four miles ahead. WTF?

He shifted in his Corolla's cloth seat, which was dotted with cigarette burns and reeked of them as well. He didn't smoke, but his older brother, who'd had owned the car before him, did. Tension and anxiety needled his gut. He felt moisture swell in his armpits, his antiperspirant no match for the fear and apprehension he felt. A glance to his mirror revealed a drop of sweat fleeing his temple. He rarely sweated. But today felt different. Like sitting on needles, the plodding traffic amplified his angst because it also heightened the weekday pain he wanted to escape. But it wasn't the source.

His plan that day was to pull a lunch-hour ruse on his co-workers. A covert operation. In his back seat were eight quarts of his wife's soup, the Asian Tofu Udon. At about 10:45 AM, his plan was to send an office email to all employees at his workplace. The email would read:

Lunch on me! Free, delicious soup, first-come, first-serve! Hey everyone, I got the entire office some tasty Asian Tofu Udon soup from a new Japanese restaurant, help yourself! Heat 2 minutes and enjoy. If you like it, let me know as I know the owner! - Jeff Trotman (Audits - 402)

He wasn't afraid of the ruse itself; he was fearful of its outcome. He felt as if he was poking a bear. Would they like it? Ignore it? Would the eight quarts sit there untouched? Assuming half the office ate in the breakroom, he calculated that eight quarts would be plenty. Perhaps too plenty.

As the traffic crawled into the city, the odd anxiety swirled in his stomach and intensified with each mile. At first, he compared the emotion with a drive to the dentist for a root canal. But that wasn't it.

Up ahead, the flickering lights of fire trucks and police cars came into view. As Jeff approached, he saw an 18-wheeler jackknifed in the opposite lane. Every driver gawked. While an accident on Chicago's freeways wasn't unusual, what was unusual was the spectacle it caused. Its trailer was split open as if a superhero had ripped it apart, its cargo splattered across the freeway. Fruit and their sloppy innards painted the road a vivid orange. He guessed it was mangos. When he crank-opened the dirty window of his Corolla to get a better look, the sweet smell of cantaloupe floated into the cabin. The scent was welcoming and soothed his stomach, guiding his thoughts back to his childhood summers. Before his brother went the way of a juvenile delinquent, they'd spent a month at his uncle's cabin in Wisconsin. After swimming for hours, his aunt would roll down to the lakeside with a platter of fresh canta-loupe, watermelon, and other fruits he didn't know existed. The fruity aroma sparked a fiery reminder of what he was working for... his family's freedom. His childhood summers were all about creative exploration. The ability to do nothing or do everything. The kind of freedom that exists only before the rat race steals dreams and bribes souls.

His youthful reminiscing also struck him with additional insight. His appre-hension and stomach pains weren't about fear, they were about judgment. Like the kind of judgment when you go to a new school, and the principal stands you in front of the classroom and says, "Boys and girls, meet Jeff, he's new."

He left his window open until diesel fumes from passing semi-trucks overtook the scent of cantaloupe. The fruity fragrance disappeared, but so did his worries. Judgment, fear of failure, all of this was just part of the pro-cess, he thought.

Once he arrived at work, the morning's workload moved effortlessly. Instead of fearing the 10:45AM email, he anticipated it. The message was armed, queued, and waiting. He watched the seconds tick down to 10:45 on the old-school clock outside his office, and on the button, he sent it. *Whoosh!* sounded the "email sent" notification.

And then he exhaled relief and waited. And hoped.

A few minutes after 11, Hank peeked into his office and knocked on the open door. About forty, Hank had the body of a twenty-year-old Bulgarian weightlifter but the face of a sixty-year-old cardiac patient. His face glowed a deep shade of red and acne scars pockmarked his square cheeks as if some-one had targeted it for BB-gun practice. With a gray buzzcut and flat jawline, Hank could have been a military drill sergeant. If not, Central Casting was missing out.

"Hey boss, where's this new Japanese place? I googled it and found nothing. That soup was dope."

Jeff looked up and smiled. "Actually, that soup is from a dear friend of mine who is starting a soup business. She wanted feedback, so she asked me if I could put some in the break-room for people to try."

"She's starting a Japanese restaurant?"

"No, a soup business," Jeff answered. "Canned soup."

"No shit? It didn't taste like it was from a can." He scratched his temple. "So why does the carton say it's from a Japanese restaurant?"

Damn! Jeff reflected as he nervously tapped his foot underneath his desk. He paused, realizing he didn't really plot this strategy thoroughly.

"She said she wanted an unbiased opinion and to see if the soup could pass as restaurant quality."

He laughed, "It did. Where can I buy a few cans, a Trader Joe's or something?"

"Not yet, she's still working on getting them into the stores. If you want to pre-order a few cans, I can tell her. She's giving 20 percent off on all pre-orders, four bucks for a 12 oz can."

Hank nodded and then swiftly pirouetted, exiting Jeff's office.

Damn! he thought again. Did Hank take offense to the fake Japanese restaurant label? Or maybe it was because he was acting as a middleman, something sounded scammy, like an MLM, not a soup startup. Before Jeff could reach any conclusion, Hank returned. This time he didn't knock; he stormed in and slammed his palm on the table. *Wham!* The loud percussive noise rolled Jeff back into his chair, knocking over the photo behind his desk. His co-workers outside his window stole several inquisitive looks as if they hoped to witness office drama. But there was none—only triumph.

Hank announced, "Count me in for five cans." He lifted his palm, and a twenty-dollar bill was left lying on the table.

By the day's end, Jeff would leave with $248 in cash from eleven co-workers who would order sixty-two cans total. He'd also get six interoffice emails about the soup, inquiring about the mythical Japanese restaurant. With thirty-five employees at his branch, Jeff thought eleven orders plus six queries were phenomenal. Nearly half, he reasoned. Moreover, he adequately explained why there was no restaurant behind the soup. His "fib" was mostly met with indifference. Only one person was angry—not because of the experiment but because she was stoked about a new Japanese restaurant opening. He profusely apologized in all cases.

"But that's not even the good news," he chimed to his wife after work. "I only brought enough soup for 24 people. If 11 people asked about it, that's nearly half a thumbs-up rate. I don't know what's normal for the food business, but that sounds pretty damn good."

Seated on a kitchen stool, Sam legged a swivel toward Jeff, her eyes narrow and arms crossed. "So let me get this straight. You lied and said my soup was from some restaurant? And then you didn't even admit it was from your wife?"

Jeff explained that he devised his ruse because he was looking for solid, unbiased feedback. "When I deliver the soup, I will tell them it is from my wife. I will explain everything just as I explained to you." He paused, but joy was not dressing his wife's face. He continued, "Put it this way, Samantha: you buy stuff from friends and family because you feel obligated, not because you like the product." He motioned downstairs toward the front door. "We buy Girl Scout Cookies from our neighbors out of obligation, not because we like them." He snuffed, "Well, I like the cookies, but you don't."

She finally softened and then asked, "Promise me you'll tell them the truth."

"I will."

"To be honest," she said after uncrossing her arms, "I'm not surprised it was a hit. People at the hospital love my soup too. But half your office liking it seems too good to be true." She flipped a blond lock out of her eye, her lips pursed. "Wait a second. What if they went back for seconds or had more than a serving? Then half your office didn't like it. Didn't you say this Hank was a big beefcake?"

Jeff nodded. "Yeah, built like a brick shithouse. If anyone ate more than a serving or two, then the percentage of people who liked it would be less." He scratched his temple. Then, "Not sure if the data tells a story, but people liked it enough to buy." He held up cash, beaming ear to ear. "Our first sales, baby! Should we frame it on the wall?"

Sam grinned like she was holding back laughter.

"I'm serious!" Jeff said, holding one of the dollars up toward the 1/5/10 Planasy on the wall. "I say we pin this up there to remind us why we're doing this."

"I don't need a reminder," she replied, "I just hope when you deliver the product next week and tell the truth behind your little trick, the,"—she raised her fingers in quotes—"'the brick shithouse' doesn't put *you* in the shithouse."

THE ETHICAL ENVELOPE PRINCIPLE

Pushing Ethical Gray Areas Can
Foment Negative Skew

In my first book, *The Millionaire Fastlane,* I mentioned that I listed fake employees on my website. When my business was growing, I hired my best friend for customer service, and as such, there were many office jokes. One of these jokes evolved with several fake employees being listed on my website. As the months passed and the joke faded away, I realized that these additional employees made my company look larger than it was. This might have been a skew[S32] when others (or potential competitors) were evaluating my business. I didn't think much of it except when I wrote my book years later.

Sometimes authenticity can bite you in the ass. What some see as "rule breaking" others might see as pushing the ethical envelope. As with many things in life, the Ethical Envelope Principle affirms that *ethics are subjective and what one finds acceptable behavior, another will find it unethical.* In short, there is no right answer.

After my book was published, I soon learned that some readers found my "funny but fake" employees unethical, despite my humorous motives. It wasn't illegal but broke unwritten rules. For some of my readers, my confession of this practice turned into negative-skew[S36]. While I have no regrets, I completely understand their opinion. Whenever you break the rules[S44] and it becomes public, people might take offense. Thus negative skew is created.

In Jeff's case, using fake restaurant cartons to gauge market feedback could create negative-skew with potential customers, assuming they find out. Fibbing about "buying lunch" also is a risk, one I wouldn't take. The point is, anytime you authentically break the rules and test ethical boundaries, some will take offense. Ethics are subjective. If you think an action might be ethically sketchy, here's a rule that I always use: If your action became public, would you regret it, or would you need to apologize profusely? If yes, it's probably an action you should avoid. In my case, I willingly broadcasted my "fake employees" story in my book because I knew I meant no malice. Breaking rules doesn't mean breaking laws, but it could test the gray area of ethics.

- Ethical gray areas can create negative skew and lost sales.

- If your questionable action became public knowledge it would require an apology, it is probably something you shouldn't do.

THE PAYMENT PROVES PRINCIPLE

Money Talks, Opinions Walk

74

In 2009, my friend was in pre-launch mode for a new product in personal security. Tens of thousands of people voiced an opinion on how great the idea was. He even received national press. He presumed to be sitting on a big winner. However, when it came down to actually buying the product—spending the cash—buyers stood on the sidelines with their wallets locked. Ultimately the product was a failure. He validated the idea in the arena of friends, family, opinions, and email addresses instead of in the arena of proof—*money*.

The Payment Proves Principle asserts that *in business, the only opinions that matter are the ones attached to money.* Money is a verifiable vote. Of course, money doesn't have an opinion, but its possessors do. And when money flows into your pockets, money is given a voice. It says, "Yes, you've convinced me of value so here is my hard-earned money."

So, when Mom says your business idea sounds great, don't believe her. When Jimmy the bartender says your idea about a new liquor line sounds awesome, be skeptical.

A *trivial-validation* is when someone voices a positive opinion about your idea, including someone within your target market. While trivial-validations might be encouraging and feedback loop connecting[S46], they still constitute an opinion, making it no better than buying Girl Scout Cookies from the next-door neighbor. If trivial-validation is the only data you have for your idea, that's okay. It just means your idea remains riskier and more speculative than one with money behind it. Sadly, high fives and Facebook likes don't pay bills or put kids into college. Trivial-validation can be exciting, and it can jump-start your business. However, the first milestone worthy of champagne is when trivial-validation turns into cash-validation.

Cash-validation turns presumptions, speculations, and hypotheses into truth. Money is the only thing that validates an idea 100 percent: a sale, a pre-order, or an investment. While an email address is the next best thing to a payment, it's still trivial. Yes, you can work with a massive list of email addresses, but ultimately those email addresses need to convert to cash. Just like done kills doubt[P49], payment proves. And in the competitive marketplace for ideas, money constitutes an official vote at the ballot box. Winning polls doesn't make victors; winning elections does.

☑ KEY CONCEPTS

- The only proof of a valid idea is actual cash-validation, or money—pre-orders or sales.

- Trivial-validation is any favorable response that isn't money—an email address or likes and comments.

- An idea supported by trivial-validation is riskier than one validated by cash.

- Likes, comments, opinions, and email addresses don't pay bills.

THE FORGIVENESS PRINCIPLE

Let Relative-Value Forgive Your Sins

75

D ave's Killer Bread was co-founded in 2005 by Dave Dahl, a high school dropout, an ex-meth addict, and a convicted felon. If you're not familiar with Dave, he successfully relaunched and rebranded his family's bread business. It went from a floundering local company to a national brand in thousands of stores worldwide.

He didn't allow his negative backstory to dampen his enthusiasm or steal his future. Instead, he leveraged his story as a part of his value-skew and brand, organic, non-GMO, healthy bread. Dave's Killer Bread was acquired in 2015 for $275 million. And now, one-third of Dave's workforce are ex-convicts, making their hiring practice a piece of their branding skew and world-changing mission.

The point of this story is The Forgiveness Principle: *If you offer the world something valuable, the world doesn't ask about your past transgressions.* Relative-value is utterly ignorant to your faults and historical failings, or your *life demerits.*

A life demerit is anything that you perceive as detrimental to your self-worth as a person or an entrepreneur. It's that negative voice in your head promoting the negative narrative so your dead dream can stay dead.

In any transaction where you are the value provider, the only thing exchanged is money. Buyers don't ask for your college transcripts or your credit scores. They don't ask about your bad driving record, your loveless marriage, or your last five failed businesses. They don't need a play-by-play on your last church confessional. Everything—from excuses to misdeeds—all are blasted out the window. When you have something people want, you're never too young, too old, too broke, too uneducated, too straight, too gay, too white, too black, too short, too introverted, too this, or too that. *Can you solve my problem and at what price?* Ex-cons take note: value wipes the slate clean.

Please don't confuse this with negative skew[S36]—negative skew is advertised and public; life demerits are *private* and *personal.* When someone has what you desperately want or need, their backstory can fade to black. In the case of Dave's Killer Bread, their relative-value proposition wasn't lifesaving at all—it was freaking bread. It proves that all our excuses about why we can't get started are all self-funded delusions. When you have what the market wants, you'll earn more than money; you can earn an unseen and unadvertised benefit: redemption.

☑ **KEY CONCEPTS**

- If you offer relative-value, the world generally ignores your past transgressions and personal faults, or life demerits.
- Seekers of value don't know (or ask) about your life-demerits—if you have what the market wants, money will flow.
- Relative-value is incredibly redemptive, especially for those with troublesome histories.

JUST A FRIENDLY COMPETITION
SATURDAY JULY 15TH, 2017 - 8:44 AM
(8 days later)

The next week, on an early Saturday morning, the Trotman's would repeat the soup experiment. This time, it would be Sam at the hospital. The break-room soup-drop would be minestrone. Sam reported that the minestrone from Harlucci's Italian Deli was a second-shift favorite at Mercy when she worked those hours, so it was a good gambit to push minestrone to the third shift.

By the end of her night and into the morning, she had nothing to report. While some ate the soup, no one asked her about it. When she came home that morning to tell Jeff the bad news, she found him at the kitchen table behind his beefy desktop computer. To his side were an HP printer and a multi-slot attaché, an old-school adding machine, and a stack of papers with Neve on top. Soft jazz spirited the background.

"This your new office?" Sam questioned.

"Our office." He peeked up from the computer and then glanced at the whiteboard on the wall with the framed dollar bill. "I need an actual office, a real space that reminds me of our goals." He muddled his lips. "Our little desk in the bedroom wasn't working. Whenever I go in there, I feel like sleeping, not working."

Sam scanned the table. "Not a lot of room to eat."

He motioned to the other half of the table and the two empty chairs. "There's plenty of room. I don't mind eating at the counter or behind the computer." He started clacking at the keyboard and returned his gaze to the screen.

Sam dropped her bag on the table with a noticeable thud. Jeff's head didn't budge, but his eyes peered up. He noticed her hair was straggled; her black scrubs she normally wore was replaced with hospital-grade mint scrubs. Jeff noticed the overnight change of clothing and beckoned, "What happened to you?"

Sam laughed, "Oh, just another day at the office. One of my patients had an excavation site cave in on him, burying him alive. Everyone in the ER was covered in mud and I had to change."

Jeff's eyes widened. "Dead on arrival?"

"No, no." She winked. "The medics saved him."

Jeff nodded nonchalantly and then threw her a pointed look. Sam knew what he was asking without him saying it. And for the next two minutes, she told her husband the bad news. The minestrone experiment at the hospital was a failure. Sam clarified, "I'm sure it's the work hours. People on the third shift have strange appetites. The wee-morning is more suitable for donuts and coffee than minestrone."

Jeff surprisingly brushed it off. "Not a big deal, I've been getting quotes for production and we're looking at thousands of dollars per SKU."

Her eyes narrowed, puzzled. Jeff smiled deviously and asked rhetorically, "Oh, you want me to explain?"

"Yes, but please, no mansplaining. I have a degree in nursing, not an MBA."

Jeff clarified, "A SKU is each soup flavor we produce. The minestrone is a SKU, the Asian udon, the creamy potato; we only have money for one SKU. And since I already presold 24 cans of the Udon, our decision is simple. Your Asian udon is our winner."

"How much are we looking at?"

Jeff looked at his notepad. "I've talked to three co-packers. The smallest minimum order quantity is 100 cases. Each case has 32 cans." He flick-tapped his pen on the table and continued, "No one would give us an exact price until seeing the recipe, but we're looking at a fixed cost as low as $1.19 per can or as high as $2.30. At 3200 cans that's about $3800 on the low side and $7,360 on high."

Sam's mouth gaped, her face shocked. After grabbing a handful of pistachios from the bowl on the kitchen table, she said, "That's our entire emergency fund. We'll need to dip into our retirement accounts."

Jeff nodded. "I figure we use half our emergency fund and don't touch the retirement account. We put the rest on your Visa. Mine is still hurting from my T-shirt accident."

She cracked a couple nuts and tossed them into her mouth, unfazed. "I don't understand," she said, chewing. "Why can't I just cook for myself to get started? That way we can afford as many SKUS as we'd like."

"It's against the law. You can't sell food cooked from your home kitchen."

Sam shook her head. "No, I'm not talking about our kitchen, but a kitchen we rent."

"Rent what?"

Sam laughed. "You want me to girlsplain?"

He smiled weakly and then nodded. Sam continued, "We rent a commercial kitchen."

Jeff froze and looked up. "There's such a thing?"

"Yes, and I'm not talking about one of your co-packers. My cooking shows

I watch on TV always mention them. We can find a commercial kitchen that rents by the hour and we can cook our own small batches and start selling small from there. Maybe we can get some good feedback before we make a big order with a co-packer."

Jeff wedged back in his chair, rubbing his forehead almost embarrassingly.

Unsure of he was stunned or just confused, Sam leered at him. He broke the silence with a hillbilly singsong. "Well, gawd damn."

"What?"

"I didn't know that. Strong work, darling. This makes things a lot easier. We can really tinker with the recipe before committing big dollars to a large order. You want to be in charge of finding the kitchen since you're the one that will be in it?"

"No problem." She smiled then walked into the kitchen to the coffee maker. "What are we thinking of naming the business?"

She poured herself a cup.

Jeff shrugged. "It's probably one of the most important decisions we'll make. It needs to be perfect, something that embodies a mission."

Sam interjected excitedly, "How about Kindly Kind Kitchen? Our mission is to be kind, and all our soups will be vegan and responsibly sourced. And I want a portion of our profits to go to an animal rescue or some type of charity. And I want our label to be earthy and happy."

Jeff butted in. "Whoah, hold on. Lots of ideas but I don't think Kindly Kind Kitchen is a good idea."

"Why?"

"Duh, Kindly Kind Kitchen? What if we have a bunch of lazy customers who don't want to say all that and instead say KKK? KKK is a bad association, and I don't think we need to have that type of implication lingering around our brand."

A light-hearted flute melody started playing from Madison's bedroom, an odd juxtaposition with the current topic.

"Good point," Sam admitted. "I never thought about how others might perceive the name, just how I wanted it to be perceived." She sipped her coffee then asked, "How about Happy Farms?" Jeff shook his head reluctantly. "It's not bad, I guess. Just doesn't move my meter much, and we don't own a farm. Don't think we should settle for anything but the best."

"Hmm, how about Vegan Varieties?" Sam offered.

"Not bad again, but we should avoid the word 'vegan' as it is another word that could have negative associations."

Sam retorted loudly, "It's not negative!"

"Listen, Sam, I'm not talking about the word and what it means to your other vegan friends. I'm talking about non-vegans. Say vegan to a non-vegan and they immediately think dry, bland, chewy, and tasteless. Had I mentioned our soup was vegan at work, we probably would have lost half our sales. Let's just stick with the word plant-based. That way we can appeal to a larger audience and not alienate others."

She set her cup down on the table. "You're right." She begrudgingly nodded and smiled. "Again. You've been on a winning streak, and I don't like it."

He dropped Neve to the table. "Let's give the business name a week or two to think about." He hesitated then smirked wily. "In fact, I say we turn it into a competition." Jeff, always the competitor, loved beating his wife in trivial matters: who could hold their breath longer, who could balance an egg on their forehead, a round of corn hole in the backyard. Whenever she'd lose at something, no matter what it was, he'd blame her vegan diet, alleging she was missing protein or fogging her brain up with too much tofu. Of course, Sam cared about Jeff's impromptu competitions as much as she cared about dairy farmers. Jeff declared, "The person who thinks up the business name gets an hour massage from the other." He rubbed his hands together, devilishly, and then added, "For every week for the next month."

She popped another pistachio in her mouth with confidence. "Deal."

THE ENVIRONMENTAL HACKING STRATEGY

Change the Weather to Make Progress Easier

76

M*y 600 Pound Life* is a reality show on the A&E Television Network featuring morbidly obese patients and their struggle to lose weight. Anytime I watch it, I want to throw my drink at the television screen. Even rationed viewings destroy my faith in humanity.

Anyway, the goal for the patients on the show is to lose a moderate amount of weight. Then they can get approved for gastric bypass surgery. Most of the patients fail at sustained weight loss, even after the surgery. Every failure shares a commonality, and I'm not talking about excessive junk food consumption. After Dr. Nazzicharian warns the patient of the mortal urgency for a proper diet, they go home to an environmental nightmare.

Every failure is preceded by an environment that doesn't encourage change, but a continuation of the status quo. Each patient is surrounded by enablers consisting of friends, family, and even parents. My favorite is that the family claims support for their obese family member but not enough to stop filling the house with Oreos and Ding Dongs. *Oh, we love Johnny and don't want him to die of a heart attack, but we don't love him enough to stop buying the junk that is killing him.*

In one case, the poor man was 850 lbs. Mostly bedridden. Couldn't walk through doors. Terrible lymphedemas. But the most disgusting and frustrating thing of all wasn't this man's plight. It was that his mother enabled him.

Oh, he gets angry if I don't get him what he wants.

Are you fucking kidding me?

Your kid is eating himself to death, and your only concern is to not make him mad? You want your four bacon-double cheeseburgers? Great, I won't be your courier; go get them yourself. It's like trying to rehabilitate an alcoholic in a bar or a crackhead in a crack house.

Even after losing 200+ pounds and getting the help he needed, this poor guy above ended up suffering a heart attack and dying on the show. Tragic but not unexpected. But hey, at least his mother didn't make him angry, and she was helpful enough to bring him two loaves of bread, six perogies, and three bags of Skittles.

If you want any chance at success, from weight loss to Unscription, your environment must be engineered to help. Not hinder. It's called *environmental hacking*.

For example, I never write unless my workspace is clean and organized. Over the years, I noticed a pattern in my writing effort. If I wrote in a cluttered and disorganized workspace, my writing would also suffer from similar chaos. Worse, no writing would happen at all.

If your goal is to eat carrots every day, your environment will largely determine success or failure. If eating carrots means a daily visit to the store, I'm betting you'll fail. The target goal is environmentally inconvenient. If you bought a big bag of carrots and laid them in the middle of your refrigerator, I'll bet you'll meet your goal. One environment is designed for failure, one for success. This is why bodybuilders prep their meals a week in advance: they're reshaping their environment to make goals more attainable.

The first key to manipulating your environment is to understand that you have the power to do so. Yes, your setting can be controlled. But only when you're willing to confront your sacred excuses.

For instance, my life has two chapters. My life in Chicago was the depression chapter. The dream chapter began in Arizona. I recognized young the need for sunshine in my life. I changed my location and hence, changed the weather. But before doing so, I had to embrace the change dyad[S42] and confront my sacred excuses...

> *Oh, you can't leave Chicago, you grew up here!*
> *You don't know a soul in Arizona!*
> *But you won't see your family for months on end!*

Once I realized every excuse was not a real reason for staying, I left. I knew I needed the sunny weather to succeed. Without it, my career as an author would not exist, and to be honest, I'd probably be strung out on Prozac due to a vitamin D deficiency.

The point is, manipulate your environment so that you move probability toward success[S59]. Find the city that empowers you to seek excellence and new skills[P39]. Apply to a startup incubator. Tweak your grocery list and arrange your refrigerator so you eat the best diet. Find the gym that gives you the best workout. Planet Fitness is brilliantly branded as a non-judgmental gym for those who don't want to be around grunting bodybuilders and bare-waisted fitness models. Their value-skew is literally an environmental hack for the self-conscious. Surround yourself with people who uplift your goals and don't belittle them. If your friends are Scripted rat racers who troll your dreams, it's time for new friends, or keep them a few zip codes away. My forum has thousands of people who are pursuing Unscription. Visitors get a daily exercise in environmental manipulation.

You can't win a race towing a wagon filled with bricks. You know your optimum environment—find it or make it. Never ignore it.

☑ KEY CONCEPTS

- If you want to improve your chances at success, hack your environment.

- Environmental hacking makes positive action easier and progress-stalling inaction harder.

THE FINICKY FELINES PRINCIPLE

Two Finicky Felines Doesn't Make a Market

Christmas 2020. I purchased an expensive cat condo for my family's two house cats. After the large box arrived on our doorstep, we spent an hour putting it together. This cat-tree came equipped with ladders, dangling mice, and private cubby holes perched high in the sky. I almost wished I was a cat. After finishing, we placed the towering tree next to the cats' favorite window and then watched. And waited. And waited more.

Within minutes, they both started fighting over the new item in their space. Except they weren't fighting over this lavish cat-tree, they were fighting over the cardboard box it came in. Fast forward a few weeks, and they still haven't touched the cat-tree, but damn, they sure love that box!

I mention this story because my cats' behavior best symbolizes how you should approach any market: like a room full of finicky cats. Remember, magnetizing money[S24] doesn't involve chasing cats, but making them come to you. Whenever you poke the market, or what I call the *marketmind*, you'll never know what comes back at you. The marketmind represents the total market that *should be* interested in your product. My cats *should* like a cat-tree. The Finicky Feline Principle is *a reminder that even the best products or services will have a considerable breadth of dislikers.*

Whenever you interact with the marketmind, dangling cheese, baiting worms, or offering soup, expect your share of finicky cats. You expect one thing (*They'll love this cat-tree!*) and get another (*Darn, they love the box, not the tree!*) Many times, these unexpected outcomes don't reflect a true market consensus. And false flags may appear in the form of negative opinions or indifference.

Think of it this way.

The marketmind is like the stock market. Outside of a few companies making news, the market moves as a holistic entity based on macroeconomic and geopolitical events. The market can be up two percent for the day while one stock is down 40 percent. Yes, a plummeting stock is a tiny piece of the market whole, but it doesn't prove the consensus. It's like taking the Pacific Ocean's temperature in Costa Rica while expecting it to be the same in San Francisco.

As such, when your product interacts with the marketmind, you never know if you're getting an accurate consensus of the marketmind or just a tiny reflection of a few individuals. Furthermore, the marketmind only reacts on the basis of perceived-value.

A phrase I always preach to aspiring entrepreneurs is this: *Not everyone loves coffee.* Despite coffee being a global $150+ billion-dollar business, not everyone finds coffee tasty. If you harvested the most delicious coffee on the planet and offered it to someone who simply doesn't like coffee, you'll get rejected. As a collective, nobody can predict how fragments of the marketmind will react to a given stimulus: your advertising, your product, how your customers use your product, customer service, brand, and packaging; everything is a variable! This is why business plans are about as accurate as monkeys throwing darts at the stock pages.

The best you can do with the marketmind is to go fishing and see what happens. Drop a piece of cheese into the rat race construct and then watch. When a marketmind fragment expresses an opinion about your offer, apply the 3A Method[S55]. Is there something actionable or skewable[S32]? Is it someone who doesn't like coffee? Is this opinion a pattern reflective of the collective or a random stock? Is there meaningful-validation[S88] to outweigh negative opinions? Don't let two finicky cats make you errantly believe that the other 63 million cats in the world would rather have a $3 box over a $300 cat-tree.

☑ **KEY CONCEPTS**

- The marketmind is like a stock market, but instead of representing all stocks, it represents all people who are in your target audience.

- One opinion represents a tiny piece of the marketmind, but it doesn't prove the consensus.

- *Not everyone loves coffee* represents a divergence in the marketmind from the consensus, which may or not be known.

- Marketminds react holistically on the basis of perceived-value, not necessarily to true- or relative-value.

A BRAND IS BORN
MONDAY, JULY 24TH, 2017 - 4:44 PM
(9 days later)

Home from work early, Jeff found his wife lying atop their bed. She was wearing nothing but her Ritz Carlton bathrobe as if she were chilling at the spa. Her hands were clasped behind her head as if she'd just had the best sex of her life. Monday was her day off, so it wasn't unusual. But she wasn't watching television or reading a book; she was gleaming with a shit-eating grin. Jeff looked around, confused. "Where's Maddy?"

"Band practice." She twirled her hair. "She'll be home in an hour, RyRy."

Jeff's eyes flared wide with anticipation.

"You feeling frisky?" He quickly loosened his tie.

"No, keep your shirt on." She snickered. "I'm actually feeling stiff." She rubbed her neck and sat up, maintaining the grin. "Our bet. You lost and I want my prize." She gestured to the nightstand. Jeff spied a bottle of massage oil and an exfoliating brush.

He frowned and then sat next to her on the bed, glaring at her intently. "Wait a sec, we have to agree on a business name. You don't win just because you say you win. We haven't discussed anything."

She laughed again, "Oh, I win. Because I found the name of our business and our brand story. It isn't just good; it's excellent. And if you don't like it, I'm firing you as CEO. And as a husband." She tried to flick her forefinger on his temple, but he jerked away.

He let loose a dramatic sigh. "Fine, let's hear it."

Sam folded her legs like an eight-year-old about to reveal a secret. "Heroic Kitchens." Jeff's nostrils flared but he said nothing. She repeated, "Heroic Kitchens. It's perfect. Any time someone buys one of our soups, we will donate a portion of the profit to an animal at a rescue sanctuary."

Jeff's frigid stare remained. He asked, "You're allocating our profits when we don't even have any?" He grimaced, but Sam's smile remained. Jeff carried on, "So you want to donate a portion of our profits to animal shelters like the humane society or the pound? That is"—he said rubbing his face—"assuming we even make a profit?"

Sam said, "No, we're not donating profits toward pets, but animals who somehow escaped the meat trade—cows, pigs, chickens, any animal who we can give a story and a name to."

"So we're rescuing farm animals?" He shook his head. "I'm confused."

"No, not like that." She angled closer. "There are hundreds of animal sanctuaries around the world. Many of their rescued animals have incredible stories of survival. A lot of them need medical attention, or at least food. We simply sponsor one of the animals and include that as part of our mission. I say we even go as far as putting the animal's story on our labels, so the customer knows exactly who they are helping when they buy a soup from Heroic Kitchens. We can fill our website with these stories, a list of all the animals we help. And we're helping people be healthy. It's the perfect business that makes a difference."

Jeff restrained a nod. Sam continued, pace quickening, "And with a name like Heroic Kitchens, we can move into other plant-based lines, like snacks or cookies. Maybe even ice cream. Not just soup!" Her husband sat silent and shook his head, glaring at the floor. Sam's felt her chest get heavy, anger swelling into throat. This name was perfect, and Jeff was feigning indifference. Her smile melted into a dead stare.

Jeff slapped his palms on his knees and then lurched up from the bed, frowning.

"What? You don't like it?" Sam rebutted, anger creeping into her face. Jeff unbuttoned his shirt and threw it on the floor. Confused, Sam scowled, "Uh, what exactly are you doing?"

He walked to the nightstand shirtless and grabbed the bottle and the exfoliating brush. "I'm thinking I don't want to get massage oil on my good shirt."

He climbed on the bed and commanded, "The CEO of Heroic Kitchens wants you to disrobe."

THE PERSONALITY AND PURPOSE STRATEGY

78

Humanize Your Corporation with a Personality and a Purpose

Some years ago, I sold my Lamborghini. After a mild summer with plenty of sunshine, I realized that I no longer drove it. Yes, it sat in the garage collecting dust. When I first bought the Lamborghini, the brand resonated with my Unscripted, "defy society" identity. I saw it as a symbol of divergence and uniqueness. But it also represented gaud and ostentatiousness. For me, as an introvert, those traits were not desirable. I sold it because as I aged, I preferred obscurity over unwanted attention.

I tell this story because all successful brands do a great job at honing a corporate personality and a purpose that ratifies their customer's identity. As consumers, we don't want to do business with corporations; we want to do business with entities who have relatable stories to ours. Or we do business with brands that affirm our identity or purpose.

In my case, the Lamborghini brand and what it represented didn't change—my identity did.

Productocracies[S71] go hand in hand with a powerful brand image. Behind every disciple[S39], a clear brand identity reinforces loyalty. Branding, however, is a complicated business—so complicated that people make careers of it. For amateurs, branding means a slick logo, a pithy slogan, and some gold-foil stationery. For experts, branding is more... *It is the art of personifying a business with human qualities and characteristics, so it reflects or affirms your customer's identity.* A well-executed brand identity reinforces your customer's identity and, as a result, becomes a value-skew[S32] in the buy decision.

Consider the brand Harley-Davidson. How would you describe their core group of customers? Risk-takers or conservative "play-it-safe" types? If you live YOLO and carefree, would buying a Harley enhance your identity or damage it? How about Nike? As a highly recruited athlete, would a fortune spent on Nike clothing arm your identity or weaken it? How about the person aspiring to get fit? The Nike brand becomes an extension of identity. Think about how these brands weave into identity: Louis Vuitton, Apple, Wrangler, Ferrari, Volvo.

While branding isn't within this book's scope (there are many books on the art, and it is an art) it starts with profiling your target customer's identity.

Who is your perfect customer? What do they wear, where do they live, what does their life look like? What goals do they have, or who do they aspire to be? From there, give your business a personality and a mission that would affirm or build on that identity. Would a vegan or an animal lover like to buy soup that also donates money to rescue shelters? Absolutely. The company's mission goes beyond the product and is purpose-driven with an identity as if it were an actual person. And because its target customer shares a similar identity, skew and brand value is created.

People are loyal to brands and relationships, not corporations or businesses. Make your business feel like a person with a soul and a personality. Build friendships, and those friendships will turn into money.

☑ **KEY CONCEPTS**

- The more your corporation is "branded" like a human personality, the more the marketmind will view your business favorably.

- Your brand personality should affirm or strengthen your customer's identity, creating an additional value-skew.

- People naturally want to do business with people, not faceless corporations.

THE "GOOD ISN'T GOOD ENOUGH" PRINCIPLE

Aiming for a "Good" Likely Ends in a Mediocre

The day I wrote this principle, I received one email that grabbed my attention. Now mind you, between my forum and my books, I get dozens of emails per day, from testimonials to solicitations to administrative nuisances. This particular email had the following subject line:

Your books are more valuable than my MBA! (No, not kidding!)

When I opened the email, a reader (thanks, Chris!) it read as follows:

... I have gained more practical and valuable business knowledge and actionable ideas from your books (and from reading the posts on your forum) than I did from my entire MBA program...

...these are not just books; they are invaluable reference manuals too. My journey to Unscripted begins today.

As you can see, this reader believed my work delivered tremendous value. He would classify my books as "excellent." Such an email is indicative of a Productocracy[S71] as well.

I tell this story because if you want to succeed at anything in life, you have to do good work. Or better, excellent work. That doesn't matter if you're a lawyer, an entrepreneur, or a short-order cook.

Sadly, the secret to "good work" cannot be found on the Internet. In fact, if you go on the hunt for it, you'll instead find the gateway to mediocrity.

Let me explain.

Ever hear the cliché "done is better than perfect?" Or the variant, "perfect is the enemy of good?" Google the "perfect enemy" phrase, and you'll get 184 million page results. The good folks parroting this platitude aren't saying anything new or novel, and they aren't helping you build a Productocracy. Remember, 99% thinking won't get you 1% results.

Here's the big problem: Perfection is often confused with excellence. As such, people don't shoot for the stars, they shoot for "good enough." The "Good Isn't Good Enough" Principle asserts that *if you aim for good, your likely outcome will be mediocrity or worse, poor.* How likely? My guess is about a whopping 84 percent chance. The fact is whatever performance standard you target becomes your best-case scenario. Think about that.

If I want to make $10,000 more next month or lose ten pounds, these targets become my best-case results. Hence, they become outlier outcomes. If we plot potential outcomes on a normalized distribution curve, the "best case" would be at the flat end of the bell curve. Mathematically, it's a two, or worse, three standard deviation outcome. However, the expected results occur in the curve's meat—the middle. The "meat," or the center of the bell curve has a 68% probability of occurring. Simply put, if you make "good" your target, you subconsciously handcuff yourself with a 68 percent chance of producing mediocrity. Worse, you strap yourself with a 16 percent chance of producing garbage.

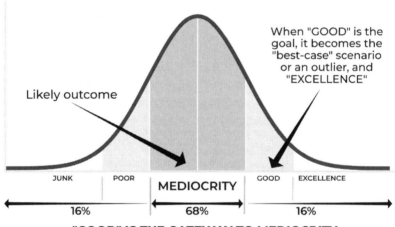

"GOOD" IS THE GATEWAY TO MEDIOCRITY

The answer to the plague of good is simple: Target excellence as your best-case scenario. Make excellence a goal. Don't confuse this with perfection. Excellence is about doing the best you can do. Once excellence becomes your objective, then the middle of the bell curve shifts to good, the most likely outcome. Mediocre and poor also shifts, nearly becoming improbable, a two-standard deviation outcome. This is how you end up with the "good" in our trusted aphorism.

So how do you aim for excellence? Treat the *minor* details of your project with excellence, and the *major* result will turn out pretty damn good. For instance, writing excellent scenes is guaranteed to give you a good screenplay. Writing excellent code subroutines and functions will get you good software.

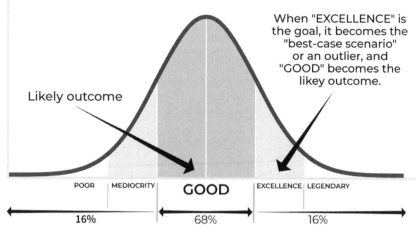

"GOOD" IS THE GATEWAY TO MEDIOCRITY

Not perfect, maybe not even superior, but good enough to incite markets and maybe hit a Productocracy.

When *minor* details are approached with a "good enough" philosophy, your *major* outcome will likely degrade to fair, or poor. The sum of the fair parts doesn't create excellence, much less good. Twenty mediocre scenes won't make a good screenplay. The result is ineffective relative-value[S26]. And that doesn't sell inventory, it doesn't magnetize money, and it certainly doesn't create value-skew.

For example, here's how I approached excellence in writing this book. I role-played as if I was a college senior with weeks before graduation. To graduate, I absolutely need an "A" on a short life principle that might help a new entrepreneur succeed. Every chapter in this book is written with this premise: Make it an "A" or don't pass and graduate.

With this performance strategy, I know many readers will think my book, the final outcome, is good. Some, like my reader Chris with the MBA, might think it's excellent. And, of course, some will think the book is just okay. But here's the hook... very few (2 percent) will judge the book as sucks. Moreover, I can sleep well knowing I did my best, regardless of the market outcome.

Target excellence and shift your potential outcomes. Good becomes probable, mediocrity, improbable.

- When you target "good" as a goal, you make good the best-case scenario.

- If an action-series were standardized on a normal bell curve distribution, the "best case" outcome becomes an outlier, and the expected outcome is the middle, or mediocrity.

- If you aim for good, you are 84 percent likely to produce mediocre or worse work.

- If you aim for excellence, you are 68 percent likely to produce good work, and a significant portion of the marketmind will find value in your work.

A PARTY FOR A PAYDAY
JANUARY 1ST, 2018: 12:01 AM
(5 months, 8 days later)

3 - 2 - 1 - Happy New Year!"

A crowded dance floor of drunken partiers cheered in celebration. Confetti rained from above, blotting out the massive steel and glass windows which plated the dark sky. A stranger next to Samantha blew a whistler far too close to her ear, but she didn't care.

The Trotmans kissed and then hugged, their long embrace immune to the revelry around them. The crowd jumped and yelled like newly minted lotto winners. Jeff stood back and eyed his wife's protruding belly. He held up his champagne and gestured a toast. After another long kiss, they slow-danced, despite the frolic circling them. The rowdy crowd chorused *Auld Lang Syne*. Sam gazed into her husband's glimmering brown eyes, a clue he also felt the scene. She rested her head on Jeff's shoulder as if they were in the third verse of *Open Arms* by Journey. She whispered, "I can't remember the last time I was this excited about a new year."

When the Trotman family first decided to start a business nearly one year ago, they didn't expect to be here. Not this soon, especially after false-starting with a knife sharpening business. How they ended up at a New Year's Eve party at the Grand Hyatt was a story in itself. Even in tight financial times, they were closer to their dream than they could have ever imagined.

Their failed knife sharpening idea was soon replaced by a vegan soup business, a clear gap in the market that Sam identified as a vegan herself. Better, they had a recipe that was proven to be damn tasty, as verified by both vegans and non-vegans alike.

Still, their business barely had $17,000 in sales. With startup costs and many mistakes, their company also lacked a profit. Furthermore, they weren't ready to hire a co-packer. After Sam located a commercial kitchen, she was cooking once a week, canning, and labeling. Many obstacles still laid ahead, but many were overcome. They were overjoyed by their progress. They both felt alive. Mornings weren't as disquieted. Food tasted better. Their real jobs were more tolerable. Life had optimism and hope.

The last six weeks leading up to their celebratory New Year's Eve was a blur. Jeff had extra time to devote to the business because of the holidays while Sam cashed in vacation days. During that time, they solved one problem after another: from their brand positioning to authoring a story behind the company to getting a website launched with order-taking ability.

Their credit cards hemorrhaged at the growth, and the $33,000 they had saved over five frugal years was now down to $21,000—not because they'd spent it, but because December was a blood-bath for the stock market. When the Trotmans saw their balances decline from the increased volatility (and the loss of control surrounding it), it steeled their resolve. Still, their frugal ways adopted in their "lean years" now played a significant role—instead of money going into a market they couldn't control, it was going into a business they could. They aimed for those mysterious, asymmetrical returns.

Still, their burn-rate could have been worse. Jeff almost overpaid a "web developer" $6,000 to build an eCommerce website. Neither Jeff nor Sam had a clue about how eCommerce websites were made, so the $6,000 price tag seemed reasonable. After Sam did an hour of research, it turned out their web developer was simply installing WordPress with a WooCommerce plugin, something they could do on their own. If not, they could hire someone very inexpensively to do it. Certainly not $6,000. Bullet dodged.

Then a failed Kickstarter campaign cost them money. Despite paying $997 for a terribly expensive crowd-funding training seminar, the Kickstarter project didn't meet their threshold goal. Jeff followed the tactics precisely as suggested by the training materials, but it failed to deliver any meaningful sales. Jeff wasn't sure if he had been conned by a bro-marketer or just failed at marketing messaging. He lamented, "Hard to sell a taste they can't taste." He wanted to try again with a new campaign angle; Sam wanted to try a new channel. They would need to decide later.

Then a big disaster came as an unfortunate surprise. After canning, their soup only had a shelf-life of 15 to 17 days. No one got sick; thank the rancid smell for that. But it was their first major problem, an unnerving one that shook the foundation of their resolve. But it didn't last long. Sam solved the issue just days later. Because they didn't hire a co-packer (or have access to their consultants), Sam hired a food chemist for one hour. She discovered all the details on flavoring and preserving secrets, what spices to use and not use, what plant-based food is susceptible to spoiling quicker, and other tricks of the trade. "It was the best $250 I ever spent," she recalled. And she was right. She tweaked her recipe, and the soup stopped spoiling.

Meanwhile, Jeff started implementing one of his marketing ideas: exhibiting at weekend craft fairs and art shows. Since it was winter, he only found two to attend. The first one was an epic failure, one for the *Guinness Book*, if ever such a world record existed. After six hours, Jeff had sold exactly zero cans of soup. Yes, zero. Foot traffic wasn't a problem, the place was jam-packed, and Jeff ran out of business cards. "Business cards don't pay bills!" Sam would later heckle when Jeff reported 190 disappearing business cards as a 'bright side.'

Sam had named the company, exposed their near-fatal website hire, and solved their spoiling soup problem. As such, Jeff *felt* his biggest challenge was getting out-hustled and out-smarted by his wife. Sure, they were a team, but he wanted to be the Captain Kirk of their business. Hopeful for a different outcome at next week's craft fair, Jeff knew something had to change. He had to assess the problem, then adjust. As the old saying went, it's insane to expect different results when you repeat the same thing. So he changed tactics.

Next week at the fair, Jeff would sell out of every can of soup he'd had in stock—120 cans total in two hours. He'd leave early with nearly $600 in sales, a far cry from the zero cans sold last week. A drastic change in tactics changed the outcome drastically—*all because Jeff gave a free sample to anyone who walked by.*

As Jeff left the craft show early, his chest fluttered in excitement and anticipation. A smile was plastered on his face that didn't crack the entire drive home. He thought to himself, *This soup is like a drug—all I have to do is get someone to sample it, and they're hooked.* As he sped home, he saw himself jumping on the mattress like a pre-teen boy with tickets to a new *Star Wars* flick. His small win at the craft show fired something in his soul that went beyond monetary rewards. It was a passion and a tolerance for the process, a self-respecting peace knowing he was making a difference. Working on his business was now a habit, as much as watching Cubs games had been ten years ago. And though he still had a thankless job as a thankless auditor at a thankless company, that job suddenly became more bearable. It was no longer the ends; it was the means. And yet, all these feelings curiously confused him. He wasn't passionate about this plant-based stuff like his wife. But he was on fire for this business and what it represented. It gave his life a purpose and a direction, all while the world found value in it. He couldn't imagine what he'd feel like if he sold millions of cans, not hundreds.

When Jeff returned home from the art fair, his wife was seated on the couch with Madison watching TV together. Jeff laughed as he saw *The Brady Bunch* airing, specifically the episode where Jan gets biffed in the face with Greg's football.

Jeff dropped his briefcase and asked, "So is this what you guys do when I'm gone, *The Brady Bunch*?" Sam put her hand on Madison's knee, a signal to pause the TV. Sam glanced at the clock on the microwave and then scoffed. "Oh, boy." She grimaced. "You're home early. That can't be good."

Jeff grinned and threw his hands in the air, releasing a wad of money that rained like confetti. Madison giggled and leaped up from the couch and tried to catch a few bills. Jeff continued, "Sold out baby! In only two hours!" He firmly fixed his hands on his waist as if he was about to battle a rival rapper. "Check. Your move."

Sam smiled incredulously, but her eyes twinkled. Jeff's competitive insecurities were amusing, if not ridiculous. Jeff gyrated his hips flamboyantly as if he was pole dancing. Sam chuckled. "My move? How about we celebrate at the Hyatt on New Year's? You can educate the peasants on how you made it rain money." She hesitated and then motioned to his hips, still pulsating in ridiculousness. "And if you want to get lucky, I suggest you leave your goofy dance at home."

That New Year's Eve was the Trotmans' first "paycheck" from their business. Of course, none of them took a paycheck, but it was their reward. As the last confetti fell, they continued their embrace until Jeff retreated and faced his pregnant wife. As if divine timing was paying attention to the moment, the song changed, a more fitting melody to their mood: Eric Clapton's *Wonderful Tonight.*

He smiled and asked, "May I have this dance?"

She pulled him close. "You may do as you please."

THE GOLD STAR STRATEGY

Celebrate Victories Commensurate with the Win

80

In elementary school, good work was rewarded with a gold star. In business, you need to do the same. Every expensive car I've ever owned, from Vipers to Lamborghinis, has been a "gold star" gift to myself. While your build your business, it's essential to reward yourself, even for the small wins. It might be months, perhaps years before you can draw a steady paycheck. The same applies to asymmetric returns. As such, you'll want to reward yourself for milestones reached. Here are some milestones you should celebrate.

- Your first prototype
- Your first product ready for sale
- Your first successful import, if applicable
- Your first sale
- Your first great review
- Your confirmation of a Productocracy (a big celebration!)
- Your first profit, even a few bucks!
- Your first polymorphous pay
- Your first paycheck
- Your first employee
- Your first lucrative partnership or distribution agreement
- Your first profitable month
- Your first profitable year
- Your first sign of asymmetrical returns
- A business valuation that exceeds $1 million, $5M, and beyond
- Your net worth exceeds $1 million, $2M, $5M, and beyond
- Your liquid savings exceed $1 million, $2M, $5M, and beyond
- You sell your company

Obviously, the cost of your gold stars shouldn't endanger your progress or limit future options. Rewards could be a massage, a nice dinner at a restaurant, a weekend staycation, or a New Year's Eve party. Better, a reward that fits into your 1/5/10 Planasy[S12] is a great idea. Once the asymmetric returns begin, the gold stars can get more extravagant, and you can start crossing off 1/5/10 milestones.

☑ **KEY CONCEPTS**

- Celebrate personal and business victories with "gold stars," or rewards commensurate with the victory.

- Rewards should not endanger or regress your progress.

- A reward that fits into your 1/5/10 Planasy is a great reward.

THE FRUIT TREE STRATEGY

Hunt for Fruit Trees, Not Peeled Fruit

81

I read a book recently about business growth strategies. Much of it, while entertaining, was *peeled fruit* tactics. For instance, one startup grew by hacking Craigslist—while that worked in 2011, it doesn't work in 2021. Likewise, if I wrote a book detailing how I built an Internet business from zero users to millions, most of it would not be very helpful. The methods and strategies I used five years ago, much less fifteen years ago, are peeled fruit tactics. *What's actionable today, most likely, won't be actionable tomorrow.*

The unfortunate reality we face as entrepreneurs is that actionable advice has the lifespan of peeled fruit. Once the fruit is peeled, and marketers get a hold of it, the clock starts ticking. Within years, sometimes months, that particular strategy stops working.

While some peeled fruit is worth investigating and deploying, most of your growth will come from *fruit trees*. Fruit trees are new strategies, mediums, or channels that haven't been mass promoted into the mainstream. And you only uncover them via the 3A Method[S55]. If there is a new social media platform that isn't yet mainstream, there's a good chance it could be an emerging fruit tree ready for exploit—years ago it was Facebook, then Instagram, then SnapChat, then this, then that, then repeat forever… Remember, change is constant[S42] and is the launching pad for new millionaires and billionaires.

For instance, on my forum, an entrepreneur posted his experience finding a fruit tree: legal voice-mail marketing. He reported insane ROIs. Within days as people discovered the fruit tree, the thread grew to three pages, and dozens of comments as people rushed in to use it. At some point, the tactic will become adapted and overused. The "insane ROI" will disappear.

Once the tactic becomes saturated, peeled fruit marketers swoop in and sell the strategy as some super cool new marketing tactic. These marketers will often use fresh fruit tree tactics to sell their past, rotten fruit tree, which has now become peeled fruit. Once their current fruit tree loses its effectiveness, the whole process repeats—find a new fruit tree to sell the older one that no longer works. Meanwhile, they make a fortune selling the cycle. There's a good chance that Jeff's $997 Kickstarter Masterclass was a peeled-fruit strategy. I've yet to hear of any entrepreneur who exploded his business because they paid $4997 for a super-secret marketing tactic plus six free bonuses. As entrepreneurs, we have to be on the prowl for any strategy that can grow our business, peeled fruit, or otherwise. *Just be wary of marketers selling marketing strategies*—you're better off observing their methods over buying them. You don't want to invest $10,000 in a fruit tree when in truth, you're getting peeled fruit about to go rotten.

☑ **KEY CONCEPTS**

- Strategies and tactics that work today won't work tomorrow.
- Usually, effective strategies of yesterday (peeled fruit) are packaged into expensive programs and marketed as effective strategies of today.
- Fruit trees are unique marketing strategies or new media channels not bastardized by internet marketers and guru schemers.

THE DEMONSTRATION STRATEGY

Demonstration Is Gold, Description Is Dirt

82

The last time you bought a car, I'll bet you test drove it. The last time you sprung for some cologne or perfume, I'll bet the same thing. You smelled it. Roll the towering corridors of Costco, and you'll smell tasty morsels at a sampling cart staffed by a grandmotherly attendant. Eat in the aisle, pay at the cashier.

The most powerful sales strategy for a Productocracy[S71] is a demonstration. This can be a video walkthrough, a free trial, or a free sample. The Demonstration Strategy *serves to minimize risk, present pre-purchase value, and foster reciprocity*. It's like arming the sales process with a laser-sighted rifle.

The first demonstration perk is risk elimination. What is more likely to compel a sale? A sign in the window that reads, "Our Unscripted Cookies are a decadent mix between creamy peanut butter and rich dark chocolate imported from Belgium," or a free sample? End risk for your potential customer, and you'll grab more sales. In this case, eating a sample before buying guarantees that the customer's relative-value[S26] expectations will be met.

The second perk is it allows your customer to see what life is like without your value. If your customer freely samples the product and instantly loves it, you win a sale along with a guaranteed non-return occurrence. Trust comes before lust. And if consumers are lusting after your product(s), you could also charge a slightly higher premium.

In the application and video game business, a demonstration is the industry's backbone with the "freemium" business model. Here's how: 1) get your customers to try it for free and 2) get them hooked, so they want to pay for it. A video game that has you entertained or enthused in minutes will hook you into paying. My business also used the freemium tactic long before freemium was even a buzzword. My most significant value-skew[S32], the Unique Selling Proposition, or USP, allowed advertisers to try my service risk-free. Getting advertisers to join was a breeze because, at the time, the industry standard was "Pay 100 percent upfront." My customers only paid when I sent them a customer. My purpose was demonstration: give potential clients a risk-free evaluation and hook them into paying for the service only after they found valuable customers.

No matter what you're selling, you must apply some form of demonstration. In the infomercial business, potential product placements that can't be demonstrated are principally rejected. Without the demonstration's visual power, these big infomercial companies know that they're going to war with sticks and stones. You have to go into battle with the laser-sighted rifle.

In another example, my publishing company gives away the first five or six chapters for every book I write. My purpose is to reduce the risk for my reader. After a chapter or two, a potential reader should know if they like the content and my voice. Second, I'm trying to hook them. In every book I write, I pay strict attention to the early chapters because that is where the demonstration occurs. It is where the sale is made or lost.

The final demonstration perk is reciprocity. Psychological studies show that if you do something free for a stranger, they are more likely to return the favor. While the other bullets exude more sales power, everything helps.

Studies have reported that the power of demonstration is impressive. One firm said that beer sales were boosted by 71 percent when national retailers hosted beer sampling. Frozen pizza samples? Exploded sales by a whopping 600 percent![1] Mind you, this is what corporations are willing to reveal. It's unlikely that any company would announce a sales strategy capable of spiking sales by hundreds of percentages.

Of course, none of this matters if your product is garbage. Demonstration and its results can often be the first sign of a Productocracy, or lack thereof.

☑ KEY CONCEPTS

- A Productocracy's most powerful sales tactic is demonstration.
- An effective demonstration lowers or eliminates customer buying risk, gets buyers hooked, and taps into reciprocity—all of which improve probabilities for sales.
- The "freemium" business model is a form of demonstration, particularly in video gaming.

---

1 - https://www.theatlantic.com/business/archive/2014/10/the-psychology-behind-costcos-free-samples/380969/

THE GAMIFICATION STRATEGY

Play Life Like a Video Game to Be Won

83

Hundreds of aspiring entrepreneurs visit my forum daily where they freely post their questions and their struggles. One common struggle voiced on the forum is video game addiction. A phenomenon once reserved for teenagers, we now have grown adults joysticking their lives down the drain. And they can't stop. My unscientific theory into this epidemic is a combination of three things. First, video games are a coping mechanism for the realities of rat race life. Just like junk food, sports, and television. Second, video games can be played in relative comfort[P3] where failure is anonymous and consequence-free. Fail at a video game, and you press RESET to try again. Success is marginalized to a RESET button, all while eating pizza and reclining on a La-Z-Boy. Third, and most importantly, video games are designed for addiction. Like most coping mechanisms, addictive components fire our feedback loop[S46], giving us a false sense of success. These are the same elements that drive success and transformative passion, spiking dopamine. Once you taste fictional success, your brain wants more.

The more I study technology, religion, and science (quantum physics is a real mind-bender), the more I wonder if life is a technological simulation. All of us could be avatars for some advanced civilization, and God isn't some ephemeral bearded man on a throne but a pimply-faced teenager who pressed the "ON" button. Regardless of what you believe, our reality is what we process through our five senses. And those senses should be telling us that life has to be more than working five days a week for half a century, paying bills, and then dying.

Once you realize your role in the rat race religion[P5], your goal should be crystal clear: Win your freedom and be happy in its pursuit. Yes, happiness NOW, not LATER. Attack entrepreneurial life as if it were a role-playing video game (RPG). Do so, and you move probability[S59] because the same "leveling-up" mechanics apply. In any RPG, you have to become a problemologist[S30] to advance through the game. As such, you're continually investigating, identifying problems, acting, assessing, and adjusting[S55]. As skills and resources accumulate, so do your opportunities and their results.

Many RPG video games are a team effort involving parties. A warrior will join with an elf who offers complementary skills. When the warrior can't cast a spell, he joins with a wizard. Likewise, to win at entrepreneurship, you'll also need a team: employees, freelancers, contractors, joint venture partners. In business, wherever you are weak or in need, hire or outsource. Many entrepreneurs want to "do it alone" because they also want control or fear delegation. Going it alone might win some battles, but it rarely wins the war.

Finally, the game of entrepreneurship is riddled with resets and game restarts. No one wins the game on their first play. They play and repeatedly fail until skills are honed, learning is done, and wisdom grows. Over time, your character builds and gets stronger. Problems are solved more comfortably, gold starts to accrue, and bigger wins are scored. Leveling up is one step closer to a rat race escape. And then one day you'll discover, hey, my life is so incredible I don't need junk food, television, or video games.

☑ KEY CONCEPTS

- Video gaming is endemic to how dismal and hopeless life is for most people.

- Video gaming is destructive because it allows unlimited anonymous failure while stimulating our dopamine centers with fictional success.

- Look at life as a real video game with problems to solve, rewards to be won, teams to build, and freedom to obtain.

ONE GIANT STEP FOR TROTMANKIND...

MONDAY, MARCH 5TH, 2018 - 10:11 AM
(63 days later)

Beachball in her belly, Samantha was weeks from birth. Instead of taking unpaid maternity leave, she opted for a lighter workload, going from four days a week to two. The extra days gave her time to work on the business. Jeff continued to utilize his lunch hours, often cold-calling distributors and other "whale" accounts. Without a dedicated full-time employee, progress was slow, albeit steady.

The sun peeked out from the gray sky for the first time in months. Despite a brisk temperature that couldn't crack 60, spring freshened the air. Sam glanced out the window and saw convertibles with dropped tops. People walked about without jackets. After five months of unmerciful Chicago cold, 59 degrees might as well be 82. She texted Jeff: *Sunny day = good omen.*

Like a changing season, the Trotmans entered a new phase in their business. And new phases come with new risks. Today was the big day: Their first order with their selected co-packer, two SKUs costing nearly $10,000 for 100 cases each of Asian Tofu Udon and Creamy Potato Bisque. After weeks of sampling and about a dozen FedExes back and forth with their co-packer, they finally got their two recipes nailed down. While their co-packer wasn't the cheapest, they offered organic ingredients plus storage and fulfillment. Shipping two skids of bulky cans from North Carolina to Chicago and storing them in a townhouse garage was, as Jeff put it, "amateur."

Since their New Year's Eve celebration two months ago, they'd cautiously moved ahead. Now, hard decisions needed to be made. While their sales were growing, it was a slow crawl with peaks and valleys. While five or six orders a day from their website was encouraging, it put them in a gray area. They weren't selling enough to warrant a big order with a co-packer, but they were selling enough to make Sam's weekly visit to the commercial kitchen a royal pain in the ass.

"This is starting to become a chore," Sam reported. "You know I love to cook," she said to Jeff, "but these weekly visits to the kitchen are starting to take their toll." Jeff followed with a confession of his own. "I haven't been marketing as much. I know every sale means less inventory, and less inventory means you need to go back to the kitchen. And with you being on the verge of birth, you need to start going easier, not harder."

Sam agreed. "Yes, I don't think we can continue with this 'dip our toe in the water' strategy. We need to dive in and just do it. Freeing me up from the kitchen will also give me more time to get our message out. I'd like to implement that influencer strategy you mentioned."

Most of their sales were coming from the unlikeliest of places, their businesses' social media accounts, Instagram, TikTok, and Facebook. Sam would post soup photos or make plant-based memes and tag them with vegan-related tags, and like clockwork, two or three sales would trickle in with each post. The strategy's effectiveness had Sam considering hiring a marketing and public relations firm, at least until they wanted a $15,000 retainer.

In the meantime, Jeff was trying to secure commercial wholesale accounts.

They understood that their venture's real growth wouldn't be from occasional website sales but in getting their soups on the store shelves where plant-based soups are virtually non-existent. Jeff cold-called and emailed food distributors, but no one was biting. At this point, he would have loved to hear back from someone and get a literal rejection instead of a literal ignore. It seemed as if the food industry was like a high-school clique; if you weren't sitting at the cool-kids' table in the cafeteria, you had to fight your way there or do something shocking. But for Jeff and Sam, they felt they were being ignored. According to Jeff, always the numbers guy, the soup had a 50 percent conversion rate on anyone who sampled it. But Sam wasn't sold on that metric and reasoned it was an anomaly. She argued, "The old ladies at Costco who do the free sampling are always fighting off a mob. And a lot of that junk is processed. I'm afraid you're just catching people when they're hungry."

But she would later become a believer. Jeff showed her their customer list, which at the moment was just under 4,000 people. "See these marks?" He pointed to a column on the spreadsheet. "Those are repeat buyers, and according to the numbers, our reorder rate is already at 21 percent. And we don't even know if the other buyers already ate the soup."

This data sold Sam, combined with a slew of emails from random strangers raving about the soup, statements like "OMG it's about time!" or "My carnivore husband loved it!"

It was time to charge ahead.

When it rolled into the lunch hour, Sam's phone rang. "It's done," Jeff said flatly on the line as if he'd just made an appointment for a prostate exam. "Next month you'll have an $8,900 charge on your Visa. We'll have to dig into whatever's left of the emergency fund." He paused. "By this time next week, we'll be the proud owners of 6,400 cans of soup."

"I thought our first order was going to be ten thousand dollars?" Sam asked.

"I begged the manufacturer to do better. Told him how we're a struggling small business living in a dump." He laughed. "Guess he felt sorry for us and waived the credit fees plus gave us a three percent discount."

"Nice," she said, walking over to the window and moving the curtain aside. The sun was even brighter, the melting snow reflecting its rays into a blinding sheen.

"Well, I should get back to work," Jeff said. "I loathe thinking about that credit card bill when it comes next month. Between the Fed-Exes and the kitchen rental, we're near our limits."

"Or you can look at it from the bright side like today's sunshine," Sam stated. "When we sell all those cans, we'll quadruple our revenue. And have $25,000 in profit to buy more. And who knows, maybe pay some of it off."

She paused and then glanced at the whiteboard on the wall. She spoke forcefully. "Remember Jeff, it's *nail and scale*, not *worry and scurry*."

THE LEAP OF ZEROES PRINCIPLE

Don't Fear a Leap of Zeroes

84

Ionce found an uncashed check in my car for $11,000. As I told this story in the first *Unscripted* book, the check was squashed between my seat and the center console. After I got over the shock of not missing it for a month, I could only smile. I'd made the *Leap of Zeroes* many years earlier. When I started my business, a two-zero expense, say $500, was a lot of money. Now, it is about as significant as buying a Slurpee from the Quik-Trip.

At some point in your evolution from consumer to producer[P22], you will need to make a Leap of Zeroes. Like a leap of faith, The Leap of Zeroes Principle *is an inflection point in your business when bigger decisions with bigger price tags must be made.* This could be new equipment, hiring new employees, a warehouse lease, or a seven-figure loan. My first Leap of Zeroes was years ago when I was broke. I spent thousands of dollars on a premium domain name. At that point in my life (and business), it was the largest purchase I had ever made, and making it felt like going "all in."

If you've ever swum in a cold pool or a lake, you know it's better to just dive in. An inch-by-inch "toe-dip" creep into the frigid water prolongs the pain and amplifies the fear. Furthermore, it also gives you a chance to talk yourself out of it. At some point, you need to steel your loins and just jump.

If your business proves to be a Productocracy[S71] while showing signs of leverage[P16] and asymmetric returns[S21], don't fear making the Leap of Zeroes. And yes, it will feel like a huge risk. But it isn't when given some rat race perspective... *Investing $10,000 on two skids of plant-based soup is risky, but financing $50,000 over six years on a new Chevy Tahoe isn't?* As they say, people spend more time planning their week-long vacation than they do planning for their financial futures.

The problem is your transition from consumer to producer doesn't automatically cancel the scarcity mindset. It doesn't cancel your memory of financial struggles. It doesn't swap perspectives on what constitutes a good investment... buying soup to build a business? Or buying a Tahoe to build your ego? When you're taught to pinch every penny and save every dime, the idea of spending $10,000 for a business venture seems foolish. Risky. Outlandish. This is normal... but expected.

So how do you know when a Leap of Zeroes is needed? Two criteria: 1) Reasonable and 2) Necessary. First, the expense must be reasonable. There is nothing unreasonable about buying inventory for your new business. It is also necessary. Without this "leap," the Trotmans cannot move forward. Most often, a Leap of Zeroes is required to move the business to the next level. This is an important distinction—some large expenses are neither reasonable nor necessary. Yes, spending $15,000 to retain a public relations firm might help the business. But is it reasonable and necessary? No, neither.

When significant sums of money with more zeroes appear in your life, both on the expense and revenue side, it's part of the Unscripted process. If you don't fear the zeroes in business, then the zeroes in your personal life will also start to change. And one day you might find yourself unfazed at finding five or six figures stuffed in between the seats.

☑ **KEY CONCEPTS**

- At some point in your business, you will need to make a "Leap of Zeroes," which is a large expenditure that is required to move your business forward.

- A "Leap of Zeroes" expense should be reasonable and necessary.

- As your business grows, so will your personal "Leap of Zeroes" by way of larger numbers—more income, more saving, and more taxes.

THE MILLIONAIRE PAYCHECK STRATEGY

Hire Yourself for Seconds and
Get Paid Millionaire Rates

I once earned $180,000 an hour. I kid you not. Here's how I did it, and here's how you can make a similar rate of return on your time. Every few years, I host an annual Unscripted conference at a beautiful resort in Arizona. If you haven't hosted a fairly large event at a hotel before, let me be clear. Everything is overpriced, from food to audiovisual equipment. Before you guess that I profited $180,000 in ticket sales, let me correct you pronto. This conference is basically run at cost, and I barely draw a profit.

As I prepared for the conference and reviewed my order, I noticed a line item for curtains that backdropped the speaking stage. It was a whopping $1,500. My jaw dropped. I immediately fired off an email to the event coordinator. I asked, "Can you do better for this price? $1,500 for curtains is a bit exorbitant for a curtain rental, considering we've hosted this event at your venue for many years."

The event coordinator was happy to remove the $1,500 curtains from my bill and still provide them. Boom! Just like that, 30 seconds earned me $1,500. If you "hourlyize" that rate of pay, it comes to a staggering $180,000 an hour.

[30 seconds X $1,500 = $3,000 a minute]
[$3,000 a minute = $180,000 an hour]

If someone offered you a temporary job that paid $180,000 per hour for some risk-free work, would you take it? You would instantly, as I would too. That fact is, anytime you're about to spend money, *hire yourself.* Take a few seconds, at most a minute, and seek a discount, a promo code, or a negotiation. If you're successful, you will earn a staggering return on your time, usually an hourly rate that amounts to thousands.

Last year, I purchased a software subscription that retailed for $129 a month. Before I clicked "Submit" on the order page, I did a quick internet search for a coupon code. I found one that discounted the service to $89 a month. Within thirty seconds, I saved $40. If you "hourlyized" the return on my minor fragment of effort, thirty seconds, it amounted to a return on time invested to a whopping $4,800 per hour.

[30 seconds X $40 = $80 a minute]
[$80 a minute = $4,800 an hour]

And because it's a monthly subscription, the 30 seconds continually pays $40 in savings every month. Seconds of my time kept $40 a month in my pocket, residually for as long as I remain a customer.

Hiring yourself also goes beyond coupon codes and Internet shopping. As Jeff was faced with his first order's daunting cost, he asked for a better price. Those seconds paid handsomely. Negotiating for a new car or a new appliance? Uttering the phrase *Is that the best you can do?* only takes seconds, but the hourly return on those seconds can amount to hundreds, if not thousands. In real estate, a few days of patience can yield tens of thousands of dollars.

Whenever you make a purchase, *hire yourself*, and aim to get it for less. No, you're not cheap, but you do want an instant payday at millionaire rates of return. Keep in mind: This is a defensive strategy[P12], and the game is won on offense. However, money is still money. Not seeking millionaire paydays is no different than tossing money out the window of a moving car. Transform tiny blocks of your life into millionaire paydays, and one day, you will be a millionaire.

☑ KEY CONCEPTS

- Anytime you spend money, hire yourself and earn a huge rate of return.

- Combined with an offensive approach, negotiating in all circumstances can earn huge rates of return, usually at millionaire pay rates.

- Searching for coupon codes, patience, and merely asking *Is this the best you can do?* can save you thousands and earn you a huge return on your time.

EFFIN' GRANDMAS?!
MONDAY, MARCH 12TH, 2018 - 3:01 PM
(7 days later)

Before the co-packer could pack their order, Jeff and his wife noticed an immediate shift in their approach. While they were already committed, they went from a brisk walk to a sprint. Having 6,400 cans of soup stored in a North Carolina warehouse (and a pending credit card bill) added another layer of seriousness. Jeff would mention, "Can you believe we're doing this? It feels surreal. My stomach is in knots, and I'm not sure if it's excitement or fear."

But with each day, each order, and each email raving about the soup, the excitement would chip away the fear. Until one day, it simply disappeared. They had a new normal working alongside their current jobs; Jeff would deal with operations and wholesale acquisition, Sam marketing and outreach. Their business amounted to a second job, but oddly, they didn't quite equate their business work with actual work.

Jeff would spend lunch hour at his job submitting orders into their fulfillment processor. If there was any time left over, he'd make a call or two to a food distributor or a specialty grocer. On the days she worked graveyard, Sam would spend the later hours of her afternoon prospecting and marketing. On her days off, Sam would work the business in the afternoon and evenings as if it were her own job. Jeff tasked her to focus on plant-based influencers with a large social media presence. They learned fast that when an Instagram or YouTube user raved about the soup, it would generate instant sales directly proportional to their followers. The first time it happened, an Instagram user with 3,900 followers posted a photo of the soup and raved about it. It generated 12 sales nearly instantly and ended up being one of their biggest sales days.

When it happened again a mere four days later, the same math repeated. Someone with 11,000 followers generated 41 sales… Another new record.

Once Jeff analyzed the numbers, he remarked, "Oh my, it's like printing money. We just need slew of influencers to taste it." If anyone raved about the soup on social media, Jeff deduced that minimally one-third of one percent (.003) of their followers would buy. He barked more numbers at Sam. "If we can get one of these skinny soy-boys with one million followers to plug us, we

310

can sell 5,000 cans in a matter of minutes. At a $2 margin, that's an instant profit of $10,000, for mere minutes of work!"

Sam shook her head and then glared at her husband's douchebaggery, remarking rhetorically, "Soy-boys?" She crossed her arms. "Mr. Jeffrey Trotman, let me warn you. You can't be saying stuff like that. If one of our customers heard you, we'd be done in a flash."

His eyes peered over the desktop computer still parked on the kitchen table. Sam saw his face flash worry. He reclined back in his chair, his lips contorting into mush. "Crap, you're probably right." He paused then clarified, "When I was at work and gave Hank his soup order, he laughed when I told him the soup was vegan. He said, 'Wow, I liked soup for soy-boys?! Amazing!'"

"No need to explain, Jeff, I forgive you. Try to remember you're the CEO of a company now, not a playground bully. Be mindful of what comes out of that mouth of yours. Strangers who feel betrayed won't be so forgiving."

Two days later, they would get their first big break. Sort of. It was a call from Philadelphia. It wasn't a big break in terms of money—the order was only for one case—but it was more of a beaver dam breaking, complete with a message from the beaver. When Sam got the call from Papa Tony's Italian Deli at 5 PM, she couldn't believe it. She asked for clarification. "Pardon me if this is none of my business, but why would an Italian deli in Philadelphia want to order a plant-based soup?"

"South Philadelphia," corrected the man on the phone in a Rocky-like 'Yo Adrian' Italian accent.

"I'm sorry," Sam offered, "South Philly. You get a lot of requests for vegan soup?"

The question drew silence. Sam imagined the man on the line to be about 300 bills, a jogging suit that had never been jogged in, and a pinky ring to round out (no pun intended) the look.

As the silence hung, Sam wondered if her question crossed a line or if it was just "Yo Adrian" thinking.

The deli owner finally spoke, almost sounding remorseful. "We get a lot of old people asking for it. You know, grandmas and stuff. So I found you on the interwebs. Came up on the first page."

Sam threw the phone a puzzled look. "Older people are asking you for vegan soup?"

"Yeah, yeah…" he said but broke into a negative, "but I don't think they like it. I had a few tell me they want it for their grandkids. Mrs. Carlucci told me her grandkids won't eat anything with meat in it. And if they can't eat at Grandma Carlucci's, they won't visit Grandma." A pause, then louder, "Can you imagine that? How do you go to Grandma Carlucci's and not eat her meatballs? They're to die for. Those grandkids of hers, they should lop off their damn fingers for showing such disrespect." He scoffed. "No meat, my God, what's this world a-coming to?"

Sam didn't comment but thanked the man and took his order. It was their first wholesale account, but more importantly, it hinted at just how many tentacles they had working for them.

After Sam hung up, she uttered under her breath, channeling her husband's piss-poor impersonation of Al Pacino, "No shit, effin' grandmas."

THE FIRED CUSTOMER STRATEGY

86

Fire When You Tire

Years ago, I remember a customer in California who would call several times a week and occupy hours of customer service time. When billing rolled around, she'd be back on the phone contesting every line-item, bit-by-bit, minute-by-minute. After several months of dealing with this melodramatic client with too much time and obviously not enough work, I asked the rep to investigate her average bill size. It amounted to about twelve bucks. Specifically, I was paying someone five hours at $25 an hour to "manage" this person as a boss and as a customer.

I whipped out my "nice but firm" writing style and ended the relationship. Keep your $12.87; I'll stop spending $125 trying to earn it.

Fun fact for business owners: Every current and potential customer is your boss. The bosses pay you for work, or in our case, for our relative-value. However, what isn't often considered is how much value do our bosses bring to us? If it isn't enough, fire them. When they bring you more trouble without the marginal benefit for that trouble, dump them.

What few realize is that business transactions are a mutual agreement between two parties and then a value exchange. When one party is aggrieved, and the balance goes out of whack—on either side—someone must fire the other. If you're paying me $20, you expect at least $20 in value. If I come up short, I get fired, and you go to another company. But on the flip side, if you're yielding $10 in revenue but costing me $50 in expenses and/or ball-busting drama, you're going bye-bye.

Because most consumers have been bombarded with the conventional wisdom *the customer is king, many* customers go instant asshole, then instant apeshit when something isn't right. The *customer is king* mentality has given them a license to treat business owners and their employees like used cat litter. This happens often on my forum. When it's clear a user is trolling my forum to distract and disrupt, posting such statements as "You're all wasting your time" or "You'll never get rich," I have no problem removing them. They're not visiting my forum for enlightenment or business building.

In another example, I once had a paying customer call me a fraud in several forum posts because I didn't return his email within two hours. Mind you, he sent the email at 6:27 in the evening. Because I eat dinner like every other human on the planet, his request for a refund was not answered within his expectation profile[S39], which turned out to be "as soon as I fucking send it." After waiting an hour, he decided to have a temper tantrum. When I read his request (about three hours after his first email), I promptly refunded his money. Then I promptly banned him. Sorry, but your $59 doesn't give you the right to libel me while dropping a stink-bomb inside my house—in the words of our most loved/hated ex-President, *You're fired!* Refund? Hell yeah, how fast can I do it?

But MJ, that isn't SUCS as you preach, you're a hypocrite!

No, champ. When I tire, I fire.

Don't believe the lie. Customers aren't kings, they're presidents—and presidents can be booted out of office with just one vote... *yours.*

☑ KEY CONCEPTS

- Your boss is your customer, and they can fire you, but you can also fire them.

- Fire problem customers when the value they bring sinks below their cost.

THE HINDSIGHT STRATEGY

Think Consequentially and Expose
Process-Killing Choices

In 2012, a medical-device CFO making $200,000 a year thought he'd score some internet points by videoing himself berating a Chick-fil-A employee at a drive-through window. The two-minute YouTube video went viral and stoked a national outrage. When the dust settled, he was fired from his job. The man also lost over $2 million in stock options and, as of March 2015, is now unemployed and on food stamps.

One bad decision can invalidate thousands of good ones.

Pete Rose bet on baseball, and his life was forever changed. Tiger Woods crashed his Lincoln amid a marital infidelity cover-up, and things were never the same. Michael Richards, known for playing Kramer from *Seinfeld*, used racial slurs during a stand-up comedy routine and lost his reputation instantly. Bill Buckner erred in the World Series, tarnishing an outstanding baseball career.

What's the common thread in all these stories?

One event can destroy a process. Even one you didn't intend. An action lasting minutes can kill a process that took you decades to build. The process builds the event (I finally got my CFO dream job!) while an event (Let's berate this minimum wage employee!) tears the process apart.

Yes, one reckless decision can ravage your life or destroy your business in an instant. A one-night stand can kill a marriage. An inappropriate slap on the butt to an employee can destroy a career. And a drunk driving accident can ruin lives. An action that spans mere minutes destroys a lifetime of process, killing livelihoods, relationships, and reputations. Think about that for a minute. One impulsive decision (or mistake) has the staggering power to invalidate thousands of well-planned ones. Your dream house took two years to build, but one carelessly placed cigar burnt it down.

The event kills the process. But the reverse does not apply. One positive action cannot erase thousands of negative ones. Eating broccoli for one day won't help you lose the weight that took years to accumulate.

The unfortunate reality of the event/process dichotomy[P28] is that the consequences of our actions are unfairly weighted toward the bad ones. In Jeff's case, if some of his customers discovered that he had pejoratively stereotyped them as "soy-boys," it would jeopardize their business.

Your defense for exploiting process-killing choices is consequential-thinking. *Consequential-thinking* extrapolates consequences while assessing risk and probability. Think before you act! Before embarking on a risky action, ask the questions: What are this action's worst- and best-case consequences and their reasonable odds? Are these outcomes worth the risk? Why are you betting the house to win a free hamburger? To be edgy? Are you risking your health to inflate your ego? A proactive mind answers these questions in seconds. Once reviewed, catastrophic threats to your process can be exposed, and bad decisions can be avoided. In effect, consequential-thinking brings hindsight into the present.

☑ **KEY CONCEPTS**

- One event lasting minutes can destroy a process that took years to build, but the reverse does not apply.

- Poor decisions are weighted negatively and can be process-killers.

- *Consequential-thinking* extrapolates consequences while assessing risk and probability, bringing hindsight into the present for better decision-making.

JUST ANOTHER DAY AT THE OFFICE...
THURSDAY MARCH 15TH, 2018 - 5:12 PM
(3 days later)

"Who died?" Sam asked her husband when she returned home from the grocery store. Jeff was hunkered down at the corner of the kitchen table, now their de facto office, grimacing at his desktop. Bella greeted Sam, tail wagging furiously, followed by an intensive sniff of the food haul hoping to find a treat.

Without looking up from his screen, Jeff replied, "No one died."

Bella barked a rare bark as Sam unpacked the paper bags. Bella clung to her heels, still hopeful for a goody. Jeff sat silent, keyboard clacking away. He let loose a harsh breath. And then another.

After the groceries were put away and Bella got her treat, Sam lingered over to her husband. She slowly slid the chair out and sat. She pulled the back of his desktop screen and asked, "All right, what's going on?" His eyes shifted up, but his head didn't move. "Well, right now, I'm trying to stop the bleeding. I've placed some pay-per-click ads at Google. We've gotten some clicks but no orders. I've already burned through $200. I'm not sure why we aren't selling anything: our ad copy, our website's design, the wrong market. Not sure, this stuff is a fucking science. I'm having a déjà-vu when I tried to sell T-shirts."

"Is it anything to be really worried about?" Sam asked. "I mean, we keep selling soup, our customers love our product, and we've made progress."

"Yeah, I know. It just feels like it's always ten steps forward, nine steps back." He sighed. "Guess it's just another day at the office."

Sam nodded and then asked, "You know, March Madness started today. Might be a good distraction for you."

He huffed. "I could care less about that nonsense right now. Not sure I will ever care about it again." He swiveled the computer around and pointed to the screen. "We've got to figure out how to get here."

Sam moved closer and recited what she read: *Veggie Con —The Plant-Based Convention.* She looked at Jeff. "Well, that looks promising, and you know we love Vegas... It says they expect over 30,000 attendees and 200 exhibitors."

Jeff leaned back, folding his arms. "Yes, very promising, except we can't afford to exhibit. I've spent the last two weeks trying to figure out how to make it financially worth the risk. Cleaning out our retirement accounts and spending every dime of profit we've made thus far is just too big a risk. We'd be going all-in without a safety net."

Sam sat quietly for a moment and then wondered aloud, "Is it one of those Leap of Zeroes? Something we need to do to move forward?"

Jeff answered quickly. "No, not at a five-figure price tag. It would be great to go, but the cost is neither reasonable nor necessary."

"Wow, that's insane. Obviously, that's not startup-friendly when you have to be a millionaire to get a booth." She hesitated for a long moment as if unsure of something. She finally spoke. "I've been having some struggles as well. Getting influencers to try our soup is like pulling teeth. I send several dozen emails a day. Instagram, Twitter, YouTube, even started using some of the influencer platforms. Mostly everyone ignores me, which is frustrating because we know how well free sampling has worked for us."

Jeff rubbed his temple, a hint he'd not only heard Sam, but he was still trying to solve their trade show dilemma.

"On the bright side," Sam continued, "Becky said she would take over your craft-fair duties as long as it isn't more than twice a month. I told her we would pay her ten percent of whatever she sold. Based on the last six shows you did, that's about $150 for six hours of work."

Jeff nodded, eyes still locked on his screen. "I don't think my niece is vegan," he stated and then continued, "People ask if I'm vegan, and when I say no, it seems a bit contradictory. It probably comes across as a money grab to them, just some carnivore trying to make a buck on a trend."

"Well, I could see why," Sam replied. "Our soups are based on my story and my love of animals, not necessarily yours. And no, Becky isn't vegan, your sister told me she's a pescatarian. She only eats fish. But yes, moving forward, we should probably keep you away from the public. Some vegans might not like hearing that my husband likes dining on ground animal organs encased in pig's intestinal lining."

Jeff pursed his lips and finally looked up from his computer, contempt darkening his eyes. With a disgusted scowl, he shook his head. Sam snickered. "Oh, I'm sorry, darling, I meant to say that you like sausage."

THE TRIANGULATED VALUE STRATEGY

88

Relative-Value Casting: Don't
Quit Three Feet from Gold

There's an old motivational story about a miner who quit digging three feet from gold. He had the right idea, location, and tools, but he gave up when his early excavation uncovered nothing. As a result, he sold his mine to another miner who continued the dig. And well, you know what happened next.

Thousands of entrepreneurs suffer the same fate every year. They have the right business idea and the tools to unearth gold; they just misjudge the "adjust" in the 3A Method[S55] and fail. Hence, giving up too early. Not because they lack motivation, but because they fail to triangulate their offer and understand the sales system. Nothing is worse than working on an idea and quitting only to learn later that another entrepreneur executed it perfectly into a multi-million-dollar enterprise.

If you have a great idea and the makings of a hit, *relative-value casting* will expose it within the sales system. It will also confirm a quitting decision, the hard verdict that says, "Yes, it's time to quit and move on to a new idea."

Relative-value casting is like fly-fishing, the process of casting a line in the water over and over. You can have the tastiest bait in the world (your relative-value), but without the right sales system, you'll never catch any fish. Yes, escaping the rat race is like fishing. In effect, this "sales system" is your business system[S19], the machine that converts relative-value into a profit.

Here are the five components of the sales system.

1. Relative-Value (The Bait)
2. The Message or Offer (The Hook)
3. The Channel (The Boat)
4. The Reach (The Frequency or Depth)
5. The Closing/Conversion (The Fishing Pole)

RELATIVE-VALUE (THE BAIT)

The bait, your relative-value, is your product or service. The four components that follow should confirm (or triangulate) relative-value, a venture worthy of commitment. If one of them is deficient, the system breaks down, and no fish are caught. The result is a false flag on failure where you might judge your idea isn't worth a continued pursuit.

CHANNEL (THE BOAT)

Your boat is the marketing, retail, or wholesale channel and is needed to take you to sea, or the market. If you think about the TAM in terms of a body of water, the boat gets you access to fragments of the market, like a fishing hole. Different boats take you different places on the sea. Without a channel, you can't reach the fish and present them with the bait. So are you leveraging the right channel with the right targeting measures? Or is there a better medium to reach your audience? If you're advertising a facial cream on a gun and knife forum, it's the wrong channel. If your Facebook ads target "all adults over twenty-one," you're targeting the wrong audience. You must continuously test varied channels and targeting options by using the 3A Method; acting, assessing, and adjusting. Your product might not suck, but the channel and the audience it hits do.

MESSAGE (THE HOOK):

Your hook is your offer. It is the messaging and presentation of your relative-value (the bait). If your product rocks, but your message is deficient or flawed, or the hook is too obvious (pushy, exaggerated), you fail. I'm confident the most common false flag on failure evolves from messaging. Your copy is weak, the photos blurry, your call to action doesn't exist. Your design and UI look like they were done with GoDaddy's web tool. The fact is that many great products die because of flawed offers and poor presentations: messaging failure. In the end, you could hit the right medium and saturate the right reach—but a poorly constructed offer sinks the boat before you get started. I'd guess most launch failures are from failed messaging, not from failed products!

REACH (THE LINE):

Your line is your reach and market penetration for your relative-value offer. If you have a great product combined with a great marketing message, but your line doesn't go deep enough, not reaching enough fish, you fail. If your ad had only one hundred impressions or thirty-two clicks, your conclusions will stem from an inadequate sample size. No matter what the industry, conversions need large samples. Just because you burned through one hundred dollars at Amazon and nothing happened, it doesn't mean failure. Ensure your sample size is adequate to warrant conclusions about its data. I'd recommend at least 5,000 impressions and/or 500 clicks. The right channel and the right targeting, but the wrong reach, might falsely flag failure.

CONVERSION (THE FISHING POLE)

Your specialized-unit is offered at the right channel and in the right quantities. You've got a fantastic offer, and your customer is hooked. The problem is, your fishing pole breaks, and the customer swims away. Your fishing pole reels in the catch with a conversion, or your ability to close the sale. For websites, this would be the order process, or perhaps a store policy. Did someone want your value but didn't want to pay for shipping? How easy is it to go from "I want this" to "I bought this"?

Countless entrepreneurs have a great idea with a strong value-skew[S32]. But when they fail to triangulate that value with the right CHANNEL (boat), MESSAGING (hook), REACH (line), and/or CONVERSION (pole), that great product goes unseen, and hence unbought. Your specialized-unit's true-value can't be proved (or disproved) unless you "3A" these four components.

Looking back at my past business failures, I succeeded in producing relative-value, but failed at relative-value casting. I failed in acting, assessing, and adjusting each component.

It really is like fly fishing ... you might cast your line a hundred times before snatching a bite. Never quit until you've thoroughly "3A'd" this system. Do so, and you won't abandon a gold mine with three feet left to dig.

☑ KEY CONCEPTS

- Marketing to potential customers requires a five-point sales system with each component working synergistically.

- The five components to a selling-system are 1) relative-value (bait), 2) message (hook), 3) channel (boat), 4) reach (depth), and 5) conversion (pole).

- A failure in one or more of these components will result in no sales, and possibly a "quitting three feet from gold" scenario.

- If all five of these components are tested with the 3A method, it will determine moving forward or quitting.

THE SCAIDA STRATEGY

Catch Fish: Craft Hooks and Sell More with SCAIDA

89

After I earned my finance degree from college, I realized that a number-crunching job, even temporarily, was worse than bathing in muriatic acid. So I stayed and got a degree in marketing. It was then I learned one of the oldest marketing formulas in existence, and yes, it still is relevant today. While a lot has changed, behavioral economics and what motivates humans has not.

As entrepreneurs, half our battle is creating something people want. The other half is convincing them to buy it. When casting your relative-value[S88], one piece of the sales system is your hook, the messaging that shifts a potential customer to a buyer. With a producer mindset[P22], I'm always observing other business owners and their actions. More often than not, small-business owners rarely wander outside of their self-centered bubble. As a result, they craft toothless hooks. Instead of selling solutions and benefits, they sell features and self-aggrandizing jargon. *We objectively e-enable compelling technology with backward-compatible collaboration for mission-critical apps in native environments!* Remember, no one cares[S24].

As consumers, we buy things to solve needs. We participate in transactions to fill voids. You don't buy a McDonald's Happy Meal, you buy a screaming child quiet. You don't buy a drill; you buy a hole. You don't buy a Lamborghini; you enhance an ego. You don't buy a piece of software; you buy a convenient solution. As problemologists[P29], we must demonstrate[S82] our solution, not the facts and features of the solution. Does the fact that you are the largest cannabis laboratory in Colorado solve my problem? It doesn't until you translate that feature into a benefit.

Compelling hooks and the entire sales process can be scaled down into a simple, acronymized model called SCAIDA.

[SC] SELF-CENTERED

Going back to Ptolemy[P23], the earth-centric astronomer, everyone is the center of their universe. As such, people don't care about your business—they only care about what it can do for them. Your entire offer must lead and then linger in the spirit of pure, unadulterated self-centeredness. What can your business do for me? How will it make my life sexier, more comfortable, or more livable? In historical marketing parlance, it's called WIIFM, or *what's in it for me?*

[A] ATTENTION

You Won't Believe It: See How Time Has Ravaged These 67 Gorgeous Celebrities of the Last Century...

Ever see a click-bait headline like that and then get stuck clicking 67 times to see the entire list? LOL, I have. And it's all because of A, attention. Grab attention with a compelling, benefit-oriented headline or a shocking picture that lures eyeballs. In my case, the image was a time ravaged celebrity, and the benefit was curiosity. Since I grew up in the last century, I was praying not to find Phoebe Cates on the list. Whew, she wasn't!

Anyway, with Attention, the goal is to grab your customer's attention with your offer's primary benefit. If there are many benefits and value-skews[S32], focus on the top one, more commonly known as your USP, or unique selling proposition.

[I] INTEREST

The art of creating more *interest* in your offer happens when you stack value-skews. Interest is where you expand on the benefits of your offer beyond the primary one. Make *what's in it for me* more compelling than the primary benefit. Leave the customer declaring, "Wow, not only do I get my main issue solved, but also get X, Y, and Z!" Example: "Wow, not only do I get email leads for my business, but the phone calls are free?" If possible, don't describe; demonstrate by offering a free trial, a free sample, or a video walkthrough.

[D] DESIRE

Desire drives up the interest with more value-adds on top of your primary and secondary offer. Desire could be free bonuses, discounts, extended trials, sweepstakes entries, or add-on upgrades. Wrap up all these extra bonuses by telling the potential customer how these other benefits will help them, on top of the primary benefit. "Wow, I can get a 15 percent discount if I pay yearly instead of monthly?" Solidify Desire with a slew of positive testimonials.

[A] ACTION

Action is a call to close the sale. Nowadays, the most effective way to do this is through a scarcity statement.

Limited time only!
Offer expires in two days!
Only 100 spots are available!
Only 500 in stock!

Then stack your scarcity statement with a FOMO (fear of missing out) through social proof, peer testimonials, and user raves from satisfied users. Social proof creates a FOMO element, but it also strengthens desire because it's an uncompensated third-party validation.

Fail to hook your offer with SCAIDA and you'll fail to get bites. The sales-system collapses. Combine this fact with the other casting elements, and you see why most businesses fail. There are multiple points of failure that go beyond the value you create.

Your customer is Self-Centered: grab his Attention with a benefit-oriented headline or an impactful picture; generate more Interest by stacking more benefits; build Desire by demonstration and how your relative-value solves problems proved by positive testimonials; take action and close with a scarcity statement and more raves…

… Congratulations, you just got a degree in marketing, and it didn't cost you four years and $50,000.

☑ KEY CONCEPTS

- An ineffective hook cripples the sales-system.
- An effective hook deploys SCAIDA; an appeal to Self-Centered interests, an Attention grabber, an elevation of Interest and Desire, and a call to Action through scarcity and/or FOMO.
- An effective hook translates features and facts to benefits and solutions.

THE ASYMMETRIC TRACTION PRINCIPLE

Most of Your Success Will Come from The Least of Your Channels

The Pareto Principle is the idea that 80 percent of X is caused by 20 percent of Y. In business, Pareto applies to sales channels: 80 percent of your sales will come from 20 percent of your marketing effort. Namely, the Asymmetric Traction Principle: *the majority of your company's growth will happen from a minority of your strategy.* Your most significant revenue sources will come from just a few channels—the rest will be minuscule or worse, be a crash and burn.

Back to our fishing metaphor: Some boats take you to better fishing holes within your market.

There are eight major marketing channels you can use for growing your business, and within those eight, you'll find dozens of subsets. The good news is there are hundreds of marketing options available for experimentation. The bad news is, only a few of them will be responsible for your growth. Yes, you're looking for needles in haystacks. Those eight major marketing channels are:

BUSINESS DEVELOPMENT / JOINT VENTURES / PARTNERSHIPS

Influencers, affiliate relationships, and joint ventures with other companies. **Application:** A YouTube influencer agrees to review my book or accepts it freely.

DISTRIBUTIVE MARKETING

Channels, distributors, and other wholesale or retail firms who sell your product. **Application:** Selling my audiobook on Audible.

EMAIL / TEXT MARKETING

Sending potential or existing clients new offers and sales. **Application:** Text messaging a client who abandoned their shopping cart, and messaging customers about new products/offers.

PUBLIC RELATIONS

Free media, press releases in major media, podcast interviews, and contributing articles to media outlets. **Application:** Writing for *MarketWatch* or *Forbes* while plugging my forum.

SEARCH ENGINE AND REVIEW MARKETING

Target favorable rankings in the search engines and review services for a particular keyword. **Application:** Yelp, Google

ONLINE ADVERTISING

Paying to advertise to a target audience, pay-per-click advertising, display ads, and pixel remarketing. **Application:** Google, Pinterest, Facebook, Instagram, Etsy, etc.

ONLINE CONTENT OR VALUE MARKETING

Content marketing, blog articles, online tools, forums, blogs, free calculators. **Application:** The Fastlane Forum, the Unscripted Network, and GradeMyBusinessIdea.com

OFFLINE MARKETING

Direct marketing (mail), billboards, vehicle marketing
Application: Mailing a potential client a free sample

Using the 3A Model[S55], your job as an entrepreneur is to find those channels that work best for your business. This process involves a lot of trial and error as you cycle through the media and triangulate your bait[S88] with varying experiments.

In my first business, most of my revenue came from three channels: search engine marketing, business development (affiliates) and pay-per-click advertising. In my publishing company, most of my income comes from three channels: Amazon, audiobooks, and content marketing, via community development through my forum. In every instance, I didn't find (or build) these channels instantly, but over time, exposed through a series of trials and failures.

Not every channel or marketing medium will work or give you a positive ROI. Suppose your expectations are set too high, and you quit after evaluating just one or two channels. In that case, you risk a failed casting[S88], followed by a false flag on relative-value[S26] or a Productocracy[S71]. For instance, advertising on Facebook can be a complicated task. Campaign management is a career in itself. If you give up after spending $100 and conclude that your product sucks, your conclusion is likely flawed.

Additionally, as you cycle through channels, you'll want to target the larger road opportunities. Interstates, freeways, and boulevards are better than roads, lanes, and driveways. If you spend two weeks schmoozing a YouTube vlogger with 100 subscribers, you're targeting a driveway that will likely have little effect. Conversely, the YouTube channel with 1,000,000 subscribers is a freeway. Focusing on the bigger roads ensures asymmetric yields[S21] on your effort that move the needle[P67] faster. A purchase order from Bob's Hardware store on Maple Ave is different from a purchase order from Walmart.

Whenever I get an interview request, I first decide: Is this an interstate or a driveway? Because podcasting has become ubiquitous, most interview requests I get nowadays are driveways and not worth my time. I only do interstates, freeways, and boulevards.[1]

When in doubt, go bigger. Every business is different. Uncovering the best channels for driving traffic and customers is part of being a problemologist[P28] And because marketing is dynamic, this process is infinitely iterative. What works today at driving customers to your business won't work tomorrow. Yes, effective marketing is like peeled fruit[S81].

☑ KEY CONCEPTS

- Pareto's Principle applies to marketing strategy: 80 percent of your sales will come from 20 percent of your effort.

- There are eight general marketing strategies for reaching your market, each representing dozens, sometimes hundreds of options, all of which need to be Acted, Assessed, and Adjusted.

- Be preferential to larger audiences to improve chances of asymmetric yields.

---

1 - If you are just getting started and struggling to build an audience, I would recommend taking every interview offer you get!

BURNING OUT
SUNDAY APRIL 1ST, 2018 - 12:05 PM
(17 days later)

I t was the longest, most hellacious week the Trotmans could remember. And it wasn't over. Sam was lying on the couch, staring at the ceiling. Jeff was in his office, which now commandeered the entire kitchen table. Family meals, when they had any, took place on the couch or stooled at the kitchen counter.

Gripping Pinky, her stuffed animal companion, Sam snarled from behind the couch, "It's never over! I just finished Saturday's orders, and now there's another fourteen sitting there!" She was exhausted. They'd postponed their Saturday board meeting to Sunday, but it looked as if Sunday's rescheduled meeting was also in jeopardy.

Earlier that week, Jeff had pressed his wife to have their weekly weekend conference at a restaurant, forcing them out of their routine. But as Friday passed into Saturday, it became clear that neither had the energy to groom themselves, much less leave the house. And Sam was struggling with late-term pregnancy irritations; frequent urination, swollen ankles, heartburn, and difficulty getting comfortable.

The hectic week started with Jeff re-listing his Kickstarter with a different angle, unbeknownst to Sam. Instead of focusing on the soup, which he couldn't do since no one had invented taste through a computer screen, he focused on their story behind the soup. After revealing Sam's struggles to find healthy vegan options in soups, he described her love affair with animals, the primary reason she was vegan. In his Kickstarter brief, he described Heroic Kitchen's mission: donating a piece of the profits to a rescued animal at a real rescue sanctuary. His wife had already found dozens of rescue shelters that wanted to be part of it. As he reviewed the many animals who needed sponsorship, a job normally reserved for Sam, he was overwhelmed with grief.

Every animal had a shocking story.

A cow tagged in the ear as G32, now named Houdini, had escaped the slaughterhouse gauntlet. Several sick pigs dumped like trash next to a pig farm. There were even some chickens. Jeff wanted to pick them all, but he could only select one.

He ended up choosing Mookie, a golden retriever who only had two functional legs and one that needed amputation. Saved from the Yulin Meat Festival in China, Mookie's story struck Jeff like a brick in the face. Not knowing dogs were a delicacy in another culture and often tortured for "flavor," he was sickened to learn the about Mookie's story and his rescue. The details were so horrific that Jeff felt his heart implode as if were being sucked into a black hole.

Jeff contemplated Mookie's photo submitted by the rescue. The dog's haunted eyes bored sorrow and betrayal into Jeff's soul, a vanquishing that made him nauseous. After a moment, he had to look away, fearful the traumatic photo would besiege his dreams. He needed to see no more— Mookie would be chosen for help.

In his Kickstarter brief, Jeff relayed Mookie's story, walking a fine line between the horrific details and the emotional rescue. Mookie now had a real story of hardship and heroics, and that story made him real with a heartbeat and a will to live. Suddenly the world wanted to donate to his well-being through the magic of soup.

He'd reached the project goal in a matter of hours.

He had once experienced a similar process at the craft fair; a dismal failure was reversed into a profound success by a mere shift in tactics.

Sam, now up from the couch, shuffled to a chair at the table. She fell into her seat, her head propped on her hands which she elbowed on the kitchen table. She woozily pleaded to her husband beside her, "Can you take care of today's orders? I need a break."

Jeff nodded smirkingly and stood up, walking to the pantry. Sam heard rustling until he approached with a bottle and placed it on the table.

"Champagne? At noon? While I'm 38 weeks pregnant?" She looked up at him. "Did you snag a big account today?" He stood above her and nodded at the bottle. "This is just sparkling spritzer, but to answer your question, no."

Perplexed, she continued, "We hit new sales records for a weekend?"

"Yes, but that's not what this is for."

"You inked a joint-venture with Beyond Burger or Impossible?" He mashed his lips and shook his head. She whacked him on the knee with the back of her hand. He sat down and smiled with the asset still under lockdown. "Well, tell me!" Sam admonished, plopping her head back into her hands as if it were a pillow.

Jeff revealed his big Kickstarter success. "Could be thousands of cans, hundreds of cases!" he reported, giddy.

Sam managed a half-smile and said flatly, "It's great news. Fantastic, actually." She paused. "But I'm so exhausted with the hospital—even desk duty—that the last thing I want to think about right now is more work, even if it is ours. There's never a break with this business; it runs twenty-four seven and never closes."

Jeff remarked, "Yeah, isn't it wonderful? We're making money every day of the year. This is what DeMarco was talking about. DeMarco! Remember him? The Unscripted thing? It won't be like this all the time, this is just our process, remember!?" He didn't wait for her to answer, adding, "We're building our business system with poly-pay, or whatever DeMarco called it."

Sam remembered when and why it had all started. "Polymorphic pay," she corrected. "Of course I remember. I'm just burned out." Her hooded eyes sank heavier as she leaned back and cradled her belly.

He continued, "If this Kickstarter thing goes as planned, we're looking at thousands of dollars. And Mookie, our sponsored rescue dog, will have the money for surgery."

She nodded—another anemic smile as if unimpressed with his news.

Jeff repositioned himself in front of her and sat in the chair backward, leaning on its back. It creaked in opposition. "But that's not the big news," he said as if he'd had too much caffeine.

She attempted to perk up, raising her forehead. "Yes, more news?"

"Yes."

The silence hung again. Always the numbers guy, Jeff continued, "Our sales just went over $100,000. And with today's orders, our monthly cash flow generation just went over $6,000 per month. That's not even with the Kickstarter thing. Sales have gone up every month, and I'm not talking about a few hundred bucks. Last week I ordered another lot with our co-packer, and I only had to charge 20 percent of it. Because we're not spending a fortune on advertising, our net margin is 48 percent. Better, our reorder rate is 19 percent."

"Nineteen?" Sam mumbled weakly. "That doesn't sound good."

"Actually, it is wonderful. Remember, Samantha, when people buy soup, they don't eat it right away. It often sits in the pantry until rainy weather, the flu, or something. If we're at 19 percent already, it probably is a lot better." He held up a stack of papers. "These are customer testimonials, people who love our soup, or love that we're making a difference with rescue animals."

She feigned another weak smile and tried to muster joy for the moment, but the numbers to Sam were just that—numbers. She felt a kick in her belly, and she gasped, her grip firming on his.

Jeff motioned to her belly. "My darling wife, let me put it in perspective for you." He cradled his hands around her face, caressing her cheek as if he was consoling a sad child. He said calmly, "Our business has made enough money—and has been making enough money for the last two months—that you can quit your job." He leaned in, louder. "Tomorrow."

THE COMMITMENT & BALANCE PRINCIPLE

Expect Commitment to Wear the Mask of Imbalance

91

Whenever I hear, "Thank God it's Friday," I can only shake my head in disappointment. What a tragedy: *Thank God that five days of my life are over, only so I can get drunk the next two days so I can forget about repeating the same five nauseating days next week.*

In Buddhism, "the middle way" is about a balanced approach to life, that an optimum existence is a path found between materialism and spirituality. While I believe this to be true, I don't believe you can find a "middle way" in today's rat race culture. When you're sacrificing five days of work for two days of freedom, is that a balanced approach to life? Nope, more like unfair and unbalanced.

The Commitment and Balance Principle affirms that if you want to live the "middle way" for most of your life, *you'll need to embrace commitment, and sometimes that commitment can wear the mask of imbalance, at least temporarily.* Before Buddha found the middle way, he practiced asceticism. The extreme imbalance of minimalistic living (and nearly dying) is what compelled his discovery of the middle way. In a lot of ways, our journey will be similar, but without the dying!

When I was building my web company, there were many twelve-hour days, sometimes lasting weeks. Sometimes I would decline dates, parties, and nights out. And yes, some of my relationships temporarily suffered. Likewise, when I wrote my first book, I checked myself into a beach condo and wrote for thirty days. It was eat, write, sleep, lift. This book as well: I disappeared for weeks straight and needed heavy drinking and illicit drugs to get me through it. Okay, just kidding about the drugs, but not kidding about the long hours. In short, balance was nowhere—I was living like the ascetic Buddha.

When something is a commitment, things can go unbalanced. Does Elon Musk (and his multiple divorces) give you fuzzy feelings of a balanced life? Probably not. The truth is, *today's* top producers lead anything but balanced lives. But *yesterday's* top producers probably do. For instance, think balance and unfocused priorities is how Michael Phelps won twenty-three Olympic gold medals? How about Michael Jordan and his six NBA championships and four MVPs? These guys lived and breathed their profession. But today, after their prime, I'm betting they live pretty balanced lives.

Exceptional results come from extraordinary commitments that culture will label as unbalanced. When people preach "balance," they're talking about a balance amongst culturally endorsed priorities. Everyone wants six-pack abs, the big bank account, and the creative freedom to do work that matters. The problem is those same people also want to eat McDonald's every day. They want to watch every *Bachelorette* episode. And they want to buy all the hot brands—all while cashing a government welfare check. For them, "imbalance" is an implied threat to priorities—priorities which are either frivolous or comfort-seeking. If "imbalance" means giving up the ice cream, then balance represents the status quo.

I have no idea who won last year's World Series. Yet there are people in my life who can recite entire lineups and baseball stats from teams fielded in 1976. Unless you're a player or a professional gambler, watching a meaningless baseball game that has no impact on your life is a terrible waste. As they say, the most important things in your life seize your time. When meaningless bullshit is your priority, balance is like a goal stuck in wet cement.

Prioritize your priorities beyond rat race coping mechanisms. Please do so, and suddenly its weekend cheese might feel like a cheap joke. Today I lead a "middle way" life the way I want. How? I was committed and willing to meander into the world of the imbalanced.

☑ KEY CONCEPTS

- The rat race makes balanced, or "middle way" living nearly impossible.
- Commitment can often cause things to go temporarily unbalanced.
- Embrace unbalanced periods of your life to seek lasting balance.
- Your actions express your priorities.

THE SELF-DIRECTED PINK-SLIP STRATEGY

92

Don't Quit Your Day Job Until
Your Business Makes You

I get several dozen emails per week regarding my books. Most of them are encouraging, but every week, a few have me concerned. The worrisome messages are the ones that demonstrate reader impetuousness and malformed expectations. Bluntly speaking, just because you read one of my books doesn't mean you should quit your job or drop out of college. Such actions reflect a reader who is not process-driven but event-oriented.

> *Quitting college to start a business is an event.*
> *Quitting your job to start a business is an event.*
> *Starting a profitable business is a process.*

My recommendation? Don't quit your job unless you've got the following four guidelines flashing green.

1. Existing sales with adequate profit margins
2. At least a six-month runway (cash flow) to support an owner paycheck
3. Scale and growth potential (Can revenue increase 10X within the next twelve months?)
4. Evidence of a Productocracy

Quitting a job (or college) is a huge decision. In my opinion, reading a few books about business isn't a license to make reckless decisions. In short, don't quit your day job until your business *makes* you quit your day job. The Trotmans are at the precipice with rising sales and a verified Productocracy. Quitting won't endanger their living situation, or their business. Your family's basic living essentials shouldn't be part of your risk equation. Starting a business while homeless and starving might light a fire under your butt, but trust me, the Hollywood ending is unlikely.

- Quitting your job or college is an event, launching a profitable business is a process.

- Don't quit your day job until your business forces you.

- Existing sales, six months of cash flow, scale potential, and evidence of a Productocracy are all green lights to quitting your job.

THE STORIFICATION STRATEGY

Put It in a Story: If You Can Make Them Care, You Can Make Them Buy

93

Like many pounds worldwide, the animal shelter in Maricopa County, Arizona, is jam-packed and overflowing. Hundreds of dogs wait to be adopted weekly. Dozens more are euthanized for no reason other than over-crowding and indeterminate temperaments. Simply too many dogs, not enough adopters.

And yet, when any dog is offered for adoption on television (say a local morning show) and given a backstory—strayed, abandoned, abused, or whatever else—the phone rings off the hook. The dog waited in a cage to be adopted for eight weeks but had no takers. But put her on television? The dog would only have to wait eight minutes. The backstory transforms the dog from a faceless number on a clipboard to a creature with depth and sentience.

Bottomline: attach a powerful story to your company and its products, and you will sell more. Stories are how we make sense of the world. And when the right story resonates with your customer's identity, either through their humanity or their ego, you create positive value-skew[S32] and a more compelling argument for their sale.

Stories and their powerful effect on buying psychology have been proven.

One such experiment came from SignificantObjects.com, which demonstrated how narrative can impact any object's perceived-value. At Significant Objects, everyday thrift-store items were purchased cheaply and then resold on eBay, except with one difference: A powerful story was linked to the objects. As a result, items purchased at an average of $1.25 were sold for many times more, nearly $8,000 in total. A one-dollar jar of marbles was given a story and sold for fifty dollars. A one-dollar wooden apple core was given a story and sold for over one hundred dollars. And dozens more.

Perhaps the most iconic use of storification comes from the J. Peterman company, which started as a mail-order fashion catalog in 1987.

As Peterman explains…

How did we do it? By breaking all the rules. Our 'Owner's Manual' catalogue only featured one item per page, we used paintings of items versus photography, and each item was accompanied by intensive romantic copy. These were all things the "experts" said we couldn't do.[1]

By tying each product to a story, or as Peterman explains, "romantic copy," each product carried a unique value-skew. For instance, here are some of the words behind the story of a simple flannel shirt: "symphony," "yarn-dyed plaid," "cheeky," "sumptuous," "immensely cozy," all tied together in a cute little narrative. This is how a company can sell a hundred dollar flannel shirt that looks no different from something you find at Kohls for fifteen dollars.

You cannot underestimate the power of story for creating skew and making people *possibly* care. With Ptolemying[S24], we already identified that no one cares. Putting a story to your business can weaken this truth because our egoic selfishness likes having our identity validated while being a part of the narrative. *I adopted that dog on television!*

Quite possibly, the most important page on your website isn't what you're selling—it's the story revealing WHY you are selling it. Studies have proven that the "About Us" page is one of the most frequently visited pages on a website. I estimate my forum's "about us" page has been hit more than two million times.

Tell your audience WHY you are in business and give them a story they can identify with. If consumers identify with either you or your product, you will sell more and stack your skew.

☑ KEY CONCEPTS

- Attach a powerful story to your company or its products, and you will sell more.

- Storification can invalidate Ptolemying and make people care about your business.

- The "About Us" page is one of the most frequent visited pages that buyers read.

- A good backstory for your product/company is a value-skew.

---

1 - https://www.jpeterman.com/Philosophy

WHAT IS SEEN CANNOT BE UNSEEN

TUESDAY, APRIL 3RD, 2018 - 12:04 AM
(2 days later)

Samantha didn't quit her job, at least not the next day.
Despite her employer, who was about as ruthless as a Scrooge before the "undigested bit of beef," Sam did the honorable thing. She gave her two-week notice and still worked. She wouldn't abandon her patients or co-workers.

Once Janice, Sam's 'I can't live without my bacon' co-worker found out, she questioned Sam at her locker. "Are you transferring to another hospital after the baby is born? Or moving to private practice?"

"I'm getting out of nursing," Sam quipped. "Remember, I said that Jeff and I are starting a business selling plant-based soups." Janice furrowed her brow and glowered with confusion. Sam read the look and clarified. "Like the soup you asked the recipe for?"

"Oh yes," she said, leaning on the locker, "the creamy one with potatoes and bacon?"

"Yes, but there's no bacon in it."

Janice shook her head, perplexed. "But how does it taste like bacon?"

Sam sighed and then feigned a half-smile. "You didn't read the recipe I gave you?"

Janice shrugged and smiled sheepishly, a mist of sweat embracing her plump reddish face. Sam guessed her systolic blood pressure was a shade north of 160.

Sam raised her index finger and lifted an eyebrow. "Smoked paprika, Janice, smoked paprika."

While Sam soldiered through her Monday at the hospital, Jeff started the week with a failure. Two weeks ago, he'd paid for a half-page advertisement in the local weekly shopper called *Windy City Green Living*. As the sales rep said, "Our magazines are distributed for free at all grocery stores countywide." Jeff couldn't refuse the opportunity and promptly charged $1,500 on his credit card. Heroic Kitchens would have a half-page ad in a magazine that focused primarily on green, sustainable living. The ad was beautifully done (in-house by the publisher), complete with a coupon code for tracking. It hit the stands last Tuesday, but by the weekend, Jeff knew it was a failure. Only seven orders.

It reminded him of his T-shirt fiasco—he'd spent $1,500 to make twenty bucks. With his wife teetering on exhaustion, he secreted the failure from her.

But redemption wasn't far behind.

His next gambit was unconventional, crafty, and perhaps a bit devious. It was an ingenious strategy that involved hiring a private investigator. Well, not a traditional PI, but an online records PI, someone who had access to firewalled records and data. Again, all unbeknownst to Sam. Not because he needed her approval but because he liked surprising his wife, like the time he offered free samples at the craft fair. It rained money then, and he hoped this tactic would cause money to rain as well. He also wasn't sure she'd approve, and frankly, he didn't care. It was time to be bold and intrepid. As her due date approached, she shouldn't have been working as hard as she was.

As for the private investigator Jeff hired, it was about one thing: *mailing addresses*, specifically, the physical addresses of social media influencers in the health and fitness space, primarily plant-based. Because this data was mostly withheld or not widely available, a PI legal "special access" to certain records was needed.

After Sam complained about the struggles of reaching influencers, he reasoned he'd hit them with blunt force: a FedEx package containing a soup sampler kit. Jeff speculated that for anyone who received an unexpected FedEx package, the delivery would warrant special attention. Even torn open in curiosity and intrigue. For Jeff, the spectacular conversion rate on free soup samples was too hot to ignore. The more that people tried it, the more sales they got, or in the case of influencers, they might plug Heroic Kitchens to their followers. He also knew that people with plant-based interests wouldn't throw away a perfectly good can of soup.

The tactic worked brilliantly.

Within ten days, the tactic resulted in two "shout-outs" from influencers on YouTube and Instagram. Analyzing the numbers, Jeff hypothesized that it had a 66 percent success rate since he had only sent three FedEx packages. Combining with nearly 1,000,000 followers, the two shout-outs from these two channels (which only amounted to about 90 seconds) sold nearly 28 cases, 869 cans to be exact. Jeff had paid $55 for the online investigator and $129 for the FedEx packages. The tactic drummed up nearly $5,000 in new business and 640 new customers. Many of which would hopefully reorder, or better, storm into their local Sprouts or Whole Foods demanding that they supply Heroic Kitchens.

After Sam endured her final late shift at Mercy Hospital, Jeff rewarded her with the good news. It took them three days to fill the order, and that was with Jeff's niece's help.

Once Sam settled into an at-home groove and distanced herself from hospital drama, her stress slowly faded despite a baby kicking at the gates. As she typed away at her computer, she commented, "I work almost as much as I did as a nurse, but this doesn't feel like work." She said, "The hours fly by, and I know we're making progress on our goals. Every time we sponsor a new animal, I love knowing we're making a difference." She rubbed her belly. "And a happy mommy means a happy baby."

Their unborn baby was days away. Maybe hours.

Still, Jeff persevered with his day job. Since starting the business, his view of his job and its work improved. So much that he was in line for a promotion, a promotion he didn't want.

While his business sucked up his lunch hours and most of his free time, it gave his job meaning. And his life. It impressed him that trivial matters like baseball games and who won some stupid reality TV show had no place in his life. He had a more important purpose. Not just a common purpose, like taking care of your family, but it was a cause that made a difference in the world. It was a mission that he could see transcending years, if not decades. His job that he once hated played a role in this equation, and it made it tolerable. Thoughts of giving his resignation crossed his mind, but he told himself he needed to win a major store shelf first. Heroic Kitchens was making sales, but they weren't in any big retailers.

When Jeff arrived home from work that evening, he found Madison at the kitchen table playing on her iPad.

"Hey sweetie, I have your dinner." Maddy looked up. Her father had two bags of Burger King and held out one of them. Since BK started offering the plant-based Impossible Burger, Sam and Maddy found it to be acceptable fast-food. Maddy, also vegan like her mother, stood up and grabbed her bag, the jingles on her iPad still tolling. "Thanks, Dad," she said softly while maintaining focus on her screen.

"Where's your mother?" Jeff asked.

Maddy gestured to the back of the couch and made a shushing motion to her lips. She whispered, "Mommy cried herself to sleep."

"What?" Jeff's eyes burned with concern. "Did she tell you why?"

"She was looking at the sick animals who needed help. It made her sad. She said she had to pick two tonight but couldn't." Maddy shrugged and then turned heel to go to her bedroom.

"Hey," Jeff said before she could leave, flashing her an anticipative simper. Maddy smiled sheepishly and returned to her father. He rustled her hair and kissed her forehead, whispering, "Thanks pumpkin, good night."

After Maddy retreated into her bedroom with her dinner, Jeff peered over the mountain of cushions and saw his wife sound asleep, eyes twitching in full REM. Her eyes were red, and tissues littered the floor. Nestled between her belly and her chest was a stack of sponsorship applications. Animal rescues around the country were asking Heroic Kitchens to sponsor their animals. Each paper detailed a rescued animal who needed help, complete with their story and a photo. His wife promised she'd pick two animals for their next co-packing order. Ugh, another thing to do before bed, Jeff thought.

He grabbed the applications and walked to the kitchen, putting his wife's plant-based burger in the refrigerator. After plating his fries and double-bacon cheeseburger, a real one, not that plant-based crap, he sank into his chair behind the kitchen table.

He let loose an exasperated sigh. He had already worked eight hours that day, and another few remained. The co-packer was expecting the order tomorrow morning. With each order they sent to their co-packer, they would change their rescue animal. His wife picked. He wrote the copy. The information would then be sent off to a freelancer in Southeast Asia who would redesign the label. While this was cumbersome, it was one of their skews. Each soup label featured a rescue animal complete with a brief introduction and a photo. The animal's full report would be QC coded to their website, which would encourage email acquisition, coupon distribution, and brand loyalty.

After a long Monday, he was exhausted like his wife. But two animals needed to be selected. He flipped through the pages quickly, looking for any notation that she'd made a sponsor decision before falling asleep.

Nothing.

He sighed again and then took a bite of his burger, followed by a handful of french fries. The chair creaked as frustratingly adjusted his sit. He just wanted to relax and shower off the workday, so he considered picking blindly.

Before he could just grab any application, a photo caught his attention.

At first, he couldn't recognize what he was looking at, so he started to read. It was about a pig named Sniff who was rescued from a pig farm in North Carolina. Well, not really a pig farm, but on the dirt-road leading *from* the farm. As he started reading, his heart felt mortally wounded. The pig's body was smothered in a dirty pink, a tapestry of open sores, abrasions, and wounds. Found nearly dead and sun-dried in a ditch, Sniff had squirmed off an NFFS truck, a cute acronym that meant "not fit for slaughter." The truck transported sick hogs for euthanasia, a death sentence of neglect or lethal injection, a fate no better than the slaughter guillotine that awaited the healthier hogs. But Sniff had other ideas. As the truck left the farm, it was speculated that he managed to get his emaciated body through the truck's fence-gates, wriggling himself free of the bed and falling into a roadside culvert. Two days later, as the vultures circled for the coming feast, an animal activist found Sniff. Presumed dead, the activist noticed the pig's nostrils sniffing when touched. In that moment, Sniff was born, or one could say, reborn. Now at Shady Acres

Rescue forty miles away, Sniff was still struggling to recover from his trauma and the sickness which got him on the "NFFS" truck.

Jeff shook his head and moved on.

The next was a meat cow called Spock. But Spock was born deformed and unable to grow into an official "meat cow." At just a few months old, Spock was purchased from a cattle farmer. The rescuer reported that the farmer complained, "I got no use for deadstock, you can haul him out here for ten bucks." It took a second for Jeff to make the connection, but deadstock must have been livestock that was worth nothing. In other words, also destined for the NFFS truck. Two photos were included in the application. One was a full-body picture of Spock standing awkwardly while eating. His hind-quarters appeared to be disproportionate to his front legs as if afflicted with cerebral palsy.

Jeff flipped the page and reviewed the other photo.

It was a heads-only portrait.

He locked with Spock's eyes in the photo.

Spock's almond-shaped eyes were intensely black but shimmered in a glassy reticence as if he was still unsure of his fate and the new humans charged with his care. Jeff studied the photo as Spock's eyes continued to bore into him.

He laid the application on the table and swallowed hard, turning away. Then he glanced back at Spock's picture, the cow's eyes still locked onto his own.

He never gave much thought to cows, or as they called them, cattle. His wife always argued that cows and pigs were just as intelligent as their Bella. That they exhibit emotions, joy, and fear. They smell, taste, feel, and that they even mourn for their babies. Worse, they feel pain. He looked away from Spock's picture again hoping to sever the new neural connection.

But it was too late.

He heard his wife's voice echoing in his head. *There's no way to humanely kill something that doesn't want to be killed—if it's not your life, it's not yours to take.*

He cursed to himself, *Damn it Samantha, quiet!*

Next to Sniff and Spock's application sat his dinner, a bacon cheeseburger... a real one. He lifted the bun and glared. Sniff could have been the bacon and Spock the burger. Literally. Except whoever sat slaughtered and processed on his bun didn't have the fortunate opportunity to receive a name. Or a story. Or the luck to have escaped the genocide of their species.

Like a dam bursting in his head, he suddenly understood his wife.

He wasn't eating meat for a necessity like an Inuit in the Alaskan tundra; he was eating it for pure flavor. Convenience. An entertainment apparatus at a tailgating party.

Sweat misted on his forehead as his mind didn't like his dissonance exposed to the light, but his soul knew. Smelling the burger, Bella begged next to his chair, giving her best plead. Her tongue dolloped in drool while her dark almond eyes glared in anticipation. As he gazed into Bella's innocent eyes, he saw no difference from Spock's. Then he thought the unthinkable. Bella's fate in another culture could be the same as those animals he aimed to save, destined to be guillotined so some hurried consumer can have their drive-thru dollar meal. How could he participate in this closed-door insanity? He loved animals just as much as his wife. If he couldn't slash Sniff or Spock's throat, how could he pay someone to do it for him? His wife's didactic lectures, which always landed on his deaf ears or erupted in a contentious spatter, suddenly made sense.

His wife cried herself to sleep, and now Jeff was struggling to hold the tears at bay. To Jeff, veganism was a dogmatic topic they danced around. But reading these stories, looking at the photos, it now meant something else.

He gave the rest of his burger to Bella, who gobbled it up in three seconds. Picking up the pen, he marked Sniff and Spock's sponsorship applications.

They would be Heroic Kitchen's next two sponsor animals.

And Jeff would become their biggest cheerleader.

THE BURNT BRIDGES PRINCIPLE

Burnt Bridges Can't be Rebuilt

At some point, after your business starts growing, your job will become an impediment. And it will be time to quit. At first, it might seem like a good idea to tell your boss to shove it. It might seem tempting to walk into his office and kick him in the ass with your steel-toed boots, causing a stir. But it isn't.

The Burnt Bridges Principle is a reminder that *most new business ideas are unearthed from jobs and it is always best to leave your job on good terms.* My first profitable business idea was spawned from my low-wage job. And if you have a job, it's likely your business will be related to your work. If so, you don't want to slam any doors on your future business. Perhaps your current employer will become a customer? Or can your co-workers become potential hires?

If it's time to quit your job, congratulations. But please, leave the steel-toed boots on the floor. Starting a business after being arrested for assaulting your boss is, well, starting off on the wrong foot.

☑ KEY CONCEPTS

- Most new businesses are spawned from jobs, or opportunities discovered in a job.
- Always keep bridges open in case you can leverage your past career contacts.

THE GOING WIDE STRATEGY

Consider "Going Wide" to Expand
Your TAM (and Your Profits)

95

Since I adopted a plant-based lifestyle, eating at fast-food restaurants has become near impossible. Up until recently, most chains offered few, if any, meat-free options. Then in August of 2019, Burger King started selling Impossible Whoppers, a plant-based hamburger. Suddenly I found myself rolling to Burger King a few times per month. This itself was rare because when I did eat meat, I rarely ate fast-food.

The next quarter, Burger King reported record-breaking sales exceeding expectations, which, according to the CEO, was fueled by the new plant-based burger.[1] Congratulations to Restaurant Brands International (the owner of Burger King), who figured out that "going deep" wasn't the only way to improve sales.

"Going deep" is an attempt to improve market share by enticing your total addressable market[P53] with a new offer or a new product. For example, if Burger King offered a new burger topped with a fried egg, they're trying to get more meat-eaters to eat more frequently at Burger King. In that equation, I and other vegetarians are not part of the total addressable market.

Conversely, "going wide" isn't about expanding market share but about expanding the TAM. When Burger King offered their new Impossible plant-based Whopper, their total addressable market suddenly blew up to include vegetarians and some vegans. In other words, their available market expanded by millions of people. If four percent of the US population is vegetarian as some studies claim, that's more than 13 million people who just jumped into their TAM. How would you like to wake up one day and discover that 13 million more people might buy your product?

In an example closer to home, I've only written books about business and finance. My TAM is limited to individuals with these interests. However, I also plan to write in other genres, from thrillers to general non-fiction. If my

---

1 - https://www.cnn.com/2019/10/28/investing/restaurant-brands-earnings-burger-king-popeyes/index.html

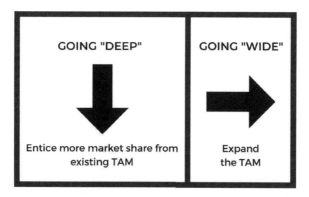

THE "GOING WIDE" STRATEGY

publishing company sells in these categories, suddenly my TAM will widen substantially. Going deep would be writing more books about entrepreneurship—going wide would be writing a murder mystery. Simply put, "going wide" is like opening a dam and expanding your sales pool.

When you're in the trenches of business, "going deep" is often seen as the only way to improve profits. *I need to sell more widgets! I need to sell more widget variations!* True, but also look to go wide. Can your business system[S19] leverage operations and economies of scale to offer another product that would expand the TAM? If the carrying cost of "going wide" is financially justified, consider it a wise move.

☑ KEY CONCEPTS

- "Going deep" is tempting your existing TAM with a new offer or a new product.

- "Going wide" is expanding your TAM with a complementary product that can leverage your existing business system with economies of scale.

- Consider "going wide" once your business system is in place and scaling economies are present.

THE PURPOSE DRIVEN STRATEGY

Be Led by Purpose, Not Passion

By twenty-five, I had five business failures banked. Five. Common themes underlaid those failures: I was either chasing money, following passions or both. As I got lost deep into the Desert of Desertion[P57], only one thing got me out: I was *purpose driven*.

Purpose is the primary driver behind motivation and perseverance. Without an intense *Purpose*, a great rat race escape is unlikely. A Purpose is the camel that gets you through the desert. A strong *Purpose*—a why—fires motivation, steels determination, and jerks you outside of your comfort zone. When hard, uncomfortable, or thankless work becomes part of the process, and it will, *Purpose* breaks through that muck. *Purpose* is the engine to persist when the prevailing emotion is to resist.

As for your *Purpose*, it can be anything. From the superficial, *I want to prove my parents wrong*, to the altruistic, *I want to save the whales*. Whatever it is, it must be strong enough to compel steady action and get you through the Desert of Desertion when a severed feedback loop isn't firing passion.

For me, my ultimate fear in life was waking up at 5:30 AM and then having to drive to the train station and waiting in frigid weather. Then I'd ride a crowded commuter train into Chicago, navigate a caffeinated swarm, hitch an elevator to the 57th floor of some obscure skyscraper, and then sit there for the next eight hours selling insurance. The reward of this tedium would be to repeat it for the next four days, for the next forty years. Writing it now gives me anxiety.

It was that story, that vision, that gave me a *Purpose*—an avoidance purpose that compelled me to work. It forced me to expose my missteps, from ignoring markets to selfish inclinations. It drove me to make the sacrifices that needed to be made. In other words, *nothing else mattered*.

Think of it this way: You're tied to railroad tracks. A train approaches, each second thunders louder. The violent vibration against your back intensifies as death advances. The ropes binding you to the rails tighten as you struggle to break free. Fear floods your veins with adrenaline. You can now see the locomotive's fog light, brighter and brighter. Louder and louder. And in a few moments, the train will strike you dead. Unless you find *a reason and a purpose* to move.

At that point as the train approaches, I'm guessing you won't have a problem with motivation or distractions. Nothing else will matter. Not season five of *Game of Thrones*, not the thankless job, not the unpaid car payment. Why? Because at that moment, your life has clearly identified its *Purpose*. To live. To survive. Or you might think of your family, and your *Purpose* is not to survive for survival's sake, but to spare them the grief. In our story, Sam wants to save animals. Jeff wants freedom from mundane work and fears an empty life. Both are valid. Your *Purpose* doesn't matter, only that it's as intense and urgent as the approaching train. With this disposition, it's impossible to dither.

If you don't look at life this way, you don't stand a chance. Except it isn't a train that threatens your life—it's time. You're born, and then you die. Regrettably, most peoples' life purpose is comfort[P3]. They don't seek to break free from the tracks; they want you to give them a pillow and a Netflix subscription. *Let me die in comfort*. And in today's culture, it is far too easy to be comfortable. It's a rat race construct.

If you need help finding a meaningful purpose, try this thought experiment: You win $5 billion. After five years, you've traveled the world, bought everything, tried everything, and provided for family and friends. After years of hedonic pleasure, what would be next in your life? What would you do? Your answer might shine a light on your *Purpose*. Get a *Purpose* and Unscript or get a job and muddle.

☑ KEY CONCEPTS
☑ KEY CONCEPTS

- A strong Purpose—a why—is the only motivational fire you can count on to get through the Desert of Desertion.

- A weak purpose compels dithering and makes you bribable to comfort and excuses.

- The "billionaire thought experiment" can help you uncover your purpose.

THE POROUS BELIEFS STRATEGY

Carry Porous Beliefs to Expose Your Poison Pens

97

In 2017, I went vegan. You read that right. Even reading it now has me coiling in disbelief. Had I foreseen the future in 2015 and told myself this, I would have hit the floor laughing. Vegan? As in PETA, kale, and tofu? Ha Ha—me balling on an NBA team seemed more likely. But it did happen. How? *Porous beliefs.*

Years prior, my dietary style was Paleo (high protein [meat] and low carb). Still, as I continued to rack up high-risk factors for heart disease, as well as an observation of my body's behavior after eating particular foods, it became clear I needed more investigation. What I discovered, both nutritionally and humanely, was so shocking (and heart-wrenching) that the shift was pretty easy. More concerning was my own hypocrisy: Was I, the author and professor of *Unscripted*, following a Script simply because *Well, that's how it's always been done?*

Beware of what you believe because it is your flight-plan. If your belief is a poison-pen[52] it will write a tale not of your liking. For example, if your poison pen is a belief in Santa, you might embarrassingly divulge to your third-grade classmates that your show-and-tell toy was a gift from Santa Claus. Believe that Jim Jones is the messiah, and you'll travel to Guyana and drink the Kool-Aid. Poison-pens can be, well, poisonous.

In all these cases, porous beliefs could have saved you from embarrassment, repeated failures, and death. A *porous belief* is anything that you believe to be true but is open to critique and investigation. Simply put, your beliefs—no matter if they're religious, nutrition-related, or political—are weakly held and unlocked, or porous to new information. And such information leads to new beliefs (canceling the old ones) and, eventually, truth.

Porous beliefs are the only way to give truth a chance. Everything must be questioned, even your most sacred convictions. If you want the truth of God, you won't find it at a Christian church, a Jewish synagogue, a Muslim mosque, a Buddhist temple, or at a particle accelerator. The truth is found at all five.

You've never been conditioned to seek the truth; you're conditioned to confirm your biases. This is why you watch the same news stations, read the same blogs, and attend the same church. You're not seeking the truth; you're seeking to confirm your belief. Known as a *confirmation bias* in cognitive science, this is why political derision is the worst it's ever been. Today's media no longer reports the truth; they're reporting narratives and confirming biases. For example, if you believe former President Trump is a racist xenophobe who was a Russian agent, you're tuned into Rachel Maddow. If you think he was the second coming of Ronald Reagan, you're watching Sean Hannity. The problem is, you're not going to get the whole truth at either—but likely bits and pieces from both.

When your beliefs aren't porous, the truth will bounce off them.

A solid belief is immune from new information, no matter how pertinent. Worse, such new information suffers from another failure in cognitive mechanics: *the backfire effect*. It has been psychologically proven that our convictions actually get stronger when we're presented with conflicting evidence adverse to our beliefs. This is why political arguments on Facebook are pointless, regardless of evidence. Facts bounce with impunity—you could have video proof of a politician slaughtering puppies, but voters wouldn't care. *Nope, that's my guy.*

Truth is not pushed to your iPhone in an alert. It's not found on Yahoo's home page. It's not that trending news story curated on Facebook or Twitter. In today's culture, the truth is an enemy to the rat race and the ruling elite, which wishes to keep the scam alive. The fact is, *if you're not seeking the truth, you're not getting the truth.*

Your evolution as a human being, not just in business, relies on porous beliefs. If you're not changing every few years[S42], it's because your beliefs are behind concrete. *Truth* bounces like it fell on a trampoline. And *truths* are always the best basis for decision-making. If you want to change your life, start auditing your beliefs to expose poison-pens. What beliefs are causing problems in your life? I challenge you to get a notebook and journal every choice you make for the next week, including the belief that compelled it. Then beside each choice, write down its payoff and its short- and long-term consequences. Years ago when I contemplated suicide, a belief-audit exposed the poison pen that put me there.

BELIEF AUDIT:

- Poison Pen: Network marketing and business training programs purchased from late-night infomercials can help me succeed.

- Action: I joined a network marketing company.

- Payoff: I'm part of a team! I'm the CEO of my business!

- Short-term consequence: I haven't made any money. Moreover, I've wasted six months and alienated a lot of friends.

- Long-term consequence: I've been doing this business for two years and have nothing to show for it. I now have a closet full of unused products I can't sell.

Here's a thought audit exposing a poor dietary habit.

BELIEF AUDIT:

- Poison Pen: The food I eat really doesn't impact my health.

- Action: I ate a pint of ice cream.

- Payoff: It was delicious; I felt great while eating it!

- Short-term consequence: Felt some guilt, got really tired and bloated after, and had acid reflux all evening.

- Long-term consequence: Obesity, low self-esteem, unhappiness, low energy, higher medical bills, diabetes.

Believe whatever you want—but please, believe it only after you have investigated all available information and audited your beliefs. Seek the truth, not a confirmation of your biases. As Mark Twain famously said, "What gets us into trouble is not what we don't know. It's what we know for sure that just ain't so."

☑ **KEY CONCEPTS**

- A *porous belief* is anything that you believe to be true but is open to critique and investigation.

- Most people aren't interested in the truth; rather, they are seeking to confirm biases, which is why they watch the same news programs, visit the same websites, and go to same church.

- If you are the same person today as you were five years ago, it's likely your beliefs are not porous, but concrete.

- The best foundation for decision-making is truth, not belief.

- Truth isn't curated to mainstream news: if you're not actively seeking the truth, you're not getting the truth.

BENDING THE KNEE WITH GLEE
SATURDAY, APRIL 7TH, 2018 - 7:00 PM
(4 days later)

The deep-fried Brussels sprouts, the sautéed asparagus, and the teriyaki tofu steak."

The waiter wrote the order, nodded, and retrieved the menu from Jeff. He snuck a glance at his wife, who was leaned back in her booth, stunned, eyes wide as limes. Sam giggled. "Tofu steak?" she recited incredulously, face plastered with skepticism. She flicked her head back and forth, channeling her best impersonation of a southern Black woman who took shit from no one. "You trying to get something from me later?"

Jeff turned and smiled, an expression not of lust or laughs but of love and adoration. Sam saw his eyes gloss over, and her chuckle faded into a warm smile. She felt Jeff's hand on her knee under the table. This seemed more than a horny husband. "What is it?" she asked.

"I'm now plant-based. For good."

Sam laughed and slapped the table. "You, vegan?" She quickly glanced at the date on her phone and then said, "A late April Fool's joke?"

"Don't label me as a vegan," he corrected, eyeballing his wife. "I am a plant-based libertarian who owns guns." A pause, then "And no," he shook his head, "it's not an April Fool's joke." He stared at her wondering if she'd believe him. He added, "I wouldn't do that to you."

Sam's smile melted into disbelief. Jeff didn't yield into laughter or a devious grin, his face was chiseled in seriousness. After locking eyes in a silence, Sam realized it wasn't a joke. Three seconds later her tears erupted. Watching his wife sob, Jeff himself had to hold back his own.

Twenty minutes later, Sam was told the story and how he'd crossed the chasm. Her veganism was a combative issue in their marriage. Jeff tolerated her shopping list, and Sam tolerated his "flesh eating," as she'd call it. Outside of occasional barbs between each other, they learned to live with it. Neither expected anyone's mind to change.

Once her tears abated, Sam placed her palm on his wrist and whispered, "I'm proud of you, Jeff—how you've grown as a man, how you've grown our business, and how—" Before she could finish, the waiter interrupted them with their food.

After dinner and the shock of Jeff's dietary announcement, they got down to business. Since Sam had quit the hospital and was now Heroic Kitchen's only full-time employee, Jeff received daily updates in real-time via text message as they happened. "We picked up another wholesale account!" and "We snagged Derlinger Distributors!" were the two big messages Sam had sent for the week. The wholesale account was a small chain of plant-based grocery stores in the Northwest. The other, Derlinger's, was a medium-sized distributor that had a small slotting in the health food section at all Kroger stores. It also got them listed on Vitacost, Kroger's online health store. When Jeff got home from work that day, Sam reported the details nonchalantly. He wondered if she knew that Kroger had over 3,000 stores in 200 cities. It was an account that Jeff had been working on for months and during his lunch breaks.

When Jeff questioned her lack of enthusiasm on such a big deal, Sam clarified. "I read the contract. It says we grant them the option, but not the right to put our brand on their customer's shelves, including Kroger."

"Meaning?"

"Meaning that they don't have to do anything. They simply carry our brand and can distribute it to their buyers if they're interested." She paused to let him assimilate it. Then, "In other words, we ain't going to wake up next month and find our soup in 3,000 stores."

"Damn. Why you got to be such a buzzkill?"

"There's more. They also want us to change our labels. They think they're amateur, too earthy, and lacking cohesion. They said the smiling cow thing is overdone, and that it also implies dairy, something really stupid to do on a plant-based brand."

Jeff finger quoted, "'They said?' You spoke to Dicky, didn't you?" Dicky was Derlinger's VP of sales, a trust fund brat heir to the Derlinger Distribution Empire, a big fish in Cedar Rapids, Iowa's small pond.

"Yes," Sam answered. "He was really helpful. Knows a lot about the industry, what's liked by buyers, and what isn't. Said he's been in the business for 20 years."

"20 years?" Jeff scoffed, "He's only 30 years old!"

"Well, this thirty-year-old happens to be in charge of $100 million in wholesale volume a year and wants us to make our sponsored animal a larger part of the label." Jeff shook his head. Sam added, "And change the entire color scheme of all three of our soups."

"Three?!" Jeff cursed. "We have two."

Sam remarked, smiling, "Not if we want Derlinger to carry us."

THE THREE STRIKES STRATEGY

Observe Negative Echoes:
Three and You're Out!

98

Six months after *The Millionaire Fastlane* was released, it was painfully clear: the book cover I designed and loved, sucked. Countless people in my target audience voiced distaste about the design. Colored in lime green and tangerine orange, countless folks commented. From "ignore the cover" to "hideous," the evidence in my 3A Method[S55] revealed a big problem. Instead of allowing my ego to justify its desire to be right (these people are wrong and don't know good design when they see it!), I embraced change[S42] and swapped the cover for a new one. Nearly ten years later, I've never heard another complaint about it.

It's inevitable. You can't avoid it, and you simply can't stop it.

Your product sucks.
Your website stinks.
You're a scammer.
You're this, you're that.

While Assessing in the 3A Model, you'll eventually hear negative feedback about you or your product or business. Whenever you counter a negative market echo about your product or business, it's either *meaningful-* or *trivial-invalidation*. While cash-validation[P74] proves you offered perceived-value[P25], meaningful- and trivial- invalidation proves you do not. Money fails to move into your pocket because you either failed in your skew presentation[S32] or failed elsewhere.

After encountering a negative echo, your first job in the Assess component of the 3A Method is to determine what kind of invalidation it is. Meaningful-invalidation has actionable intelligence. As the owner of a publishing company with myself as its primary author, a negative echo with actionable intelligence might be, "Not interested; you lost me at the foul language," or "Your stuff is too verbose."

Whenever identical patterns emerge with negative echoes, it's likely a skewing opportunity to improve your value array. Remember, removing negative skew[S36] is value-skewing. To determine this potential, I use a three-strikes scale: one meaningful invalidation is a curiosity, two is a concern, and three is critical. Hit three strikes, and it's time to reconsider the tactic and Adjust. If three people withheld their money because of the same gripe, you could bet many others did too. Assessing, then Adjusting to meaningful-invalidation allows positive skew to accumulate and stack atop your offer. More skew equals more sales[S32]. While one opinion isn't a consensus, it can reflect it.

In another example, if you're advertising a new party game you invented, a meaningful-invalidation could be "looks boring" or "too complicated." Not a fun thing to hear after you spent six months and $6,000 from your 401(k). Instead of getting angry, probe further. Why did she say it looked boring or complicated? Even if you don't hear back from the negative echo, it could indicate a problem in your packaging, advertising, or presentation.

The other type of invalidation is trivial. Trivial-invalidation contains zero actionable intelligence and can be ignored. These negative echoes usually fall into the category of cynics or coffee-haters[P77]. In one instance, one happy reader recommended my book to his friend, who replied, "Meh, millions of people tried that business shit and failed." This ignorant statement harbors nothing actionable other than proving my bias that most people are absolutely beyond saving. And that's great because the rat race needs its rats. In other cases, the intelligence cannot be used. For example, over the years many people professed that they originally passed on reading *The Millionaire Fastlane* because of the title. This negative echo wasn't something I could fix without losing the central theme of the book. The fact is, you could create the most fantastic product ever invented, and many people in your target audience still won't like it. And many times, those folks tend to be the most vocal.

Identify what's actionable and meaningful in your Assess[S55] routine, then discard the rest. And while the haters are hating Monday through Friday, you'll be Unscripting...

☑ KEY CONCEPTS

- Whenever you counter negative feedback about your product or business, it's either *meaningful-* or *trivial-invalidation.*

- Meaningful-invalidation is factual and potentially actionable; trivial is opinion and not.

- Three meaningful invalidations are critical and should compel corrective action.

- Adjusting meaningful-invalidation creates more positive skew.

THE OBSERVED MODELING STRATEGY

Use Observed Modeling to Expose Trade Secrets and Best Practices Hiding in Plain Sight

Most mainstream gurus who have carefully cultivated a public brand are full of shit. At least, the shit they sell. If you want to learn from these gurus, *stop buying what they SELL, and start studying what they DO.*

Years ago, when I developed a front-facing user interface (UI) for my ground transportation and travel business, I modeled it off the most trafficked travel businesses like Expedia and Travelocity. I knew that these big, well-funded companies tested the best converting UI variations. The winner of their tests was whatever they consistently presented on their website. I simply modeled it. In effect, I was able to reap the rewards of their work and on their dime.

What works best and what doesn't is right in front of your eyes. Study it, then model it. Take any highly competitive industry with deep-pocketed budgets, and you can easily "extract" the best-practices by *observed modeling.* Then you can extrapolate those results to your business.

Again, want to learn guru secrets? Don't *buy* their shit; study *how* the sell their shit. If you see the same ad on your Facebook feed for months, you can bet that variation makes money. Observe the copy, the photo, and the landing page. Assess how you likely fit into their target audience. By reverse-engineering every public-facing ad component, you'll unlock the best practices for what is working and what isn't. Likewise, see the same infomercial on television over and over? Again, you can assume it's making money. Observe every nuance, and suddenly, you'll know what works in the infomercial business.

As an author, observed modeling works fantastically. If you search the web for writing's best practices, you'll discover much conflicting information. One writing "expert" says you should never use adverbs. *He* haphazardly *shuffled the cards. She* frantically *called the police.* Another expert says avoid passive voice and don't swear. Fuck that. ;-)

Observed modeling reveals the best practices. Any time you read a best-selling author who has sold millions of books through a prominent New York publishing house, you're getting what works and what's acceptable. When that book hits the shelf, multiple editors have reviewed it. And not just any editor found on Upwork, but the best editors. If John Grisham wrote, "He cleverly avoided the question," you can bet for damn sure that using adverbs is acceptable.

Winning formulas aren't a secret. They're advertised in broad daylight for all to see. Look at the best, observe, reverse engineer, and model. Assess, adjust, repeat[S55].

☑ **KEY CONCEPTS**

- Best practices and trade secrets often hide in plain sight.
- Observing and modeling highly successful processes can help you mimic the same success without the trial, error, or cost.

THE NO JUDGMENT STRATEGY

Sideline Your Biases and Wipe Your Tears with Millions

100

Some years ago, I made a million-dollar discovery on my forum. As the website grew, it eventually became beneficial to monetize that traffic with advertising. Most users didn't care, but others did. One publicly complained about the ads. A few others followed, voicing the same opinion. It was a meaningful-invalidation that went beyond three strikes[S98]. Embedded underneath the complaints was an opportunity[S36]: disgruntled users said they'd be happy to pay for an ad-free forum.

I thought the suggestion was ridiculous. Why? My personal bias scoffed, "Wuh? I'd never pay to surf a forum ad-free, so why bother? I don't mind ads!" Despite my sentiment, I listened to my users. I offered an ad-free version of the forum for a mere $7.99 a month for anyone interested. On top of ad-free viewing, I also added several other benefits, including what many felt as more important: privacy and less dreampreneur noise. In one decision—merely using the 3A Method[S55]—I found a 7-figure fortune hiding underneath my forum pages. Had I allowed my bias and my desire to be right, I'd be poorer today. Simply put: *It pays to test your wrongheadedness.*

In another example, observed modeling[S98] proved that interruptive pop-up lightboxes are more effective than any list-building strategy. *Get your free report! Join our list and get a free coupon!* After nearly twenty years of web surfing and probably 20,000 pop-ups, I can't recall ever giving my email address to one of these interruptions. They don't work on me, and I hate them. Yet, despite my hatred and disdain for the strategy, the concept is widely used, and still today. The verdict is clear: It works. My opinion, null and void. My ego, bruised.

You see, when it comes to execution, your personal biases do more damage than good. In another story found within my forum pages, a young fitness consultant wanted to break free from the time-for-money trade. While she earned a decent income, she was overworked doing email consultations that fell outside her consultancy scope. She asked the group for suggestions. From automating to scaling to reforming her clients' expectations as a fitness consultant and not as a therapist, dozens of tips poured in. Many of them useful.

Sadly for this woman, her biases ruled her world, and she let them dictate her actions, or I should say inactions. She flat-out rejected every suggestion, preceded by a personal excuse as to why it wouldn't work. Every recommendation was dismissed, countermanded, or excused away based on her personal worldview and biases. Her conclusion bordered on the ridiculous, tantamount to saying *because I don't use supplements, so neither does any woman on the planet.*

Look, business is hard enough. Don't make it any harder by letting your personal tastes and narrow frame of mind corrupt the real world. Your perception is rarely the reality. When it comes to wealth and freedom, a debt-free dream house and a Lamborghini parked in the garage does wonders to assuage a bruised ego. Accept wrongness and get rich or believe your rightfulness and stay poor.

☑ KEY CONCEPTS

- Personal biases can often prevent good ideas and best practices from being executed.
- Your perception is rarely the reality.

THE RAT RACE LOSES ITS QUEEN
SUNDAY, APRIL 15TH, 2018 - 8:00 PM
(8 days later)

On April 15th, Tax Day, Samantha would give birth to the family's second child. While they awaited the infant's arrival at the hospital, Jeff was seated at his wife's bedside. Sam gripped Pinky while practicing her breathing. As she huffed, Jeff's phone was blowing up with text messages. She shot Jeff an annoyed look. "Just tell everyone I'm doing fine. And turn that damn thing off!" She pointed to the hospital sign admonishing cell phones to be silenced.

Jeff shook his head, beaming. "Uh, actually, those are orders." He turned his phone around and swiped the list. "See?" After scrolling through several, he put the phone away and added, "No texts from family, at least yet."

For the next two hours, Jeff would keep an eye on his silenced phone. Their health insurance was a worthless Obamacare bronze plan. *Funny how the "Affordable Care Act" made my health insurance anything but affordable,* he thought. Hopefully enough orders would ring through cover the hospital co-pay. He hated to divert any attention from his wife and her labor, but Jeff was fascinated. The business had reached a new threshold of activity.

Earlier that week, Heroic Kitchens had started sponsoring several plant-based and animal rights podcasts. And before he and his wife left for the hospital that morning, he got word that another campaign went live: Heroic Kitchens would sponsor the *Earthy Earthlings Edict*—a weekly email news-letter with over 630,000 subscribers interested in sustainable living. His bet was on the podcasts doing better than the newsletter. He couldn't have been more wrong. In a matter of hours, they'd sold over 3,000 cans, mostly tied to the newsletter.

The podcast sponsorships also did well, but comparatively speaking, $1 spent in podcast advertising yielded $3.50 in profit, but $1 spend in eNews-letter sponsorship yielded 10X—$37.00. Once Jeff learned that a simple email was generating thousands in business, he sent emails to their homegrown list. Because their rescue animals were QC coded on their soup labels, they would get dozens of subscribers per day. On a whim, Jeff sent their email list a five percent off coupon, and the response amazed him. Dozens of orders poured in—at a mailing cost of nothing.

Between the marketing initiatives and their in-house list, the numbers sparkled neon green in Jeff's head. His fascination grew into delight as he marveled at the mathematical power of the system he and his wife created. He pinched himself and nothing changed. It was not a dream. Spend $1 here earn $3.50—that's a 350 percent return. Spend $1 there, and it turns into $37, or a 3,700 percent return. Of course, he could spend $1,500 and only earn $90 as he had with his *Windy City Green Living* newspaper advertisement. Still, every channel, every medium that reached their audience, essentially rolled the dice on creating another money printing press.

At that moment, Jeff was hit with resounding clarity.

He understood how millionaires and billionaires became millionaires and billionaires: They weren't buying indexed-funds and hoping for eight percent a year, they were hunting for printing presses that generated asymmetric returns. They would sell products and services and reap a ridiculous ROI, hour by hour, day by day, month after month.

Jeff was not used to earning money unless he was at work. And he certainly wasn't used to making 3,700 percent on a money investment. And now that their business was a legitimate enterprise, he knew it had to be worth a lot of money… the kind of money that would have taken them decades to save.

Sam moaned in pain and kicked him out of his mathematical trance.

He was in a hospital delivery room.

The rhythmic beeping of medical machinery and the odor of hospital sterility jogged his memory. The last time he had been here was with the birth of his nine-year-old daughter Madison. Back then, their lives were upside down and lifeless. Utter distress and bleak futures. While he was proud when Madison was born, the moment suffered in a raw emotional undercurrent. Between the thankless jobs, the rising costs, the foresight of a hopeless future filled with nothing but weekend distractions, the memory felt impure, soured by circumstances. Madison's birth was but an hour old, and there he was, consumed by uneasiness. He snapped out of the memory but couldn't help but feel a flit of sadness and regret, a heartache that he didn't give his precious newborn daughter the moment. And the guilt that he'd allowed it to happen. Nine years ago, the rat race had stolen this moment from him. Now the rat race was on its heels. Retreating. If the rat race was a game of chess, he felt like he'd just taken its queen.

He returned his attention to Sam and scooted closer, grinning. He reached for her hand and began to slowly caress her fingers. Her pain-filled face cracked with a smile, and she pantomimed him a kiss. Her face was drawn and pale, her long blond hair frazzled and scattered, but her eyes were twinkling with joy and anticipation, a luminescence that Jeff had seen more frequently since she left nursing. Jeff hoped she was feeling the joy he was. It was profoundly different. It had depth. Velocity and longevity. He knew his children would have parents who wouldn't miss a moment. And that he was the author of his family's story, not a job, not Wall Street, not some economic forecast from some central banker.

Jeff would not think about business for the rest of the night.

He'd absorb the moment, the hour, the evening with his wife, and anxiously await the second time he would become a father.

When his son Micah was born, no words could describe his elation.

It was an emotion he never knew existed.

THE CHOOSING HAPPINESS STRATEGY

The Five Levers of Joy: Make Happiness an Easy Choice

One of the happier moments in my life continues today. No, it wasn't a marriage or the birth of a child; it was self-sufficiency. I remember the day like it was yesterday. I had recently moved from Chicago to Phoenix, and it was a beautiful sunny day in January. Meanwhile, in Chicago, it was cold and snowing. As I left the bank after making a deposit, it hit me that I had acquired the skills and wherewithal to never need a job again. In hindsight, this was the moment that my "happy switch" flipped ON. And get this—I was still (relatively) broke. Twenty plus years later and that happiness still remains. And now today, it has luminesce and is more impervious to externalities like politics, one-star book reviews, and social media loudmouths.

This might be hard to believe, but you too have a "happy switch." And at any moment, you can turn it on. The problem is most people need an external stimulus to move this switch. For example, your happiness switch might flip ON when you get a job promotion or win money at the casino. But shortly after that, it flips OFF again, only to wait until the next external provocation.

This dance between happiness and the external environment is the wrong way to live.

Ultimately, happiness is a choice. It evolves from the inside, not the outside.

I realize this is easy for me to say when my stomach is satiated, my bank account is full, and my bills are paid. But the truth is, I've made happiness an easy choice. How? I focused on what makes happiness likely. Specifically, you can make happiness such an easy choice that your "happy switch" has no choice but to be on. There are five "research-supported" levers of joy and a fulcrum to target if you want happiness to be your "new normal."

The fulcrum is a present moment awareness. It is an understanding that both past and future thoughts are mind fragments, and that the only time that exists is now. Eckhart Tolle, the author of *The New Earth: A Guide to Spiritual Enlightenment*, calls this the *Now*. If you live to 65 years old and each second represented a "now," you would have enjoyed 2,051,244,000 Nows. The question is, how many of those moments were spent dwelling on the past or hoping for a future? How many Nows were enjoyed in pure happiness? Probably not many.

For example, even been to your kid's recital or baseball game, but your mind is at next week's meeting? Have you ever cursed a sunset as it blinded your drive home from work? Have you ever relived an old sightseeing video on your smartphone while realizing you don't even remember being there? Life is chaotic. And amid all that chaos, living in the Now is nearly impossible. As such, happiness becomes a moving target in the future, fleeting and all too often, rare. Our brain makes happiness a tough cat to catch because we're always *thinking fractally*.

If you're not familiar with fractals, they are recursively chaotic systems driven by an infinite feedback loop. Think of it this way: If you multiply any number by half (0.5), you'd never get to zero. Each outcome just becomes smaller and closer to zero, but zero, numerically, always remains unreachable.

In life, a *fractal thought* is a future precondition that must occur before you grant yourself happiness, usually starting with a "when." *When* I get my dream job, *when* I get out of debt, or *when* I get married. Someday[P4] is a fractal thought. As a result, anxiety and unhappiness are the distance between now and what you want in the future. Namely, you rob the present. The chasm between those two states is the ever-moving fractal, like a Mandelbrot set.

The problem is fractal thinking makes happiness conditional to a variety of prerequisites. *You haven't given yourself the right to choose happiness.* Because the fractal is recursive and driven by a feedback loop (your new car, new gadget, or whatever else sparked joy), it perpetuates itself in a Pavlovian response. The fleeting moments of joy we experience in our consumption and vanity goals are *transient happiness*, the cheese, the impetus for our rat race[P5] existence. Ever feel invigorated buying a new car, and then just weeks later, the joy fades, but the five years of payments remain?

Sadly, the permissive moment of transient happiness only temporarily stops the fractal from moving deeper into the rabbit hole. After the faux happiness fades, the anxiety returns because we're now on the hunt for the next happiness condition. You got the Mercedes C-Class, but now you're gunning for the S-Class.

Furthermore, fractal, anxiety-producing thinking doesn't end with just a "when." For instance, how much money is enough? When the answer is "more," it's a fractal mind-fragment because "more" is unattainably infinite. When you're always moving the goalposts, the search for fulfillment never ends. The end result is your life punctuates with fleeting moments of transient happiness while *pure happiness* peeks over a distant horizon. You're working hard for milestones and goals, but misery bridges the chasm between the achievements.

The truth is, most people are imprisoned in a time machine dreaming of a future that may never come. Others are stuck in the past, reliving old wounds that steal the seconds, the extinguishing moments of Now.

Whenever your mind dwells on the past or future, the joy of Now is lost. Anxiety, fear, or impatience becomes the baseline. Or moments are hollowed out while you're smothered in your smartphone. Ever go to a concert, and everyone is watching and recording it through their smartphone? Instead of enjoying the moment's full sensory experience, absorbing the sights, sounds, and smells, the moment is cheapened when viewed through a two-dimensional facsimile that can only be marginally experienced in the future. It's the ultimate waste of the moment; sacrifice 100 percent of the Now to enjoy 25 percent of it later.

Life's past anxieties and future chaos can only be tamed with moments of appreciation in the Now. Pure, lasting happiness occurs in the present when transient happiness is not present. Even if you're focused on a happy memory, the thought of that memory happens Now. If you're thinking about a dreamy future, the same thing: the idea occurs in the Now. Now is the only place where pure happiness can switch on. And any thought that takes you away from the Now is a raincheck on joy.

That said, the first happiness lever is *gratitude*. Embrace the process[P28] and your current station in life. No matter what it is, feel it, live it, and don't let it pass without your appreciation. Anytime I walk into a grocery store and see aisle after aisle of food choices, I am smacked senseless with gratitude. Be happy about the awesomeness surrounding you: a warm bed, a hot shower, a house that gets you out of the stormy weather with food on the table. You can do all of that and still be excited about the future. Yes, stop and smell the coffee but also the dirty mop water.

The second lever is family and friends, specifically, *positive relationships* with people who support your goals. Show me someone rich in good relationships, and I'll show you someone who is pretty darn happy. Please don't mistake "family" to automatically mean blood relatives. In many cases, as reported on my forum, some family members can be toxic to happiness. Some are even abusive. You can't choose your blood in such cases, but you can choose what you do about it. All relationships are a choice that impacts your story[S2]. Your "family" is your support network, not necessarily that stepbrother who called you a loser for 25 years.

The third lever is freedom, or *autonomy*—the ability to feel in control of your life, to stockpile options, mobility, and whatever else you want to do. This is what caused my happiness switch to permanently flip. And scientists agree where evidence now supports autonomy's significance in its happiness role. *The Journal of Personality and Social Psychology* cited "autonomy" as the number-one contributor to happiness. When you're flipping off strangers from your car because another commuter cut you off in rush hour traffic, you have no autonomy. According to data from the US Census Bureau and the Centers for Disease Control, New York City was ranked as the unhappiest American city. Yes, the home of Broadway, Central Park, and Times Square isn't fostering happiness. Could a lack of autonomy be inflaming the misery? Autonomy was behind my happiness switch flipping on.

The fourth lever comes from fulfillment or purpose. Broadly speaking, fulfillment is contribution and self-development. It's the feedback loop[S46] and knowing that you're making a difference and doing meaningful work. It's having an active dream and the autonomy to pursue it. It knows that *You* today are better than *You* yesterday. It's when the "whens" are not flashes of happiness but times of euphoric elation layered atop existing joy.

And finally, the fifth lever is your *health*. Physical well-being. Neglect your health, and the other levers become severely marginalized, or worse, disappear. If you're sick or bed-ridden, nothing else tends to matter. Don't make a fortune only to lose your health. To live unbalanced for short periods is expected. Living unbalanced for forty years is not.

While it isn't within the scope of this book, significant research proves these dimensions of happiness. The psychological self-determination theory (SDT) supports autonomy (freedom) as well as connectedness (family) as a critical factor in happiness. Studied by researchers Richard Ryan and Edward Deci from Rochester University, SDT posits that the best forms of motivation and engagement, including persistence and creativity, come from our experience of autonomy, competence, and relatedness. Specifically, Deci and Ryan postulated that these needs, when satisfied, enhance self-motivation and mental health (well-being), and when thwarted, do the opposite.[1] Basically, intrinsic improvement and growth (fulfillment), autonomy (freedom), and relatedness (family) are core constituents of happiness.

Moreover, research also shows that freedom has a significant impact on health and morale. In one study, Yale psychologist Judith Rodin encouraged nursing-home patients to exercise more control over their choices, from the environment to facility policies. As a result, 93 percent became more alert, active, and happier.[2] Some lived longer. Another researcher, Angus Campbell, author of the *Sense of Well-Being in America*, concurs with autonomy's significance and perhaps knew before all of us. Commenting on a University

---

1 - Ryan, Richard, and Edward L. Deci. "Self Determination Theory and the Faciliation of Intrinsic Motivation, Social Development and Well-Being." January 2000. http://selfdeterminationtheory.org/SDT/documents/2000_RyanDeci_SDT.pdf.

2 - " Salmansohn, Karen. "The No. 1 Contributor to Happiness." Psychology Today. June 30, 2011. http://www.psychologytoday.com/blog/bouncing-back/201106/the-no-1-contributor-happiness."

of Michigan study, he stated: "Having a strong sense of controlling one's life is a more dependable predictor of positive feelings of well-being than any of the objective conditions of life we have considered."

Much of this research also explains why specific jobs are incredibly fulfilling and why everyone doesn't need to be entrepreneurs. If your job provides autonomy, connectedness, and a feeling of competence, you've made your happy switch an easy flip.

Happiness is a choice, but let's be honest. Not all of us have the mental fortitude of the Dalai Lama, Gandhi, or the Buddha. When your low-paying, low-fulfillment job feels like a mandatory prison sentence, the happy switch becomes a difficult flip. For the rest of us who want better odds at happiness, make a commitment to your Now, while targeting the five levers to flip on your happy switch: gratitude, autonomy, purpose, self-development, relationships, and health. The seconds are dripping away. You likely have millions, if not billions of Nows remaining. *Don't wait to be happy; choose to be happy.*

GRATITUDE
RELATIONSHIPS
AUTONOMY
PURPOSE
HEALTH

THE "NOW"

THE HAPPY "SWITCH"

PRESENT MOMENT AWARENESS

THE FIVE LEVERS OF JOY

☑ KEY CONCEPTS

- Happiness is a choice, a switch in your head that can be flipped on at any time.

- Fractal thinking is a raincheck on happiness based on "when" something happens, like "When I get my dream job, I will be happy."

- Transient happiness is the temporary joy felt from an external stimulus, buying a new car, or accomplishing a goal.

- Pure happiness occurs in moments of present moment awareness, or the Now.

- The five levers that influence happiness are gratitude, autonomy, purpose and improvement, supportive relationships, and health.

- Pure happiness, which is transcendent and lasting, can only happen in the Now.

THE WEALTH ACCELERATION PRINCIPLE

Accelerate Wealth: Grow Your Net Worth by the Business Multiple

Here's an interesting fact: If you invented a household product, your net worth would increase by a factor of 16 for each dollar of profit you earned—or 1600 percent. If you earned a $200,000 a year profit, you'd be a multimillionaire. How? The average multiple for businesses in the household goods industry sells at a 16 multiple. In other words, for every dollar you profited, your net worth would go up by a factor of 1600 percent.

The truth is, the rich don't get rich because they save nickels and dimes from their Starbucks celibacy. They don't get rich because they're paid well from their cushy job. They get rich because they enjoy recurring asymmetric returns[S21], 300 percent, 500 percent, 1600 percent, sometimes every month. They get rich because they tap into the Wealth Acceleration Principle, *an economic reality called the* valuation multiple *which gives business owners the power to explode wealth.* In public finance, it's called a PE, or a *price to earnings* ratio. I call it a wealth-acceleration factor.

As I write this, Netflix's PE is 87. That means that Netflix, as a business, is worth 87 times its profits, or earnings. Doing that math, that's about $230 billion. If you want to own a piece of Netflix through shareholder ownership, the share price you'll pay is "87 times earnings." If a billionaire wanted to buy Netflix, they'd need to start their bid at around $230 billion as it is the asset's market value.

Likewise, any small business you own will also be subject to a PE valuation, often called "the multiple." Multiples in private enterprises range from 1.5 to as high as 30 or more. For example, the first time I sold my business, I sold it at a multiple of about 4.5. The second time was around 3. This means that anytime I grew my company's bottom line, profits, my net worth accelerated by a factor of 300 to 450 percent. As a business owner, any time you grow your business, you receive a net worth gain equivalent to the industry's average multiple. Here is a sample of average industry multiples:

INDUSTRY	MULTIPLE
Advanced Medical Equipment & Technology	24.81
Advertising & Marketing	11.10
Apparel and Accessories	12.58
Freedom old	15.52
Legal Services	9.73
Maintenance and Repair Services	9.73
Management Consulting Services	9.73
Commercial Printing Services	10.07
Computer Hardware	11.76
Constructing and Engineering	8.22
Construction Materials	10.75
Consumer Publishing	10.07
Corporate Financial Services	20.56
Department Stores	11.22
Distillers & Wineries	15.54
Employment Services	9.73
Vegetable, Fruit & Nut Farming	13.81
Food Retail & Distribution	9.75
Other Food Retail & Distribution	9.47
Healthcare Facilities & Services	12
Household Products	16.10
IT Services and Consulting	11.79
Medical Equipment, Supplies, and Distribution	21.35
Non-Alcholic Beverages	17.58
Personal Products	21.35
Recreational Products	13.36
Software	24.35

Source as Feb 2021: https://www.equidam.com/ebitda-multiples-trbc-industries/

While smaller companies have much smaller multiples, these figures represent how large (and outrageous) some multiples can get. Still, the numbers are impressive. Moreover, the more significant the impact your company makes, the larger the multiple becomes. For example, if you start a business in the personal products industry, say deodorant or facial cream, and your business succeeds, expect your net worth to grow at a substantial rate. According to the chart, a large personal products business sells at a 21 multiple or a wealth acceleration factor of 2,100 percent. Of course, a smaller company with a few million in revenue likely won't sell at 21X profit, but perhaps five or ten. Still, where can you get 500 and 1000 percent returns?

Don't believe me?

Native Deodorant, a small start-up with just a few employees, was recently bought by Proctor and Gamble for $100 million—in all cash. Native didn't disclose profits before the acquisition, but if its earnings were a mere $5,000,000 a year, the multiple would be 20.

For online businesses, the average multiple tends to be in the two to five range. Assuming an average multiple of three, it means your net worth will rise by 300 percent any time you improve your enterprise's profitability. Yes, a whopping 300 percent! Know any investments that have the opportunity to grow 300 percent in one month? One year? A business can—and it is the same mathematical magic that powers a strong Unscripted offense[P12] and asymmetric returns[S21]. Once you wield this power, saving $10 a week and hoping for eight percent a year just seems awfully ridiculous, about as absurd as marathoning across Canada.

☑ KEY CONCEPTS

- The rich get rich because they enjoy asymmetric returns, 300%, 500%, sometimes 1000% every month on their marketing initiatives—spend $1, earn $10.

- The valuation multiple is a business metric which prices business assets.

- Depending on your business and your industry, the valuation multiple also is your wealth acceleration factor and can be as low as 150 percent or as high as 10,000 percent or more for public enterprises.

- Smaller companies start with smaller valuation multiples.

- Anytime you grow your company, your net worth increases by a factor of the multiple, sometimes more (The reverse applies as well.)

THE BIG LIST STRATEGY

Grow Your List, Grow Your Profit,
Grow Your Valuation

103

In late 2020, Insider Inc., parent of *Business Insider*, announced it was buying a controlling stake in digital media startup Morning Brew for a whopping $75 million.[1] The interesting thing about this story is Morning Brew is just a list of email addresses. Specifically, it's a newsletter with 2.5 million readers (and over $20M in revenue) spread out across three different industries.

No matter what your business, from an internet software service to a new Asian restaurant, the bigger list you have, the bigger your paycheck will be. A list is a big part of your asset's valuation. In digital marketing, the old adage (ten years being "old") is "tell me how big your list is, and I'll tell you how well you're doing."

Any business, from a global operation to the local coffee shop, absolutely must have a website. While sales are its primary goal, your secondary goal for your website must be list building. If you haven't yet, start immediately capturing email addresses or phone numbers. How? The same Unscripted logic applies to list building: offer value. In direct-marketing circles, a free value offering is called a lead magnet. It could be a newsletter, a free resource, an extended trial, a discount, or a contest entry.

And yes, compelling copy is critical. Because consumers covet their phone numbers, much less their email addresses, asking them to relinquish personal contact details is a skill in itself and worthy of your next best book to read[S66]. While some consumers might see email/text marketing as intrusive or annoying, make no mistake: it is the fastest and easiest way to generate a lot of money fast.

My friend owns a personal grooming company that employs various tactics to capture email addresses: from spin-to-win popups to exit coupons. His favorite capture magnet is a $10 gift card popup on exit, which in his words, astonishingly has converted as high as 70 percent. When explaining the conversion rate, he divulged that a gift card frames perceived-value much better

---

1 - https://www.morningbrew.com/daily/stories/2020/10/29/business-insider-buys-controlling-stake-morning-brew

than a standard $10 coupon. Both are the same, but their perceived-values are not. In another example, a forum user once reported that his text message marketing conversion rate on his abandoned shopping cart was a staggering 43 percent. Yes, you read that right: 43 percent!

My lists total over 100,000 email addresses. If I hit that audience with a relative-value[S26] offer, I'm guaranteed to convert those email addresses into cold hard cash. For instance, let's say I host a two-day seminar for $1,000 and blast my list with the date, time, and price. I'm guaranteed to generate $100,000 in a matter of days, assuming I limit my seminar to just 100. While I have no plans on hosting a seminar while joining the ranks of a guru hustler, can you see why coaching workshops and "secret seminars" are such a big hit in the internet market racket? Professional list builders are monetizing their list.

In the end, your lists are a big part of the asset you're building. They can be monetized, sold, and receive a valuation. You own them like you would a money-printing press in your basement. If (or when) you ever sell your business, the size of your list can dramatically impact your top-line offer.

That said, don't confuse list building with growing your social media account. *The Millionaire Fastlane's* Facebook page has approximately 160,000 likes. In 2013, a post on this page would reach 30,000+ people within a day. In a blatant money grab to force me to advertise, the mobsters at Facebook now show that same post to 300 people. Gee thanks. In short, a list owned by Facebook and a list owned by you are two different things. Remember, if one megalithic corporate entity can squash your business in a matter of minutes, you're job proxying[S27]. Yes, big social media presences have value, but they're not as important as what you own, monetize, and can sell. A bigger list draws bigger profits, which draws a bigger valuation.

☑ KEY CONCEPTS

- No matter what your business is, collect email addresses as they are a valuable asset.

- Email marketing has been a "fruit tree" marketing tactic since the internet was invented and continues to offer the best bang for your marketing buck.

- Don't confuse your private email list with social media followers— you own the list, or you own nothing.

VIVA LAS VEGAS!

B ecky just graduated; we can hire her," Sam said, cradling Micah while nursing him with a bottle. With two months of full-time work under Sam's belt, Heroic Kitchens had grown beyond a two-person operation.

"Let's not," Jeff bounced back, too fast for Sam's comfort.

"Why not? You have an issue with your niece? She does a good job at the fairs, and she needs a job."

"Because," Jeff stated, finger quoting the air, "'needing a job' and being my niece does not qualify her for the position. And neither does her status as a vegan."

"Again, she's pescatarian," Sam corrected.

"Look, Samantha, our first employee is a pretty big deal. And we've built us a business that is really starting to take off." He turned into the table and flipped through *Neve*, the raggedy notepad he'd used for his entire life. "Our revenue this month is on pace to be over $28,000. At a 37 percent net margin, that's over $10,000 in profit. Throw in my salary at my job, and we'll make almost $15,000 this month." He swiveled, facing his wife. "We've never made that much before... ever."

He flipped to the next page, holding up a hefty $510,000 written in black marker and underlined. "At our current sales, profit, growth rate, toss in your salary, our business is already worth over a half a million dollars."

Sam flashed disbelief. "Excuse me? How do you figure?" She walked to the crib and laid Micah under a blanket, glaring back.

"I do this stuff all day at work: valuations, audits, numbers. And I'm telling you, our business is already worth a half-million." He shook his head. "The point is, we can't hire my niece, at least not as our operations manager. We're not running a hobby or a charity. We're onto something big here, and we shouldn't treat it like a lemonade stand." He paused, then gestured to the crib. "We now have two children to care for."

"Didn't you say our margin last month was 43 percent? Why did it go down to 37?"

"Nothing to worry about. As we continue to add wholesale accounts, it will continue to go down. The margin on wholesale is half that of retail." Jeff then added, "Plus your salary." He tossed his notebook back on the counter and then lamented, "But we still can't afford the trade show."

Sam flashed a mercurial smile.

He noticed. "Please tell me you didn't already hire Becky."

"No, no." She grabbed a seat next to him. "But I do have a surprise."

Jeff didn't like surprises and preferred to be the one giving them. He led in with an "And??"

"We're going to the trade show. I got us a space."

Jeff gawked, ready to blurt something, but Sam muzzled his mouth with her finger. "And it will only cost us $3,000, not $30,000."

Jeff lurched his head back, unable to disguise his shock. "What, how? There are no spaces for $3,000, I checked. And double-checked! What on earth did you do?"

Sam laughed. "I picked up the damn phone. You forget we have a full-time employee now." She gave her husband a crafty wink. "Anyhow, I called Tottingham's Tofu; they have a booth. You know we use them in our Udon soup for one of our ingredients. I phoned Shirley, their sales manager, and asked if they could rent us a space... within their space. Like a sublease."

Jeff shot his wife a sly look, impressed with her creativity. It was a formidable match to his private-investigator/FedEx gambit that had yielded dozens of influencer shout-outs.

"Holy hell, you sub-leased a trade-show booth? I never thought of something like that."

"Yes, and they agreed, especially since we use their tofu in our soups. They saw it as a win-win. When we succeed, they succeed. And they get three thousand dollars." She paused and then added, "And get this, they gave us enough room so we can set up a sampling station." Sam whacked him on his thigh, butt unavailable since it was seated. "So get ready to saddle up and go to Las Vegas... you're going to be a busy boy..."

Jeff smiled and licked his lips like a salivating dog.

Sam stood and glared him down. "Sure you don't want to hire your niece?"

THE PHONE AND FEDEX STRATEGY

Pick Up the Damn Phone

The Undercover Billionaire on CNBC chronicles a successful entrepreneur who is dropped in a small town with no resources and tasked with creating a million-dollar business in ninety days. The billionaire who accepted the challenge was Glen Stearns, the founder of a national mortgage company. While the billionaire came up short on the challenge (he created a barbecue restaurant with a $750K valuation), it was enlightening for culture to see that "no money" and "no skills" isn't truly a barrier to success. The only barrier is the crap in your head.

That said, the show was a big topic on my forum. Every episode was discussed. One forum user, Kyle Keegan, the host of the Kill Bigger Podcast, was so impressed by the show that he sought to meet the billionaire at the restaurant he'd created. When he made the suggestion to the forum community, mostly everyone dismissed the idea, including myself.

A few weeks later, the meeting would happen. Kyle and several other Fastlane Forum members would meet the billionaire in Erie, PA. How does an average Joe hook up with a billionaire for lunch and talk shop? Quite simply, he didn't do what was conventional. Conventional would have entailed sending an email, which Kyle did. But a day later, Kyle did what most wouldn't: he picked up the phone and started dialing.

In today's technology chaos, sometimes going "old-fashioned" is how you get above the noise. Sadly, too many young people nowadays don't know how to use the phone. Worse, it is feared as if it were a bloodthirsty demon. Fact is, a phone call is always treated more urgently than an email, as is an in-person visit. Also, sending a FedEx to reach a prospect is another method of contacting the right people free of noise. And if your competition isn't using these tactics, it might give you an advantage. Sometimes if you want unconventional results, you have to do what is unconventional, or what might be considered "old-school."

- Don't be afraid to pick up the phone when appropriate.
- Your competition likely isn't using the phone, why shouldn't you?
- A phone call, handwritten postal letter or courier packages, and other "old-school" tactics have more urgency and sometimes work better for getting above the noise.

THE WIN-WIN STRATEGY

Use WIN-WIN Analysis to Solve Seemingly Unsolvable Problems

105

Years ago, when I owned a B2B (business to business) service for ground transportation companies, I wanted to place a full-page advertisement in a trade magazine. I don't remember the exact amount, but it was expensive—too expensive for a small company that was yet to eclipse $1M in revenue.

To solve my problem, I deployed a *Win-Win Analysis.*

A Win-Win Analysis is simply one question: *Is there a third-party agreement, a joint venture, or an unconventional deal that can solve this problem and be a "win-win" for the partner?* Oftentimes there is.

To solve my problem—*I can't afford a full-page advertisement*—I had a talk with the managing editor for the magazine. Instead of an ad, I offered to write for the trade magazine on various internet topics. In those articles, I was able to mention my company several times, using examples and results. It was a win because I didn't have to pay for advertising, but my company also got full-page exposure. The trade magazine won because they now had valuable, publishable content, free of charge. Win-Win.

The next time you encounter a problem, ask the Win-Win question. That $30,000 trade show booth you can't afford? You might be able to get it done with just a few thousand.

☑ KEY CONCEPTS

- Use Win-Win Analysis to solve seemingly unsolvable problems by involving third parties, joint venturing, barter, or resource sharing.

THE APOLOGIZE LATER STRATEGY

Stop Asking for Permission and Give Gatekeepers the Bird

106

I was in second grade. I don't remember the exact circumstances, but the class was on a field trip. Before returning to school, we ate lunch at a Mexican restaurant. Later that day, the stomach pains hit. If I didn't act fast, I'd shit my pants at my desk. Worse, if my classmates discovered my bowel blooper, my childhood would be ruined. Without thinking, I jumped up from my seat and bolted to the bathroom.

When you want something bad enough, you don't ask for permission. You don't raise your hand and patiently wait to get called on. You get up and do it. From toilets to dreams, life is the same way. No matter what your dream is, put your damn hand down. You don't need permission to live it from anyone. Act now, apologize later.

After I sold my ground transportation business, I was discussing a new competitor with a colleague. This new competitor put a spin on the industry and had just launched in New York. We unanimously speculated that the business wouldn't survive due to numerous regulatory hurdles. That new competitor was Uber. Our opinions didn't reflect the market and proved us horribly wrong. Uber shockingly didn't wait for regulatory approval; they acted and apologized later.

Closer to home, I had a neighbor who dreamed of being an author. But instead, she was a mailbox watcher. She spent her time sending query letters to publishers and literary agents. Her action wasn't needled action[P67] or focused experiments thrust into the marketplace. Her action was about *asking*... asking for permission and a "yes" from an esteemed gatekeeper. By doing so, she denied herself *agency*—the power to act and live her dream. She's been on the Ask Train waiting for years, praying for a blessed reply from a stranger who holds the keys to everything she wants. In other words, she's still dreaming...

Had I waited for a publisher's permission to write my book, I would never have made it to market. I didn't let a stranger perched in a Manhattan skyscraper stop me. Remember, one rejection doesn't make a market consensus. When Lindsey Stirling tried out for America's Got Talent, she was chastised by Piers Morgan. "You're not good enough...to get away with flying through the air and trying to play the violin at the same time." Sharon Osbourne piled on: "What you're doing is not enough to fill a theater in Vegas." Stirling ignored the gatekeepers, and instead, was led by the marketmind[P77] proving a Productocracy[S71], a decision that made her millions.

We live in a fantastic time. The Internet has given you, the ordinary citizen, profound upward mobility. The internet has democratized agency for the world, neutering once-powerful gatekeepers and returning it to the people. Yes, Saint Peter is asleep, and the Pearly Gates are open. Thanks to the web, the ivory towers, which once courted the exalted grantors of permission, are crumbling. If you have the talent and the desire, approval or consent is no longer needed. The keys to your dream await in open pastures: your website, YouTube, Instagram, Amazon, and any other medium with an audience.

There's only one gatekeeper to target: the marketmind. Fear—not gatekeepers—is the only thing that conceals talent. If you sing, sing to the marketmind and see if it claps. If you tell jokes, tell jokes and see if it laughs. Throw yourself overboard into the marketmind and let them react to your value. Gatekeepers can suppress talent like a cork in a bottle, but talent always pressurizes in the marketmind, eventually bursting.

Millions of adults live like they're still stuck in grade school, raising their hands, waiting to be called upon to go to the bathroom. Instead of asking for bathroom permission, they're asking for permission to live their dream. They're waiting for someone to pick them out of a hat and say, "Yes." Don't crap your pants with your dead dreams; stand the hell up and get moving.

☑ KEY CONCEPTS

- You don't need anyone's permission to live your dream.
- The Internet has democratized talent and value, giving anyone the ability to go from zero to hero.
- Target the marketmind and let it tell you how good or bad you are.
- Great talent, or value, pressurizes in the marketmind and eventually blows up.

THE WEAKNESS AND TRIPWIRE STRATEGY

Hire Weaknesses While Laying
Tripwires to Foretell Incompetence

Whenever Van Halen, the legendary rock band, went on tour, they were known to give their tour promoters high-maintenance contracts with many specific requirements and stipulations. The most infamous request is known as the brown M&M clause: Each promoter at any venue was instructed to remove ALL brown M&Ms from the backstage candy dish. Failing to do so gave Van Halen the right to cancel the concert while still receiving the full tour price. When this story first surfaced, it was instantly presumed to be a case of celebrity rockstar divas. Until this day, that rumor still persists.

The truth is, Van Halen was serving up a *tripwire*, a method that detects potential incompetence and/or oversights. If you're tech-savvy, think of it as a honeypot. As David Lee Roth said, whenever this minor stipulation was ignored, they knew that they could expect other problems in more critical areas like sound, lighting, and visuals.[1] A brown M&M meant, *Oh shit, better double-check every instrument, every connection, and every detail.*

Like a touring rock band, business is a team sport. Even if you're the only employee. At some point, you'll need to hire or contract outside help from people who are more skilled than you. And when you do, a tripwire is necessary to determine if you're hiring someone with an attention to detail or attention to just getting by. For instance, whenever I post a job on a freelancing website, I always include a tripwire in my project description. For example: *With your bid, please include in ALL-CAPS if you prefer Star Trek or Star Wars (or neither) and why.*

When a bid is submitted, and this information is missing, the application is immediately denied. If this person cannot follow your simple instructions in the project brief, how will they perform with the actual project?

When decided when and who to hire, optimally, you should focus on your strengths and hire out the weaknesses. If you can code but can't sell, hire someone who has the gift of sales. If you have a growth mandate (and the

---

1- https://www.npr.org/sections/therecord/2012/02/14/146880432/the-truth-about-van-halen-and-those-brown-m-m-ms

resources created by it), you should always hire your weaknesses away. And by "hire," I don't just mean employees. It can be contracted freelancers or companies found around the world. My publishing company doesn't print books; it outsources the job to publishers in Michigan and Wisconsin. My editors? All freelancers.

While I've never run a business with many employees, I regularly leverage more talented people than I. From cartoonists to voice actors to designers, I've hired them all. And in each instance, it's always the better alternative than "doing it myself."

While I believe you can learn anything, weaknesses take longer to hone. Had I tried to learn how to draw cartoons, my timetable would have tripled, or the final product would have been diminished.

Accept your entrepreneurial role as a problemologist[P29] who project-manages solutions. As the famous UK entrepreneur Felix Dennis once alluded, his job as an entrepreneur wasn't to *do* spectacular things; it was to *hire* those who can do the spectacular things for him.

☑ KEY CONCEPTS

- A trip-wire is a hiring tactic that can help detect incompetence or a lack of attention to detail, saving you a hiring mistake.
- Hire your weaknesses, work your strengths.

THE GREAT DISHWASHER PRINCIPLE

How You Do What's Meaningless Is
How You Do What's Meaningful

As a young man, I had some cruel jobs. By "cruel" I meant as if God kept playing a joke on me. There was the job in the frozen floral warehouse where I would learn all about daisies, orchids, and alstroemerias. Then I worked at Sears as a stock clerk for a good five years, not in the hardware or electronics department, but the linen and drape center. That's when I learned about valances, tiebacks, pleats and priscillas. I won't go on, but I hope you get my point.

In each case, I hated these jobs. But I made damn sure I would *try* my best and then *do* my best. Looking back, I realize this mentality is what prepared me for more tremendous success. At Sears, I was the best stock clerk and towel folder; nicely squared, tight corners, and the linen lines perfectly aligned in unison. When I worked among the roses and carnations, I did the best at what the job demanded. But wait, there's more. I was even a great dishwasher, like, the Michael Jordan of dishwashers. While Jordan drained jump-shots, I was draining sinks with not a smidgen of streaks or residue.

There's an old saying (I couldn't find the rightful owner as many claim it) behind the Dishwasher Principle. It goes like this: *How you do anything is how you do everything.* Particularly, *how you do what is meaningless is how you will do what is meaningful.* If you're taking shortcuts and cheating your way to a law degree, that is how you will practice law—with shortcuts and cheats. And when you discover that it doesn't work in successful law practices, you'll be disadvantaged and unprepared.

Wherever you are today, you're never too good to do the grind. Nowadays, there are too many small people with big egos. Social media and the culture of likes and upvotes have inflicted many people (mostly young people) with a warped sense of superiority and an unhealthy aversion to character-developing work. All of that can be wrapped up with a tight little bow called entitlement. When the sheltered college world is left behind, they enter the real world, expecting an entry-level job with a penthouse office and a penthouse paycheck. This attitude works at one thing only: keeping you enslaved to the Scripted rat race[55] of economic slavery.

Let's be honest. The ideas in this book and their application won't be easy.

And much of it you will hate. On your Unscripted journey, how you do the meaningless things, stuff you likely *don't want* to do, is how you will do what you *want*. Even today, a decade beyond official Uncripted liberation, I still do things I hate. As a publishing company owner, I hate dealing with shipping and logistics. While these duties might take only a few hours per week, I still do them because they support my purpose[S96]. More importantly, doing what I hate allows me to do what I love: To write with creative freedom, to live passionately without restriction or reason, and to contribute in ways I could never imagine.

Once you outline your halfway vision from the 1/5/10 Planasy[S12], everything you do—even the unsexy jobs—brings you closer toward your goal. *Don't just do the work; kill the work.*

Remember, strive for excellence and give good[S79] a great chance. Confront the work as a personal challenge and a litmus test for advancement toward better outcomes and better pay. Take pride that you're writing the chapters of your life[S2].

Whatever you're doing, approach it with these three things in mind: 1) effort, 2) pride, and 3) optimism. Do it as if it were your own. I don't care if you're driving for Lyft, waiting tables, or shoveling horse manure; give it the best you have, do it well, and know you're grinding coal to make a diamond. *What* you do does not make you, but *how* you do it. If you're a great dishwasher now, I'll bet you'll be a great surgeon later.

☑ KEY CONCEPTS

- How you do the meaningless is how you will do the meaningful.
- If you cheat your way *into* an opportunity, you likely will cheat your way *managing* the opportunity.
- Give your best effort in all that you do with pride and optimism, even work that is boring or tedious.

NEW MONEY, OLD HABITS
Wednesday, July 25, 2018 - 7:15 PM
(39 days later)

U h, since when does a flight for two to Las Vegas cost $1,200?"
Sam was standing at the foot of kitchen sink grimacing at her phone. Visa had texted her about an airline purchase. Jeff was at the kitchen table, back to the wall, the light of his desktop computer glaring in his face.

He looked up, gloating. "First class, baby." He gestured to the luggage on the seat next to him. "And a new tri-fold for my new suit. I can't style in 1D wearing some crap from Walmart."

Sam furrowed her brow and pouted, "First class?" Jeff paid her no mind, not even a glance.

She pirouetted and stormed off into the bedroom. A commotion ensued as if she were rifling through a magazine. A moment later, Sam emerged and marched back to the table dropping a pile of papers in front of Jeff. It shocked him from his computer trance. He glared at the documents and shot his wife disgust. "What the hell?"

Sam grabbed the top sheet. "This is our credit card statement. See that? That shows we owe $13,200." She slammed it down and picked up another. "See this one? It says we owe $4,931."

"Why are you going through our bill pile? I'm in charge of the money."

She responded with another slam, the thuds getting louder. "This one, from the hospital for having a baby, $3,900." Another thud. "This is our business insurance due next month. $1,935. It doubled because our revenue doubled, as did our employees." Slam! "These are health insurance quotes for a family of four—every one is like a fucking mortgage Jeff." She crossed her arms. "Need I go on?"

Jeff sat startled and frozen. He let the moment marinate and then slowly, deliberately turned his computer toward Sam and pointed. On the screen was a banking page, open to their business checking account. He pointed and said, "$81,000." He smiled as if he'd just checkmated a Russian grandmaster. "That's more money than we've ever had since we've been married. Hell, when we lost most of our 401(k)s in 2008, that was only $3,000!"

Expecting Sam to dance about the news, Jeff waited. But only stern dissatisfaction steamed from his wife. The silence lingered. Back in the day, Jeff always had an impulsive taste for haughtiness: the Lincoln Navigator, the Louis Vuitton purse, his BMW. Any reason to celebrate was always a reason to spend. It's why they would never save or cheapskate their way to millions. Unless, that is, they lived until the year 2190.

He waited until her scowl melted, but it only dissolved into an empty glare.

Finally, tone softer, Sam said, "Jeffrey, I appreciate the update on our money situation, but $81,000 isn't enough to ride off into the sunset in a Rolls Royce. So why are you flying across the country like it is?"

He raised an eyebrow as if she'd just uttered a numerical falsehood, like 1+1=5.

But she hadn't.

She was right.

The large number dazzled Jeff as did the valuation numbers he knew. While the figures were promising, it wasn't near their Escape Number which accounted for the real numbers… like the cost of living, the cost of expensive woodworking tools, and the cost to retire thirty years early without starving yourself. Why was he acting like he was a millionaire?

He scoffed, turning the computer back around. He started clicking away and then muttered, "Fine, I'll get them refunded and go coach." Sam didn't move, but her eyes did a blinking glance at the chair with the suitcase. He nodded at it. "Including the suit."

Sam, now with a self-satisfied smile, dug in gloatingly. "Go ahead, you can say it."

"Say what? That we're not rich?"

"You know…"

Jeff sighed exasperatedly and then shook his head. Then, tone slow and deliberate, he said in a singsongy voice, "Samantha thank you for reminding me that you're always right."

She smiled, enjoying the banter. "Well, Jeff, if that was true, we wouldn't have $81,000 in the bank and a business worth a half-million dollars." She slapped his shoulder playfully. "It could be worse: you could be in the garage sharpening knives." She winked and trotted away, throwing him an air-kiss.

THE DIDEROT PRINCIPLE

Consumption Is Viral: Stuff Begets More Stuff

109

The first extravagant gift I bought for myself to celebrate a net worth milestone[S80] was a metallic silver 1999 Lamborghini Diablo. Even twenty years later, this car still turns heads and sells for hundreds of thousands of dollars. While I was proud of my achievement, I knew I was opening a Pandora's box of new spending. The Diderot Principle asserts that *the more stuff you have, the more stuff, or carry cost, your stuff needs.* And stuff costs money. Here's what also came with my new Lamborghini:

- $250 oil changes every few months
- $2,500 tires every few years
- $5,000 in miscellaneous maintenance per year
- $20 to $50 every time I valet parked
- $250 for every wash, wax, and detail
- $100 in fuel on every fueling
- $4,000 yearly state license registrations (depends on location)
- $2,000 to $4,000 a year in insurance
- $12,000 for the dreaded clutch every 10 to 20,000 miles

Stylish stuff often has a stylish price tag, both in purchase and use. Moreover, such garishness always demands equal garishness. Going back to my new Lamborghini, I remember having to upgrade my clothes because it felt a bit odd showing up to the club style challenged. People expected Supreme and Prada, not Sears and Payless. In a more realistic example, if you upsize to a bigger house, you also upsize your expenses. More rooms, more furniture, more space, more air to heat and cool, more home, more taxes. Consumption spirals into more consumption, and often continuous, repeat consumption.

While I learned this concept years ago and thought it was something I alone recognized, it turns out it's been known for centuries. Stuff causing more stuff was first observed by Denis Diderot, a mid-sixteenth-century French philosopher who penned an essay on the regrets of parting with an exquisite gift. The luxurious gift caused Diderot to evaluate the rest of his possessions, which suddenly seemed tawdry and out of place. Long story short, Diderot went into debt trying to upgrade the rest of his possessions—his desk, chair, art—with equally adulated items.

Centuries later, this behavioral phenomenon is known as the Diderot Principle: the likelihood that new stuff, especially stuff that exceeds our current complement of possessions, can spark a fire of spiraling consumption. The Diderot Principle also posits that we tend to identify with our possessions and strive to keep those relationships cohesive. Namely, people who drive Lamborghinis likely won't be comfortable driving it in Walmart jeans.

It doesn't matter what it is—a new puppy, a new computer, or a new pair of shoes—all consumption begets more Diodetic consumption. And consumption creates expenditures, which likely conjures the ultimate thief of freedom, debt. In short, consumption grows the rat race walls taller and more inescapable.

While there's nothing wrong with rewarding yourself for a job well done, even a Lamborghini, just know you're buying more than just a car. You're buying the car and all the stuff that comes with it.

☑ **KEY CONCEPTS**

- Consumption is viral, creating more consumption.
- Consumption, especially from affluence, will spawn more consumption, either in maintenance, or complementary items.
- Known as the Diderot Effect, consumption increases as it aims to match equal affluence.
- Consumption requires production and can steal freedom.

THE CORNBREAD STRATEGY

Invest in Cornbread Before Splurging on Champagne

110

In 2007, after I sold my company for the second time, the new owners moved the business from Phoenix, Arizona, to a hot tech district in San Francisco. I'm sure the rent increased by $30,000 per month, not to mention labor costs and everything else from coffee to cubicles. Since I knew my old company's inner workings, I never understood this reasoning, other than wanting to "look the part" of a technology company. Phoenix is not devoid of IT talent or office space.

Anyhow, it felt like déjà vu. You see, the first time I sold the company nearly six years earlier, the exact same thing happened: a fast move to San Francisco, increased costs, and increased things that didn't seem to matter. I know foosball tables and unlimited Pringles in the lunchroom are good for employee morale, but you know what isn't good for employee morale? Layoffs, pink slips, and bankruptcy. Sadly, years later, despite a different economy, a different team, and a different vision, the outcome would be indifferently the same: bankruptcy.

When starting and growing your company, cornbread must come before champagne.

Cornbread is any expense that can positively impact your bottom line, directly or indirectly: a new software program, a new advertising expense, a new employee. Any expenditure that has no meaningful or measurable effect on the bottom line is a *champagne expenditure*.

Every dollar you earn or invest in your company should go into cornbread. Until you reach the business's maturation stage, it shouldn't be spent if it cannot grow the bottom line. Extra expenditures, such as marble doors, custom-branded mousepads, and that fancy neon light for your logo, can wait. Preservation of cash and its ultimate redirection into market validation and then growth are the only things that matter.

But when cash flow ramps up, so do the temptations. Stuff begets stuff, and the Diderot Effect[P109] can inflict businesses just as it does people. Corporations are owned by people, so the same behavior travels downstream. If your business card says "CEO" (but you haven't made a dime in profit yet), does your new CEO identity demand a Tag Heuer watch and a red pin-cushion mahogany chair? Are you flying from New York to Los Angeles in business class because that's what CEOs do? It's champagne and a threat to your growth.

When cash is tight, growing a company is impossible. More sales, traffic, and users demand more resources. Every dime of revenue (and profits) should be reinvested into your company to fund whatever growth challenges await. There is a time and a place for champagne. It just isn't the third mile of a marathon.

☑ KEY CONCEPTS

- Champagne expenses are unnecessary business expenditures, while cornbread is necessary and usually directly attributed to revenue-generating activities.

- Newly growing businesses are susceptible to champagne, creating a similar Diderot effect.

- Growing a company is nearly impossible when cash-flow is tight.

- All profit should be invested in cornbread, make champagne expenditures a reward for milestones.

LOADING BULLETS IN THE BARREL...

SATURDAY, OCTOBER 20, 2018 - 11:15 PM

(87 days later)

irls, Girls, Girls...

G As Mötley Crüe blasted their ears, the air was thick with doused cigarettes and stale beer. A young woman, not much older than twenty-one, was parading her hips in front of Jeff, mostly skin aside from red lace panties about as thick as his pinky finger. He was drinking at a back table at some nondescript strip club in a not so nondescript neighborhood. If Las Vegas had a manufacturing district, he was in it. Seated next to Jeff was Dale, one of Tottingham Tofu's sales managers, his trade-booth partner that weekend.

Per Dale's recommendation, they were there to celebrate a successful trade show. With his wife managing the business at home and Becky partying on the strip with some old college friends, Jeff was planning on dinner alone. Dale had suggested a night out. Jeff obliged, not knowing a "night out" meant a sordid strip club. He feared upsetting his joint venture partner, who was the means-and-the-method behind their unlikely trade show appearance.

Dale remarked, "We've never done this well at the Veggie Con." He held up his Heineken to toast. Jeff clinked Dale's bottle and took a sip of his whiskey, his third of the night. Dale continued, "The soup sampling station really attracted them like flies." He gestured to his cellphone on the table. "My assistant messaged me and said we generated nearly a hundred more leads, double last year's count." Dale's phone lit up with a call, brightly displaying the phrase "The Wifey" on the screen. He pressed "Decline" and sipped his drink once more, his eye crinkled in deviousness. Dale continued, "I'm on commission, so your company's presence really helped."

Jeff nodded and smiled weakly. "Yeah, we did great too. Secured six new distributors and sold a boatload. My wife's going to be ecstatic when I give her the news."

Dale sold him an appraising look, lifting his head and narrowing his eyes. Jeff took another nervous drink of his whiskey.

His attendance at a strip club wouldn't bother his wife. What bothered him was the crapshoot of alcohol. His drinking history suggested a fine line between harmless giddiness and demolished inhibitions, taking with it all critical thinking.

He looked around the interior of the gentleman's club and realized a gentleman wasn't in sight. He remembered his wife's rant about "gentlemen" being code for douche. Most of the post-dinner crowd looked like they'd just finished mowing lawns or digging ditches. He and Dale were the only men dressed business-casual; the rest were dressed slob-casual. He refluxed the cheap whiskey, the bile/acid combo burning his throat.

"Why here?" Jeff said. "A strip club next to an abandoned factory? Surely there's got to be some nicer places in Vegas?"

The dancing blonde in front of him winked as she continued her suggestive gyrations. Dale angled into Jeff's ear and whispered, "I've hooked you up." He grinned, eyes glimmering with wit. Then, "Prostitution is illegal in Clark County, but I hear this place is geographically challenged." Dale coughed a laugh, then nudged Jeff under the table. "If you know what I mean."

Before Jeff could react, the blonde sat next to him. She reached under the table and began stroking his inner thigh. A skinny brunette with mustardy meth-teeth and a corpse-like body strutted from around the corner. She nuzzled herself next to Dale, who promptly gave her a kiss on the forehead. The blonde whispered in Jeff's ear, "My name's Jade." She motioned to Dale and said, "Your friend here just paid us quite handsomely to give y'all a very special dance…" She nodded to the back of the bar where a sizable blood-red curtain concealed an archway, "Let's go, cutie," Jade tittered while caressing the corner of Jeff's ear.

Jeff quickly shot his trade show partner a confused grimace. "Go ahead," Dale said, snickering, "take a load off." He slapped his left hand on the table snickering while the other hand fondled the brunette's waist-long hair. Jade's hand meandered from Jeff's thigh to his groin, her caress intensifying. She winked him a "come hither" look, and for a moment, he considered it. Her lavender perfume assaulted his senses in what should have been a welcome scent in the club's stink of mop water and cigarettes. As Jeff grappled with the situation, Jade suddenly stood and grabbed his hand. After pulling him up, she escorted him toward the red curtain to the great unknown beyond. The bass thumped "I Wanna Rock Right Now" by Rob Base as Jeff's heart sped. After a few steps, Jeff stopped, despite the tug on his arm. Jade abruptly halted as if she'd walked into a wall, nearly falling off her high heels. The sensual, seductive smile on her face evaporated. She sneered, "What the fuck? You coming or not?"

Jeff unhooked from Jade's hand. He said, "No, but thank you. You can go."

She shrugged. The sneer morphed to a smile once she realized she'd just gotten paid for a "dance" she didn't need to perform. She spun and quickly shuffled off. Jeff returned to the table and opened his wallet. After he flipped a hundred-dollar bill onto the table, he stated, "I appreciate the dance and the drinks, Dale, but I have work to do."

He grabbed his whiskey and took one last sip, lilting his head to the grimy ceiling tile. It was browned by cigarette tar as old as the Reagan administration and caked with some unknown black goo that was probably syphilis incarnate. He faced Dale and his brunette friend, who were both were painted with confusion. Jeff thought about saying, "Tell the wife I said hello" or something to that effect, but instead, he stood silently zipped. After a moment of awkwardness, he then said flatly, "See you tomorrow at the booth." He turned and left the building.

THE D.A.R.E. STRATEGY

Identify Risks That Create DAREs

111

After three vodka tonics, I felt light and free. I'd just met a woman on an internet date, and the meeting went fantastic. Eye contact, engaged conversation, a few hair-flips; my ego was surging with confidence. I hopped into my 850-horsepower Viper and started the drive home. Five minutes later, my car was wrapped around a twenty-foot date palm, destroyed. But my life, luckily, was not.

What happened? With a hot ego and lowered inhibitions, I thought I'd street-race a throaty Mustang. I throttled hard, spun out, and crossed into oncoming traffic, broad siding a tree. In hindsight, I failed to recognize a DARE, or a *Downside Asymmetric Risk Event*.

If you haven't noticed, asymmetry is a big theme behind a great rat race escape. A *Downside Asymmetric Risk Event* is when your choices have best- and worst-case consequences that are unevenly skewed negatively: *minimal upside, colossal downside*. It is a failure at consequential-thinking[S86]. When I'm street-racing on a crowded city street in a car sauced with nitrous, my upside is a fleeting burst of adrenaline and a superficial ego boost. Ten seconds of fun, eh? The downside is I crash and kill myself. Or someone else. The downside is catastrophic and lasting, perhaps eternal. The risk of this action (street racing) and its outcomes are disastrously asymmetrical. Remember, one poor decision can invalidate thousands of good ones.

Whenever you fail to identify a DARE, which could be a literal dare: *I dare you to jump off the cliff, I dare you to eat the whole bag of marijuana gummies,* you're playing Russian Roulette. Your lousy decision loads the gun. While there's a decent chance you can escape the consequences of your poor choice, there's also a chance you'll blow your head off. While none of us would willingly play Russian Roulette with a loaded gun, you are whenever you make poor choices. A DARE becomes a bullet.

Remember that medical-device CFO who thought he would video himself chiding a Chick-fil-A employee at a drive-in window? A DARE loaded the gun. His upside was some likes and comments from anonymous strangers on YouTube; his downside was losing his career and life savings. He spun the barrel and lost. Remember, as Unscripted entrepreneurs, we're trying to manipulate probability and have asymmetry work for us, not against us.

However, the real danger of DAREs are risks that are hidden or not easily forecasted—or *asymptomatic risk*. For instance, if you're speeding on the interstate from Colorado into Kansas with a broken taillight and a pound of weed in your trunk, your DARE is asymptomatic and very asymmetrical. The catastrophe is not easily seen: getting stopped by police and thrown into jail for months, perhaps years.[1]

Similarly, the new buzzword worthy of clickbait headlines on financial websites nowadays is this concept called FIRE—or *Financial Independence Retire Early*. With a ten-year bull-market behind us, this movement is based on the compound interest scam[P6]—living frugally during your youthful working years while saving and investing most of it in the stock market. The hope is to "retire early" and continue living the same frugal existence based on presumed growth rates and systematic withdrawals. Participants call this financial independence—I call it financial dependence. Why? The risk is asymptomatic and asymmetric. If the stock market crashes or goes into a three- or five-year recession, retirement turns into a reckoning. *OMG, my life savings are gone! OMG, my withdrawal calculations didn't account for three years of negative returns!*

While I respect the movement's central tenet, freedom, denial of reality is best served asymmetrically. There is a 100 percent certainty that the stock market will eventually crash, and with it, life savings will too. While most markets eventually recover, most people can't survive the duration. Freedom is the right neighborhood—relying on the stock market for that freedom is the wrong house. Newsflash: changing the prison warden doesn't change the prison. Swapping your slave-owner from a corporate job to Wall Street doesn't change slavery. In other words, FIRE is a DARE. Bullet, meet barrel.

As an Unscripted Entrepreneur, stock market crashes or economic recessions are not DAREs. If the stock market crashed tomorrow by 50 percent or didn't earn positively for the next thirty years, my lifestyle wouldn't change. I don't have to update the resume and hunt for a job. There is no DARE. In fact, during the COVID-19 pandemic, my income didn't drop. It went up.

Bet on it: The better you manage—or preferably, eliminate—asymmetrical and asymptomatic DAREs, the better life you will have. Life as an entrepreneur is filled with risk. The question is, are the chances you're risking worth the best- and worst-case outcomes? Are you risking everything for twenty minutes behind a red curtain at the back of a sleazy strip club? What kind of

---

1 - As I write, marijuana has not been decriminalized in Kansas.

probabilities and expected values[S56] are you dealing with? Think consequentially for a few seconds, and you will expose the DARES. And avoid the stupid games that have stupid prizes.

☑ KEY CONCEPTS

- A *Downside Asymmetric Risk Event* is when your choices have consequences with a minimal upside but a colossal downside.
- DAREs often involve literal *dares: I dare you to jump off the cliff.*
- DARE risks are usually asymptomatic, they are hidden or not easily forecasted.
- Consequential Thinking can help expose DAREs.
- Financial Independence Retire Early, or FIRE, is a DARE with asymptomatic risks.
- Don't risk everything for twenty minutes of pleasure behind the red curtain.

THE BACKSEAT PRINCIPLE

Bad People Open Troublesome Roads

112

When I was sixteen years old, I had an odd friend named Dave. Dave scared the crap out of me because he was unpredictable—one minute he seemed friendly and supportive, and the next he'd look at you with a homicidal scowl. One day while I was at his house, he cursed at his mother, calling her names I won't repeat here. His mother didn't discipline him; she simply shook her head and walked away. My eyes gaped like saucers. Later that same day, Dave caught a rat in the backyard and burned it alive on a leaf pyre. I objected in spirit but kept quiet, not wanting to be Dave's next victim. After the sick deed, I gave an excuse and left. It was the last time I saw Dave because I decided it would be the last time. Even in my youth, I sensed something off. Disastrous. My intuition knew I didn't want to hitch a friendship with this guy. And sure enough, I was right. I read about Dave in the newspaper some years later; he murdered a police officer.

The Backseat Principle asserts that *every person who is in or enters, your social circle puts you one degree away from their consequences.* The question is, can you identify and remove people who are liabilities to your goals? Will you allow the negative inertia of someone to carry you to dark places? Or will you be a proactive CEO of your choices?

Be wary of who you invite into your life. Start looking at people as if you were a backseat passenger in their car. Get into the wrong car, and once in a while, you'll find yourself on their detours and united to their second-order consequences. What if I'd remained friends with Dave and happened to be with him when he killed a cop?

You can't escape the rat race and Unscript from the world's economic religion[P5] tethered to human liabilities who insist on keeping you in it. Are the people in your life driving you to mediocrity, or worse, exposing you to DAREs[P111]? Or are they driving a route to growth and winning? Don't let one sordid transgression at a seedy strip club in Vegas destroy your business or your marriage. Likewise, don't let one poorly placed comment with a joint venture partner endanger the relationship. While Jeff might not have approved Dale's behavior, he wasn't privy to Dale's marriage arrangement. Perhaps they had an open relationship? The fact is it was none of Jeff's business. Still, Dale opened a green-lighted road that Jeff wouldn't willingly drive. People, both good and bad, pave the streets on our map. If your map is tarred with many troubled roads because of the people you're hanging with, eventually you'll find yourself stuck on one of them. And troublesome roads only lead to one place... *trouble*.

☑ **KEY CONCEPTS**

- Every person in your social circle puts you one degree away from their consequences.
- Look at new friends and/or business associates as you would being a passenger in a car they drive: If they crash, you might go with them.
- Bad people inflict second-order consequences into your life.

THE LOW EXPECTATIONS STRATEGY

Carry Low Expectations to Provoke High Satisfaction

Confession: I've been on hundreds, perhaps thousands of Internet blind dates. Yes, I was a serial dater years ago in the pre-Tinder era when it wasn't so mainstream. On each "date," my expectations for the meeting were simple: meet another human being and have a good conversation.

This standard of expectation made all my dates/meetings enjoyable, if not interesting. When pictures didn't match reality, I didn't get angry. If twenty seconds revealed that this woman was not the woman of my dreams, but more likely the woman of nightmares, I made the most of it—laughed, drank, tried to learn something. Expectations were always exceeded. Heck, a man in a pink dress could have shown up, and I still would have had a good time. Not because I liked being misled, but because my expectations were set so low. I made *satisfaction* the probable, likely outcome. I was there to meet another human being, and the violation of that expectation is only to be stood up[1].

The chasm between expectation and reality is a disappointment. If you want less disappointment and more satisfaction in your life, lower your expectations. While you might not be able to control reality, you can control your expectations. It's a potent weapon in your arsenal of brain tricks, and another influencer within the happiness levers[S101].

For much of my life, I've held low expectations; for myself, for friends, and for any future outcome. While some might mistake low expectations for pessimism, it is about maximizing satisfaction while minimizing disappointment. Lowered expectations do two things: First, it mentally prepares you for it if it does happen, and second, it makes satisfaction more likely. More satisfaction equals more happiness.

Think about the last time something happened that exceeded your expectations. How did you feel? Overjoyed, excited, surprised? Conversely, how about the last time you felt disappointed? What was your expectation versus the outcome? The difference between all results and your feelings about those

---

1 - I was only stood up once!

outcomes is a matter of expectation. Change your expectation, and you can change satisfaction—and keep that happiness switch on.

☑ KEY CONCEPTS

- MJ was an online serial dater back when it was for nerds and losers.
- Low expectations, which you can control, ensure high satisfaction while preparing you for the worst.
- The gap between expectation and reality is disappointment.
- Exceeded expectations creates transient happiness.

FEAR BETRAYS THE PAST
TUESDAY, JULY 30TH, 2019 - 2:15 PM
(283 days later)

Jeff stood at a towering glass window overlooking Woodfield mall, the late-afternoon sun beating down on his face. He was on the 17th floor of the Schaumburg Tower in an unfinished office suite. Bare metal girders shelled various cubes and walls, but mostly, the floor was empty. With no tenant to pay for utilities, the air was oppressively humid. His wife had texted that she would be ten minutes late, but it was now looking like twenty.

Earlier that day, Jeff had scheduled the 5 PM meeting with his wife, telling her it was about "a big business deal." He stressed her attendance was impera-tive. She must have thought it was about a new distributor or joint venture partner based on her giddy reaction.

Across the empty floor, Jeff heard the elevator ding open. He glanced but couldn't see inside. Keys jingled, but no one exited. As the door started to close, he shouted, "Sam? Back here."

The door reversed back open, and Sam peered out, dumbfounded. Jeff tried to rein in his glare. He hated tardiness.

She drifted out cautiously. She was dressed business casual in a maroon sport jacket with a black satin undershirt and a matching mid-length skirt. Scanning the barren floor, she asked, "I thought we had a meeting here? Something about a big deal?"

Jeff faced her from across the room and spread his arms outward as if he was showcasing a prize on The Price is Right. "This is the big deal."

She strolled cautiously closer, her eyes narrowing. "Come again?"

"We've outgrown our townhouse." He grinned and then fanned out his hand again. "Say hello to the new corporate office for Heroic Kitchens."

She surveyed the floor and then frowned. "I see an empty room with no offices or desks. You rented this place without asking me?"

Jeff corrected, "Leased." He strolled to the corner of the window. "This can be your office. You get a view of the mall. And in the other corner, we'll put my office." He faced his wife, her expression still hard as granite. He continued, "This place can handle a total of ten employees. And with Monica, we're now at five."

Monica, who had been hired the week before, would be their fourth full-time employee. She was a recent college graduate with a degree in marketing and a passion for Heroic's mission. Better, Monica was vegan and owned a YouTube channel with over 250,000 subscribers. She had experience as a vlogger, influencer, and marketer. Her channel already was responsible for thousands of dollars in sales, and it was how she'd gotten on Jeff's radar. They'd interviewed more than a dozen candidates, but Monica was a lion among kittens. Charged with taking Jeff's job, marketing and operations, the move allowed Jeff to focus on scaling challenges. Commercial office space was the first of such challenges.

Ten months ago, when Micah was born, Heroic Kitchens had been in a few dozen stores nationwide, and most of their sales were direct-to-consumer via their website and Amazon. After Micah's birth, Jeff cashed in all his vacation hours and exercised the company's paternity leave. It gave him a full month to work on the business while Sam dove in as a full-time mommy. It was her life's dream—the dream she'd mapped out in the 1/5/10 Planasy she'd drafted three years before. While his wife still worked part-time, it was on her terms. Better, she was making more than her old salary at the hospital for a quarter of the work. Sam trusted him with the finances, and Jeff trusted her on everything else.

When Jeff returned to his job, he gave his resignation and quit two weeks later. Initially, he'd wanted to quit once their revenue reached $2,000,000, but that would have to wait for the other $300,000 to catch up. Surprisingly, that would only take a few more months to happen.

Once the Trotmans found their optimum operational groove, the results were astonishing. Sam went back into the commercial kitchen to experiment. And experiment she did, coming out with a new flavor, a plant-based Clam Chowder. Once it was lined, engineered, and co-packed, ready for sale, they messaged their customer list (now over 100,000 strong) about the new flavor. That email generated over $80,000 in sales in one day.

More than a year after they signed with Derlinger Distributors, they were finally shelved in all Kroger stores. That blew things up. Big.

Jeff found himself working every day, from order fulfillment to customer service to managing retail and wholesale accounts. There simply weren't enough hours in the day, and they needed to hire. The problem was it wasn't going to happen from a 1,200 square foot townhouse.

Sam glared at her husband, standing in front of the large office window. From the 17th floor, she could indeed see Woodfield Mall and its empty parking lot. Like many malls around the world, it was dying a slow death. Her chest felt queasy as she thought again of her husband's impetuousness, a trait which she both loved and hated. In this case, she wasn't sure which.

Sam faced the window, happy to know her husband couldn't see her antipathy. She spoke sternly at Jeff's windowed reflection as if it would soften the blow. "We can't afford this. This is going to cost us thousands."

"Yes, $6,000 a month, but the landlord gave us a great deal. It's a three-year lease, and they will help with the build-out. We can have it done in just a few weeks. They also—"

Sam interrupted, quickly turning from the window, "Six grand every month? Are you fucking insane? That's four times the rent at our townhouse!" Her face seethed red.

"No, it's not nuts, that's the going rate for offices of this size and in this area," Jeff said flatly. "And to your point, yes, we can afford it."

His face stiffened as he didn't appreciate her aloof tardiness and now the cursing attitude. He'd managed millions at the job he'd just quit. She carried on, scoffing, "Like we could afford those first-class tickets you bought for the trade show in Vegas? How about the Lincoln Navigator we had repossessed, or that T-shirt business you bombed on?" Sam shook her head, eyes unsettled and now teary.

But Jeff didn't bite as he would have two years ago. He veered over and grasped her shoulders. "Hey, what's wrong? You should be happy." She took a deep breath and then stewed for a minute, her face trembling as if she faced a demon.

As the tears welled, she turned back to the window again, choosing to look at her husband through its reflection. Tone bitter and brooding, she said, "I am happy. That's just it. I've never been happier in my life. I'm with my kids all day, even if I'm working. I get quality time with my husband, and geez, you don't even complain about money anymore. I'm helping animals, I have a worldly mission, everything is just fucking awesome." She sniffed, "And my husband is vegan." She shook her head in disbelief and then sighed a whirlwind. "Oh yes, I'm living the dream I've always wanted."

Jeff stood back and shook his head, puzzled. She'd spoken two "fucks" in less than two minutes—something deeply emotional was stirring. He asked, "Then why the crying and acting like you just got put back on a graveyard shift?"

She sniffled and then raised her hands as if she gave up. "This!" she said, focusing on the empty, unfinished concrete floor. "I mean, this isn't cheap." She shook her head disgustedly. "I'm just afraid of you—or us," she corrected, "making a wrong decision and having to go back to the way things were."

"So you don't trust me?"

"Jeff, I've always trusted you, and that's the point. This isn't about some pricey plane tickets that can be refunded. This isn't about making a mistake on some dumb T-shirt business. This is big. And you know how you like to act first and ask questions later. If we screw this up, it could send us right back where we started."

Jeff was speechless as he stood in front of his wife, dumbfounded. *Scarcity mindset?* he wondered quietly. Sam didn't wait for his retort and lingered to the window again, continuing her avoidance. The silence lasted for an eternity, except for a police siren, which passed on the road below, followed by two more.

Finally, Sam turned and faced him, her eyes blood red and lips trembling. "I... I..." but she didn't finish and turned around again.

Now getting impatient, Jeff asked, "What on earth is going on, Sam?"

Another silence.

He prodded, "Samantha?"

In the eerie quiet, she mumbled, "Pinky."

Unsure if he heard her, he repeated, "Pinky? Your old stuffed animal?"

She didn't answer and stood motionless, her back still to her husband.

Jeff strode over to her and tapped her on her shoulder, his impatience turning to disorientation. He said softly, "Hey, Pinky's at home exactly where you left her."

She quickly turned to face him, and what Jeff saw frightened him. Gone were his wife's tears. Her jaw was clenched, and her cheeks were flushed a blood red. Her bright blue eyes were now a shadowy green. She vigorously shook her head, seething in anger. Her voice thick and petulant as if she was a teenager, she said, "NO SHE'S NOT."

Jeff shrugged, bewildered.

Sam relented, "When I was ten years old, we had a lamb at our ranch named Pinky. My father came home with her one summer, and I instantly fell in love with her." She gazed vacantly at the floor. "She was this cute little fluffy furball, and I spent most of the summer with her. One of her eyes was bright pink, which is why we called her Pinkie. We weren't sure if she was blind in that eye, or if it was just some genetic defect." She paused to sigh, her face maintaining its hardness. "I remember she had these long and curly eyelashes, almost cartoonish. She used to fall over and wriggle on her back like she was dancing to La Cucaracha. Her little legs would flop around like she was playing the air drums. She loved getting her belly rubbed, and it was her way of asking for one."

Jeff let her talk, but he wasn't sure where she was going or how this had anything to do with renting an office.

Sam carried on, simmering in the thought. "When Pinky was hungry, she'd give you this tiny, adorable squeal and her lips wouldn't even move. I remember thinking that she sounded like a dolphin." She paused and bit her tongue, face tightening. "Anyhow, I guess it was my fault. When my father brought her home, he said not to get my hopes up, that Pinky would only be visiting for the summer. So, I spent every day with her, knowing that my pops was probably just doing another trucker or a rancher a favor. A ten-year-old doesn't think about the reasons, I just saw that I finally had a pet." She finally looked up at her husband, her anger morphing into revulsion. "My parents wouldn't let me have any pets, not even a cat."

Jeff felt his eyes start to well when he realized his wife was sharing something she'd never shared. Sam continued, the horror in her eyes losing its battle with remorse and sorrow. "For three months, I nursed Pinky with bottles of fresh milk. The Alstons up the road had dairy cows." She looked oddly at Jeff as if this fact was common knowledge. "Pinky and I, we'd play hide-and-seek in the haystacks, fetch, we'd even nap together whenever my father was on the road." She paused, two tears escaping both eyes. "It was one of the happier summers I could remember, at least, until Pinky disappeared."

Jeff finally spoke. "Your father made good on his promise and returned her?"

Sam didn't move but her face drooped, her eyes glazing over vacantly as if she just aged ten years. She continued, "That's what my mom said, yes." She wiped a tear on her blouse. "I cried myself to sleep for days. I wouldn't eat. After three days locked in my room, my Pop ordered me to the supper table because it was Thanksgiving. After finishing the meal, I asked to be excused so I could go back to my room. When my father gave me a stern no, I blew up. I told him I hated him and wished him dead. I yelled and yelled, demanding to know where he took Pinky." Sam shook her head, hatred now burning out her tears. She looked at Jeff and said, "And you know what that bastard said? He just looked at me with this sick expression, I can see it as clearly as if it were today. With this self-satisfied grin, this gleam in his eye as if he got some type of joy from teaching his daughter a lesson, he said, 'Samantha, you just ate Pinky. That's life—and life don't give two cents about your feelings.' And then he snickered and smiled while forking another slab of Pinky into his mouth, chewing obnoxiously and sucking gravy off his fingers as if it was his last meal before a death sentence."

Jeff's eyes flared, his heart feeling like a cinder block just dropped on his chest.

"After that, I vomited all over the dinner table. I remember seeing bits of partly digested meat and green beans splattered all over the dinner table. The odor was horrible, and I wondered what part of my best friend did I puke on the table? Her belly I rubbed so many times?" She shook her head, the anger returning. "My mother just sat there like an obedient shrew while my father continued eating and slurping. He made me clean it up before I could go back to my room."

Jeff tried to hold back his sobs but couldn't. He drifted to his wife and embraced her, causing her to erupt in tears. He whispered, "I'm so sorry, sweetie. I never knew."

After a tearful silence, she pulled back. "My relationship with my parents was never the same. Then they dragged me into church a week later where the priest gave a sermon on love and compassion." She scoffed sarcastically. "My motherfucking father had as much compassion as a starving wolf in a hen house. His workshop was wall-to-wall bucks and antelope that he killed sport hunting." Jeff thought about Sam's earlier rants about hunters and gentlemen. "The hypocrisy pissed me off so bad, I glared at him the whole time." She fled from the memory and looked up at her husband. "When I didn't go to his funeral, my mother disowned me, which is why she wasn't at our wedding. Stuck up for that asshole till his last breath. She's a wretch who married a wretched excuse for man."

Sam stepped back and collected herself, the weight of the heavy memory lightened. Wet mascara shaded her with a black pallor. She pulled a tissue from her purse and wiped her face. She spoke plainly, "I'm sorry, but whenever I'm happy, I expect to have my heart broken. I wake up every morning waiting for someone to wake me from this dream, waiting for someone to shake me into reality, waiting for someone to drop the bomb and say that none of this is real, and it will all disappear. I'll go back to the hospital, you'll go back to your job, and we'll see each other for a few hours a week. And the kids get their part-time parents." She paused and then confessed, "I'm sorry. I've just got this bad sense that the summer is ending, and my heart is about to be broken again."

The sun was now setting, her husband standing in a blinding sunbeam. He took a deep breath and moved back into her space. It took Jeff a moment to figure it out, but Samantha was terrified of having her happiness disappear in the dark of night, like Pinky did those many years ago. From childhood trauma to early relationships, she was used to having her joy stolen. Interrupted. Snatched away like an insect in a Venus flytrap. When her mother no-showed their wedding, it soured the event. For her, the bigger financial burden of commercial office space must have jolted her fear into overdrive.

Jeff studied her and then put a finger to her chin. "Sweetheart, our summer can last the rest of our lives. This life we created isn't going to be Pinky." Sam wiped a new tear away from her cheek and looked up at her husband, sniffling, the setting sun drowning out his face.

"Hey, I got this. This office is the right decision, both financially and for our business." He paused. Then he said, "I know how busy you've been with Micah, but I've been busy too. I don't think you understand how much our business has grown since our little boy was born." He took a step back, smiling. "Do you know why I don't talk about our money problems anymore?"

She shook her head weakly.

Jeff continued, loud enough that his voice echoed on the empty floor. "Because we have no money problems. We're out of debt. Everything is paid, your student loans, my loans, all the start-up costs for the business, everything is paid for. Even with all the investment into the business, I'm still able to save tens of thousands of dollars a month." He paused, waiting for her to react, but her face was still traumatized from the tears. He knocked playfully on his skull and gave her a dumbfounded look. "Are you listening to what I'm saying? You've trusted me to handle the money, and I have. Not only is our business worth several million, I've saved close to a half-million dollars. At the rate we're saving and the value of the business, we're nearly at our Escape Number and could technically retire in a few years." He threw her a pointed look. "So, Mrs. Cleaver, the dream that you're living right now ain't going nowhere, and it soon will be in our own home. Summer will continue until we're old and with grandkids."

She blushed and wiped more of the blackness that drizzled her face. Apologetically she said, "I just get scared anytime I see you spending money on things I don't understand. After we got married, you spent money like we were rich." Her face finally broke a weak smile. "Girls from Idaho generally don't need Louis Vuitton purses. I'd rather have an ATV."

Jeff chuckled then nodded. "I get it, but I've also learned a ton about myself in this process." He lost himself in a moment, then continued. "I realize that all my impulsive spending, the Navigator, that purse, I bought all that stuff to medicate my own unhappiness. A bribe so to speak. But now"—he hesitated and walked toward the window—"it's different because we can afford these things. And we aren't medicating our boring lives, we're celebrating how great it has become."

He appraised the view out the window over the freeway. "Sometimes I wonder where we would be if we'd just accepted the inertia of our lives. Micah probably wouldn't be here. We'd both be miserable."

"Or divorced," Sam added quickly. "We never saw each other."

He turned back to his wife, conviction in his voice. "Our business can afford this, but more importantly, we must afford it if we want to keep growing. Our mission for our family and our mission for the animals depends on it. We can't take our foot off the pedal now."

She nodded, her worry relinquishing the fight.

After they faced each other in silence, Sam nestled up to her husband, embracing him tightly as if he was the only thing between her and life itself. As they hugged, Jeff heard her crying again. But this time her tears had a different resonance. It wasn't tears of stolen dreams or slaughtered play friends; it was joy. She kissed him on the temple and then whispered into his ear, "I love you."

THE PERSEVERANCE STRATEGY

Believe it, Define it, Set the Goal, Shift the Identity, and Forge a New You

In a 1995 interview, Steve Jobs said, "I'm convinced that about half of what separates the successful entrepreneurs from the non-successful ones is pure perseverance."[1] I agree, but like many short platitudes extracted from billionaire interviews, the statement speaks of an effect, not a cause. It's like saying, "I'm convinced that about half of what separates the successful chefs from the non-successful ones is a wood fired oven." Insightful, but not very helpful if you don't have access to the oven. In other words, what exactly causes perseverance and the motivation to carry forward when things get tough?

Expectancy theory suggests that we're motivated to act and make decisions based on the expected result of our behavior. For example, if you know washing the dishes might get you a back rub from your wife, you'll likely be motivated to act. While this theory might have relevance in simple matters of cause and effect, it doesn't when it involves audacious goals in the future. Namely, when a process[P28] is required, the expectancy theory won't help you lose weight, start a business, hit your Escape Number[S15], or achieve your 1/5/10 Planasy[S12]. Kind of hard to eat celery over donuts when your decision packs no immediate visible outcome. Eating donuts, on the other hand, has immediate gratification. Without a positive feedback loop to fire passion, perseverance and willpower will simply wither away.

Unlimited motivation and perseverance for transformative goals is more like a recipe rather than a simplistic concept. Like yeast is needed for dough and dough is needed for pizza, each ingredient in the motivation recipe works synergistically to create the result. And that result is a "new you," someone who is strikingly different from the day you started. Looking back at my own Unscripted journey, the Perseverance Strategy is what got me through the Desert.[P57] The good news is, if you follow the principles and strategies in this book, you already have most of this recipe.

Belief is the first ingredient and it is the launchpad. Fix your poison pens[S2]

---

1 - https://vimeo.com/31813340

so you truly believe you can escape the rat race. There's a reason why this book is somewhat mathematical. I don't need to convince you that 100,000 units is larger than 40 years or 40 hours. I don't need to convince you that it is impossible to work 6,000 years. Of course, Belief is more than simple math. Ultimately, your inside game determines the outside game. Examine these divergent thought-forms below. Which mindsets will help you hit your Escape Number?

99% THOUGHT FORUM	1% THOUGHT-FORM
Someday	Today
Wage or Salary locus	Profit locus
Net Consumer (rat)	Net Producer (scientist)
Freedom old	Freedom young
Defense (Expenses)	Offense (Income+Asset)
Specialized-skill	Specialized-unit
Better skills = more money	Better product = more money
More time = more money	More units = more money
Optimize salary/wage	Optimize relative-value
Money is king	Time is king
Time builds wealth	Income and assets build wealth
Symmetric, monomorphic pay	Asymmetric, polymorphic pay
Positively charged to $	Negatively charged to $
Selfish inward thinking	Selfless outward thinking
Resist change	Embrace change
Luck	Probability
Ideas have value	Execution has value
The process should be fun	The process should be challenging
Event, short-game focus	Process, long-game focus
Balance	Commitment

After I spoke with that young man who owned a Lamborghini Countach, my belief shifted from resigned mediocrity, to committed advancement. I didn't know it, but I had the first ingredient to perseverance, Belief.

The second ingredient in perseverance's recipe is Purpose[P96]. Without a strong purpose, a driving "why" behind your behavior, you will be at the mercy of fleeting willpower. And willpower is a horrible motivator. In my case, my Purpose was fear-driven. I knew I'd rather die rather than suffer in a meaningless job for 60% of my life. With a powerful Purpose, I had perseverance's second ingredient.

The third ingredient is a strong Goal that stretches your comfort zones, expands your skills, and hones you into a new person. Your goals set the pace and it is why we established your 1/5/10 Planasy and its Escape Number many pages ago. It is your GPS and your lighthouse in a barren sea. Thanks to my new beliefs, I always had goals (and later, the 1/5/10 Planasy) that stretched my limits.

The final ingredient is your Identity, a critical piece of the puzzle that we haven't discussed. If your Identity isn't aligned with who you need to become, you likely will struggle. If you have a challenge ahead of you, whether it's starting a business or hitting an Escape Number, *your identity must shift to who you want to be.* "Old you" isn't good enough to reach your goals— new beliefs, a strong purpose, and a big goal must create a new identity and driving transformation toward a "new you." For most people, identity is a construct based on the *past*, past experiences, past traumas, and past careers. Instead, fabricate your identity based on the *future*.

For example, I've always loved a good steak and a meat-packed pizza. As such, going plant-based in 2017 was the hardest thing I did in my life. To accomplish my drastic dietary shift, I immediately knew that I needed to do two things:

1. Shift to a future, growth-identity and
2. Build effective anchors.

The first step is to shift from an *Old You* status quo identity to a *New You* growth identity. An Old You identity is something based on the past while the future is regarded as an optimistic construct. *I enjoy meat but I'm trying to eat plant-based.* Or, perhaps, more suitably, *I'm an engineer at Intel, and someday I'd like to quit and start my own business.* Conversely, a New You identity is future-based, what *you will become*, with the Old You regarded as a negative figment of the past. *I'm a vegan who once ate meat.* Or, *I'm an entrepreneur who is temporarily working at Intel as an underpaid engineer.*

Whenever you swap a past identity for one that is future based, you lay the groundwork for change. Because our identity seeks harmony with reality, a growth identity adjusts your thoughts and actions toward the desired change. Our identity abhors incongruence, and you will likely keep your actions aligned with it. If you identify as a financial expert, you might avoid credit card debt and other money mistakes not congruent with financial expertise.

Conversely, if the identity already matches with reality, then change becomes a matter of convenience or circumstance. Excuses, easily made. The process never builds[P28], and talent is never driven[P39]. You will always be "an underpaid engineer at Intel who would like start a business someday." Your identity asserts there is no urgency to change. Someday becomes never[P4].

For my dietary change, the first thing I did was identify as vegan. While I ate meat merely days earlier, it didn't matter because, at that moment, I shifted to my New Me identity. Moving forward, if someone offered me pizza, I refused because I identified as vegan, not as a "pizza lover striving to go vegan."

The second tactic that made this happen was effective anchors.

An anchor is something traumatically associative with Old You. For me, I heartbreakingly watched factory farming atrocities and how animals are kept inhumanely caged and then slaughtered. After watching a pig fight for its life before meeting its butchery, the anchor was seared into my brain. Add a lingering threat from my doctor who wanted me on a lifetime prescription of cholesterol pills, and my identity shifted. Effective anchors, and boom— I'm plant-based for life. My shift was hard, until it wasn't.

Identify who you want to be and how it relates to the big goals you cited in your 1/5/10 Planasy[S10]. Drastic changes in your life start subtly with a shift from a status quo identity to one of growth. And please, avoid the word "aspiring." Don't be an aspiring screenwriter; you are a screenwriter. Don't be an aspiring comedian; you are a comedian. Don't be an aspiring Unscripted[S9] Entrepreneur; you are one. After my short encounter with my stranger in a Lamborghini, my identity instantly changed to an entrepreneur. And it took a whopping ten years for that identity to match with reality.

Unlimited motivation and perseverance is not a concept, it's a recipe.

Believe you can escape the rat race.

Define a compelling Purpose.

Set a Goal that stretches comfort zones.

Shift your Old You identity into a transformative New You identity, and you'll persevere through anything.

☑ KEY CONCEPTS

- *Expectancy theory,* which proposes that you act based on the expected result of your behavior, doesn't work for distant goals that involve a process.

- Perseverance has a recipe which combines multiple principles and strategies and is responsible for goal achievement, the process behind the transformation from Old You to New You.

- Beliefs that foster an Unscripted 1% existence is the first step to perseverance.

- The second ingredient to perseverance is a strong purpose that supplants fleeting willpower.

- Perseverance's third ingredient is an audacious goal like a 1/5/10 plan or an Escape Number.

- A strong goal acts like a GPS or a lighthouse for behavior.

- The fourth ingredient for perseverance is an identity shift from who you are to who you will be with effective anchors to bolster the change.

- Your identity seeks congruence.

- A growth identity puts forth effort for congruence; a status quo identity does not.

- Don't be an "aspiring" anything—be it.

THE FINANCIAL ARMY STRATEGY

Raise a Financial Army: Start Saving for Your Lifetime Paycheck

115

Creating a specialized-unit[S18] of relative value isn't easy. Building a business system to sell thousands, perhaps millions, of those units is even harder. Even startup entrepreneurs with prior success and endless streams of venture capital financing are not guaranteed to succeed. Again, entrepreneurship is like baseball and you'll likely need to strike out a few times before getting a hit. While you wait for your business to hit that asymmetrical growth curve, you can still progress on your rat race escape. How? Start building your money-system today[S14].

If you have fifty bucks, you can be the proud owner of a third-party business system by the end of the week, perhaps as soon as tomorrow. Instead of blowing $50 on some trendy shirt that will be out of style next spring, you could buy a money-system investment, say a dividend-paying company. Your fifty bucks (no matter how you acquired it) suddenly becomes polymorphic pay. And as long as that company remains profitable and outlives you, you get a lifetime paycheck.

Think how powerful that is.

You can wear a $50 shirt a few times or get an income for the rest of your life. Moreover, your investment doesn't require you to punch in for work, submit reports, fix toilets, or contribute to the company or investment in any way. Returns are paid regardless of your status—you're only limited by what you can afford.

The problem is your lonely $50 investment might only pay four percent annually, or $2 a year. That won't move the meter. Worse, this instant business system requires something many people lack: the discipline for saving massive amounts of money. If you bought 50,000 shares instead of just one, suddenly a measly two-dollar return turns into $100,000 a year, completely passive.

Unfortunately, 50,000 shares could cost millions. Like our business, this third-party business system isn't effective unless it obtains leverage from scalable mathematics. Pounding the pavement for hours or salaries[P16] isn't going to cut it. Our business must be the leverage, which in turn can fund a money-system, and get us moving toward our Escape Number.

Once I escaped my expensive sports car blunder, I started saving money from the standpoint of raising a financial army. I knew that every dollar I saved was another soldier fighting for my freedom. Even in today's low-interest economy, every 100 pennies saved to your financial battalion, three to six procreate yearly. Accumulate enough soldiers and the compounding weapon ignites. Instead of enjoying six cents per year, it's $60,000.

And finally, one buck saved today is one you won't need to earn tomorrow. Indentured time (time lost fighting the enemy) shifts to free time.

As for raising your financial army, it begins like everything else: a belief shift. First, make every dollar spent fall into one of four categories:

1) BASIC LIVING EXPENSES

Food, shelter, transportation, insurance—in the early stages of business, your household should be run lean, like a fine-tuned infantry. And "basic" living expenses should mean the used Honda, not the new Tesla.

2) DEBT REDUCTION

If you're towing a lot of debt, don't worry. Anytime you reduce your debt, you make progress on your Escape Number. While raising a financial army is offense[P12], defense is protecting it. When you carry debt you can't afford, you create traitors: your soldiers defect to the enemy and then fight to enslave you. And then they procreate, unleashing new insurgents. The net effect is a triple-negative: 1) you lose a soldier, 2) the enemy gains one, and 3) the enemy creates more in the future.

If excess money isn't needed for living expenses or can't be reinvested in your business, pay off high-rate credit cards or loans. Start stealing soldiers from your foe. If your bank charges 20 percent interest on your credit cards, you automatically earn 20 percent by eliminating the debt. Killing debt pays instant interest. The debt is no longer giving birth to new soldiers. Treat debt you can't afford like a zombie virus.

3) CORNBREAD BUSINESS EXPENSES

It cannot be said enough. Your business anchors net worth acceleration through asymmetric returns, not pennies pinched from canceled cable TV subscriptions or Starbucks celibacy. If one dollar invested in your business yields ten dollars tomorrow, why bother with rat race investments? Massive wealth doesn't come from annual eight percent stock market returns; it comes from annual 800 percent returns from your business. If your business is a Productocracy, it will always be the best bet for surplus money.

4) YOUR MONEY-SYSTEM AND ITS ESCAPE NUMBER.

After these three categories have been addressed, save the remaining funds into your money-system. And as your business grows, so will your savings-rate. If you're making $80,000 a month, saving 80% isn't unusual, nor is it difficult. When your income blows up like Heroic Kitchens, debt can be paid in broad, swift strokes. It might take you ten years to pay off your debt in a job, whereas in a growing CENTS-based business, it might take you ten weeks.

The final step for raising your army is to make it bigger every week, even just a few dollars. Every month get closer to your Escape Number. If you're struggling with debt, now is the time to penny-pinch and cut "comforting" expenses from your life, things that not only waste your time but imbue procrastination. Is that pile of smutty gossip magazines necessary? Cancel them. Is the Beemer too Diodetic[P109] with insurance, repairs, and gas? Maybe it's time for a used Prius—or take the bus, ride your bike, or walk. Yeah, I know, not cool. But neither is working until your eightieth birthday.

When I started my army, I created a makeshift wall counter, which broadly displayed my net savings. Every day, it reminded me of my purpose and my Escape Number. It weakened temptation. I could dismiss thoughts of fancy cars, second homes, boats, and other flashy expenditures… at least until I could pay cash for them. While this might seem neurotic, I was neurotically opposed to slaving at a job for fifty years in a stiff polyester suit. I made darn sure I got closer to my Escape Number a few bucks every day.

Altogether, your end game is to create your business system and funnel excess profits into a money-system, which ironically, consists of many third-party business systems. *A business system you own funds business systems you do not.* The short- and long-term goal is identical: lifetime financial freedom[P11]. When your business kills it for the month, and you have an extra 10G flashing green on your debit card, ask yourself this: Whose army are you funding? Yours, the one working to liberate you from the world's economic religion[S5]? Or the one working to keep you kneel at its altar? Saving slow for retirement is a dumb idea; saving fast to win your freedom is not.

☑ KEY CONCEPTS

- Every saved dollar should earn you three to six cents in polymorphic pay for life, without ownership hassles.
- Outside of your Unscripted business, look at saving money as if you were raising a financial army.

- Debt payment earns you an instant yield on the interest charged: A debt payment costing ten percent in interest is like earning ten percent.

- Your business is for asymmetrical returns and creating wealth; the capital markets are for renting your wealth which pays you polymorphically.

- Every dollar earned should be directed into 1) basic living expenses, 2) debt reduction, 3) cornbread business expenditures, or 4) a money-system.

- Once your business starts to grow, savings rates can jump to 50 percent or more while debt can be paid fast, often in large bulk payments.

- Your end game is to create your business system and funnel excess profits into a money-system, a diversified basket of third-party business systems.

COVID-190,000,000
WEDNESDAY, APRIL 2ND, 2020 (2:45 PM)
(247 days later)

From his 17th floor office, Jeff stared at the threatening sky overshadowing his desk. The television hung on the wall aired CNBC, volume muted. Jeff didn't need to hear the commentators. As the tickers flashed red across the screen, the financial punditry was warning of a recession. COVID-19, a worldwide virus, was shutting down much of the world economy.

He tried to temper a smile.

People in poor health would die. Businesses would go bankrupt. Savings would evaporate—jobs lost or furloughed. But none of it would be the fate for his family or his company. When the economy crashed in 2008, his family took a beating as if Mike Tyson delivered the blows. Now he was the one landing blows, and some pandemic wasn't going to stop the fury.

Thunder rattled the steel-encased windows as the sky swirled in a dark steel gray. His door was open, and he could hear that the corporate office for Heroic Kitchens buzzed with activity.

The business was booming.

Moreover, Jeff now understood the power of real financial freedom. With their sales exploding as retail shelves were stocked with their soup, they were financially independent and leading life as Fastlane Unscriptees. Jeff would remind his wife (practically daily) about the déjà-vu their life would have endured had they not changed their strategy and started a business. With the pandemic showing no signs of slowing, unemployment would rise to 12 percent. Bankruptcies would skyrocket as would suicides. Jeff learned his old employer would merge with a new company and lay half the workforce off. There was blood in the streets, except this time, that blood wouldn't be his family's. The stock market also crashed, but this time, it had no impact on their finances. They not only held on to their investments, they added to them.

Once their debt disappeared, they started saving their excess earnings, a habit learned from their days as savings-rats. But instead of saving $100 a month from their paycheck, they were saving tens of thousands. Better, they weren't suffocating under frugality's yoke and what they couldn't do. Their favorite restaurant was the *Garden Buffet*. Before Covid, they would eat dinner there sometimes three or four days a week. It was fast, convenient, healthy, and money didn't matter. They could eat there—or anywhere—every day of the year.

From the day they conceived their business nearly four years ago, it would take them thirteen months to match their job salaries. And only four months from there to double it. Seven months later, they would be millionaires based on the asset valuation of their company. Today they were multi-millionaires many times over. And now Jeff didn't need to finance his dream car; he could waltz in and pay cash.

While they still lived in their rented townhouse, Jeff and his wife were officially shopping to become homeowners again. But not just any home—their dream home. Better, they agreed to put 50 percent down so their mortgage would be easily manageable while also taking advantage of low interest rates and mortgage interest deductions.

He glanced outside his office and saw Monica leave her desk to sidle up to the exterior window. As she admired the overcast kaleidoscope churning in the sky, Jeff thought how valuable she was. Hiring Monica had instigated a quantum leap for their business. She shared marketing operations with his wife, saturating social media influencers with Jeff's blunt force "Fed-Ex" strategy. She managed newsletter and podcast sponsorships, as well as their public relations outreach. According to their accountant, Monica's public relations efforts created over $15,000,000 in free advertising. With an impressive environmental and humane mission, combined with great soup, Heroic Kitchens received countless magazine, newspaper, and website features.

With marketing out of the way, Jeff was able to pound the phones and LinkedIn, calling on distributors and grocery C-suiters from the big guys: Whole Foods, Target, Sprouts, and other national chains. He was amazed at what he could do once his attention turned to scale. He added retail and wholesale accounts nearly weekly. Reorder percentages on individuals skyrocketed from 19 percent to 24 percent to 31 percent as soup stored on store shelves or in pantries were finally consumed. Reorders at the wholesale level were a whopping 96 percent.

As more retail and wholesale accounts jumped to put Heroic on their shelves, their net margin continued its slow decline into the low teens. But Jeff expected it. There were six employees now, many wholesale low-margin accounts, and a lot more expenses. And new competitors and copycats. Their brand was now nationally known, and their soup was in over 5,000 stores, including many of those big chains Jeff courted. With brand recognition, it became easier to push new products into the system. They didn't have to convince anyone—their reputation was known. Hard work done years ago was still paying today. With this new power, revenue soared past $10M, then $25M, and then $50M. They now had a chickpea snack line and were soft-testing a new type of plant-based pizza, another product line ripe for innovation. Costs were climbing, but so were revenue, profits, and momentum.

The decision to rent office space was the right one. It gave Heroic legitimacy and gave its employees a focus with a crystallized mission. Large six-foot photos of every animal they'd saved decorated the office walls. A great idea, but within a year, the walls were full. As more animals were saved, their photos were pinned to the wall outside the elevator landing. Called the "Wall of the Saved," the collage featured hundreds of animals and would be the first thing visitors saw when they exited the elevator.

Jeff snapped out of his nostalgia when the elevator dinged.

His wife exited with the day's mail in one hand and an open letter in the other. With her eyes fixated on whatever she was reading, she drifted toward Jeff's office, almost knocking over a flower arrangement. As her eyes lapped left to right, her face went frigid. Jeff knew the look. Whatever she was reading wasn't good news.

Once in Jeff's office, she closed the door. Holding up the document like a dirty sock, she said to Jeff seated at his desk, "Please tell me this is a mistake." Jeff shrugged and scrambled to find his glasses. When he didn't see them, his wife walked to his desk and laid the document in front of him.

"The IRS—" she said flatly, crossing her arms. She gestured to the paper. "—says we owe $220,000 dollars." Jeff picked up the document and examined it. Sam continued, "When I saw a letter from the IRS, I got scared and tore it open. I know you take care of all the money, but nothing good ever comes from those bureaucratic assholes."

"You're right," Jeff said calmly.

His wife raised her eyebrow. "About them being bureaucratic assholes? Or that this is a mistake?"

Jeff laughed. "About them being assholes." He tossed the paper aside on his desk. "Unfortunately, this is correct. Those are the back taxes we owe."

She frowned and then confiscated the tax bill from his desk. She recited, "$220,521? What are we, Fort Fucking Knox?"

"Sam, don't worry about it. The baddies in DC aren't coming to throw you in jail." He shuffled through the rest of the mail and continued, "I've been expecting this and prepared for it. We have more than enough money. When you owe this much, that means—" He stopped abruptly and stared at a legal-sized envelope that had come with the day's mail. Without finishing his thought or paying mind to his wife, he ripped it open like he was a ten-year-old at Christmas. Inside was a stack of clipped documents, at least a half-inch thick, peppered with signature stickies. He gazed at them hypnotically. He flipped a page, then another. His heart raced. After scanning several pages, he fell back in his chair, mouth agape, papers still in his lap. He sat silent, his face painted in shock as if he'd just exited the best rollercoaster ride of his life.

Sam cocked her head and eyed him suspiciously. "Okay, let's hear it. You just got a love letter from the IRS saying we owe them a fortune. You're ripping open mail like it was season tickets to the Cubs. Are you going to tell me what planet I'm on?"

He ambled back behind his desk and pointed to the couch. "Samantha, you should sit down."

She narrowed her eyes and sat down cautiously as if a bomb was strapped to her waist.

Once she settled in, Jeff spoke measuredly. "In the last few weeks, I've been busy trying to get this business to the next level and seeing what we need to do to get there. Part of that involves some forecasting, predicting things in the future, and how it fits into our overall mission." He swallowed hard. "We have to look at things not only in terms of our products and the animals we save, but our family." Sam nodded and gave a weak smile, unsure where he was heading. Jeff offered his palm in the air and continued, "This office, for example. This was a big financial decision, but we decided it was needed to move forward. Hiring our fourth, fifth, and six employees, again, big decisions. Adding more product lines, moving into snack food, again, more big decisions." He scratched his head as if he was struggling to explain.

Sam laced a long strand of hair behind her ear. "You're talking about a leap of zeroes again?"

He gave her a quizzical look and then snapped his fingers. "Sorry, it's been years since I've read those DeMarco books, but yes." He stood up and walked to the filing cabinet and opened a drawer. After rifling through it, he removed a file and held it up. "This right here should be our next leap for the business."

She raised her brow. "And?"

"It's a proposal to build a manufacturing facility. It's going to cost tens of millions." He retreated to his desk and dropped it topside.

"Millions?" Sam swallowed hard, her face flashing fear. "Why can't we just continue like we've been doing? Our sales keep going up, we're in thousands of stores, things are going great."

"It's not that simple. Our margin is starting to get squeezed. We have new competitors entering the space, some of them large companies. We use a third-party co-packer which adds to our cost; a lot of these companies don't. They own the manufacturing, and because they are completely vertical, they can crush us on price. Remember Sam, when we started this, there were virtually no vegan soups on the market."

"But our skew isn't pricing, Jeff; it's quality ingredients, great soup, and saving animals. I don't want to be the cheapest soup on the shelf."

"You're right, and neither do I. But this isn't about price, it's about cost. Walmart won't even shelve us cause our wholesale price is way too high. If our vendors think our wholesale price is too costly, and the rest of the space starts to price down, it could put some significant headwinds in our way. Nothing is stopping these big corporations from copying our recipes, and it's already happened twice. Shelves are getting crowded, and the grocers watch their margins like we watch ours."

She folded her arms. "Walmart is not exactly the target market for our brand."

"Everyone deserves healthy food options, Sam, so I'd argue it is. And that doesn't count what we're doing to bring awareness to the animal trade."

Sam reluctantly nodded and then stood up. She paced in front of the window. After a few laps, she stopped and groaned, throwing her husband a perplexed look. "So we owe the IRS a ton of money, and now you're saying that we need to spend a ton of money on a factory?" She shook her head and then gestured to the envelope Jeff had gleefully torn open. "I'm going to guess that envelope is news about some mega-loan we just got approved for? Because everything I'm hearing right now is not good news, and I'm not sure a huge loan is either." She started to fidget and get nervous, her fists clenched as she looked around wildly.

Jeff sighed and then pointed back to the couch. "Relax. Can you please sit back down?"

"Is it that bad?" She fell back to the couch and started teething her lips, sensing that summer was about to end.

"No, it's good."

She gave him a wanting look. "Well, I'm sitting. And waiting."

He held up the stack of papers, grinning. "This in my hand is a Letter of Intent from Universal Foods. They're a big food conglomerate out of Connecticut." He waited for her reaction, but none followed.

She shrugged. "New distributor?" Her husband threw another devious grin and conspicuously hesitated. After a lingering silence, Sam gave him an impatient glare as if waiting for a punchline.

"No, they want to buy our company."

"Sell our business?" She abandoned her lounge and firmed up. "I didn't know it was for sale! Is this what you've been doing locked up here in your office?"

"No, not at all. I've actually had multiple conversations with companies who are interested in buying our company, and they've all been unsolicited. However, when I started reviewing our numbers and the next steps for growth, both for our business and our family, I figured it would be reasonable to listen."

Sam sat motionless, her face signaling betrayal.

Jeff continued, his tone softening. "When we started this business, it was to set ourselves free. It was to control our destiny. It was to do something meaningful instead of just being good little rats who work all week while waiting for some god-forsaken retirement forty years later. You wanted out of nursing and to be a full-time mother. I wanted out of audits. And by all measures, we've accomplished that."

She interjected, voice stern, "But now you want to sell and throw it all away?"

He cracked a smile and stood up, grabbing the clipped documents which had arrived by mail. Looming over his wife still seated at the couch, he said, "We won't be throwing it away. We will be pushing it into overdrive. Take a look."

He handed her the papers, which she promptly snatched. He watched her narrowed eyes shuffle left to right as she read. He waited a moment for her to hit the words, for her to process what was happening, and for her to make the connection on what it meant. And then, as he expected, her mouth dropped open, and her eyes popped.

She leaped to her feet and whacked the papers on Jeff's shoulders. "Are you freaking kidding me? $190 million dollars? Please tell me this isn't one of your jokes."

Jeff took her hand. "No joke. It's real. The offer is $95 million in cash and $95 million in shares of their company. They're publicly traded, so that is real money." He paused, allowing her to comment, but she just stood, face still painted in shock. "I've negotiated terms that our company and its mission stay the same. Same quality ingredients, same animal sponsorships every month, and the same mission." Sam gave a worried glance outside the office onto the floor with their employees. Jeff noticed and said, "No one loses their job. I've stipulated that this office remains open complete with relocation options if anyone is looking for a life change." Another pause. "This option is the best for both our family and the company. Because like you, I really don't want to sign my name to a $30 million dollar loan for a manufacturing facility."

He reclaimed the documents from her hands and flipped through them. He stopped at one page and pointed, "And here it says they will hire you as a part-time consultant so you can continue to manage the animal sponsorships." He paused. "The salary is $120,000 a year. I negotiated that for you because I know how important the animal mission is to you. It's a total win-win."

She rubbed her neck, eyes still wide with shock. Unable to process the new reality, she asked, "But what will you do without this company?"

He laughed. "We'll net over $150 million dollars. Not only did we hit our Escape Number, we blew it out of the water. That means I'll do whatever I want. Who knows, maybe get a band together and play small jazz clubs. I've always wanted to write fantasy fiction novels. Maybe I'll start another company or invest in several. But I do know I will be getting my dream workshop with all the best woodworking tools." He winked at her. "And you, darling, you'll be getting whatever your little heart desires… that is, assuming we agree to do this."

Sam turned from Jeff and strode back to the couch as if she was drunk and blind, carefully taking a seat. She sat there frozen, staring at the carpet. It wasn't the reaction Jeff had thought his wife would have. Did she not want to sell? Did she want to continue the status quo? Worry welled up in his throat. He took a seat on the couch next to her and put his hand on her knee.

"Well, what do you think? This is our decision, not mine."

After a moment, she finally looked up, her eyes swimming in tears.

"I think I have the most awesome husband that ever lived. When, and where do we sign?"

THE COST OF MONEY STRATEGY

Make Debt a Function of
Cost, Not Affordability

In an early version of *The Millionaire Fastlane*, I mentioned that the only debt burden I carried was a mortgage. That admission caused me to get some reader hate mail. Some readers argued that *If I were truly financially independent, I wouldn't need a mortgage.* To some degree, that's correct, but only when judged from a rat race perspective.

All debt decisions should be based on the cost of money, not as a tool for affordability. You see, for the 99 percent stuck in the rat race, debt is a tool for *affordability.* Namely, if you can't afford something, get a loan. For the Unscripted, debt is a function of the *cost of money* or the interest rate. If I can take a 30-year loan at 2.5 percent interest and earn more on that money elsewhere in business or investments, I'll do it. Then, if I don't have a fair use for the surplus cash, I'll pay extra on the mortgage and earn the guaranteed rate on debt-reduction[S115].

Debt is not a function of *OMG I can't afford this BMW unless I get a loan,* it's a function of *OMG, the money is nearly free!*

When I bought my first dream home, I put 20 percent down. My second dream home, I paid 100 percent cash. My third home, I put 50 percent down. In every case, I could have paid cash for the house, which is how I gauge affordability. My financial decisions regarding debt aren't based on *Gee, what can I afford with the largest loan?* It's *How cheap is the loan and can I better reinvest that money instead of paying cash?*

When you know how to create asymmetrical returns, often taking debt is the better decision. Debt is a tool, and sometimes that tool goes on sale. Unfortunately, rat racers use debt as a tool to increase access to more expensive goods they usually couldn't afford. Bottomline: If you need a loan to afford it, you can't afford it.

- Rat racers use debt as a tool for affordability whereas it should be used as a tool based on its cost, or interest rate.

- Face debt decisions based on the cost of money, not on the largest payment you can afford.

- If you can earn asymmetrical returns on cash, taking low interest debt often makes sense.

THE NEW HORSE STRATEGY

Be True to your 1/5/10 Planasy: Know When It's Time for a New Horse...

117

About six months before I sold my company, I faced a difficult decision. As technology improved and consumer expectations changed, I knew my business had to change[S42]. In short, I estimated that my business, if it went unchanged, had a life span of about three more years. The changes required to keep it growing would have required several additional employees, more capital, and yes, more risks. Moreover, I no longer was challenged by the industry and felt I had accomplished all I wanted to do. I also knew that selling my ground transportation company near an apex would supply me with enough money that I never needed to work again. It was at that point I made the decision to sell.

Turns out that decision was correct. A few years later, the industry I exited would be disrupted by Uber. And the company I sold would go bankrupt, preceding a slew of customer complaints about poor customer service, a new standard that replaced the excellent customer service I'd provided. Those who managed the company were too slow to adapt[S42], and with new priority stakeholders (investors)[P37], some of the value-skews[S32] I'd offered disappeared. Ultimately, the company had to be sold at a fire-sale price.

The point is there might be a time when your personal and business goals no longer match. Specifically, the 1/5/10 Planasy[S12] you designed many years ago has mostly come true, or it is within your grasp. Your business might be screaming to grow, but such growth no longer coincides with your 1/5/10 Planasy. You either need a new plan, or you need a new direction.

Don't fear closing one part of your life to start a new one.

☑ KEY CONCEPTS

- Your business will have a growth inertia that must be gauged with your own personal goals and visions as designed in the 1/5/10 Planasy.

- Don't fear getting off a horse only to learn to ride a new one.

THE "3T" FINANCIAL STRATEGY

Evaluate Financial Decisions Through
the Prism of Time, Trouble, and Taxes

118

As I mentioned in the prior strategy, before I sold my company, I recognized that my existing business model was not sustainable as technology and consumer expectations changed. The "adjust" in my 3A Method[S55] revealed that a new business model was likely required, which itself required more capital and employees. While this was a secondary reason for selling, there was a more obvious, pressing reason: I knew that *money earned and taxed at a lower tax rate TODAY is worth far more than money earned and taxed at a higher rate LATER.* If that doesn't make sense, it will.

Whenever you're making financial decisions, you have to look at your money options beyond simple numbers, namely through the prism of time, trouble, and taxes. For example, let's say you enjoy $2,000,000 a year in net profit. Life is great, business is good, the bills are paid, and you're stockpiling cash for your financial army[S115]. And then suddenly, you're offered $20,000,000 for your business. At first, you dismiss the offer because you're making $2M a year and you can earn $20M in a short ten years, assuming things stay the same. True, but these numbers don't tell the whole story.

The first problem is time. Remember, time favors NOW over LATER, just like money. Money and free time enjoyed today is far better than ten years from now. Twenty million dollars today is worth just that. Twenty million earned over ten years discounted for time (using a five percent discount rate) is only worth $12,143,000 today. So waiting ten years to earn $20 million will cost you nearly $8 million.

And that doesn't account for trouble, our second variable. Who knows if your profits will be sustainable at $2M a year? I'm sure at the beginning of 2020, millions of businesses had a rude awakening when COVID-19 paralyzed their businesses and their profits. Waiting ten years to accumulate your $20M is subject to trouble, whether it's from the industry or just the grind to earn it.

The final consideration is taxes. As of early 2021 in the United States, the sale of business assets is taxed at the capital gains rate of 15 or 20 percent. This tax rate is far lower than earned income taxes. If you're profiting $2M a year, your marginal tax rate for state and federal taxes will be near or at 50 percent.

In short, you will need more time to actually clear $20M in after-tax money. With that in mind, let's go back to our example.

If you accept the $20M offer for your company, not only do you get the cash now, you only get taxed 20 percent on it. You'll clear $16,000,000. Wait ten years for your $20M and you'll pay 40-50 percent in earned income tax rates. In ten years, $20M after taxing will only be worth only $8,895,218 in today's dollar. Not accepting the offer will cost you over $11,000,000 and ten years of life, assuming all things hold equal. In other words, you'll need close to twenty years to get the same "after-tax" benefit of a net $16,000,000.

TAKE OFFER

$20,000,000 today, taxed at 20 percent = $16,000,000

TAKE PROFITS OVER TEN YEARS

$2,000,000 taxed at 45 percent = $1,100,000 Annual Net
$1,100,000 earned for 10 years, discounted @ 5% = $8,895,218

As you can see, it's almost foolish not to take the offer if money and freedom is your primary concern. Of course, the answer is different for everyone. You could also grow the company by another 25 percent in two years and your company might then be worth $30M, instead of $20M. The "sell or keep" question is highly personal and dependent on your 1/5/10 Planasy[S12]. Just don't make the decision on numbers alone—consider time, trouble, and taxes.

☑ KEY CONCEPTS

- Always make big financial decisions through the prism of time, trouble, and taxes.

- A liquidation event forces accelerated wealth due to time and taxes.

- Passing on a liquidation event could cost you millions, assuming conditions that stagnate or deteriorate.

- Consider your 1/5/10 Planasy when making financial decisions.

THE MONOGAMY STRATEGY

Stay Monogamous If You Want a Happy (Business) Marriage

A common confession I hear from young entrepreneurs is, "None of my businesses are successful." To which I reply, businesses? You mean like, none of my wives are happy? Why do you think there are no professional golfers who also play professional tennis? Anytime someone reports "six businesses," that's code for, "I have six businesses that suck and make no money. I'm throwing shit against the wall and hoping for something to stick."

When you own a Productocracy that prints money—side businesses and other distractions cannot tempt you. If they are tempting, your business isn't profitable, or your passion for the process has faded.

For new entrepreneurs, "trying" to grow multiple companies is like "trying" to become a world-class violinist with one hand tied behind your back. Remember, your Unscripted[P9] pursuit will meander into the realm of the obsessive with periodic sessions of imbalance[P91]. If that commitment is scattered among several interests, you won't end with one great result, but many mediocre ones. Ten ventures cumulatively earning $10,000 are not better than one that does it single-handedly. When you split your effort among assets, you build weak assets. Weak assets don't scale into multimillion-dollar valuations with leverage potential[S17], and they don't change lives.

Monogamy seals a great marriage, both in business and in relationships. If your time and emotional support are shared with six other partners, can you expect a good marriage? Will this type of relationship thrive, survive, or die?

Don't be influenced by these high-profile entrepreneurs who have twenty projects going on. You haven't sold a company for millions, and you aren't a Shark Tank investor. Every investor who appears on these business shows like Dragon's Den got there because of faithful monogamy. Years before, they committed to one business and one only. Only after striking it big, polygamy happens—diversification into multiple ventures where passions are explored and capital allocated.

Don't be a dumb-ass. Think about it. The world's most renowned entrepreneurs become known because they killed it with one project, not many. They first worked "in" their business, then they worked "on" it.

If you're new to entrepreneurship, monogamy must precede polygamy.

You have one business or none. Be loyal to one business, skew multiple value attributes[S32] Act, Assess, and Adjust on it[S55], validate a Productocracy[S71], and that business will be loyal to changing your life. Change your life first, then you can focus on changing the world.

☑ KEY CONCEPTS

- "Multiple business ventures" is code for "All of my businesses suck and make little money."

- Monogamy is focusing on one business only, like a world class athlete would train for one sport only.

- Monogamy should be a natural instinct, like finding the partner of your dreams.

- A Productocracy evolves from monogamy like a good marriage.

- Once you sell your first company for millions, polygamy can be a consideration as you move from entrepreneur to investor.

THE "LIVING THE DREAM" PRINCIPLE

Get Busy Living, or Get Busy Dying

*T*he *Shawshank Redemption* and *The Count of Monte Cristo*, two of my favorite movies, share a common theme: Men who had a dream for freedom, a freedom that would need to be painstakingly earned with time, courage, cunning, and a lot of hard work. In both stories, their dream of escape kept their souls alive and driven to do the work. Without a dream, both men would have been dead, their souls waiting for time to revert them to their maker.

Many people caught in today's modern economic religion[P5] are faced with the same reality. They're empty souls on a treadmill of time, aging in indifference, consuming in hope, saving in anticipation, and dying in regret: no hope, no future, and no chance of anything changing but years on a calendar.

The thread that binds them all is a dead dream. Dead dreams are why everyone is miserable and counting down the seconds to the weekend. Dead dreams are how people stay miserably stuck in the same dismal pattern, work, pay bills, consume, and then repeat. In fact, addiction has been weaponized to medicate misery, from the smartphone glued to our faces to the junk food spiked with sugar to the dopamine manipulating video games packed with reinforcement heuristics to the TV programs and sporting events that fill our empty lives with meaning. *Unhappiness—dead dreams—is the business model of the modern world.*

Like Andy Dufraine or Edmund Dantes did in the depths of despair, it only took one split second to change the paradigm they faced: they made a decision to dream an escape or die trying. Once these men decided, their life suddenly took on new meaning, filled with hope, purpose, and yes, even a little joy amidst prison squalor. As Andy said, *get busy living, or get busy dying.*

The Living the Dream Principle affirms that you are just a split-second away from living the dream. Resurrect the dream from the dead, give it a vision and a probability, and then relentlessly pursue it. If you didn't frame your 1/5/10 Planasy[S12] and your Escape Number[S15], go back and do it. As soon as you establish the decision framework and a goal, congratulations: you're now living the dream. Yes, it's actually that simple. When your dream is alive and pursued, profound stuff happens. Actions are given purpose. Goals are created. Plans and decisions are made, visions updated. And yes, food tastes better, jobs become intentioned and easier, and life feels more meaningful.

Surely, you've heard the old saying, *it's not the destination, but the journey.* The journey of a dream pursuit is the dream. It only needs to be alive, pursued, and made a poignant piece of your Now. If that seems counter intuitive, trust me, it isn't. When I reflect on the era I spent building my businesses, I feel great reverence and joy.

I was living the dream then. And I'm living it now.

It took me some age and gray hair to understand this, but the only moment that exists is Now. Today. This second and this word. You can only appreciate the Now, while having optimism for the future. And even if you don't reach your dream, well, regret won't haunt you. The regret of failure is transient; the regret of never trying is transcendent.

Every strategy and principle in this book are designed to improve your probabilities for Unscripted[S9] success, not just as a far-fetched dream, but an absolute reality free from the rat race. The right mental roadmap backed by the correct mathematics can make it happen.

Yes, this game is challenging, but you can make it easier by focusing on the right things: Put all 120 strategies and principles into practice, and you will move the needle on probability[S59], expected values[S56], and better life outcomes.

Enjoy the ride, my friend. Accept the process[P28] and let the passion flow from your effort[S46] and the unfolding dream it creates. Embrace your new role as a scientist[S7], and you will discover that this thing called entrepreneurship goes beyond business: It is the discovery of soulful freedom, of your true purpose, and of yourself. These are things money cannot buy.

Thank you for reading. I wish you good probability and much happiness. *Now* is the time for it to happen.

☑ KEY CONCEPTS

- Unhappiness, or a dead dream, is the business model of the modern world.
- You "live the dream" whenever you have a dream that is alive and pursued.
- The regret of failure is temporary; the regret of never trying is permanent.
- Entrepreneurship is more than a career, it's a revolution for your life and family.

EPILOGUE
(LATER IN 2022)

G od damn, Austin, they're bleeding into everything!" Charlie scoffed from his trailer at his dairy farm in Henly, Texas, just outside of Austin. He had heard the news from his bookkeeper, Martha.

"Says here they're not from Austin, but from Chicago." She pointed to the community newspaper, her voice strident above the window air conditioner behind her.

"Give me that." He snatched the newspaper from Martha and gave it a scowling look. With a cigarette perilously hanging from his lip, Charlie lifted the newspaper to his face and brokenly recited the article from the neighborhood news:

> *Forty-two acres in Henly were recently purchased by Jeff and Samantha Trotman, entrepreneurs from the Midwest who founded the worldwide brand Heroic Kitchens. Capitalizing on the sweeping consumer shift to more plant-based foods, their company was acquired for $190 million in early 2021 by Universal Foods. The two vegan entrepreneurs have relocated to the Austin area.*

He dropped the newspaper from his face and glared at Martha.

"Damn vegans! What do they want with forty acres next to my ranch?"

"Keep reading," Martha said flatly.

Charlie put the newspaper back to his face and continued reading silently.

He stopped and questioned, "They also bought the Hustle Jazz Club in Austin? What's that got to do with anything?"

Martha sighed and gestured to the newspaper, signaling Charlie to keep reading. She watched as his eyes rolled side to side for another minute. Suddenly his pale face flushed red. He lowered the paper and grimaced, shaking his head. He jeered, stumbling on his words, "Pinky's Animal Sanctuary?! They're launching an animal rescue next to my ranch!? For...For what do they call

432

it?" He put the newspaper back to his face and recited dumbfoundedly, "...for rescued pets, livestock, and other victims of the meat trade?"

Martha merely nodded and threw Charlie a sympathetic look as if he were a child who'd dropped his juice-box. Because of milk alternatives, Charlie's dairy farm had been dying for the last decade. Without government subsidies and high-powered lobbyists, it would have died years ago.

"Said they're planning to do all kinds of events, awareness projects, and social media stuff." He shook his head again. "This can't be good for business."

Martha laughed. "No, generally vegans aren't."

Charlie flicked her a cocked eye and headed to the coffee maker, tossing the paper in the trash.

"Coffee hot?"

Before Martha could answer, there were three firm knocks on the trailer door. Martha swiveled her chair toward the door and ballyhooed a "C'mon in!" Her tone was curiously jovial, and it left Charlie concerned.

In walked a young couple, perhaps late thirties and attired casually, but not dairy farm casual. The man wiped his shoes on the doormat and introduced himself. "Charlie? Hello, I'm Jeff Trotman." He gestured to the woman at his side. "This is my wife, Samantha." Charlie simpered an expression that one would associate with the boogieman, not an attractive couple from the Midwest. Jeff continued, "We're your new neighbors."

Martha was grinning ear to ear, relishing the scene. Charlie didn't move or extend a hand for a shake. After inhaling a drag of his cigarette, he eyed them with suspicion. His first inclination was to throw them out. Instead, he nodded and said, "Ah yes, I just read you bought the jazz club in town. Congrats."

Jeff spoke flatly. "Yes, thank you, but that's not why we're here." He walked forward and offered Charlie a large manila envelope, unsealed. Charlie snatched it standoffishly while eyeing Jeff up and down skeptically, as if he'd been served a lawsuit. Charlie removed a bundle of clipped documents from the envelope and read.

As Charlie scanned the paper, Jeff said, "That's an offer to buy your ranch. As you probably noticed, it's about twice the market value for it. And from what we're hearing about good old milk production, things aren't going to get much better." Charlie lifted his head from the paper expressionless and sized them up. Then he glanced at Martha, who was still beaming, wondering if she had her meat hooks in this. He continued to read and then finally broke his silence in a deep Southern drawl more representative of a Mississippian than a Texas cowboy. "Well, that's a mighty fine offer you got here. But I'm afraid I'll need some time to think about it." He took one last drag of his Marlboro and then skillfully flicked it out an open soffit window.

After a silence, Martha stood up. She held up an envelope and stated, "This is my two-week notice. The Trotmans hired me to join their team at the animal sanctuary."

The red in Charlie's face drained white, his mouth gaped wide.

Jeff added, "Hendrickson's dairy farm up Highway 5, just like yours but slightly smaller, just sold for a third of our offer. It is more than generous. And next year at this time, your farm will be worth far less, especially short-staffed. This is your once in a lifetime chance to get out of a business that"—he paused carefully selecting his words—"well, a business that needs government subsidies and deceptive advertising to stay alive. This is your opportunity to ride off into the sunset."

Charlie narrowed his eyes at Martha in disappointment, and then nodded back to Jeff. "I like your bravado, son, but like I said, I'll need some time to think about. How about you give me a few weeks, and I'll get back to you."

Jeff shook his head exaggeratedly. He then smiled and said with reserved courteousness, "I'm sorry, but this is a now or never deal. I'll even throw in two season tickets to the jazz club."

Charlie's smirk faded. He asked, "I'm sorry, but how long is 'now'? A day or two?"

"Eleven minutes," Jeff exclaimed.

Charlie jerked back, astounded. Sam flared her husband a quick glance, not expecting the salvo. "Pardon me?" Charlie said. "You want me to make a decision to sell my farm in eleven minutes?"

"Yes," Jeff said, breathing through his mouth. The air stunk of cigarettes and noxious ammonia.

Everyone but Jeff froze wide-eyed, including his wife. After an uncomfortable silence, Charlie put the documents back to his face and scanned them. The tension in the office was palpable. Martha, his chatty bookkeeper, was struggling to maintain a flat affect and looked like she wanted to bust out laughing. Charlie broke the silence, urging, "This is a big decision. Why only eleven minutes?"

Jeff answered firmly, "Because you never know when a short eleven minutes can change your life forever." He smiled. "And now you only have ten left."

THE END

:-)

Appendix A

VARIOUS ESCAPE NUMBER CALCULATIONS

Escape Number = PTEA + Money System + POM
(See Strategy #15 - The Escape Number)

1. STEP 1: Calculate pre-tax earnings need to purchase the assets (Cost of Assets / [1-TaxRate])
2. STEP 2: Calculate your yearly carrying cost for the assets. (Cost of Assets X 1.5%) plus $15,000 for every child.
3. STEP 3: Calculate your after-tax money-system, the pre-tax income which needs to be saved, which carries the asset costs via investment income.
4. STEP 4: Calculate your pretax POM number using an arbitrary percentage of your money-system. A minimum of 50% is recommended. This gives you a safety net from economic recessions.
5. STEP 5: Calculate your Escape Number by adding the pre-tax earnings cost of the assets (PTEA) to your money-system number, plus your POM.

☑ EXAMPLE #1: THE NOMAD TRAVELER

I want to travel the country in a luxury RV with my wife and child, and visit all 50 states!

STEP 1 (PRE-TAX EARNINGS TO BUY ASSETS)

Class One RV	= 1,000,000	
One Jeep (towed)	= 50,000	
After-Tax	= 1,000,000 + 50,000	= $1,050,000
Pre-Tax	= 1,050,000 / .60	= $1,750,000

Translation: To purchase $1,050,000 in assets, you will need to earn $1,750,000 before taxes.

STEP 2 (CARRYING COST OF ASSETS)

```
Asset Carry Cost (1.5% x $1.05M) = $15,750
Health Insurance:                = $10,000
Lifestyle/entertainment:         = $10,000
Existence expenses:              = $10,000
One Child (C):                   = $15,000
____
Annual Carry Cost                = $60,750
Gross Carry Cost Pre-Tax:        = $101,250
```

Translation: You need to earn $101,250 a year before taxes to support the assets.

STEP 3 (CALCULATE YOUR MONEY-SYSTEM)

```
Paycheck pot = [Carry Cost ($101,250) / Expected Yield (5%)] = $2,025,000
Pre-Tax: $2,0250,000 / [1 - 40%] = $3,375,000
```

Translation: You need to earn $3,375,000 to save $2,025,000 earning 5% to generate $101,250 in yearly passive income.

STEP 4 (CALCULATE YOUR POM)

```
POM = Paycheck Pot X 50%        = $1,012,500
Pre-Tax: $1,1012,500 / [1 - 40%] = $1,687,500
```

Translation: Your economic POM cushion is $1,012,500 which is acquired by earning $1,687,500.

STEP 5 (CALCULATE YOUR EXACT ESCAPE NUMBER)

```
Escape Number = PTEA + Money-system + POM
$6,812,500 = $1,750,000 + $3,375,000 + $1,687,500
```

Translation: To escape the rat race and enjoy your dream envisioned in your 1/5/10 Planasy, you'll need to earn roughly $6,812,500 before taxes. This assumes you saved $2,025,500 (earned from $3,375,000) which is invested in passive income investments, and you own your RV and car without loans. You also have a $1,012,500 cushion (earned from $1,687,500).

☑ EXAMPLE #2: THE SINGLE PLAYBOY(GIRL)

I want fast cars, three houses around the world, and the ability to do whatever I want!

Notes: Will be subject to 40% taxes and larger POM figures, or 100%.

STEP 1 (PRE-TAX EARNINGS TO BUY ASSETS)

House one	= 3,000,000
House two	= 1,500,000
House three	= 1,000,000
Six luxury/sports cars	= 1,500,000
────	
After-Tax	= 7,000,000
Pre-Tax	= 7,000,000 / .60 = $11,666,666

Translation: To purchase $7,000,000 in assets, you will need to earn $11,666,666 before taxes.

STEP 2 (CARRYING COST OF ASSETS)

Asset Carry Cost (1.5% x $7M)	= $105,000
Lifestyle/entertainment:	= $30,000
Health Insurance:	= $10,000
Existence expenses:	= $10,000
────	
Annual Carry Cost	= $155,000
Gross Carry Cost Pre-Tax	= $258,333

Translation: You need to earn $258,333 a year before taxes to support the assets.

STEP 3 (CALCULATE YOUR MONEY-SYSTEM)

Paycheck pot = [Carry Cost ($258,333) / Expected Yield (5%)] = $5,166,660
Pre-Tax: $5,166,660 / [1 - 40%] = $8,611,110

Translation: You need to earn $8,611,110 to save $5,166,666 which earns 5% to generate $258,333 in yearly passive income.

STEP 4 (CALCULATE YOUR POM)

POM = Paycheck Pot X 100%   = $5,166,660
Pre-Tax: $5,166,666 / [1 - 40%]   = $8,611,110

STEP 5 (CALCULATE YOUR EXACT ESCAPE NUMBER)

Escape Number = PTEA + Money-system + POM
$24,972,220   = $7,750,000 + $8,611,110 + $8,611,110

Translation: To escape the rat race and enjoy your dream envisioned in your 1/5/10 Planasy, you'll need to earn roughly $25 million before taxes. This assumes you saved $5,166,666 (via $8,611,110 in earnings) which is invested in passive income investments and a $5,166,666 POM cushion (via $8,611,110 in earnings) and you own all your homes and cars without debt.

☑ EXAMPLE #3: THE STARVING ARTIST/MUSICIAN

I don't care about fast cars or big houses, my wife and I just want to be live an artistic life free from work while enjoying life with our three kids.
Notes: Will be subject to smaller taxes and POM figures.

STEP 1 (PRE-TAX EARNINGS TO BUY ASSETS)

House   = $550,000
Two cars   = $50,000

After-tax   = $600,000
Pre-tax   = $800,000 (using tax rate 25%, not 40%)

Translation: To purchase $600,000 in assets, you will need to earn $800,000 before taxes.

STEP 2 (CARRYING COST OF ASSETS)

```
Asset Carry Cost (1.5% x $600K)   = $9,000
Lifestyle/entertainment:          = $7,000
Health Insurance:                 = $10,000
Existence expenses:               = $10,000
Children (3)                      = $45,000
____
Annual Carry Cost                 = $81,000
Gross Carry Cost Pre-Tax          = $108,000 (tax @ 25%, not 40%)
```

Translation: You need to earn $108,000 a year before taxes to support the assets + children.

STEP 3 (CALCULATE YOUR MONEY-SYSTEM)

```
Paycheck pot = [Carry cost ($108,000) / Expected yield (5%)] = $2,160,000
Pre-Tax: $2,160,000 / [1 - 25%] = $2,880,000
```

Translation: You need to earn $2,880,000 and save $2,160,000 earning 5% per year to yield a $108,000 in pre-tax polymorphic pay

STEP 4 (CALCULATE YOUR POM)

```
POM (Using 33% or .33 X $2,160,000)   = $712,800
Pre-Tax: $712,800 / [1 - 25%]         = $950,400
```

Translation: You need to earn $950,400 to save an extra $712,800 for a "peace of mind" cushion.

STEP 5 (CALCULATE YOUR EXACT ESCAPE NUMBER)

```
Escape Number = PTEA + Money-system + POM
$3,672,800 = $800,000 + $2,160,000 + $712,800
```

Translation: To escape the rat race even in this minimalistic lifestyle, you'll need to earn roughly $3.7 million before taxes. This assumes $2,160,000 is invested in passive income investments, you own your assets without debt, and you have $700,000 as an economic cushion.

HAVE AN UNSCRIPTED SUCCESS STORY?

Succeeding at Unscripted Entrepreneurship and reclaimed your life? Message me and tell me your story for an opportunity to be in my next book, Unscripted Book (3) featuring the detailed stories of those who have escaped the rat race and are now living their dream... message me at mj.demarco@yahoo.com

OTHER BOOKS BY MJ DEMARCO

The Millionaire Fastlane
Crack the Code to Wealth and Live Rich for a Lifetime
(Published 2011 - Over 1,000,000 copies sold, translated internationally in over 25 languages)

Unscripted
Life, Liberty and the Pursuit of Entrepreneurship
(Book 1, 2017)

Wealth EXPO$ED
This Short Argument I Overheard Made Me a Fortune
(2020, Short Story)

AUTHOR NOTES

When I started writing this book in late 2017, there were no plant-based soups in stores. By the time I finished in 2021, there are now several options. *Change happens quick...*

If you are going to post a review of this book on Amazon or another book retailer, please include the word "Spoilers" if you are going disclose story outcomes, plots, and/or business ventures. Thank you!!!

Printed in Great Britain
by Amazon